SOUNDING INDIGENOUS

Sounding Indigenous

Authenticity In Bolivian Music Performance

Michelle Bigenho

palgrave

First published in hardcover in 2002 by Palgrave Macmillan
175 Fifth Avenue, New York, N.Y. 10010 and
Houndmills, Basingstoke, Hampshire, England RG21 6XS.
Companies and representatives throughout the world.

PALGRAVE is the new global publishing imprint of St. Martin's Press LLC Scholarly and Reference Division and Palgrave Publishers Ltd. (formerly Macmillan Press Ltd.).

ISBN 0–312–23906–8

Library of Congress Cataloging-in-Publication Data
Bigenho, Michelle, 1965-
Sounding indigenous : authenticity in Bolivian music performance / by Michelle Bigenho.
    p. cm.
   Includes bibliographical references (p.) and index.
   ISBN 0–312–23916–5—ISBN 0–312–24015–5 (pbk.)
    1. Music—Performance—Bolivia. 2. Music—Bolivia—Philosophy and aesthetics. 3. Ethnomusicology—Bolivia. I. Title.

ML239.B6 B54   2002
781.62'6884—dc21

                                     2001056142

Design by Letra Libre, Inc.

First edition: July 2002
10 9 8 7 6 5 4 3 2 1

Printed in the United States of America.

For my parents,
Caryl and Edward Bigenho

Contents

LIST OF FIGURES

Acknowledgements

The fieldwork that formed the basis of this book was made possible by a Fulbright IIE grant (1993–94) and Fulbright Hays Dissertation grant of the U.S. Department of Education (1994–95). It was also made possible by the generous participation of the members of the music ensemble *Música de Maestros,* the members of the *Taller Boliviano de Música Popular Arawi,* the people of Yura, and the people of Toropalca. My profound debt is also with the authorities of the *ayllus* of Yura, and the members of the technical team of *Investigación Social y Asesoramiento Legal, Potosí* (ISALP). Throughout the text, quoted materials that do not have citations to published sources come from the formal and informal interviews I conducted in relation to these institutions, performing ensembles, and indigenous groups. The Anthropology Department of Cornell University provided the conditions under which I was able to complete a first stage of this work as my doctoral dissertation. I am also grateful to the Centre of Latin American Studies at the University of Cambridge for a Visiting Fellowship and for favorable conditions for writing, uninterrupted by teaching duties. Hampshire College's Hewlett Mellon faculty development grants have made it possible for me to return to Bolivia in the summers of 1999, 2000, and 2001.

I am particularly grateful to my dissertation committee members. My chair, Billie Jean Isbell, always successfully met that difficult yet necessary balance between encouragement and critique. John Borneman formed a dissertation writer's group, of which I was a member, and his insight, within and beyond that context, has been extremely valuable. Martin Hatch spent many hours reviewing my music transcriptions. I am also grateful to Mary Roldan for her suggestions in the early part of my Cornell career and on some of my first attempts at writing this document.

I am extremely fortunate to have been a member of dynamic writing groups at both Cornell University and in the Five College area, and within these contexts I have greatly appreciated the comments of Florence Cherry, Nick Fowler, Smita Lahiri, John Norvell, Beth Notar, Joshua Roth,

Stefan Senders, Pat Walker, Erick White, Barbara Yngvesson, Jan Zeserson, and Li Zhang.

Several sections of this work have been presented at conferences and colloquia, or discussed over a series of email exchanges, and within these contexts I received thoughtful commentaries that have in some cases shifted my analysis, and in other cases have provided points from which to sharpen certain debates. For these discussions I am grateful to Denise Arnold, Greg Downey, Paulla Ebron, Davydd Greenwood, Regina Harrison, David Lehmann, Bruce Mannheim, Valentina Napolitano, Robert Philen, Henry Stobart, Terence Turner, and Juan de Dios Yapita.

Many friends in Bolivia have made my fieldwork and subsequent visits a great pleasure. Sometimes they opened both their hearts and homes to me; at times they provided stimulating conversations about Bolivia's contemporary realties; and some of them provided me with commentary on the final version of this manuscript: Rossana Barragán, Gilberto Barrera, Huáscar Cajías, Martha Cajías, Hernando Calla, Julio Calla, Pamela Calla, Ricardo Calla, Miguel Cárdenas, Rolando Encinas, Alexia Escóbar, Isabel Espinoza, Javier Espinoza, Raití Espinoza, Modesto Gálvez, Mercedes Gonzales, Eluteria Gutiérrez, Elizabeth Jiménez, Thomas Kruse, Humberto Llanos, Norma Mendoza, Marlene Mercado, Silvia Rivera, Olga Sallés, Prima Sardinas, Día Severyns, Isabel Subelzu, Martha Ugarte, and César Vallejos.

For their infinite encouragement, not to mention assistance with the preparation of the book's illustrations, I can never sufficiently thank my parents, Caryl Bigenho and Edward Bigenho. I also would like to thank my brother Chris Bigenho for lending a third set of ears to my music recordings and transcriptions.

Other friendships have kept me sufficiently involved in playing music, while I engaged in writing about music. For this, special thanks go to Rolando Encinas and the members of Música de Maestros, and to the regular and itinerant participants in the traditional Irish music sessions in Ithaca, NY, Cambridge, England, and Greenfield, MA.

I am greatly indebted to Joanne Rappaport for her insightful suggestions for revisions to this manuscript, to Kristi Long at Palgrave for her support in completing the project, to Karen Graubart for friendship and much encouragement, to Margaret Cerullo for giving the entire manuscript a fresh read in its final stages, and to the students of Hampshire College who took my course, "Senses, Culture, and Power."

While I am grateful for the support and suggestions of all these individuals, I alone am responsible for any shortcomings in this project.

A section of chapter 5 formed part of an article: "Coca as a Musical Trope of Bolivian Nation-ness," *Political and Legal Anthropology Review,* 21 (1): 114–122, 1998.

A version of chapter 6 was previously published as an article: "Sensing Locality in Yura: Rituals of Carnival and of the Bolivian State, *American Ethnologist* 26 (4): 957–980, 1999.

CHAPTER 1

AUTHENTICITY MATTERS

The musicians were sweating under heavy wool ponchos—not the most comfortable attire in the late morning French summer sun—but the Bolivian delegation made sacrifices at the July 14 parade for the international folklore festival in the town of Saintes. For the most important event of this festival the Bolivian musicians wore their gala costumes, two different styles traditionally donned for the interpretation of Italaque panpipes—a highland Bolivian tradition. The impressive costumes and sounds may have differed from what many French people knew as typical of Bolivia. At least that was the intention of the Bolivian music director. The lengthy parade route did not faze the Bolivian musicians. Through their urban ritual parades at home, Bolivian musicians and dancers have extensive experience in moving sonorously and kinesthetically through the city streets. Playing, dancing, and moving forward are all performative activities which occur simultaneously. They go together as do the activities of not playing, not dancing, and not moving forward. These performative practices require skills in the calculations of space and time. To dance to the band in one's own group, the leading section of the troupe must maintain a sufficient distance from the preceding dance group. But the dance section must also avoid falling too far behind, so as not to break the continuity of the ritual parade, and possibly face disqualification by the organizational entities who judge the different troupes within these parades.

These Bolivian performance practices clashed with the way French organizers envisioned their parade of international folklore. Not far into the parade route, one of the French organizers began yelling at the Bolivian delegation. After a time lapse for translation, the message came through: "The Bolivians are falling too far behind! They should be right behind the other delegation! There should be no space between them! By radio they are telling us that the other delegations are backed up behind the Bolivians." The band in front of the Bolivians followed a performance practice that contradicted that of the Bolivians: walking forward in silence, stopping to play, and then walking forward again in silence. As the French organizers raised their voices, Rolando Encinas, the Bolivian music director, shook his head and gave the order in Spanish: "Keep a distance from that band up there or we will not be able to hear ourselves play." The French did not achieve their desired seamless parade, and the Bolivians heard themselves play and danced to their own music. The Bolivian delegation gave a performance that represented an "original" Italaque—a regionally linked indicator of highland Bolivian indigenousness as well as a marker of Bolivian national sentiment. Their musical performance, geographically and performatively split from its source as they imagined it, established its domain over the practiced place of the French international folklore festival parade route; it was a temporarily Bolivian national domain.

On that warm July morning in France, a group of musicians, known on Bolivian soil as *Música de Maestros* (Music of the Masters), performed their rendition of authentic indigenous music from their country. At play within this performance were multiple and often contradictory claims to and expectations of authenticity. The musicians' sense of authenticity extended beyond their mere appearance in native dress while playing panpipes. In order to produce a performance that felt authentic, they had to be able to hear their music and to move to it in specific ways. While the French also desired an authentic *representation* of Bolivian music, they were not concerned with the authentic *feeling* of this performance. On this trip to France, Música de Maestros had joined a dance troupe to form a delegation that performatively represented the Bolivian nation to a foreign audience. Like many other musical proposals in Bolivia, Música de Maestros dedicated its energies to performing the nation.

In his study on nationalism, Benedict Anderson argued that national communities were imagined through the spread of print capitalism and the common reading of newspapers and novels published in vernaculars; this shared textual/symbolic world held the imaginative power to enlist members in the killing of others in the name of the abstract concept of the nation (1991). There are obviously limits to thinking about national communities only through the precondition of a literate and actively reading citizenry. This book is concerned with alternative modes of feeling membership in imagined communities, modes that, through music performances, are not outside of visual representations, but are at once connected to embodied practices and sonorous experiences. If Anderson wrote about nations that read common texts, I want to lay out a nation that listens to, dances, and feels an imagined common bond, and that plays and dances, for itself and for others, the elements of these feelingful activities that bind people who do not necessarily know each other.

Lest the reader think I have discarded the politics so fundamental to discussions of national communities and reverted to a mushy apolitical celebration of music, moving bodies, and colorful folklore, let me immediately elaborate on the conditions that keep politics at the core of musically performed imagined communities.[1] The Bolivian context, like many other national contexts, is constituted by a collection of diverse communities. While languages are not always the best indicators of these communities, they are still telling of the cultural differences in Bolivian society. The 1992 census revealed that 58 percent of Bolivia's population speaks an indigenous language (46 percent bilingual with Spanish and 12 percent monolingual indigenous) (Albó 1999: 15). The indigenous languages of Quechua and Aymara are spoken in Bolivia's highlands, and more than 30 different indigenous languages are spoken by 33 different ethnic groups in Bolivia's eastern lowlands (Albó 1999: 43). Since the Spanish conquest, indigenous peoples of Bolivia have been forced into interaction with Spanish colonialism, and then with British and U.S. economic and cultural imperialism. Through these interactions, in what Mary Louise Pratt calls the "contact zones" (1991), some sense of difference has been maintained, even though contemporary elements of "indigenous" difference can be located within particular colonial underpinnings (see Rasnake 1989; Abercrombie 1998). Those who are not indigenous in Bolivian society may be labeled through the complex terms of "criollo" (Creole) and "mestizo." While the term "criollo," in the conquest period, referred to those who were of Spanish descent, but who were born in Spanish America (as opposed to the *peninsulares* who were born in Spain), its contemporary meaning is more akin to a disassociation with any indigenous heritage. In its blandest sense, "mestizo" may refer to someone who has both indigenous and Spanish heritage, but the processes of *mestizaje*, the mixing of both indigenous and Spanish cultures, could be said to have reached all areas of Bolivian society. So who is mestizo and who is indigenous? Is the term mestizo ever used in a self-ascribing way or is it always assigned by others to signal the lack or absence of an authentically indigenous heritage? These are the diverse and complex cultural affiliations through which I explore authenticity in music performances that emerge within the territory of the Bolivian nation-state.

While the Weberian state may refer to bureaucratic institutions and a monopoly over the legitimate use of force, the hyphenated nation-state pretends to place this authority and organization over a hypothetical single common community whose members reside in a single common territory (see Anderson 1991; Falk 1985; Hobsbawm 1990).[2] As in other national contexts, this mythic isomorphism of one state–one nation–one culture–one community could not be further from what actually occurs in the practices of Bolivian citizens. The question then centers around how these cultural differences are articulated through the official Bolivian nationalism of the state as well as through the popular nationalism of people living in Bolivian territory. This multicultural milieu is the prism through which claims to authenticity become reflected in contradictory and competing ways.

While conducting my research on Bolivian music performances, I often encountered similar kinds of clashes like the one I described as occurring between the French festival organizers and the Bolivian musicians. While the terms of these clashes varied, as did the participants involved in them, it became evident to me that major arguments were occurring around different claims to authenticity. On one hand, an ensemble like Música de Maestros was completely absorbed in striving for an authentic performance. They interpreted the master composers of Bolivia, and this was viewed as both a cultural and historical project. As they pursued composers' original intentions, they also conducted fieldwork in the countryside of Bolivia to present performances believed to be true to contemporary cultural originals. Música de Maestros was not alone in their pursuit of cultural authenticity, but I did not recognize this as a central issue in thinking about my work until I became aware of what I will lightly refer to as the authenticity police: people who, from a position of relative power (as politicians viewing their constituency, as Creoles or mestizos viewing indigenous cultures, as the French viewing Bolivian musicians, and so on), critiqued as inauthentic the cultural performance of others, applying some individually determined criteria of what was authentic. But those who were "caught" by the authenticity police seemed to be having a grand time, an experience that was "real" in some other way. The "real" experience for some people was the culturally inauthentic for others.

Indigenous authenticity of music performances held a special value in the Bolivian context. Bolivian society has experienced what I will refer to as a "return of the Indian," to borrow a phrase from Xavier Albó (1991). Indians have not disappeared and suddenly reappeared at the end of the twentieth century, but rather claims to indigenousness have acquired a new value and currency in both government programs and popular politics of Bolivia. Throughout Latin America, part of this "return" can be attributed to the heavy, symbolic load of 1992 and the general cry to replace the bland "500 years of contact" with "500 years of resistance." The quincentennial moment brought a symbolic return to the cataclysmic moment of conquest, and indigenous peoples throughout Latin America forced their reading of this event into public light. Diane Nelson, who framed her work on Guatemala around the significance of the quincentennial moment, pointed to the global reaction to 1992, including the naming of Rigoberta Menchú as a Nobel Prize winner and the United Nations' declaration of the Year and Decade of Indigenous People (1999: 4). Since 1994, the Zapatistas in Chiapas, Mexico, have also emphasized the indigenous core of their movement. The contemporary return of the Indian in Bolivia intersects with a particular history of indigenous politics in Bolivia, with postquincentennial trends that run throughout Latin America, and with global funding agendas within which indigenous peoples currently occupy a favored if precarious position. Through these processes, elements of indigenous cultures have become alienable things, things that have an exchange value outside of their use value within lived experience.

The privileging of the indigenous within international funding priorities is not innocent of what the anthropologist Renato Rosaldo terms "imperialist nostalgia" (1989b), the condition in which people of the West long for what has been lost through their own projects of colonization. Nor is this kind of nostalgia completely absent from the Bolivian national scene of nonindigenous Creole and mestizo citizens who often end up speaking for indigenous peoples within their work in government agencies and nongovernmental organizations (NGOs). Within this milieu, the authenticity of indigenous representations has tangible economic value in the form of jobs and projects. Following James Clifford's claim that in the twentieth century, identities have no essence in a global village of increasing closeness of the "exotic," but rather are "matters of power and rhetoric" (1988:14), indigenous identities that were once well entrenched in colonial bureaucracies have moved back into the state and into purportedly nonstate contested spaces of power and rhetoric. While the power of claims to indigenous authenticity is central to this book, as I explore the "return of the Indian" within a shift in Bolivia's contemporary narrative of nation, this is not the only form of authenticity that concerns me. In fact it is the contentiousness of authenticity itself that propels my general inquiries into Bolivian music performances in rural, national, and international contexts. Before I turn to the complexities of authenticity, I will present details of the ethnographic contexts where I conducted fieldwork, and address the multi-sited nature of this work.

Moving Through Places

The boundaries of my research were set by Bolivian music performances, but I moved in and out of local, national, and transnational contexts—all different but interconnected "ethnographic spaces" that I have brought together and subjected to the "excesses" of my analytical lens (see Stewart 1996: 39). Neither a Venn diagram nor a series of concentric circles captures the sense of my ethnographic spaces. One might imagine these spaces as concentric circles of meaning construction, but some of the circles stretch out, unconfined, in other directions.

Like other anthropologists I have constructed my arguments on the basis of extended fieldwork (from October 1993 to December 1995, and return trips to Bolivia in the summers of 1996, 1997, 1999, and 2000) and participant observation—the methodological cornerstones of British and American anthropology since Bronislaw Malinowski (1984 [1922]). Many ethnographic accounts give the impression of temporarily stationary anthropologists, rooted in one place over an extended period of fieldwork. The anthropologist Thomas Abercrombie has also called attention to the fact that many ethnographies have portrayed the anthropologist in a traveling mode only at the beginning of the text, and after narrative arrival, the anthropologist disappears completely from the story (1998: 29–30). I suspect most fieldwork is more about moving through places than staying in one place and I underscore this aspect of my ethnographic work.

In the field, everyone asked me about place. Upon hearing that I was an anthropologist, people in Bolivia always asked me, "*Where* do you work?" The implicit assumption was that anthropologists in Bolivia study indigenous or ethnic groups that can be unambiguously circumscribed for analysis. During a preliminary field trip in Bolivia I once phoned into the city of La Paz from a remote locale in the southern region of Potosí. A nonanthropologist friend answered the phone and asked me sarcastically, "So, have you found your Indians yet?" Anthropologists often make an indigenous group "theirs" even to the extent of dissuading other anthropologists from studying "their Indians"; as William Roseberry suggested, the possessive adjectives pose a significant problem for the discipline of anthropology (1989: 81–82). In the minds of many Bolivians I met, anthropologists become inextricably linked to a single *place* and its discrete group of "natives." The link to place constitutes one of the common traditional markers of identity (Clifford 1988), and in the case of an anthropologist studying questions of identity in relation to music, place assumes even greater proportions. The confusion on the part of my inquirers arose when I explained that I was conducting research in several different places.

Outside of a reference to Bolivia, I refused to define my research in terms of a single geographic place. Not even the geographic borders of Bolivian territory delimited my study since I also conducted field research while following a Bolivian ensemble in a performing tour of France. The necessity of the ethnographer moving in today's research endeavors has already been demonstrated in relation to the tracking of the music performance traditions of a particular rural community in its migration to the city (Turino 1993a). Nevertheless, my interest was not in following the music of a rural community as its members migrated to a new urban environment, but rather in looking at seemingly unrelated cases, whose point in common was national in nature, and to seek among them the links of an "imagined community" (Anderson 1991), and the kinds of cultural interactions that might occur between members of this national community and the structures of the state. Although place was important in my research, I heed Clifford Geertz's statement that anthropologists do not study places, but rather they study *in* places (1973: 22). I moved through multiple places to conduct research on the narratives of Bolivian nations as experienced through several music performance contexts.

I adopted a methodology of moving through places for various reasons. First, I wanted to get beyond the colonial underpinnings of a "my-people" approach to anthropology. Instead my fieldwork might be seen as occurring "in worldly, contingent relations of travel . . ." (Clifford 1997: 68), and those relations of travel were generated by thematic questions of music and identification processes at local, national, and transnational levels. My ethnography follows Akhil Gupta's and James Ferguson's reinvention of "the field"—a focus on "shifting locations" rather than "bounded fields," and the implicit attempt to "decolonize" anthropology through that invention (1997: 38). Within a framework of multisited ethnography (see Marcus 1998; Marcus 1995), I followed the perceived authenticities associated with different Bolivian music performances. My ethnographic work had more to do with how people imagined "Bolivia," and their own places in those imaginings, than with a single geographically pinpointed place. A thematically generated study through shifting locations also forces the anthropologist to consider seriously those "outside forces" that are interpreted, all too often, as impositions of change on an otherwise discrete cultural order.

A tension exists between the postmodern and the political-economic approaches to multi-sited research.[3] While the political economic approach might follow global economic histories in frameworks inspired by Eric Wolf's *Europe and the People without History* (1982), the postmodern approach might emphasize traveling and disembodied flows. The model of traveling cultures becomes problematic with its almost inevitable de-politicization of cultural politics (Gilroy, Lecture at Hampshire College, 2001), but the global history approach tends to set up a predetermined framework of the ways local social interactions must inevitably be shaped. In "moving through places," I focus neither on disembodied cultural flows nor on the all-determining factors of globalization, but rather on the grounded examples of the social interactions and cultural politics that articulate with the intangible but real structures of nation-states and global economies.

I methodologically moved through places in pursuit of music performances that ultimately become split from their sources. While musical expressions start somewhere with someone, music easily reaches the ears of anyone, anywhere. One could say the same of other *visible* identity markers such as traditional dress, which may be physically carried from one place to another or even viewed on television. Traditional cuisine may also move in the memory of a traveler or through a transnational business endeavor. But even a home recipe in a strange environment becomes difficult to reproduce in the absence of proper ingredients.

Music, as an identity marker, takes the prize in dissemination potential because its *audible* nature permits its spread through the exploitation of cassette and radio technology. Cassette technology allows consumers to record their own music or record from other recordings, thus greatly increasing the potential diffusion of music. Cassette recorders/players were rather common in the rural areas I worked, although the cost of batteries did impose limitations on cassette listening/recording habits. I seldom went to a fiesta in rural areas of Bolivia where there was not at least one community member recording the community's music. Putting the "read-on" technology (the ability to make one's own recordings) of cassettes in the hands of many, potentially democratizes recording and duplication capability, putting these activities at the direct disposal of consumers (Manuel 1993: 1–6; Wallace and Malm 1984), while also potentially blurring the consumer and producer distinctions so starkly delineated by Theodor Adorno (Manuel 1993: 9; Manuel 1988: 9).

I propose moving through places as a fruitful means to anthropologically study identification processes at the level of nation. National identities, like most identities, are multiple, dove-tailed, constantly shifting, and relative to different subject positions. While a view from a single village of what it means to be Bolivian enlightens the ethnographic record, it does not account for the combined mobility of music and the multiple narratives of nation that emerge through the experience of music performances. The Bolivians in the cases I examine are also on the move: rural people seeking temporary employment in other areas of Bolivia and urban musicians temporarily on international tours. Ultimately, this ethnography places on center stage the national and regional identification processes that occur in relation to being on the move. Several authors have remarked on the importance of movement in a comprehension of twentieth century identities and the importance of shifting our ethnographic projects to account for regional integration and marginalization (Tsing 1993: xi), "new forms of dwelling and circulating" (Clifford 1988: 13), identities formed "on the move" (Chambers 1994: 25), and translocal phenomena like the state (Gupta 1995: 376). I met the challenge of studying the translocal nature of musical narratives of nation through a combination of research sites, both rural and urban—through a constant movement back and forth, to and from the four cases upon which I chose to focus. If Anderson's imagined community emerges from visual readings of a shared print media (1991), the imagined community within this text emerges from shared sonorous experiences or sonorous experiences that reflect a collective memory of nation and make collective claims to cultural authenticity. I treat both competing and shared claims to authenticity because the former underline the contested experiences of Bolivia's cultural pluralism, while the latter reflect the celebratory experiences usually located in official narratives of nation.

The ethnographic examples on which I focus had little to do with a norm of Bolivian music. As examples from both highland indigenous communities and urban mestizo musicians, these ethnographic examples were all in some way exceptional.[4] Toropalqueños and Yureños, inhabitants of two highland indigenous locales in Potosí, were exceptional in that their identification processes inverted the common sense ideas about where "tradition" should be most entrenched. Both Toropalca and Yura were part of the ethnic group called the Wisijsas, a group that Viceroy Toledo divided in the sixteenth century, reorganizing these populations for the benefit of colonial organization and control. Toropalqueños and Yureños have never been under hacienda systems, the people of these regions thus falling within the classification of "original peoples" who have always had access to their own land. Today both Toropalca and Yura refer to locales inhabited by between 5,000 and 7,000 inhabitants[5] who are presently organized, to varying degrees, in terms of *ayllus:* the indigenous organization of the Andes. In 1863 the geographical spaces of Toropalca and Yura were both designated as cantons, a political division of the Bolivian state. The official capitals of these cantons are located in the villages called, not surprisingly, Toropalca and Yura. The people who live in Toropalca and Yura are usually divided into the categories of *vecino* and *comunario.* These terms refer to people who identify with two different world views, but who inhabit the same geographic space. Vecinos live outside the logic of the indigenous organizations, identify with an urban experience, live primarily from local commerce, and often view indigenous ways of life as obstacles to general progress. Comunarios are those who identify with and live within the logic of the indigenous organization or ayllu. The concept of ayllu encompasses the nested moiety structures through which rotating systems of authority and accompanying ritual practices reproduce highland indigenous collectivities. Rather than a pure Andean indigenous structure, the contemporary ayllu structures reflect an articulation with Spanish colonialism and with the republican and state structures that followed independence from Spain. On the other hand, vecinos often speak both Spanish and Quechua and champion or identify with indigenous musical expressions as a source of regional pride. "Culture" and "language" alone are not enough to mark the differences between these vecinos and comunarios; interaction between them must be comprehended in terms of structured relations of inequality.

Today, the connections between people in Yura and Toropalca are minimal and my fieldwork encountered more contrasts than similarities between the two areas. Yureños were relatively more connected to regional and national influences and appeared more "traditional"; Toropalqueños were relatively less connected and they lamented a loss of their own "tradition." Both insiders and outsiders complained that Toropalca "had no culture," or had "lost its culture." In general, Yureños admitted loss of some traditions, but did not lament the fact. Yureños' visible and audible cultural markers were too well pronounced to place their possession of "culture" in any doubt. In Yura and Toroplaca I was facing two cases that suggested that an ethnic identity based on an indigenous organization tended to be quite strong in precisely the areas that had more connections to an urban context, and comparatively weak in areas of relative isolation. The inhabitants of both of these areas were involved in processes of temporary seasonal migration. Yureños and Toropalqueños, in search of temporary labor contracts in agricultural and construction work, would travel to other areas of Bolivia and to Argentina. Their music performances reflected in distinct ways their articulations with these seasonal migrations.

In the city, a study of mestizo music performance in relation to narratives of nation that focused on the *rules* of that construction might study music ensembles like *Kjarkas*, a five-person performing ensemble that has reached national as well as international success by selling a highly stylized music, the "Andean" content of which rests heavily on their instrumentation. They usually play the *quena* (a notched flute), *zampoñas* (panpipes), *charango* (a small plucked string instrument), *bombo* (large skin drum), and guitar. Kjarkas is a model ensemble of what has come to be known as Pan-Andean music (see Wara Céspedes 1984); and they often represent what foreigners know as "Bolivian." Their music is also labeled as "national" by many Bolivians in both urban and rural contexts, although the label "national" in many cases has more to do with a consistent reference made by radio announcers. In Bolivia, the wide listening audience for the music of Kjarkas can be greatly attributed to the music selection of a few disk jockeys whose radio programs reach the most isolated corners of Bolivia. Although it was not the focus of my research, Kjarkas became a part of my research as a foil against which other musicians produced alternative Bolivian national musics.

The Bolivian Workshop of Popular Music, "Arawi," situated in the city of La Paz, developed an elaborate discourse about providing an option to Kjarkas in national music through its program of music education, research, performance, and composition. The workshop was an NGO engaged in cultural projects related to music, and as such the level of discourse about their work was highly elaborated through the proposal writing they undertook to obtain funding. I played a role in that process by rewriting, translating, and submitting one of their proposals, and the workshop received a grant from the Inter-American Foundation, an institution that has been partially funded through the U.S. Congress, and that has emphasized its support of grassroots projects.

As an NGO in La Paz, the workshop proposed to serve young people of low income families, but the ideas behind the workshop were proposed and promoted by middle- and upper-class, university-educated intellectuals. In general, the instructors who carried out the daily work of the institution had completed fewer years of formal education and belonged to a lower socioeconomic class than the authors behind the project. The workshop organizers intellectualized the anti-Kjarkas discourse within an aesthetic pyramid of music classification: "traditional" music formed the base; "contemporary" music formed the tip; and "popular" or "meso" music (Vega 1966) formed the middle tier. According to the discourse of the institution's organizers, the workshop explored and experimented with the languages of these three kinds of interrelated musics. Composers who have experimented with contemporary techniques within popular music—John Cage, John Lennon, Frank Zappa, and Leo Brouwer—provided explicit points of discursive reference for the workshop's organizers. According to the organizers' discourse, the "traditional" music from the rural areas of Bolivia should be maintained for a sense of cultural roots or origins, but that maintenance should occur through performance rather than through the deadening effects of mere collecting and archiving. Workshop organizers drew connections between the techniques and sonorities of traditional musical styles and the techniques of contemporary music. Through these arguments they attempted to decenter the assumed exclusive Western origins of the contemporary avant-garde.

The workshop organizers used the terms "meso" music and "popular" music interchangeably, but they took the first term directly from the work of an Argentine ethnomusicologist, Carlos Vega. Attempting to avoid the imprecision afforded by the term "popular," Vega proposed the term "mesomusic" to refer to an aesthetically conservative music that was characterized by the use of Western tonality and Western rhythms, was of no one particular group or class, and was common within both rural and urban recreational contexts of the modern nation (1966: 1–17). The workshop viewed mesomusic as having built up its popularity through some reference to traditional forms, along with the systematic application of tonal harmonic structures that are pleasing to the ears of the masses.

For the most part, Música de Maestros performed a repertoire that fell squarely within the mesomusic category of the workshop's classification system. In contrast with the workshop, the members of Música de Maestros did not explicitly refer to their music as an alternative to Kjarkas. Nevertheless, through performance practice they too were developing an alternative to this Bolivian "national music." They built a musical project around the theme of interpreting the works of Bolivian master composers, and they began with classic Creole and mestizo pieces of the 1930s. But within their repertoire, Música de Maestros also developed indigenous genres, striving to recreate the performance styles as they were traditionally played in the countryside. The inclusion of mestizo-Creole music and traditionally performed indigenous genres emerged from an aesthetic aim of performing Bolivian music "as it was" in a previous time and "as it should be" in a different place. Música de Maestros was aesthetically driven by a quest for cultural-historical authenticity, the authentic original in time and the authentic original in space.

My degree of integration into Música de Maestros far surpassed my integration into the other contexts of this ethnography. As George Marcus has suggested of multi-sited ethnography, "as the landscape changes across sites, the identity of the ethnographer requires renegotiation" (1998: 97). I felt distinct degrees of empathy for the different cases I examined, and in each context, I exercised different forms of participation. For example, I became a regular recording and performing musician with Música de Maestros and the membership within this ensemble *as a musician* gave a sense of insidership that was never matched in the other cases, even though I was involved in *playing music* in all of them. Behind these distinctions is the difference between being a member of a community of musicians, and being a member of an indigenous community that reproduces itself through ritual music performances. While my ethnographic work spans these two extremes, my own subject position necessarily shifted within this multi-sited fieldwork. In Música de Maestros I became something of a public persona. The presentation of Música de Maestros' third album in January 1994 was my more formal initiation to the group, and afterward, I settled into the ensemble as a regular member. In the early months of 1994, people began to comment to me: "I saw you on television last night in an advertisement for Música de Maestros." It was the first album the group had recorded under the commercial label of Discolandia and this local record company had run several television spots advertising the album, evidently with some close shots of my violin playing. Not having a television at the time, I had a strange sensation of people "knowing me" through a television image that I myself had never seen. To know how people were "knowing" me and Música de Maestros, I eventually purchased a small black and white television. Through televisual media, the authentic-sounding Bolivian national ensemble was visually revealed to have at least one foreign performer. Multiple video cameras were always filming our performances. Television channels would repeatedly surprise us with a program featuring a complete performance of Música de Maestros. Copyright laws were not well enforced in Bolivia and recordings of our performances were somewhat up for grabs when it came to advertising, broadcasting, and putting musical backdrops to images and spoken communications. Música de Maestros, as well as any other group in Bolivia, had little if any control over the public use and abuse of its recordings. While these uses of Música de Maestros' recordings and images were often viewed as a form of gratuitous advertising for a group that had not yet taken steps toward full-blown commercialization, the concern over lack of control remained prevalent, especially in reference to the dubious sound quality of most video-recordings made by the television channels.

Música de Maestros proposed a nationalist music project, but one might be struck by the members of this ensemble who were obviously not Bolivian. I was the third in a tradition of gringa violinists who played in the group. Cynthia de Pareja from the United States and Christine Bergmann from Germany were my predecessors. Through television images of performances, I became known as the "gringuita" who played with Música de Maestros. When the director of the ensemble, Rolando Encinas, was hanging posters for a concert in Cochabamba he heard a couple comment on the group: "You know. They are the ones who perform with the gringa violinist." The couple made an association between a foreigner and a Bolivian music ensemble, and my status as gringa was based not on the verification of my nationality but on the visual observation of the color of my skin. In contrast with its usual unmarked status, whiteness had become the marked category in this distinction of a Bolivian performing ensemble. Between 1993 and 1995 the membership of Música de Maestros included three foreigners: Koji Hishimoto from Japan, Oscar Carreras from Cuba, and myself from the United States. Oscar Carreras played violin and taught at the music conservatory in La Paz. When our master of ceremonies introduced the performers, he always underlined the Cuban/U.S. violin duo of the group. Fans remarked on the appeal of this alliance: through a particularly Bolivian music performance there was a uniting of citizens from two countries the governments of which have politically been at great odds. The master of ceremonies would always introduce the Japanese member of the group just before introducing the director: "From Japan, but as Bolivian as we are, responsible for many of the musical arrangements of the group as well as a master musician on our wind instruments . . . Koji Hishimoto!" Koji came to Bolivia for two months and stayed six years. With a strong music theory background, Koji did many of the musical arrangements for the group. To rehearsal he brought new musical parts, often with only one or two measures changed, as he sought to perfect a particular sound for the ensemble. Koji has since returned to Japan, but from there he continues to compose and arrange for the ensemble, sending his work by fax in the days preceding the premiere performance of new repertoire. With the inclusion of foreign musicians in this ensemble, the embodiment of Bolivianness seemed to be secondary to the embodiment of a particular style of musical performance that could be learned. While I did hear that the director received some quietly mumbled critiques for the foreign contingents in this ensemble, the presence of foreigners in this performing group remained one of the ironies of this explicitly nationalist project.

In summary, while I could have studied ethnic identities in relation to music in a context of Northern Potosi, a Bolivian locale where the "exotic" and different were anything but understated, instead I conducted research in Toropalca where "there was no culture" and Yura where external influences should have, but had not, obliterated "traditions." I could have studied the Kjarkas in terms of their representation of national music. Instead I studied alternatives to Kjarkas in the form of an alternative music school that worked in traditional, popular, and avant-garde music and with an ensemble that performed Bolivian national music, and whose membership included musicians from Japan, Cuba, and the United States. Rather than taking the obvious cases to research my topic, I sought those exceptions that could lead to an understanding of the fuzzy border area of what defines Bolivian narratives of nation as performed through music.

In this book, I focus heavily on musical experiences and representations in a country where citizens have been living under bleak economic conditions. Since President Victor Paz Estenssoro's implementation of the Supreme Decree 21060 in 1985, Bolivians have been living under the pernicious effects of neoliberalism. With this decree came the "New Economic Policy," a structural adjustment program shaped by the International Monetary Fund. These policies led to the closure of state-run tin mines, the laying off of miners, the reduction of state subsidies, the curbing of social welfare programs, and the general dismantling of what had been a powerful structure of miners' labor organizations. The Bolivian hand in the design of these policies was Gonzalo Sánchez de Lozada, Minister of Planning at the time and President of Bolivia (1993–1997) during the time I conducted this research. The effects of neoliberalism have been severe for lower and middle classes of Bolivian society. My ethnography includes an analysis of performances by indigenous and mestizo-Creole Bolivians, generally from the lower and middle sectors of Bolivian society. The Bolivians playing in these performances all demonstrated significant personal and collective investments in these musical endeavors, obviously for different reasons according to each context. But these performances are clearly no superfluous superstructure. While I will show how these performances are tied to economic resources at local, national, and international levels, I also want to take seriously "the politics of culture" (Whisnant 1983; Handler 1988; Williams 1991; Alvarez, Dagnino, and Escobar 1998)—that is, to also take seriously the work of cultural representation, to grapple with the nexus of symbolic and political economies.

Multi-sited ethnography is always in danger of sacrificing depth for breadth (Starn 1999: 15; Clifford 1997: 57; Marcus and Fischer 1986: 77–110), but ultimately this speaks to the problem and promise of microscopy in all ethnographic projects (see Geertz 1973: 21). How does one make anthropology's standard methodological move from the microscopic observation to the general conclusion, especially if the case at hand is one of national sentiment? Anthropologists have no problems making this micro to macro interpretive move when the focus of the study is a village and the ethnographer's work draws on a few key informants (for example, see Turner 1967: 131–150). I do not pretend to solve this methodological puzzle, but merely state that the micro to macro moves I make do not vary significantly from other ethnographic leaps from key informant to village and "culture," except that my interpretations do not intend to arrive at a composite of Bolivian nationness. I bring together cases involving people who often never actually meet, but who participate in the collective "fantasy" of a Bolivian society (see Luykx 1999: 18–19). Closer to a "Nomadology" (Deleuze and Guattari 1987: 23) where the goal is not holistic representation (Marcus 1998: 83), my interpretations emerge from local places and specific music performances that suggest the multiple semiotic complexes through which Bolivians of different subject positions situate themselves within a national community. For an expanded audio-visual representation of the ethnographic work of this volume, readers may want to visit the website www.anacruz.net.

Pursuing the Real Thing

In this book, I explore contested grounds of authenticity in Bolivian music performances, highlighting the space between cultural experiences that are *felt, represented,* and *exchanged* as authentic. To reveal the connection between the sensory experience of music and struggles over authentic representations, I will outline three different, but not mutually exclusive, ways of thinking about authenticity that I will refer to throughout the book as experiential authenticity, cultural-historical authenticity, and unique authenticity. I propose this framework not to define that slippery thing called "authenticity," but rather to understand the workings of competing ideologies of authenticity that have real economic and political effects. In many ways, this framework of authenticity can be read as one more attempt to bridge what Peter Wade has referred to as material/symbolic dualism, the split between culture as a way of life and culture as a set of representations (1999: 449). Wade's work demonstrated the importance of overcoming these divides that all too easily feed an innocuous depoliticized view of "culture" as separate from real "politics" (1999: 454). I coin these terms of authenticity as mere heuristic devices—all caveats in place—and these different ideologies of authenticity should be seen as mutually inextricable. The devices work toward an understanding of the symbolic work involved in performance, representation, and the creation of alienable cultural things. Circling around these disputes is the question of who has the power to represent indigenous authenticity, and it is the indigenous presence within Bolivia that initially places authenticity centerstage in the pageant of national politics. While I will take up multiple claims to authenticity in music performances, the representation of indigenous authenticity occupies a central position within many of the Bolivian music performances I studied, and this work is an attempt to unravel the wider implications of this current fashion.

An experientially authentic performance is "real" because it is felt as a "groove." It is the transformative sensory experience that the Bolivian ensemble, Música de Maestros, sought to recreate within the context of a French folklore festival, as described at the opening of this chapter. The experientially authentic is not unlike the ritualized origins that Walter

Benjamin associated with the original uses of art (1968: 224). The experientially authentic performance roots people to places through bodily movement and the achievement of a performative "oneness" (Keil 1994b: 98) with sonorous events and other people. Experiential authenticity sits on that sharp edge between bodily pleasure and pain. It is at once the "grain in the voice," the enjoyment one feels upon listening to a singing voice (Barthes 1985), what makes one want to dance, as well as what makes the blues (see Smith 1992). To borrow a term from Charles Keil, experiential authenticity is about "feelingful" activity (1994a), which is not completely encompassed in any rendering of "meaningful" activity.[6] Experiential authenticity constitutes what people attempt, but often fail, to capture in any representational or recording process; it eludes symbolic representation even if most other claims to authenticity are attempts to represent this groove.

Experiential authenticity refers to the entire sensory experience of music performances, the event that becomes a "sensory metaphor" characterized by synesthesia: when one sense experience, by contiguity, draws an associative relation with another sense experience (see Shore 1991: 18). This sensory feeling of music performances establishes relations between people and physical places. The resulting connection between people and places differs significantly from the ties nation-states draw between people and places. These differences will become apparent through a contrast between highland indigenous space defined through Carnival music and a relation to place articulated through a people's struggle to be recognized officially by the state as an indigenous collectivity.

Experiential authenticity is obviously tied to the embodied experience of music performance, but my project is not one of glorifying this kind of experience—which would be an inversion but ultimately, reiteration of the mind-body dualism (Stoller 1997). I follow Maurice Merleau-Ponty's suggestion of the fundamental interrelatedness of mind and body (1962; Grosz 1994: 86). As Elizabeth Grosz has suggested, Merleau-Ponty did not valorize one side or another of this pair, but rather took up the space between these oppositional terms (Grosz 1994: 94). In the reference to experiential authenticity, I also want to avoid essentializing "experience." Robert Desjarlais, in his work at a homeless shelter for the mentally ill, revealed the essentializing of "experience" that occurs within the best-intentioned social science research that claims to present people's experiences in everyday life instead of presenting monolithic social structures; he critiqued an approach that sees experience as the be-all and end-all of analysis, what the anthropologists mired in structuralism have been missing.[7] Experience, too, is relational. Experiential authenticity is a way of thinking about the relation between performances and representations of performances, something more akin to the ritual use-value of art (Benjamin 1968: 224). In music performance, it is an authenticity that is not alienable; it is connected to a shared experience with others, a fleeting moment of the groove, a listener's great night at a concert. Experiential authenticy is often only grasped from the moment of retrospective reflection. If I am in the groove now, I am likely to talk about being there after the fact, and the process of talking about it is already directing this authenticity into the realm of representation. I find the concept of experiential authenticity useful to distinguish between the "real" as a kind of corporeal discourse of the groove, a Durkheimian collective effervescence, or heightened multi-sensorial interaction, and the "real" as what is represented as culturally or historically "correct." In this vein, I take up the space between musical experience and musical representation, between feeling the groove and constructing a representative narrative of cultural-historical origins. Sensory hierarchies are scrambled and reordered in this move from feeling to representing the groove. Rather than the multisensorial condition associated with experiential authenticity, cultural-historical authenticity moves into a less embodied realm of practices that prioritizes narrative forms and what can be visually represented and perceived.

Cultural-historical authenticity is within the realm of the always slightly imperfect representation, as it purports a continuity with an imagined point of origin, situated in a historical or mythical past. I combine cultural and historical authenticity because of the shared issues of representation, but it is important to mark the principal difference between the two: claims to cultural authenticity usually place subjects outside of history, while those of historical authenticity situate subjects within a historical trajectory. While Música de Maestros, in the opening scene of this chapter, attempted to find the groove of a particular performance, in their overall musical project, they explicitly sought to perform culturally and historically authentic renditions of Bolivian music. But the music of this ensemble was not the music that made most Bolivians want to dance. For many Bolivians, *cumbias* fit that bill, much to the dismay of many middle- and upper-class citizens who referred to this music as a "dangerous invasion." Cumbia is a song-dance genre of Colombian origins, but the cumbias danced in Bolivia—orchestrated with electric guitar, bass, and keyboards—were often Mexican- or locally produced. These contrasting responses to cumbias mark class and ethnic cleavages whereby one person's groove is another person's inauthentic music. From the perspective of some Bolivians, people who are considered "indigenous" are not supposed to dance to the modern commercialized music; they are supposed to embody the nation's foundations of cultural authenticity. In a similar spirit, Rey Chow extended Walter Benjamin's ideas on the art object's aura to colonial and postcolonial fascinations with the "authentic native" (1994: 140). Chow draws this link by rethinking "the aura of an art object as that 'historical specificity' which makes it unique to a particular place at a particular time" (1994: 139). The authentic native takes on an aura whose power may be harnessed by native subjects themselves or by national elites, but in either case the power of this authenticity is structured by the native's position in relation to the nation-state. Thus cultural-historical authenticity is crucial to the founding narratives of nation-states, and in some cases is even assumed by some citizens as their own burden as they feel nostalgia for and mourn the loss of their own culture.

My work in two highland indigenous places in rural Bolivia will show contrasting examples: Toropalca, where people felt general nostalgia for the culture they perceived themselves as having lost; and Yura, where people felt no nostalgia for lost culture and viewed their own authenticity in ironic ways. In terms of general narratives of modernity and disappearing cultures, the surprise in this comparison is that Toropalqueños, those who mourn their lost culture, live in a place relatively less traversed by modernization processes than their Yureño neighbors to the north. Cultural authenticity also takes center stage within folklore festivals. In three folklore festival contexts—one in rural Bolivia (Toropalca), one filmed in La Paz for world television broadcast, and one in an international folklore festival in France—Bolivians represented themselves to themselves and others, and sometimes they entered into contradiction with the image of indigenousness that international audiences associated with a Bolivian identity.

Cultural-historical authenticity often builds on a foundation of narrative structures. For example, the ensemble Música de Maestros performed music that fit within Bolivian narratives of nation, not necessarily those promoted by the state, but those with which musicians and their audiences could personally identify. One of these points of identification, through which multiple generations came to find pleasure in the performances of Música de Maestros, was the Chaco War, a war Bolivia lost to Paraguay (1932–1935), and about which I will say more below. Music performance is one venue through which people establish a sense of belonging to local and national communities, as both performers and listeners, and this sense of belonging is felt through a particular representation of one's past and the relationship of that past to an individual's present situation. This link is made through shared narrative forms that attribute to the history of nations the "continuity of a subject" (Balibar 1991: 86).[8] I would suggest that the Chaco War and the "return of the Indian" are two crucial axes around which contemporary narratives of Bolivian nations are presently structured.

With the term "unique authenticity" I refer to the idea that something is authentic because it is singular, new, innovative, and usually perceived to emerge from the creative depths of a composing musician's soul. This kind of authenticity raises a set of questions about composership and ownership, and once again recalls Benjamin's concept of the work of art in its model of individual creation, the work supposedly emerging from a spark of individual genius, the spark igniting the aura of a work (1968).[9] The generating logics behind unique authenticity include the romantic individualized view of artistic production, principles of constant innovation, and the idea of creators as proprietors of their works. This is the founding myth of modern concepts of authorship and copyright. Unique authenticity opens the debate about the presumed division between art created by individuals and culture created by collectivities. This kind of authenticity is part and parcel of the process whereby musical experiences become alienable objects, where a potential exchange-value of a performance assumes priority over any use-value of a performance.

As an issue, unique authenticity surfaces around the general recognition of music's separation from its purported source. If music performances make people feel rooted to place, these performances also are easily recorded, duplicated, and shifted to other places. As Steve Feld has indicated, "Music becomes a particularly poignant locale for understanding roots versus rootlessness . . ." (1994a: 269). Music, linked to specific places through performance practices, instills in people's memories the sensory metaphors central to local and national identification processes. As these musically induced sensory metaphors become split from their perceived original sources—what Murray Schafer labeled and lamented as "schizophonia" (1977)—they enter representational processes and a symbolic struggle that is often expressed through competing claims to both authenticity and ownership.

Schafer took a tragic view of the technological advances that contributed to an increase in schizophonia—"the split between an original sound and its electroacoustical transmission or reproduction" (1977: 90)—placing the creators of this displaced music in a state of alienation. Schafer however ignored the symbolically generative process that occurs when sound, split from its sources, enters a new context. For some authors the new contextualization after schizophonia is merely alienation, mass duplication, commodification, and a loss of social meaning (Attali 1985: 87–132). Steve Feld, invoking the language of Benjamin's "The Work of Art in the Age of Mechanical Reproduction" (1968), takes a different view of schizophonia, a process-based view that looks on not only "the process of splitting but on the consequent status of 'the copy' and contestation of its 'authenticity' as it seeks to partake in the 'legitimacy' granted to an 'original'" (Feld 1994a: 260). Feld opts for a study of "schismogenesis," taking a term from Gregory Bateson, to discuss the recombinations of sounds previously split from their sources (Feld 1994a: 265–271). I share Feld's view of schizophonia and schismogenesis as processes to be accepted rather than lamented, and I focus on the reshuffling of sensory experiences that occurs as part of these transformations. While sonorous domain over place is established through multiple sense experiences, the separation of sound from place and its recontextualization embodies a process of separation and reprioritization of these multiple sensory experiences. In this book, schizophonia and schismogenesis become crucial issues, not only in the international travels of Música de Maestros, but also in an analysis of cassette productions for two highland indigenous areas of Bolivia (Toropalca and Yura). These production processes underscored indigenous self-representation as well as the issues of indigenous authorship, prescribed by laws of the Bolivian state. James Clifford suggested that in the process of collecting art and culture, authenticity is *produced* through the process of taking the object out of one context and placing it in another (1988: 228). Recording may be taken as an analogous way that music is collected and through which cultural-historical authenticity comes up against a logic of unique authenticity.

The concept of unique authenticity enters this text in other telling ways: through an analysis of Música de Maestros, an ensemble that claims to interpret uniquely authentic works by "master" Bolivian composers; through the avant-garde compositions of a music workshop in La Paz, through the battles of this institution over the ownership of a fundable proposal they wrote, and through questions of authorship/composership in indigenous compositions. The central point of including unique authenticity within the discussions of this book is to challenge the art/culture divide by focussing on the hidden connections between felt experience of music (experiential authenticity), representational practices in music (cultural-historical authenticity), and the way experiences and representations become alienable objects within a political economy of culture.

These three ways of conceptualizing authenticity are my heuristic devices, but Bolivians use an array of adjectives to refer to the different music performances of this book: "Andean," "national," "Bolivian," "indigenous," "traditional," "Creole," "mestizo," "Toropalqueña," "Yureña," "native," and "electronic." "Andean music," usually indicated by instrumentation and costumes, is produced for an international as well as local audience. Performers of "Andean music" can get away with wearing just about any combination of clothing that harks to an imagined highland Andean culture: ponchos, sandals, hand-woven materials, special hats, and so on. "Andean music" could have origins in any Andean country: Peru, Bolivia, Ecuador, Colombia, Argentina, or Chile. Depending on the origin of the ensemble in question, "Andean music," to an international listener, may be *música nacional* (national music) to a Bolivian listener. "National music" was a phrase I heard urban and rural Bolivians use to refer to Andean ensembles of Bolivian origin, the Kjarkas ensemble providing the most prominent example. The instruments used by Kjarkas—quena, zampoñas, charango, bombo—mark the sonorously imagined realm of Andean music.

I will closely examine two sets of urban music performance contexts which explicitly or implicitly challenge the Kjarkas-type ensemble as "national music:" a music workshop run as a cultural nongovernmental organization (NGO) and Música de Maestros, the ensemble featured at the opening of this chapter. In these cases the modifier often employed shifts from "national" to "Bolivian" and the content of "Bolivian music" takes multiple forms. "Bolivian music" can refer to the "Creole" and "mestizo" genres in which many local composers have demonstrated their talents. "Bolivian music" can refer to avant-garde compositions by Bolivian composers. Finally, "Bolivian music," from the subject position of an urban context, can refer to "indigenous" or "traditional" music from the countryside. The workshop and Música de Maestros may refer to any of these kinds of music as "Bolivian music." In this ecumenical sense "Bolivian music" means "music created by Bolivians."

In the two rural areas where I conducted fieldwork, Toropalca and Yura, individuals did not refer to their own music as "Bolivian," "indigenous," or "traditional." Through local place references, people in Yura and Toropalca referred to their own music as "Yureña" and "Toropalqueña," and when Yureños and Toropalqueños compared their own music to other kinds of music—usually prerecorded—they would use the adjectives "native" or "autochthonous," to refer to their own music and juxtapose this with the adjectives "electronic" and "national" for music not produced through their own embodied performances. These overlapping semantic fields, each defined by different subject positions, give multiple meanings to a study of Bolivian music performances. I draw them together to explore music performances in relation to Bolivian imagined communities and the role that different kinds of authenticity play in the process of musically performing the nation.

The semantic oppositions that emerge here—Spanish and indigenous, modern and traditional—point to the numerous debates over the meaning of modernity in Latin American contexts. For example, the concept of "hybridity" provides a way of moving beyond these oppositional cate-gories (García Canclini 1995), and it also provides a response to the "eth-nic absolutism" and "the litany of pollution and impurity" (Gilroy 1993: 2). While hybridity, as one form of strategic essentialism (Spivak 1988: 13)[10] allows us to break down our own dualistic categorizations of the Spanish and the pre-Columbian, the modern and the traditional, and the urban and the rural, the concept of hybridity stops being strategic and continues as merely one more essentialism when we confuse our terms of analysis with social life itself, when we celebrate hybridity as one more dif-ference that maintains the first two terms against which the third seems so gloriously contestatory.

What I am suggesting is not necessarily contradictory to García Can-clini's original proposition, because his concept of hybridity is above all a call to transdisciplinary study—that is, that we cannot understand the com-plexities of social life if we insist upon a disciplinary division of labor, in his case, between sociology, anthropology, and communications (1995: 2, 176). Like García Canclini, I am concerned about the inevitable slippage between our modes of knowledge construction and our representations of cultural life. In the Bolivian context, such slippage may occur in debates about mes-tizaje, but the problems begin when any hint of a celebratory mood about mestizaje leaves unaddressed the political baggage that this term has carried since the 1952 revolution, baggage I will begin to unpack in the following section. As one begins to weigh this baggage, it becomes crucial to recognize that in the middle of many hybrid cultural processes, one of the principal avenues of contemporary Bolivian politics runs directly through contested realms of authenticity. Another form of strategic essentialism—not that of the social analyst, but rather that of oppressed citizens who are struggling for a stronger political position in Bolivian society—involves the reclaiming of authentically indigenous subject positions. In other words, anthropolo-gists may have stopped looking for the pure and authentic, and settled for the constructed view of cultural identities, but many Bolivians have not. In fact, the pursuit of indigenous authenticity is a principal site of contempo-rary Bolivian politics.

FLAGS

As a violinist with the ensemble Música de Maestros, I was a part of the Bolivian delegation to France that I described at the beginning of this in-troduction. During those street parade performances that required strong wind players, my role shifted to flag-bearer. Dressed in a costume that al-luded to the highland indigenous woman's dress, I carried the flag for this

Bolivian delegation in France. But I did not carry an official Bolivian flag because the delegation had forgotten to pack one. As a prop for one of their dances they had packed a *wiphala,* a rainbow flag, first claimed by the highland indigenous Aymaras, and since appropriated by many different groups in Bolivia that make claims to indigenousness. To underline the juxtapositions involved: I, as a U.S. citizen dressed in a highland indigenous costume from Bolivia, carried a Bolivian indigenous flag at the head of a Bolivian national delegation at an international folklore festival in France. What do nation, nationality, and nationalism mean in this context? And by extension, to the focus of this work, what are the different kinds of musics under the rubric of Bolivian music performances? My flag-bearing experience in France illustrates how much indigenousness has become an index of Bolivianness in the international sphere. Indigenous issues have taken center stage, even within official imaginings of the Bolivian nation-state. This return of the Indian has occurred against the backdrop of official national ceremonies.

Official Bolivian nationalism is still constructed in terms of wars, both won and lost, and through the public education experience, both rural and urban. On August 6th, Bolivian independence day, students in schools throughout Bolivia parade in uniform to salute the national flag and the independence war heroes, Sucre and Bolivar, often arranged as an altar (Figure 1.1). Bolivar was briefly the president of the newly independent republic in 1825, and his presidency was followed by the presidency of Sucre, a military man who set the foundations of the Republic on reformist and modernizing politics. These heroes and the holiday mark independence from Spain and the founding of the Bolivian republic, an event safely distanced from contemporary political questions. But for most of the Bolivian population, independence from Spain did not mean inclusion in a national project. This was a Creole independence and one that followed the squelched indigenous rebellions in 1780, those associated with Tupac Amaru in Peru and Tupac Katari in Bolivia. In fact, these early republican governments only included Spanish-speaking literate men, "at best only a quarter of the national population" (Klein 1982: 153). Through the nineteenth to the beginning of the twentieth century, as Bolivia's famed mining of silver shifted to tin, a political-economic structure developed around the interests of Bolivia's leading tin barons. Called the *rosca* (literally, spiral, or screw thread) by Bolivians, this political-economic conglomerate ruled Bolivia from the end of the nineteenth century through the early twentieth. With civic parades Bolivia also officially celebrates the Day of the Sea, a day to remind citizens that Chile took Bolivia's access to the sea in the War of the Pacific (1879–1883). In this conflict the mine owners took a pacifist pro-Chilean stance (see Klein 1982: 159), already proving that eco-

Figure 1.1   A Bolivian Independence Day (August 6th) altar as saluted by the citizens of Toropalca (photograph by author).

nomic and nationalist interests do not make easy bedfellows. While independence from Spain and the loss of access to the sea are emphasized in contemporary state rituals of Bolivian nationalism, other dates are downplayed in official state-sponsored celebrations.

The more recent historical events of the Chaco War (1932–1935) and the 1952 Revolution deeply mark contemporary Bolivian society. In the Chaco War Bolivia fought Paraguay over a relatively unpopulated piece of territory, supposedly rich in petroleum (see Albó and Barnadas 1990: 182). Bolivia lost the Chaco War, but although some museums have had exhibits on this event, the state has no official rituals through which to mourn this loss. Yet this event, more than any other in Bolivian history, is continually referenced by contemporary historiography as the moment of inception for a Bolivian national community (see Arze Aguirre 1987; Montenegro 1943: 235–239; Rivera Cusicanqui 1986: 45–48). This war marked the moment when Bolivians of different regions met in the trenches and recognized in each other a shared position of subordination in relation to the rosca that had been ruling the country. The Chaco War is a specific event around which Música de Maestros have constructed their repertoire. As another key event in relation to Bolivian nationness, the 1952 revolution stands similarly without state-sponsored ritual pomp. In the museum quarter of La Paz, on the colonial street of Jaén, where the music workshop located its antimuseumizing musical activities, one could not find a museum dedicated to the 1952 revolution (see Luykx 1999: 29–30), even though a commemorative site does exist in the Plaza Villarroel. The 1952 revolution brought inclusive citizenship policies, nationalization of mines, the Law of Agrarian Reform (1953), syndicalization of peasants, and a state ideology of cultural mixing (mestizaje). Wrapped up in party politics of the National Revolutionary Movement (*Movimiento Nacional Revolucionario*, MNR)—the party in power in 1952—the April revolutionary date becomes a holiday or a day of "labor flexibility" according to the existing local party politics. While the Chaco War and the 1952 revolution go relatively uncelebrated by official nationalism, I will show that they are precisely the events that today significantly mark Bolivian national music.

These revolutionary changes were followed in the 1960s and 1970s by several, often violent, military dictatorships until 1982, when Bolivia was characterized by "if not democracy in the full sense of the word, at least the orderly transfer of power" (Luykx 1999: 3). The 1980s mark the beginning of a shift in Bolivian national narratives, from a culturally homogenizing model to a pluricultural model, and during that decade both Música de Maestros and the workshop were founded. The shift from the culturally homogenizing narrative (1952) to a pluri-multi narrative has occurred within the context of the neoliberal New Economic Policies and the Decree 21060 (1985), which shut-down numerous mines and forced unemployed miners into the euphemistic category of *relocalizados* (the relocated ones; see Nash 1992).

Between 1993 and 1995, Bolivians were re-imagining their nationhood and new narratives of nation took more concrete forms through legislation and new bureaucratic rituals of state. The Law of Popular Participation was a sweeping reform of state-citizen relations, a legislative monument to "civil society." As a decentralizing law that nominally recognized indigenous organizations, Popular Participation was ironically one of the "three damned laws." Such was the epithet, coined by government opposition, the teachers union, and the *Central Obrero Boliviano* (Bolivian Worker Union or COB), for the laws of Educational Reform, Popular Participation, and Capitalization. Passed in 1994, during the presidency of Gonzalo Sánchez de Lozada, these three laws *together* aimed to completely restructure the Bolivian state. The government of Sánchez de Lozada, marking the MNR's return to power, initiated other changes that underscored the field of "ethnicity"—the formation of a Secretariat of Ethnic, Gender, and Generational Affairs; the promotion of bilingual and intercultural education through the Law of Educational Reform; and the choice of a highland indigenous (Aymara) Vice President (Victor Hugo Cárdenas). All of these developments marked a shift in Bolivia's previous narrative of nation—a shift from the 1952 class-based homogenizing model to a contemporary pluriethnic narrative of celebrating cultural differences (see Bigenho 1996: 490–494). Radical in its time, the 1952 proposal sought to include Bolivia's indigenous populations as equal citizens within the state, breaking away from the colonial and early republican dual national model, which was rooted in a tribute to be paid by the indigenous population. The revolutionary project eventually encompassed a land reform (1953) that dismantled large landed estates or haciendas, giving land to the former "Indians," then called "*campesinos*" (loosely translated as "peasants") under the slogan, "the land belongs to those who work it." But not all campesinos in Bolivia had been under hacienda systems. For example, Toropalqueños and Yureños were not under hacienda systems and some form of their indigenous organizations or ayllus, still exist in these areas, even though these "indigenous" organizations must be viewed as shaped by colonial administrative policies. Those who have had access to their own lands through indigenous organizations have often viewed the Agrarian Reform's institutionalization of private property as a threat to these indigenous structures.[11]

In contrast to the reforms of 1952, the more recent national narrative in Bolivia emphasizes a mosaic of cultural differences, even "nations," united under the single nation-state of Bolivia. To exemplify this trend I turn to several texts or project histories—the results of conferences or dialogues in which different sectors of Bolivian society explicitly discussed alternative ways of imagining "Bolivia." The following titles give some indication of the spirit of these discussions: *For a Different Bolivia: Contributions to a Popular Historical Project* (*Por una Bolivia diferente: aportes para un proyecto histórico popular,* CIPCA 1991), *The Pluri-multi or the Reign of Diversity* (*Lo pluri-multi o el reino de la diversidad,* ILDIS 1993), *The Revolt of the Nationalities* (*La revuelta de las nacionalidades,* UNITAS and Cuadros 1991).[12] While readings of official multicultural politics might be classified within the bland celebration of differences, in Bolivia, popular sectors initiated some of these new imaginings in radical ways. The Aymara indigenous political movement, *Katarismo,* began in the 1960s and the 1970s—drawing on the name "Tupac Katari" of the 1781 rebellions—and intersected significantly with the peasant union politics of the *Confederación Sindical Unica de Trabajadores Campesinos de Bolivia* (CSUTCB) and the formation of indigenous Aymara intellectuals in La Paz. The effects of these Aymara-centered politics have been felt throughout Bolivia's politics of multiculturalism. For example, the CSUTCB, in its second congress (June 1983), proposed the concept of a plurinational state. Their initiative, while never fully addressed within the Bolivian government, provides an intriguing example of multicultural politics as they intersect with class-based organizing. This example provided a glimmer of hope against what Charles Hale has labeled as the "hegemonic divide" and the most lasting tragedy of the conquest (1994)—what I will gloss as the oppositional positions of leftist and indigenous politics.

While the politics of cultural difference have the potential to turn in radical directions, they can also follow bland depoliticized paths. Class has not disappeared in Bolivia, but it has taken a back seat to the prominent politics of cultural difference, and the Bolivian government's politics of culturalism have already been critiqued by some authors as a relativist disguise of the same old project of molding liberal citizens of the nation-state (Arnold and Yapita 2000). Consistent with global trends of late capitalism (Harvey 1989: 341; Jameson 1991: 318), the contemporary narrative of nation backgrounds class and foregrounds multicultural issues. The Bolivian state has moved from denying cultural segmentation to celebrating it. A national narrative of respecting cultural differences may not be shared by Bolivia's elites and the governments that follow Gonzalo Sánchez de Lozada's tenure. For example, with the subsequent presidential election of Hugo Banzer Suárez, a previous dictator of Bolivia, the Ministry of Ethnic, Gender, and Generational Affairs was dissolved. Nevertheless, I would argue that global factors are contributing to the continuation of the pluricultural national narrative. International agencies have also placed indigenous cultures high on their funding agendas. In Bolivia these international resources propel many activities of government institutions, nongovernmental organizations, and the professionals employed within them. The 1952 revolutionary ideology of mestizaje also rested heavily on class-based organizing (strong miners' unions and the unionization of the peasants), which, with the closure of mines and the resurgence of indigenous politics, has waned considerably in the contemporary Bolivian context.[13]

The Chaco War, the 1952 revolution, and Katarismo are all flags that punctuate a popular emotional understanding of Bolivian history, and they are crucial to understanding the "return of the Indian" through music performances. In the following chapter I take a closer look at experiential authenticity, what moves people to dance, and the contradictions of feeling and representing music performances.

Chapter 2

What Makes You
Want To Dance

Your Groove, My Noise

Many Bolivian musicians in La Paz expressed absolute disdain for cumbia music, and yet during my fieldwork, this genre was probably the single most popular music in both urban and rural contexts. Its presence was ubiquitous in almost any social gathering that involved dancing. While the cumbia genre is usually associated with Colombian origins, many of the recordings that made their way to Bolivia emerged from recording productions in Mexico. The strong distaste for this music—Colombian, Mexican, or even the locally modeled sound-alikes—was often framed in terms of a sonorous invasion of Bolivian territory. Cumbias had seeped into Bolivia, and according to some people this music was seen as polluting the sonorous environment, clogging radio waves, social contexts, and public spaces.

Whenever I rode a bus in Bolivia my travels were almost always accompanied by music. During the overnight bus trip between La Paz and Potosí, the driver inevitably listened to music. When the control to block the noise from the cabin did not work properly, the passengers had to listen to the driver's selections throughout a sleepless night. The driver's selection invariably favored cumbias as performed by an ensemble of electric guitar, bass, and keyboards. Middle- and upper-class Bolivians feared this music was replacing or negatively influencing genuine Bolivian musical expressions. The fears of the infiltration of cumbias into Bolivia often manifested themselves in the contexts of the urban entrance fiestas, ritual parades in which troupes dance to different genres of Bolivian folk-loric expressions. In the context of these *entradas,* politicians would call for disqualification of any group that danced to a musical adaptation of a piece that was obviously of foreign influence. One is reminded of Paul Gilroy's question of whether or not "this impulse towards cultural pro-tectionism [is] the most cruel trick the west can play upon its dissident af-filiates" (1993: 33). These attitudes recall Mary Douglas's key treatise on pollution and taboo wherein she suggests that modern ideas of defilement are framed as matters of hygiene or aesthetics (1966: 35). Nevertheless, many Bolivians placed these aesthetically dangerous cumbias at the cen-ter of their listening and dancing activities.

In this chapter I attempt the impossible: to *write* about the sounds of Bolivian music. As I throw all musicological cautions to the winds (see C. Seeger 1977), my purpose is not to use language to provide a sonorous map of Bolivia, but rather to first take seriously the connection between the sounds of music and the sounds that make Bolivians want to dance, and second examine why some people's dance music is so threatening to other people. In my discussion, kinesthetics are as important as sonorities. I assume that "the groove"—a term I will gloss as that which makes one want to move to music—is a principal source of pleasure in music perfor-mance practices. The groove is not a linguistic translation of a Bolivian term, but rather a concept I will use universally to refer to a particular way of feeling a musical experience. Charles Keil has suggested that the groove is created through "participatory discrepancies," the state of being in synch and slightly out of time with the other musicians (1994b: 98). On one level, participatory discrepancies are about both maintaining the tension be-tween individual players and including those tensions within a collective performance. For example, the members of the Guarneri String Quartet talk about the strength of their ensemble emerging not from each musician matching their sound with others, but from a collective maintenance of each musician's particularities (Blum 1986: 5). There is a difference be-tween these micro-level tensions that entice a body into movement within musical practices, and the social tensions that exist between those who dance and those who remain critically on the sidelines. This chapter em-phasizes the "feelingful" side of Bolivian music performances[1] and exam-ines the conflicts that emerge as the experiences of some Bolivians clash with the representational practices of others. How some Bolivians want to represent the cultural practices of others enters into direct contradiction with the ways these groups experience music performances.

Cumbia in Bolivia keenly exemplifies a music that juxtaposes the cul-turally authentic and the experientially authentic, between what is repre-sented as Bolivian and what makes one want to move. And this dynamic around cumbia is replicated in other Latin American contexts. Cumbia is a genre through which Texas-Mexican (*Tejano*) artists are making a musical splash. As Cameron Randle, an executive of Arista Records told the anthropologist, Manuel Peña, who was researching Tejano music, "'It's considered the musical passport to Latin America, you know—the cumbia'" (Peña 1999a: 197). And in Peru, cumbia andina, disparagingly called "chicha" by those who do not listen and dance to it, combines Peruvian *huayno* melodies and Colombian cumbia rhythms within a distinctly electronic instrumentation, and this music has formed a basis of identity for the sons and daughters of highland migrants in Lima (see Razuri 1983; Romero 1985; Turino 1990). While I do not want to dismiss or downplay the commercial side of this "passport," I find it more revealing to reflect on the tensions between those who feel threatened by this music and those who locate an experiential authenticity within this music. Discourses of cultural authenticity have been used to commercially market another's music, and "world music" as sold to white Western audiences is a prime example of this move (see Gilroy 1993: 99; Feld 1994b). Another side to this regime of cultural authenticity is a kind of policing of the very experience of musical pleasures. While claims against cumbias may be made as statements against commercialization and the ruin of particular cultural and aesthetic forms, it is also a claim that remains blind to the power of music that moves people to dance. While this chapter explores the different musical sounds that formed both central and peripheral roles in my overall research, I will highlight the symbolic and discursive battles that surrounded these *felt* and *represented* authenticities, how one person's real music experience is another person's object of ridicule or source of anxiety over musical boundaries of Bolivian national music.

In presenting these grooves I work loosely within a system of classification developed by the Bolivian Workshop of Popular Music, "Arawi." I do so not to make sure each sound is properly located in its niche, but rather to simultaneously reflect on classificatory systems that reveal modes of thought, as well as carve conceptual boundaries through which the authentic becomes defined, disputed, and contested. The workshop imagined their musical activities within a pyramid that included "traditional music" at the base, "mesomusic" at midlevel, and "contemporary music" at the top. "Traditional" was often accompanied by the adjective "peasant" (*campesino*) or completely replaced with the word "autochthonous." Within the workshop's activities, "traditional music" referred to the wind instrument genres from the Bolivian countryside in which a single kind of instrument was played by twelve to twenty musicians, and each kind of instrument was associated with a performance style, with specific melodic and rhythmic patterns.

In Bolivia, this troupe style of playing has become one of the contemporary markers of a culturally authentic indigenous performance. The workshop found the need to distinguish between this performance style and the style of Pan-Andean ensembles like Kjarkas, ensembles whose members used indigenous instruments, but played them as solo artists within a professional performing group, playing genres that had little or nothing to do with the instruments' purported original uses in a rural community.

In outlining this distinction, the workshop's organizers turned to Carlos Vega's concept of "mesomusic" (1966). When Vega wanted to discuss music that was not "learned" (*música culta*), he found the term "popular" entirely too ambiguous (1966: 2). In response to this conceptual dilemma, Vega coined the term "mesomusic" to refer to: "the aggregate of musical creations (melodies with or without words) functionally designed for recreation, for social dancing, for the theater, for public acts, classrooms, games, etc., adopted or accepted by listeners of the culturally modern nations" (1966:3). Vega placed mesomusic, an aesthetically conservative music, squarely within the modern nation-state, and he perceived mesomusic as coexisting with fine-art music in the urban context and with rural folk music in the countryside (1966: 3–4). While the workshop organizers described their classification in terms of a pyramid, Vega gave more of a sense of a diamond in which the wide center is occupied by mesomusic which influences and is influenced by both art music and folk music. In fact, Vega explicitly took mesomusic out of any hierarchical structure and attributed its pervasiveness in societies to its function as a music of recreation, of capitalist production and consumption, and of cultural transformation: " . . . mesomusic is the instrument of all the groups of the world that are absorbing the cultural irrigation of the West" (1966: 16–17).[2] The workshop organizers saw Vega's concept of mesomusic as occupying multiple interstitial spaces that were likely to be influenced by both the traditional and contemporary wings of the institution's activities. Mesomusic is dance music and as such it occupies a prominent place in this chapter. In Bolivia, mesomusic might include cumbias, the music of Pan-Andean ensembles like Kjarkas, the band music that accompanies the dancers of urban entrance fiestas, and the better part of the repertoire of Música de Maestros.

Contemporary music formed the tip of the workshop's classification pyramid. Workshop organizers took as a guiding premise the idea that many of the performance techniques and preferred aesthetics of Bolivia's traditional indigenous music were precisely what composers in other parts of the world referred to as "contemporary." To buttress this claim, workshop organizers would consistently refer to the overblowing techniques that are often the preferred performance aesthetic for several vari-

eties of Bolivian duct flute instruments. Contemporary or ḁ
music seems to represent the antithesis of dance music—if suc
terization is possible. Its sounds usually do not compel people
Where then is the groove in contemporary music? How is this m
ingful? I will address this question through the soundscapes of ꜱome of
the workshop's performances.

In the next section, I turn to the grooves of Torpalqueños and Yureños,
whose music might fit in the workshop's category of "traditional music."
While Yureños and Toropalqueños often referred to their own music as
"autochthonous," they too danced to those "dangerous" cumbias.

The Autochthonous and the Dangerous

I heard the sound of the Toropalqueña *flauta* for the first time in the Fiesta de Comadres in Sarapalca, a ritual celebration at the start of Carnival
season. The flauta is a six-holed, vertically played wooden flute. North of
the village Toropalca, the community of Sarapalca had notoriety as the
place where flauta players gathered to compose the new tunes or *huayños*
for Carnival. Toropalqueños play two sizes of flauta: large (*jatun*) and
small (*juch'uy*).[3] Everyone in Toropalca told me that to study the music of
the region, I must begin at this fiesta. "That is where they create the music
to the sound of the water and the wind," they told me. Even in Yura I
found references to Sarapalca as a pilgrimage site for meeting to create
music, although this was described as something Yureños "used to do."

Sarapalca's notoriety in this sense proved to be based more on discourse than on contemporary practice. On the Thursday before Carnival
in 1994, the community of Sarapalca celebrated the Fiesta de Comadres,
the principal fiesta of their local indigenous authority. Sarapalqueños created two huayños during this fiesta. One of the huayños was created while
listening to a cassette recording of a tune that a relative, working in Argentina, had composed, sung, recorded, and sent home for the festivities.
But at this fiesta, numerous flauta players did not appear from all over the
region. There were six flauta players at most, and all but one were from
the community of Sarapalca. As I went south to the village of Toropalca
the flauta players became even more scarce.

In 1994, two aspects stood out about the sound of the flauta in the village of Toropalca: first, few musicians played the flauta, and second, the
flauta performances included women's songs (see Figure 2.1). Everyone
lamented the absence of flauta players and commented on the migration
to Argentina that was taking young men away from the area. No one commented on the fact that the women, through their song and lyrics, were

Figure 2.1   Toropalqueños play the flauta (photograph by author).

definitely the musical leaders in flauta genres. As a few flauta players struggled to extract a melody from their instruments, the women of the village belted out songs with incredible force as they continued to dance in a circle around the musicians. Toropalqueña village women sang in strong, high-pitched voices, with breathy strident timbres. In Toropalca, women's voices filled a void of flauta sounds, and became a point of departure for my study of music in that area.

Many of the women who sang were vecinos—people who lived outside of the indigenous administrative structures (ayllus) and whose aspirations for local progress often imitated modern urban styles. The vecinos of Toropalca had a very strong presence, and in relative terms, the indigenous structures there were rather weak. The vecinos of Toropalca had taken up the mission of maintaining certain traditions they viewed as characteristic of the region, assuming some of these traditions as their own—as Toropalqueños—even though "Toropalca" more often referred to the canton, the state organizational structure, rather than to the ayllu.

At the suggestion of a few of the singers, I began a collaborative project of creating a book of songs for the local school. I enlisted the help of Toropalqueña women singers in the collection and translation (from Quechua to Spanish) of their own songs. Students from all over the canton of Toropalca came to the boarding school in the village, so a songbook for the school would reach much further than the population of the village itself. The cassette that I eventually produced for Toropalca also re-flected the extensive participation of these women and the inclusion of their songs.

The women of Toropalca composed most of their own songs in Quechua, singing in a style that suggested a clear melody to the listener. I recorded these women singing in fiestas and in individual and group in-terviews. At the fiestas, the women sang without any inhibitions, but they were much more self-conscious about singing in the context of inter-views. Outside of the fiesta context, if the women missed hitting a pitch, they often stopped singing mid-phrase, or sang in a hushed, barely audi-ble voice, rushing to the end of the song, completely outside of the meter and rhythm of the fiesta performance. Although I was not surprised by their self-consciousness in one context and the lack of it in another, what emerged in the interviews was their consciousness of the musical instru-ment of the flauta as a necessary element for the representation of a cul-turally authentic Toropalqueña music. I will explore this further in chapter five, but here I want to emphasize that although the singing of Toropalqueña women was the center of the groove in Toropalqueños' Carnival experience, their own representation of a culturally authentic Toropalqueña music focused on the use of a traditional instrument that was scarcely present in Carnival of 1994.

In contrast, the Yureño Carnival was characterized by women silently dancing to a dense sound produced by numerous men who played the flauta. Yureños played one size of flauta, a medium size between Toropalca's two extremes.[4] Yureños accompanied the flauta troupe with a *caja,* small, vertically hand-held drum with a taut string across the back. They played in troupes of ten to forty musicians, and each troupe repre-sented one of the four indigenous organizations (ayllus) of Yura. Yureños valued collective volume as well as length of performance, and these were the criteria of a competition in which all troupes played simultaneously their own pieces for as long as they possibly could.

In Yura, I learned to play the flauta, an experience that gave me the op-portunity to confirm one of Henry Stobart's findings on the performance practices of these kinds of instruments—the preference for crossed fin-gerings (1988). Fingerings are crossed when stopped holes are alternated with open holes to produce pitches that could also be produced with se-quentially stopped holes (Stobart 1988). Crossed fingerings cause more disturbance to the vibrating column of air, thus producing a rich series of harmonics and a preferred timbre—what Stobart's informants called "*tara*" (see Stobart 1996a). I did not encounter discursive references to this performance aesthetic, but Yureños extensively use crossed fingerings in flauta performances. The preferred flauta sound in Yura was overblown, hoarse, gruff, and accompanied by men and women whistling the tune or huayño through their teeth.

In 1995, Yureños began the flauta season in the January Fiesta of Kings and continued through the activities of Carnival, and these two fiestas continued to be intricately tied to the ritual reconstruction of indigenous structures (ayllus) and the reaffirmation of indigenous authority systems (see Rasnake 1989). In all of these activities Yureños played the flauta in groups that represented the four principal ayllus of Yura: Qullana, Wisiqsa, Chiquchi, and Qhurqa. Each of these ayllus had their own huayños, which Yureños, during the ritual moment of the fiesta, easily distinguished from a distance. As a faint sound of flautas progressed up the river valley toward Yura, someone would comment, "Ayllu ____ is coming." During the 1995 Fiesta of Kings and Carnival, with conscious attention to the different motifs, I too learned to distinguish the huayños of the different ayllus. But unlike my conscious learning process that enabled me at any time to identify these pieces with one of the four ayllus, I found Yureños at a loss, or unwilling, to make these distinctions outside of the ritual moment. The implications of this differentiated listening experience are explored in chapter six, in which the themes of the spatial identification of ayllus and the significance of competitive musical performance frame a discussion of "feeling Yureño" during Carnival and representing oneself as Yureño to the Bolivian state.

The height of the Yureño Carnival rituals was the musical competition around the ayllus' ritual center—a column called *el rollo*. From the very center of the musical competition, the rollo itself, I listened to what at first seemed like a cacophony of sounds: all four ayllus playing their own huayño at the same time as they circled around the rollo. All musicians played loudly, doing everything possible not to be thrown off into the melody of a different ayllu. This type of musical competition—with everyone playing at once—actually produces a preferred sonorous aesthetic sought in the annual reproduction of the Andean fiesta (see Bigenho 1993: 232). In Yura, the musical competition continued into the early morning hours. The next day Yureños would discuss the unofficial winners of the competition, the ayllu whose huayño was heard all alone at the rollo before silence set in for a few early morning hours.

While some flauta players continued to play at the plaza, at about 11:00 P.M. some Yureños moved to houses where people were dancing to cumbias. This "dangerous" music was particularly popular among young Yureños. Yureños even had their own home grown ensemble that played and recorded with small labels in Potosi and Cochabamba; ironically named *Amadeus*, this group's electronic sound—in genres labeled "disco," "rok latino," "*tarqueda*," "cumbia," and "huayño"—provided the dance

Figure 2.2   For Carnival, the women dress "as good Yureñas" (photograph by author).

music in many fiestas of Yura, as men and women danced together to songs with titles like "Ay wan[t] you." Young men and women in Yura, dressed *"como buen yureños"* (as good yureños) in *unkus, aymillas,* and *ajsus,*[5] danced the night away to the electronic sounds of the likes of Amadeus, *Grupo Bryndis, Brothers,* and *Grupo Maroyu.* The morning after an evening of cumbia dancing, the men took up their flautas again to join the ranks of their respective ayllus, and the women danced together in a circle around them (Figure 2.2 and Figure 2.3). Only from the vecinos of Yura did I hear disparaging comments about the current flauta tunes being lifted from "all those cumbias they listen to." For most Yureños, the juxtaposition of what the workshop would call "traditional music" and "mesomusic" posed no dilemmas in daily practice.

Figure 2.3   For Carnival men dress "as good Yureños" and play the flauta (photograph by author).

While women's voices overpowered the weak sounds of flautas in
Toropalca, during the dates of Pentecost and San Juan (June 24), I heard
a strong representation of the breathy sounds of *ayarachis* instruments.
Ayarachis are reed panpipes with two rows of seven tubes.[6] Ayarachis were
played at a calm, deliberate tempo, and the deep sound of large drums,
slung over the shoulders of the ayarachis players, often overpowered the
melody as carried on the panpipes. Toropalqueños played ayarachis in a
circle facing inward, moving around the circle in small dance steps.
Women, hand in hand, formed a dancing circle around this inner circle of
musicians. A larger dancing crowd formed several concentric circles
around the inner circles of dancers and musicians. While Toropalqueño
musicians indicated that the ideal way to perform this genre was by donning large ostrich-feather headdresses, I never observed this "full dress" in
any of their ayarachis performances. In the next chapter I will return to
the theme of the culturally authentic performance as visually imagined
through costumes that accompany specific musical expressions. After several repetitions of the *huayllas,* the term for tunes played on ayarachis, the
panpipe musicians, all of them men, stopped playing and simply sang for
one or two repetitions of the piece.

Unlike many panpipe performance traditions in the Andes, ayarachis
are *not* played with interlocking technique. In interlocking technique,

each musician plays a panpipe with the tubes needed by the other musician to complete a melodic line; the melodic line is created by playing in paired instruments (*arca* and *ira*). Many researchers of Andean panpipe traditions have highlighted this interlocking performance practice, which requires cooperation among musicians (Turino 1993a), and which represents an expression of symbolic dualism (Baumann 1996: 30; Sánchez Canedo 1996: 84). The research fetish for interlocking technique has been replicated in many urban-based attempts to represent the most authentic indigenous performance. In the imagination of Bolivian mestizos and Creoles, interlocking technique carries the heavy symbolic load of collective cooperation as expected of the properly authentic indigenous community. Ayarachis carried a heavy symbolic load for Toropalqueños themselves, but because these instruments were played in unison, interlocking technique and its ideological implications were not part of their symbolic work.[7]

Yureños and Toropalqueños played zampoñas, the panpipes performed through interlocking technique, but this instrument and its genre remained much less significant in terms of the way Toropalqueños and Yureños represented themselves as autochthonous, to themselves and to others. Zampoña groups, often comprised of school students who bought their panpipes in the city of Potosí, participated in fiestas, festivals, and civic activities, but these instruments were not paraded by Toropalqueños or Yureños as defining instruments of the region. For Toropalqueños and Yureños, their own sense of cultural authenticity was rooted in the flauta, and additionally in the case of Toropalca, in the ayarachis. To emphasize zampoñas and interlocking technique in these contexts would be to play into what, for a Western imagination, is a very powerful trope of Andean authenticity: the communal and cooperative music performance. The powerful symbolism of interlocking technique will emerge again in my work, but in reference to the staged performances of Música de Maestros, and their attempts to represent an authentic highland indigenous performance aesthetic.

During the last months of 1995, I conducted a series of listening interviews in Yura, asking Yureños to talk about different recorded selections of music. Yureños, like many people in Bolivia's rural areas, had access to radio and cassettes, media through which they have developed a sonorous knowledge of different musical expressions. In the listening interview I included Yureña flauta music, a song from the group Kjarkas, the huayño "Bien le cascaremos," played by the ensemble *Norte Potosi*,[8] and a Peruvian song (huayno). Yureños generally did not recognize *the ensemble* Norte Potosi, although they often said the music came from the region of northern Potosí. The also did not recognize the foreign selection as Peruvian. While the responses on Norte Potosí and the Peruvian huayno were mixed, most Yureños did not hesitate to identify the music of Kjarkas, and they often named the ensemble and tagged it with the label "national music." This is the label that radio stations repeatedly assigned to this music. But I will suggest that the content of the label "national music" is increasingly empty. In this case, "national music" is a signifier of a nation stripped of its national signified. I turn to a discussion of the sonorous significance of Kjarkas, the ensemble against which both the workshop and Música de Maestros reacted by performing alternative national musics.

WHAT'S WRONG WITH KJARKAS

In 1986 I had enthusiastically attended a concert of *Proyección Kjarkas* in Lima, Peru. Not knowing if it would be a sellout, I had been stalking the theater for days before the performance to make sure I had a ticket. The concert fulfilled all of my listening expectations. I cheered with the crowds as the handful of musicians, in their ubiquitous ponchos with long fringes, gave an animated performance, demonstrating individual virtuosity on "typically Andean" instruments like the quena, zampoñas, and charango. I sang along with all of the hits of the time: "Bolivia," "Way yay yay," "Llorando se fue."[9] It was only after the show that I began to wonder why this ensemble was called "Proyección Kjarkas" and not just "Kjarkas." As I realized that this was not the real thing, I felt somewhat cheated. I had only heard a copy, a replica, a mimesis of the original Kjarkas. Nevertheless, in the moment of the performance itself they had completely satisfied my expectations of Andean music. Kjarkas and their "clones," as workshop organizers called them, have been producing the tourist music of Bolivia. It was the music I heard accompanying a video on Bolivia that the airline screened as I arrived in La Paz. It was the music I heard when I was on hold to speak with an agent of the Bolivian airline. Kjarkas's music has permeated the tourist side of Bolivia and responds exceedingly well to a Western sense of an aestheticized exotic other.

Between 1986 and 1993 I learned to dislike Kjarkas and I underline *learned* in the sense of the intellectualizing process it entailed. I learned to dislike them precisely because I realized how well they responded to my Western sense of the exotic other, and as an anthropologist, my consciousness of this fact left me uneasy. I also realize that this disillusionment was rooted in yet one more problematic attempt at the pursuit of my own sense of the authentic. To many of the workshop's organizers and instructors, Kjarkas and their clones were empty of any inherent musical value and did nothing to contribute to a uniquely Bolivian music. Workshop organizers proposed that young people should do anything *other than* clone themselves from Kjarkas.

As I began to distance myself from my "learned distaste" for Kjarkas, I came to see this ensemble's work in relation to my larger arguments about shifting narratives of nation in Bolivia. Gilka Wara Céspedes drew an association between the Kjarkas ensemble and the 1952 revolutionary narrative of nation (1993), and while this narrative was culturally homogenizing in its implications for indigenous groups, it was also a narrative that brought to the urban context a new recognition of Bolivia's peasant cultures. Groups like Kjarkas could play peasant instruments that previously would have been excluded from mestizo-Creole urban performing contexts because of the negative connotations associated with these instruments. Mestizo-Creole musicians and artists, who lived through these transformations, consistently emphasize this change of Bolivian musical practices, and as such this shift should not be underestimated. The aesthetic opposition to Kjarkas by musical projects of the 1980s and 1990s needs to be understood in terms of a turn to narratives of nation that are alternative to the 1952 revolutionary one. In the 1990s, what was "wrong" with Kjarkas was that they had passed their prime time, not in the sense of their music performance capabilities, but in the sense of their articulation with a popular narrative of nation. Nevertheless, the aesthetic arguments against Kjarkas did nothing to brake the continued popularity of this ensemble in the 1990s, particularly after their release of an album that easily moved Bolivians to dance.

When Kjarkas released their recording dedicated to "*saya* Afro-boliviana," I was given one more intellectualized reason to dislike the group. Saya refers to a musical expression attributed to African-Bolivians, descendants of slaves in Bolivia, but in the commercial rush the label "saya" is often conflated with another genre, *caporales,* a dance genre in which the male figure is the quintessential slave driver. While I was in Bolivia, the Kjarkas' saya album was extremely popular. I danced to its rhythms along with crowds of Bolivians in a middle-class dance club in La Paz (El Loro en Su Salsa), at the August 6th (Independence Day) celebrations in Toropalca (Nor Chichas, Potosi), and at a school graduation party in Yura (Quijarro, Potosi). So if so many people loved to dance to it, what was wrong with this music? Saya-caporal was a clear example of the clash between experiential and cultural authenticities. What was the best dance music for Bolivians of many different social classes and ethnic groups was considered an artistic aberration and even a swindle of authentic African-Bolivian self-representation. When I was conducting fieldwork, Robert Templeman, an ethnomusicologist, was conducting research with African-Bolivian musicians who play saya music. Interpreting this music as an expression of a social movement, Templeman addressed the exclusion of African-Bolivians from state-sponsored activities that celebrate ethnic differences, even as he recognized changes that were occurring as a result of this social movement.[10] Kjarkas recorded caporales music and called it "saya," touching off a debate about distinguishing "real saya"—an African-Bolivian musical expression from the Yungas of La Paz—from "caporales"—a genre and rhythm now present in all of Bolivia's major urban entradas.[11] Urban entradas are a general symbolic meeting place of many different sectors of Bolivian society, but the middle- and upper-class Creoles predominate in the caporales dance. With a whip in hand and huge bell-lined boots that sound off with each decisive step, the caporales male dancer symbolizes the slave-driver, the *capatáz* (see Figure 2.4).

The saya-caporal debate permeated the musical scene of La Paz, leading to apologetic attitudes on the part of some composers and questions of cultural ownership of musical genres on the part of others. At one concert, before performing a piece, the singer/songwriter Jaime Junaro publicly apologized for the composition "No me dejes," which he had labeled as "saya-caporal." The singer/songwriter Luis Rico gave a similar preface to a piece he called "La saya del caporal." A composer of the workshop received criticism from African-Bolivians for composing in the genre of saya a piece that was to accompany the final credits of the film *Cuestión de fé* (1995), the implication being that this genre "belonged" to a specific cultural group—African-Bolivians—and should not have been appropriated by composers from other cultural groups. The implicit principle at work in the claim of the African-Bolivians was an expanding notion of proprietorship over culture, a movement fraught with problems and contradictions that I will explore further in chapter seven (see Brown 1998). The composer for the movie countered that he himself was a *Bolivian* composer and in his attempt to compose *Bolivian* music, he would draw upon any Bolivian genre he pleased. The poetic license invoked by the composer was considered something that undermined African-Bolivians' own politics of culture.

Why did Kjarkas use the musical genre of caporales but call it saya? If aestheticizing the exotic other to a Western ear gained them popularity abroad and at home, the manipulation of saya aestheticized a different other to many Bolivians. In a country that was discursively steeped in multicultural politics, the easily identifiable other within Bolivia was vanishing. A pluriethnic mosaic left confusion about who the other was in Bolivian society. Discourses addressed the ethnic groups of Bolivia's lowlands as well as the Quechuas and Aymaras of the highlands, but the situation of the African-Bolivian remained differentiated within these

Figure 2.4   In the city of La Paz, men dance caporales in the Entrada del Gran Poder (photograph by author).

frameworks that recognized identity claims on the basis of indigenous language, social organizations, land access, and claims to nativism (even if these claims were structured through a history of colonial experiences). The African-Bolivians, who were brought to Bolivia through the slave trade, still remained to an extent at the margins of these discourses; at the margins of the previously described pluri-multi discourse, the African-Bolivian represented the other internal to Bolivia and caporales is the aestheticized mimetic view of that other. Kjarkas sold this aestheticized other to Bolivians, in the city and in the countryside, the same way they sold a different aestheticized other to the tourist who dreams of lone Andean flute players—true descendants of Incas—playing on Andean peaks. By playing caporales music (a slave-driving signifier) and calling it saya (an African-Bolivian signifier), Kjarkas successfully played upon a mimesis internal to Bolivia.

Caporales is a principal rhythm danced in all of Bolivia's urban entradas: Gran Poder in La Paz, Virgen de Urkupiña in Cochabamba, Ch'utillos in Potosi, and Carnaval in Oruro.[12] As part of the latent, but ever-present urban fiesta, the brass band rhythms of caporales, *morenadas, diabladas,* and *llameradas*—types of entrada dances—haunted my weekends as troupes rehearsed for the ritual moments of these fiestas.

Dancing to the Band:
What the Military Did
for Bolivian Soundscapes

The sounds of bass drums, trumpets, trombones, tubas, baritones, and crashing cymbals ultimately mark Bolivia's entradas. Throughout Bolivia, the brass band is an ubiquitous sonorous sign of fiesta. The sponsors of rural fiestas in Toropalca and patron saint fiestas in Yura brought the brass sound from the city, sometimes only three or four musicians. Principally providing dance music in the evenings, these imported ensembles blared out popular pieces in the genres of caporales, cumbias, and huayños. People in Toropalca and Yura danced enthusiastically to this band music, even though they often sarcastically referred to these groups as "pure tin cans" (*pura lata*). As well as setting apart the brass sound from the sound of their own indigenous or autochthonous instruments, the expression "pure tin cans" also indicated the listeners' perceptions that these band performances in their villages were not exemplary brass sounds. But bringing a brass band from the city brought prestige to rural fiesta sponsors (*alferes*), and demonstrated a sponsor's willingness to spend money for the success of the fiesta. The band from the city, no matter how bad it sounded, carried the mystique of the urban.

The apparent ubiquitous nature of the brass band in Bolivia has much to do with the military. In Bolivia, military service has been mandatory for men since 1904, but upper-class Bolivians have been quite successful at avoiding conscription, leaving the lower-class sectors of Bolivian society to serve in the armed forces and to learn the instruments of the brass band.[13] The presence of brass bands throughout Bolivia's soundscapes can be credited to the formation of military bands in the beginning of the twentieth century—"the State's great contribution to popular music" (Rossells 1996: 108). Military bands, characterized by their mobility within national territory, were called upon to play for fiestas and ceremonies (Rossells 1996: 109). These bands—greeting and dispatching regiments in the Chaco War of the 1930s—became a national musical expression. In the extensive liner notes to her recording of music from the Chaco War, the singer-songwriter and sociologist, Jenny Cárdenas goes so far as to say that during the Chaco War, bands were part of the military "logistics" of the conflict, accompanying soldiers in rest areas, raising spirits, and sparking patriotic sentiments (1999: 4).

As the regiments were sent off to fight in the Chaco War, cavalry boleros (*boleros de caballería*) were often the genre played by military bands (see Rossells 1996: 108–113). In their third compact disc, which focused on themes of the Chaco War, Música de Maestros recorded the cavalry bolero, "Brigada Fantasma," composed by Rigoberto Sainz. The piece was performed in a very slow ¾ meter and went through a complete repetition with different orchestrations in each repetition. The piece lasted nine minutes when it was performed in its entirety. When the ensemble had a limited performance time, the director would opt to play only the final repetition, but in its formal performances, the ensemble usually played the entire bolero. While this solemn music moved almost no one to dance, it remained as a powerful reminder of the Chaco War, sonorously indexing a point of national Bolivian origins. During the Chaco War, movement through spaces was often accomplished to the sounds of a band playing a cavalry bolero—sounds and movements through which Bolivians were establishing a common point of national identification.

Brass bands have remained central to an array of popular activities, and when they accompany dancers in urban entradas, the bands once again provide a means of connecting people and music to particular places (Figure 2.5). I danced in three entradas of the Fiesta del Señor del Gran Poder—"the minimum," I was told, if one expected protection from el Señor del Gran Poder, a Christ figure who is central to this fiesta as celebrated on the Saturday before Trinity (see Albó and Preiswerk 1986). As a participant, I was worried about the crowds encroaching on the dancers' pathway, but I was assured that during these fiestas, the dancers "owned" the streets as they dance through them. During the early part of the parade, the police kept pedestrians out of the dancers' path of movement, but domain over the street weakened as the day wore on; the police tired of pushing back the crowds and dancing on the edges of the troupe meant continuous encounters with those who had imbibed ample amounts of beer. This partially explained why the early entrance slots of the Gran Poder parade were so coveted, worth a major gift to the organizing association[14] or even worth coming to fist fights over a disputed position. When there was a backup of dance troupes and a group could not move forward dancing, the entire parade stopped in place for a break. The band stopped playing; people stopped dancing; no one moved forward; everyone relaxed and had a beer. In the urban entrance fiesta, participants were only supposed to *dance* through the entrance route; urban spectators yelled "sleepyhead" (*dormilona*), heckling participants who, upon arriving late for the entrance of their troupe, ran from one place to the next with an idea of "catching up." And if dancers dared to show fatigue and desist from dancing as they progressed forward, they would inevitably receive hisses from the crowd and wry commentaries about the lack of energy demonstrated in their participation. An urban fiesta route was supposed

Figure 2.5   A brass band plays in the Entrada del Gran Poder, La Paz (photograph by author).

to be marked both sonorously and kinesthetically; place was marked by dancing and sounding off through the streets over which one established a temporary domain.

Symbolic interpretation of the brass band underscores the folly of assigning any affiliation to a musical instrument or ensemble. Band instruments may be sonorous fixtures of the Bolivian military and thereby associated with the interests of the nation-state and Western forms, but band instruments are played by and their music is danced by the popular sectors of Bolivia, including mestizo and indigenous peoples in urban and rural sectors. The brass band as an ensemble playing in an entrada took any genre—a recorded cumbia as easily as a highland huayño—and processed it as a musical expression with which Bolivians could feel that effervescence of experiential authenticity. But within Bolivia, Creole and mestizo politicians would shore up the representational authenticity of the entrada by frowning on, or even disqualifying, troupes that danced to bands playing cumbias or any music of "foreign influences." And on an internationalized stage, the brass band never entered the construction of a culturally authentic Andean musical expression.

A close look at the groove in the repertoire of Música de Maestros brings out similar issues about musical experience and representation. But the following discussion turns to the ways people learn music and the social hierarchies that are ideologically structured and reinforced through the contradictions of feeling and representing music.

Is It in Two or Is It in Three?

On a November afternoon in 1993, Rolando Encinas, the director of Música de Maestros, met me at the San Francisco Plaza in La Paz and showed me the way to his apartment that doubled as a rehearsal room and living space. A mutual friend had put us in contact when Rolando told him that one of their violinists, Christine Bergmann, had just left Bolivia to return to Germany, her country of origin. Before departing, she had participated, as one of two violinists, in the recording of the ensemble's third compact disc. As the date approached for the formal presentation of the recording, Rolando was looking for a musician to complete the violin section. As I listened to the soundscape of Música de Maestros for the first time at Rolando's apartment, I thought to myself, "Is this Bolivian?" The sounds did not match with my schema of Bolivian music. The mestizo-Creole music of Música de Maestros was not likely to be known by an international audience. It was not the music sold to a foreign aesthetic that craved the commercially molded sound and image of an Andean "native." I have heard some North American listeners react negatively to Música de Maestros's recordings with comments like: "It sounds so heavily orchestrated." "The orchestration puts me off." "It's not what I expect to hear in Bolivian music." Música de Maestros's recordings did not have those rough edges and "muffled grooves" that for an outsider often establishes the pleasure of listening to an authentic "world music." (Feld 1994a: 284). Nor did their music fit the internationally known Pan-Andean groove. In listening to Música de Maestros, I heard an orchestration thick in instrumentation. Granted, there were the sounds from quenas, charangos, and zampoñas, which indexically mark the Andean. But what was outside of my typically Andean schema was the large ensemble sound and the use of viola, cello, French horn, and concertina. The full group consisted of 24 musicians and there was general concern about "not sounding like Música de Maestros" if too few musicians played a performance.[15] Unlike the five and six-person ensembles like Kjarkas and clones, the large size of the group was key in creating the unique sound of Música de Maestros. Another Bolivian musician described the ensemble for me, "They play Bolivian Creole music and have been concentrating on songs from the time of the Chaco War." While I had a vague idea of what Bolivian Creole music might be and a very clear idea of the historical implications of the Chaco War in Bolivia, what I heard that day was outside of my general sonorous associations with Bolivia.

The next day I returned to the director's apartment for a rehearsal. The fact that the group worked with written music eased my speedy incorporation into the ensemble. About two-thirds of the ensembles' members did not read music, although they were in the process of learning through informal classes that the French horn player gave at the director's house on Fridays. The other third read music, but the group in general relied heavily on acute ear and memory skills. While my poor memorizing skills left me reading music until the day I left Bolivia, most of the other musicians played everything from memory.

The repertory of Música de Maestros included *cuecas, bailecitos, carnavales,* huayños, fox trots, and what they called "works" (*obras*). A cueca is a song-dance form that follows a standard structure of introduction, theme, repetition of the theme, *quimba,* and the *jaleo,* and musicians use this vocabulary to discuss and rehearse cuecas. The musical structure follows the dance form, a romantic dance between a man and a woman. The introduction gives the dancers time to find a partner and the necessary handkerchief. Once in place the woman dances the introduction as the man claps. During the dance, both the man and the woman will wave their handkerchief above their head as they move close to and away from each other. Although the cueca is a dance of conquest, the man and woman never touch during the dance—almost, but not quite. In the first and second rounds of the main theme the partners dance around each other; in one round the partners move half-way around each other; in another round they make a full circle around each other. The quimba is a delicate, intimate section. As one Bolivian told me, that is where the man is quietly making his proposal to the woman. While some cuecas have a quimba that softly repeats the main theme, others will move into a different key, returning to the original key for the closing jaleo.[16] The jaleo repeats the main theme in a loud dynamic. If the cueca has lyrics, they inevitably begin the jaleo with a simple "la la la," sung to the rhythm of the specific cueca, and end with a repetition of a main line from the theme. As a signal of the woman's acceptance and thus a successful conquest, this section is energetically danced. Bolivian audiences, know the structure of the cueca and the listening public usually claps a specific rhythm during the jaleo. The same cueca is always played and danced twice in a row.

The cueca became one of my favorite genres, to the extent that musicians in Música de Maestros called me "*la cuequera*" (the one who likes cuecas), and at one of my farewell parties they indulged me with a playing of all the cuecas in the ensemble's repertoire (about 16 in 1995). Performing this genre did not come easily to me; getting into the groove of cueca forced me to examine closely the question of reading and feeling music. As a classically trained musician, the issues I faced in this difference were replicated within the entire ensemble, which included both classically trained reading musicians and self-taught musicians who played by ear. This fundamental difference surfaced within a debate over whether the cueca should be counted in two or in three.

At the center of this debate is the question of how microlevel soundspaces are subdivided and stressed. In the cueca, such subdivisions and emphases can lead to simultaneous presence of a feeling of two and a feeling of three. The *same* musical time-space of six subdivisions (eighth notes) can be grouped to give a three-beat feel (¾) or a two-beat feel (⁶⁄₈):

I I I I I I (total of six subdivisions)
II II II (stress and grouping to bring a global count of three, ¾ meter)
III III (stress and grouping to bring a global count of two, ⁶⁄₈ meter)

The Bolivian genres of cuecas, bailecitos, and carnavales can usually be written in two (⁶⁄₈) or three (¾). A tally of the violin parts for Música de Maestros as of 1995 brought the following numbers:

total recorded cuecas: fourteen
cuecas in two (⁶⁄₈): nine
cuecas in three (¾): six ("Rosa Carmín" had two arrangements, one in ¾ and one in ⁶⁄₈)

When I first entered the ensemble I struggled with the 2–3 feeling of the cueca and other genres with this characteristic. Like the cello, viola, violin, and French horn players from the Bolivian Symphony Orchestra, I came to Música de Maestros with a formal training in music reading. Nevertheless, since 1987 I had also been expanding my own musical training in my weakest area: ear and memory skills.[17] My classical training, which gave me the ability to read a piece at first sight, thrilled the director, but there was some part of this music performance tradition—like every music performance tradition—that could not be found on a printed page of music. For those who only read music, these secrets of a tradition become real stumbling blocks if a musician has not had sufficient immersion in that musical style. At first, I found that the only way I could get through the cueca, was to think in both two and three, or to think in two or three depending on a particular measure. I eventually became comfortable with the slightly off-balanced feeling I had to experience in order to perform a cueca.

Figure 2.6   This violin part for the cueca, "Rosa Carmin," is written in two (6⁄8) (transcription by Koji Hishimoto for Música de Maestros).

The two-three dilemma became the center of an explicit debate about how the director was marking the entrances to cuecas. Although the scores for these genres were sometimes written in 6⁄8 and sometimes written in 3⁄4, Rolando usually counted off these genres in three, no matter how the pieces were notated for the reading musicians. Some of the musicians from the symphony orchestra complained, "How can we play this in three when it is written in 6⁄8?" Koji Hishimoto, a Japanese musician in the group who had long since jumped over this hurdle in his own playing, attempted to smooth things over by writing "3⁄4" in place of "6⁄8." He even began rewriting entire music parts in 3⁄4. Figures 2.6 and 2.7 show two different violin parts as used in Música de Maestros's performances: one written in two and the other written in three. But one of the symphony

Figure 2.7   This violin part for the cueca, "Rosa Carmin," is written in three (¾) (transcription by Rolando Encinas for Música de Maestros).

orchestra musicians said, "You lose the whole feel of the cueca by putting it in three." In the spirit of accommodation, Rolando began counting off in two (⁶⁄₈) all entrances to cuecas, the primary genre of complaint. But not all of the cuecas were written in ⁶⁄₈. Rolando always played performances from memory, not distinguishing, nor needing to distinguish between ¾ and ⁶⁄₈. Confusion continued among the reading musicians, as Rolando still sometimes marked off entrances in two, even for cuecas written in three.

In trying to accommodate requests from the reading musicians, Rolando's marking in two sometimes left the ensemble on shaky ground at the beginning of the cueca. When the tempo of a piece did not quite click, when the musicians were not quite together, the tempo and rhythm would be described as "moved" (*movido*). This term referred to situations in which we had not quite reached that goal of the performing

artist: "a sort of atonement, or, even more literally 'at-one-ment,' an expert reconciliation of oneself with another style of doing and being"
(Ness 1992: 11). Something in the tempo was out of place; something in
the rhythm was out of place. It lacked the sense of being together. When
Rolando counted off in two the entrances to very slow cuecas, usually
those that came out of a Chuquisaca/Potosi tradition ("El Olvido,"
"Noche Tempestuosa," "Suspiros," "Gloria"), the first few measures of the
piece were often "moved." At such a slow tempo, the preparatory bars
given in two left too much time for the tempo to be "moved"; too many
unmarked subdivisions left the musicians grasping at ambiguous silences
to find the tempo of the piece. Although the director never adamantly refused to give an entrance in two, in performance practice, he slipped back
into directing the cuecas in the three to which he and the rest of the ensemble were more accustomed.

I propose that the very groove of the cueca, bailecito, and carnaval is
in precisely this ambiguity of meter—sometimes in two, sometimes in
three, sometimes in both at once. The two-three tension of the cueca
forms the "participatory discrepancy" that makes one want to dance; as
Keil suggested, participatory discrepancies can be found in the tension
generated by a complex relationship between meter and rhythm (Keil
1994a: 59). The groove of the cueca genre works between two primary
meters, the feeling of being simultaneously in two and three. Written
music, which forces these pieces into one meter or the other, leaves these
genres' underlying ambiguities to the interpreting musician. The written
parts of cuecas, as prescriptive representations[18] of potentially authentic
performances, can never fully represent experiential authenticity.

A classical music training and ethos is laden with a heavy dose of ideology that can do much to solidify a rigid approach to reading the score,
a reading that seems to ignore, deny, or place in a secondary position the
feelingful side of music performance. I would argue that this ideology
emerges in even more exaggerated ways in a classical music training of a
country like Bolivia. The ideology of the classical musician is drawn into
the fight against the deluge of folk, traditional, and mesomusics that flood
most Bolivian soundscapes, and within this ideology hierarchies are imposed: the written score over the performance, the musician who can read
the score above the musician who cannot read it. But I want to emphasize
the ideological work of this attitude. Some classical musicians take very
seriously the connection between feelingful activity and music performance. When Arnold Steinhardt, a violinist with the Guarneri String
Quartet, wrote about individuals who greatly influenced his musical education, he described the then elderly Arthur Loesser, pianist and scholar,
who by dancing the different movements of the D minor Partita for vio-

lin, gave Steinhardt a lesson on how to play Bach (Steinhardt 1998: 293). Similarly, dance experience guided many of Rolando's directing approaches in crafting the sound of Música de Maestros.

While Rolando read music well, he could follow a melody even faster by relying on his ear and memory training. I once asked him if he had listened to other quena players as part of his training. "No, not really. I didn't listen to anyone intentionally, trying to learn their technique, their style." Rolando has a unique style of playing the quena. Many people "in the business" in La Paz, through sound alone, could recognize his quena playing. As a wind instructor of the workshop told me, "He records quena for so many different people. I can recognize his playing right away. I've even seen music videos where there is a another quena player synching the part, but the sound is so obviously Rolito's." Rolando was an autodidact child prodigy on the quena, but he was also a dancer. From the age of eight he was performing and recording professionally in Bolivia, and he both played and danced with touring folkloric groups. The living room of his mother's house in San Pedro (neighborhood of La Paz) remains a visual shrine to his early performing. The walls are still plastered with postcards from all over the world, as he had written home during his tours of Europe, Canada, Japan, and the United States. Record jackets of his recordings with other groups form a border around the wall of postcards. Rolando's musical experience has always been connected to dance; he even performed as a dancer when Música de Maestros toured France in 1996, and in studio recording sessions I often saw him "find" a tempo by dancing the piece.

The sound of Música de Maestros was created through a combination of instrumentation, sheer numbers of musicians, and the manipulation of sound technologies. But the sound of Música de Maestros also developed around the inclusion of viola, cello, bass, and French horn players, musicians from the National Symphony Orchestra who entered Música de Maestros in 1993. The III and IV albums exploited this unique instrumentation, the timbres of Andean or mestizo associated instruments (that is, quena, panpipes, charango, mandolins, guitars) mixed with the timbres of instruments associated with a Western classical music tradition.

While the violin is often used in Andean and mestizo music,[19] the inclusion of low-register orchestral instruments gave Música de Maestros a distinctive sound. Emphasizing a bass line went beyond an inclusion of the corresponding instruments. In the recording studio Rolando made the aesthetic decision to emphasize a bass line. At this time, Música de Maestros made their recordings by having the musicians individually lay down their tracks, channel by channel, one at a time. In the final mix, every recorded instrument could potentially be manipulated for volume and sound effects. Rolando and Koji worked together on the sound mixes of the III, IV, and reissued I and II albums, and they often disagreed on the relative dynamic levels that should be assigned to the different instruments. I watched some of these mixing sessions in which Koji tended to turn up the instruments carrying the melody, and Rolando tended to turn those down and turn up the guitar, bass, viola, and cello. Rather than open a dispute, Rolando, smiling mischievously at me, would turn up slightly these bass instruments in the final mix—when all hands were at the board turning knobs just so, in just the right place of the music, throughout the different sections of a three-minute piece on which three hours had just been spent setting the mix. Outside of the studio Rolando justified his decision, relating it to his knowledge of music through dance experience: "No, I had to do that. Koji knows so much about Bolivian music. He has learned so much and his judgement is impeccable. His ear is perfect and he has ample knowledge of harmony. But he still has not interiorized the importance of, for example, the guitar in our music. That is the line that makes you want to dance. If you don't hear that, there is no cueca, there is no dance. When I am dancing, that is what I want to hear." As a performer with Música de Maestros, it is the guitar line, above all others, that I want to hear clearly in my monitor. During a performance in which every instrument is amplified and the sound systems are less than ideal, hearing the guitar line has often saved me from crossing with 24 other musicians who played together without a formal conductor.

Feeling a piece in both two and three, hearing a strong bass line or *bajeo* of the guitars, hearing a dense orchestration of indigenous, mestizo, and Western classical instruments—these were the elements of experiential authenticity for a performance of Música de Maestros.

PLEASURE IN THE ABSENCE OF GLUE:
THAT MUSIC MAKES ME NERVOUS

In Ithaca, New York, in 1992, one of the workshop's organizers, Jesús Durán, had me listen to a compact disc recording of the Contemporary Orchestra of Native Instruments (Orquesta Contemporanea de Instrumentos Nativos, OCIN), an ensemble of the Bolivian Workshop of Popular Music "Arawi." The title piece of the disc, *La Doctrina de los Ciclos* (1990) by Oscar García, was inspired by a text of the writer Jorge Luis Borges. The piece for two quenas began with sounds reminiscent of birds repeating a call, but meter and rhythm were absent and the variations and repetitions sounded completely unplanned. One voice of the quena, in a slower crying sound, then pierced through this thick background and was followed by the second instrument. Overblowing created an especially eerie sound throughout this section. A silence preceded the following short section, which, in almost creating a flowing melodic line, distinguished itself from the previous sections. But this was only taunting those who might have expected something more lyrical. The section was pinpointed by silences between solo statements by the quenas, each one stabbing the final pitches of the phrase. Another silence led into the following section, which created punctuated sounds with wavering pitches. It sounded as if the musicians were using a lip trill, exaggerated vibrato, and/or overblowing to create these crying sounds in a free meter, each quena answering the other in an overlapping manner. One quena then played a pitch from which followed an extremely slow glissando, while the other quena "accompanied" the first through a series of pitches with a general downward contour. A final high pitch was overblown before the next silence. Again an almost lyrical section was abruptly interrupted by what sounded like arguing birds. Silences filled the beginning of the next part, punctuated by lower-pitched bird sounds that then led into the original bird call, ending with an acoustical fade-out. The piece then ended after a repetition of the very short almost-lyrical figure and a final lower-pitched wail, each of the quenas in the general range of a semi-tone apart.

Like my first appraisal of the sounds of Música de Maestros, I asked myself: Is this Bolivian music? As I silently asked this question and the workshop answered it for me in their proposal-writing discourse—something I will address in chapter four—I also felt myself consciously assuming an open mind about this avant-garde music. This was an attitude I assumed after a childhood filled with a good deal of "ear stretching." This was a project to which my parents dedicated their energies after, to their great dismay, I had assessed Igor Stravinsky's "Rite of Spring" as a piece that "sounded like a bunch of wrong notes." Of course Stravinsky's music almost seems like mesomusic now, and particularly in relation to the avant-garde music of the workshop. As I kept an open mind and open ears, it was not until I began to consider the music-movement nexus that I asked: Where is the groove in this music? While Stravinsky's "Rite of Spring" was ballet music and its driving rhythms could certainly be said to make someone dance, the workshop's avant-garde music left behind both tonality and meter; this was no dancing music.

My most immediate reference point to what I heard in the workshop's avant-garde was the name John Cage—the master composer/guru of contemporary music who described composing as the organization of sounds and silences (1961: 62). In fact, Cage was dedicated to taking what he called "the glue" out of organized sounds: "Where people had felt the necessity to stick sounds together to make a continuity, we four [Cage,

Wolff, Brown, Feldman] felt the opposite necessity to get rid of the glue so that sounds would be themselves" (Cage 1961: 71). The existence of the groove, at least in the examples I have discussed here, seems to assume the presence of "glue"—the presence of exactly what Cage wanted to eliminate. Connecting the workshop with Cage is not simply my interpretive move. For workshop organizers "John Cage" was a common reference, as were other names in the contemporary music scene—Leo Brouwer, Jacobo Koellreutter, and Frank Zappa. Workshop organizers were quick to reiterate the idea that contemporary music, through the conscious avoidance of tonal harmony (a hierarchical system built on a seven-tone scale, which assigns greater importance to the first and fifth steps, and which constructs chords in a general progression through dissonance and toward an apparently inevitable resolution), is a musical way of aesthetically breaking out of a dominant world order. Susan McClary discussed this order in terms of regulating desire: "[Tonality,] with its process of instilling expectations and subsequently withholding promised fulfillment until climax—is the principal musical means during the period from 1600 to 1900 for arousing and channeling desire" (1991:12). For the workshop, avoiding tonality was about opening up the expectations of works. From one workshop organizer I received a copy of Umberto Eco's *The Open Work*—a text he took seriously in conceptualizing the institution's contemporary music project. According to Eco, a musical work, not structured on the predetermined patterns of tonality, contributes to a more open reading and a greater indeterminacy of the work; the unforeseeable conclusions of the work depend more on the performers in their specific performative time/spaces (Eco 1989: 15). The open work, constantly "in movement," invites the performer to "make the work together with the author" (Eco 1989: 21). Workshop compositions also tended to avoid meter and predictable rhythmic patterns. Workshop compositions used aleatory techniques. For example, using what Erhard Karkoschka would call "action notation" (1972: 3), a series of note fingerings and approximate time in which to play those notes might be the only indications to the musician, with the ultimate direction to "watch the conductor."

Taking Eco's ideas, the workshop organizers saw moving out of tonality as revolutionary in and of itself—a way of sonorously "fucking up the system" as one organizer told me. In our discussions, the organizers often juxtaposed their contemporary music with the protest songs that emerged within the Latin American New Song (*Nueva Canción*) movement of the 1960s and 1970s. They thought of their "open works" as a more challenging approach to a politicized musical expression. In their critique of New Song, workshop organizers emphasized that these political/artistic expressions depended on the content of lyrics while ignoring what they considered to be the more powerful side of song—the musical sound. Like Theodor Adorno's approaches to the music (1976; 1973), the workshop considered aesthetically revolutionary musical forms as more radical than lyrics with revolutionary content, and the anti-Kjarkas discourse of the institution was not unlike Adorno's overall dismissal of popular music forms.

This aesthetically revolutionary project was performed through the OCIN. For the organizers of the workshop, the OCIN was the "fun" ensemble of the institution. I am referring to a type of intellectual fun that can perhaps only be enjoyed by those who have sufficient education and who work within the consciously developed discourses of challenging a social system by challenging the tonal system that embodies it. The homology of the tyranny of tonality and the tyranny of society is not new within Western discourses on music (Adorno 1973; Attali 1985: 7; Eco 1989: 139–140; McClary 1991: 12; Shepherd 1991: 96–127), but its full meaning as presented by the workshop organizers was somewhat lost on the students of the workshop who preferred participating in the traditional and meso- music ensembles, within comfortable tonalities and reassuring chord progressions or within perceived culturally authentic indigenous performance practices. While students who came to the workshop showed more enthusiasm for participation in these other wings of the institution's work, an implicit rule seemed to require all students of the workshop to participate in the OCIN (see Falk 1993). I found no hard and fast rule at play here, but rather an informal understanding that participation in one sphere of the workshop should be accompanied by participation in the OCIN. Perhaps another way of viewing it is that during my work, I never met a workshop student who came to the institution because s/he wanted to play in the OCIN. Composers for the OCIN had great fun hearing and seeing their works performed, but I would suggest that the students of the OCIN were unintentionally precluded from that fun.

I say "unintentionally precluded" because the workshop's organizers certainly wanted to shatter the preconception of contemporary art music as being beyond the understanding of all sectors of a society. In a tongue and cheek newspaper article, in *Ultima hora*, December 5, 1993, titled "Contemporary Music is Within the Reach of All Ears," the workshop's coordinator, Oscar García claimed anyone can listen to contemporary music, just like they listen to any other sound. He proceeded to explain physiologically how one hears, thus claiming that it cannot be difficult to listen to contemporary music. He continued by noting that people in Bolivia have no difficulty understanding Bach, Brahms, Beethoven, and Bartok, composers who have come from such foreign contexts. Nor is contemporary music elitist, claimed his article; even if a composer is elitist, the work is immediately separated from its creator and distributed to an audience according to the mandates of those who work in the media. The media ended up as García's real culprit since they decided who was smart enough to listen to *música culta* (cultured or learned music). But contemporary music in and of itself, he argued, was not elitist. In spite of García's call to a popularizing of contemporary music, his arguments and discourse—unmistakably from the perspective of an upper-middle-class intellectual—still flew over the heads of the students in the workshop. Anyone can listen to contemporary music as sound, but can anyone feel a groove in these glueless sounds? In response to the accusation that modern music was too intellectual, Adorno responded by denaturalizing tonality—showing that there was nothing natural about this way of organizing sound—by discussing the sensuous experiences of composers of modern music and by suggesting the intellectualist pursuits in which composers of tonal music have to engage (1973: 11–12). But Adorno's argument is constructed from the perspective of the composing musicians and still does not address how listeners may experience modern music. What does a person need in order to experience this sound as a pleasurable interlude?

I would suggest that the pleasure of listening to the OCIN was achieved, not through the groove, as I have been discussing it in this chapter, but in the combined juxtaposition of "native" instruments and avant-garde composition techniques. The contemporary music component of the workshop's activities reflected similarities with the "Affinity of the Tribal and the Modern" as encountered in the Museum of Modern Art's "Primitivism in 20th Century Art," analyzed by James Clifford (1988). While the modernists were recognizing primitive artifacts as "powerful 'art'" and locating these objects within a modernist family of art (Clifford 1988: 190), in the workshop's contemporary music, Bolivian musicians were claiming to have been avant-garde before the avant-garde. The use of indigenous instruments in this avant-garde provided the main pillar of this aesthetic and ideological project. The workshop did not simply compose avant-garde Bolivian music, but rather they did so with the use of traditional indigenous instruments, the origins of which were imagined to stretch back for centuries. In their ethnography of reading the magazine *National Geographic,* Catherine Lutz and Jane Collins commented on the diverse imaginaries at work in the juxtaposition of the traditional and the modern in a single image and that the U.S. consumer of this image finds pleasure precisely in this jarring juxtaposition (1993: 110–115). Similar sonorous imaginaries may have been at work in the workshop's juxtaposition of the traditional indigenous instruments and avant-garde aesthetics. But these imaginaries were not necessarily shared by the different social classes represented within the workshop. Unlike the traditional and meso- musics of the workshop, the novelty of the OCIN did attract invitations to perform in Colombia, Chile, and on the salt flats of Uyuni for the 1994 total solar eclipse. Students of the workshop enjoyed the travel these performances entailed, but the pleasure of this music was not easily made popular; its groove was still elusive.

Some Bolivian musicians I met could not tolerate listening to the OCIN. In 1993, I performed a new work with the OCIN. Composed by Oscar García, his piece titled "El silencio del olvido" (The Silence of the Forgotten) experimented with a combination of instruments from the highlands as well as the eastern lowlands of Bolivia. At the same time the composition explored the timbres of the violin—an instrument also played in the eastern lowlands of Bolivia. The violin part was based almost entirely on the use of fingered harmonics. Pitch was left to the interpretation of the performer, within the scale of one of the indigenous wind instruments played in the piece. Meter and rhythm were left completely open to the interpretation of the performers. The piece might be temporally described as sections of unsubdivided time; the musicians moved from one section to the next according to cues given by the director. The only explicit instruction in the violin part called for a rise into the upper registers at specified moments of the piece.

When I played this piece with the OCIN at the Contemporary Music Festival, I had just begun to rehearse and play with Música de Maestros. Out of courtesy to a new member of the group, or perhaps out of curiosity to hear their new violinist, several members told me that they were going to attend the concert. The day after the performance a member of Música de Maestros politely but honestly told me what he thought of the music he had heard: "It makes me feel anguished. . . . It makes me nervous. . . . After all the horrible noises I listen to every day in the city, why would I want to listen to that? . . . It was almost painful to my ears. . . . I only stayed because you were performing." For this listener "El silencio del olvido" created a constant and unresolved tension. He went on to tell me that he had enough tension and stress in his life without listening to that music. He compared it to annoying sounds of the streets of La Paz, when car drivers are sounding their horns. For him, all of this was noise. In spite of explicitly elaborated discourse about contemporary music and its accessibility to people in all walks of Bolivian life, appreciation of these workshop compositions still remained within *pleasurable* listening reach of a few intellectuals, and the composition's juxtaposition of the native and the avant-garde created much of its appeal. In spite of the popularizing intentions behind this contemporary music project, this music remained exclusive through the impossibility of dancing to it. And for some listeners, hearing these sounds from a still position was like being subjected to painful sounds of a busy Paceño street. These musical examples place center stage the complex relation of pleasure and pain. The groove might be framed in terms of an experience that, with minor exceptions, is generally known, and is enjoyed through the repetition of this known experience. While the contemporary music of the workshop could not be further from this groove, the pleasure of these musical experiences may be felt alternatively in the listener's encounter with the unknown. In an attempt to move beyond Adorno's critique of the intellectualist accusation made in reference to "modern music" (1973), in chapter four I will return to this theme of the pleasures in facing the unknown. Sometimes only a fine line separates what moves one to dance and what leaves one completely unsettled, and the unsettled state may also be perceived as pleasurable.

In this chapter I have highlighted experiential authenticities through reflections on what makes people want to move and dance to music performances, and why one person's groove or pleasurable experience is another person's inauthentic performance, stolen culture, or even noise. In the next chapter, I turn to one of the principal stages for cultural-historical authenticity: the folklore festival.

Chapter 3

"Time!"

Dressed in our white shirts, black vests, and black pants, the members of Música de Maestros stood backstage in anticipation of another performance for a French audience. In France we accompanied a Bolivian dance troupe, *Conadanz,* and its members were both our most loyal supporters and our sharpest critics. One of the dancers surveyed us in our standard performance garb and yelled: "Look at yourselves. What is the difference between you and the French delegation? You look just like [the French]. Identical. You're not Bolivian. What you are wearing is not Bolivian. You should be wearing ponchos and *abarcas.*[1] Now that is Bolivian." Some of the members of Música de Maestros tried to answer her, but their words fell on deaf ears. Not only were we performing for a French audience, but in that audience tonight was the French patron who had befriended the dance troupe and connected them to this series of folklore festivals. He was a cantankerous benefactor whose attendance at other performances had brought vicious critiques about costuming and presentation, on and off the stage. The dancer quoted above critiqued a music group that, when in their own country, explicitly presented themselves as performers of Creole, mestizo, and indigenous genres. While Música de Maestros was in Bolivia their costumes were never an issue, but in France the official dress of Música de Maestros was criticized for not looking Bolivian enough. Implicit in this critique was that Música de Maestros did not look indigenous enough. In spite of Música de Maestros's efforts to present a diverse repertoire, within French folklore festivals "Bolivia" meant "indigenous," and more specifically "highland indigenous."

This chapter explores the performance transformations that occur in the contexts of folklore festivals. The folklore festival exemplifies a performance in which cultural authenticity is privileged over any sense of experiential authenticity. Folklore festivals are about displaying an authentic representation of a particular cultural expression, but these representational practices can be undertaken by both those who claim membership in that culture and those who remain outsiders to that culture. The shift to a staged cultural display transforms the performance, and performers often buttress the more consciously pursued transformations with tales of arduous research and claims to finally "getting things right." Other transformations more directly respond to commercial sensibilities or future prospects. For example, the dancer's dismay at our costumes, which seemed to her more French than Bolivian, could be attributed to her very real desire to be invited back to France for other folklore festivals.

Performers, as well as audiences, may be quite aware of the differences that exist between the performance as seen onstage and the original performance that is supposedly being represented, and I use the term metaperformance to illuminate the awareness and certain acceptance of this difference. In a metaperformance, performers may have a Goffmanian "primary framework" (1974: 47) in mind even as the displayed performance strays from the performer's concept, in order to satisfy the imagined authenticity of a different context and audience. While "all representations posit an absent original event, whether such events are understood as fictional . . . or 'real'" (Wurtzler 1992: 88),[2] what characterizes the metaperformance is the conscious perception and degree of acceptance, by performer and sometimes even audience, of the gap between the "real" performance and its representation.

In this chapter I will also focus on other transformations that are not so explicitly recognized, even though their implications are extensive. These transformations include shifts in temporal frameworks and the privileging of visual rather than kinesthetic and aural pleasure. The temporal transformations that occur in the festival contexts limit the possibility of getting into the grooves I described in the previous chapter. To reiterate, the groove that invites us to dance consists of "participatory discrepancies," the sensation of being simultaneously in synchrony and slightly out of time with others (Keil 1994b: 96–98). Within the time constraints of the folklore festival, bodies moving in a groove are replaced by bodies in timed choreographed movement. The shift to a temporally limited performance moves sonorous and kinesthetic experiences to a secondary plane—secondary to the visuality of costumes and choreographed dance. While music is still vital to these performances, the decentering of groove leads to struggles to establish domain over visually perceived cultural representations, and those involved in the struggle for representation often imagine different cultural authenticities.

The temporality of these folklore festivals is characterized by trunca-tion, sequencing, and a forced sense of equality. Feeling the groove emerges when one is involved in long continuous segments of music per-formance. In a fiesta context of the Andes, different groups of musicians perform simultaneously, each striving to encounter and remain within their own pulse, each in a competitive mode with the other music groups. Folklore festival organizers eliminate simultaneity in order to present cul-tural material separately under the guise of equal terms, and within a lim-ited time frame. In the name of fairness to all, folklore festival performances occur through brief sequential segments, each musical group occupying a different sequence of the predetermined time frame. Thus, within folklore festival performances it becomes quite difficult to encounter the pulse or groove.

The structures of folklore festivals recombine sensory experiences in ways that epitomize many cultural performances within a late-capitalist world system. In a way, this chapter begins to respond to Arjun Appadu-rai's call to analyze globally variable synesthesia, as global capitalism shifts modes of reading, hearing, and seeing (1990). In the metaperformances of festivals, music and dance—as well as aural, kinesthetic, and visual ex-periences—become reshuffled in complex ways. I agree with Keil who ar-gues that music and dance cannot be analytically separated, but Keil also proposes that "[s]tyles of music intended for dancing have a way of evolv-ing into music for listeners only" (1994a: 56). In this process the chasm between performer and audience becomes entrenched. In the festival, dance often rejoins the music that had become "for listening only," but these dance forms often exaggeratedly reference the imagined sources from which they originally split. And as choreographed, learned dances, they may differ from the collective kinesthetic effervescence of experien-tial authenticity. Festival contexts rearrange the relation between music and movement, and between aural, kinesthetic, and visual experiences, and this rearrangement—splitting followed by recombinatory practices— leads to a privileging of visual display and a backgrounding of aural and kinesthetic experiences.

On the surface, folklore festivals are neither traditional ritual perfor-mances for the performers nor straightforward commercially motivated ac-tivities. A ritual performance might be represented in a folklore festival, but the faith behind the ritual has shifted; the performance serves as ritual to a regional or national identity. Performers in folklore festivals often make lit-tle or no money; spectators at festivals are not big paying audiences, if they pay at all. Expenses are covered by municipalities, church organizations, or international foundations, and a moral motivation outside of and beyond commercial interest is often invoked to encourage participation in these commercially lost causes. In other words, one should participate in festivals to demonstrate solidarity with a cause or simply to show other communities and other countries the "real way" of being Toropalqueño, Bolivian, and so on. Performers do receive other benefits from festival participation: international notoriety, national coverage, present and future travel opportunities, and enticing prizes. Although performers and organizers may clash in the reshuffling of privileged sensory experiences, performers in festivals are usually more than willing participants. As performers, they willingly take on a role of a particular identity, usually in a subordinate position to another more encompassing identity. As Robert Cantwell suggested in his study of the Festival of American Folklife, we seem willing "to objectify people socially 'below' us and to coax out their complicity in the process" (1993). In this way festival contexts almost always involve an exercise of power, often cloaked in paternalism. These metaperformances are the rituals of more encompassing identities and in this way the festival is the cultural meeting point of local and translocal processes, a place to examine the discrepancies between peoples' own perceived cultural authenticity and the way others imagine them as authentic. Folklore festivals are about performing the nation—the unified Bolivian nation to an international audience, and the multicultural Bolivian nation to a home audience.

I will explore Bolivian festival performances in three contexts: a folklore festival in the local context of Toropalca, a Spanish-organized, internationally televised "Concert for Indigenous Peoples" as filmed in Bolivia, and an international folklore festival in France.

FESTIVAL AND FIESTA TIME

In the afternoon sun of an August day in 1994, Toropalqueños—both vecinos and community/allyu members—gathered around the soccer field for a folklore festival. I had just come from a cooking party where the village women had prepared an elaborate lunch for the Bishop who was visiting from Potosi. The Bishop had come to Toropalca to inaugurate a new church that was constructed to replace the church the river had carried away. The folklore festival had been scheduled immediately after lunch so the Bishop could see the cultural presentation before a four-hour drive back to the city of Potosi. For reasons that remained unclear, the Bishop could not stay for the festival and he promptly left after the sumptuous meal.

The festival was organized by a Belgian woman who had been volunteering in Toropalca for over 20 years. This volunteer—I will call her Doctora—took up residence in Toropalca to work as a medical doctor. Through her treatment of tuberculosis patients and her lay work with the Catholic

Church, she had become an established and respected figure in the village. In 1994, no priest was in residence in Toropalca; to lead mass a priest occasionally came from Vitichi or Caiza, villages at a distance of a two- or three-hour drive from Toropalca. In the absence of a resident priest, the Doctora acted as the principal organizing agent of Catholic religious activities: organizing seminars to train communal catechists; preparing individuals for weddings, baptisms, and confirmations; and leading "celebrations" (instead of mass) on the Sundays when a priest could not be present. Rather than promote a collective exploration of how a particular local way of life might be viewed through Catholicism, an approach I saw implemented in Yura, the Doctora put her energies behind the strategy of training individuals to be catechists in their communities.[3] In Toropalca, the Catholic faith was cultivated through individuals and their life-course rituals. Unlike Yura where the priest led discussions about local customs as a means of raising an awareness of a group's indigenous identity and collective power, in Toropalca the Doctora tolerated local "customs" and beliefs with ambivalence. At times I heard her scold Toropalqueños for not maintaining their traditions, but at the same time she had no tolerance for the general intoxication that usually accompanied any "tradition" in the Andes. Even though she was officially retired, as a Belgian volunteer, in 1994 she continued her work in Toropalca, not only because of a sense of service, but also because Toropalca was where she felt most at home.

The Doctora, in conjunction with vecinos in Toropalca, proposed to inaugurate the new church construction with a folklore festival, which was planned to coincide with the patron saint fiesta of the village: August 15th, The Lord of the Poor. The planning of a folklore festival brought references to other folklore festivals held recently: one in Calcha (a nearby canton) and one held in the Toropalca community of Ketacochi for the celebration of Pentecost. From these previous experiences, the Doctora was adamant on at least one point: she wanted to have prizes, but they all would be identical. As she said, "I don't want the people fighting over the prizes. These fights are never ending." In an attempt to eliminate competition and impose an equality of the participants, the Doctora would award her prizes for mere participation. Meanwhile the vecinos in Toropalca asked me to make a "contribution" to the folklore festival. They suggested that I purchase another tier of prizes that would be awarded precisely through competition and assessment by appointed judges.

In persuading me to donate prizes they told me, "That way the people will go all out with their costumes and everything." Of course, I thought to myself, why wouldn't they go all out with their presentations? But an earlier petition on the part of the local community of Lamachi had already indicated that Toropalqueños themselves did not include the cost of

"typical dress" within their quotidian management of economic resources. In Lamachi I was told that the ayarachis instruments were supposed to be played with a special costume—a headdress of ostrich
feathers. When I was in Lamachi for the fiesta of San Juan, community
members told me of their intention of going to the festival with ayarachis.
In my position of someone interested in "traditions" and "music," they
asked me to sponsor the reappropriation of this music's proper dress. I
politely refused the request, giving as my excuse an unfairness to the other
competing communities of the Toropalca region. Of course my reasoning
was not unlike the Doctora's; I hoped to keep up the rather impossible
myth of my equal treatment of all communities in Toropalca. But behind
the request to finance costumes, I read a particular attitude toward lost
cultural authenticity. They framed the loss in terms of visually perceived
costumes, and "typical dress" came to depend on a kind of charity without which Toropalqueños claimed they did not have the financial resources to present themselves as authentic. This Toropalqueño logic of
"typical dress" was in stark contrast to the concept of dressing "like a good
Yureño." Yureños wore what in other contexts would be called "typical
dress" because that was the way to be literally a good Yureño: that was the
way to formally receive outsiders; that was the way to show off one's weaving during Carnival; that was the way to gain respect; that was the way to
accumulate symbolic capital. Yureño dress was costly, but I never heard
anyone ask to have these costs underwritten. In their request that I support the festival in general, the vecinos of Toropalca assumed I would
favor the maximum demonstration of "the typical." I located my concerns
elsewhere. Eliminating competition was obviously impossible, but know-
ingly going against what the Doctora had planned was also problematic.
This was, in spite of all the participants, the Doctora's "party," backed by
Church money for the inauguration. I finally discussed with the Doctora
the theme of competitive prizes, and she seemed to agree, with reserva-
tions, to my limited plan of support. Knowing that outsiders were prime
candidates to nominate as judges, I made my contribution under the condition that I would not act as judge for the festival.

When the Doctora made the invitation to all of Toropalca's communities, she also began asking vecinos to accommodate these delegations in
their houses. The village Toropalca, unlike Yura, did not serve as a regional
ritual meeting place. In the village of Yura, specific patios were designated
as "belonging" to a particular ayllu and during fiestas these patios were
filled with community/ayllu members who otherwise would not have a
place to stay. The community members of the Toropalca region had no
equivalent of Yura's patios. In Toropalca's festival, collective pressure was
applied and vecinos were assigned the task of accommodating specific

communities upon their arrival from the surrounding hamlets. In the festival organization, vecinos occupied the symbolic position of hosts and the comunarios or community members from surrounding hamlets, who might be considered as members of the indigenous organizations or ayllus, assumed the position of invited guests. I will take up the disjointedness of Toropalqueño indigenous identities in chapters five and seven, but what I want to emphasize here is the overwhelming dominance of vecinos in local interactions, and the patronizing position from which vecinos wanted to promote the display of indigenous authenticity. But the comunarios were willing participants in this cultural pageant.[4]

Starting from the housing accommodations to every last detail, the Doctora organized the logistics for the arrival of Toropalca's communities. She contracted trucks to bring in the community delegations and to take them home at the close of the festivities. The parish provided them with dry rations, wood for cooking fuel, and bread. The Doctora had a steer slaughtered to provide meat for all who came to the village. Details that would have been "second nature" in the ritual meeting of Yureños, were spelled out in a printed brochure. In the brochure, people were told to bring: bedding, dishes, cooking pots, "typical clothes," and "autochthonous instruments." An "important note," in capital letters, ended the brochure's instructions: IT IS PROHIBITED TO DRINK ALCOHOLIC BEVERAGES DURING THE PROGRAMMED ACTIVITIES (*ESTA PROHIBIDO SERVIRSE BEBIDAS ALCOHOLICAS DURANTE LOS ACTOS PROGRAMADOS*). The programmed festival activities were distinguished from the unprogrammed fiesta activities, with the expectation of abstention from alcohol consumption in the first and its inevitable consumption in the latter. But programmed festival activities were inserted within a week-long fiesta, alcohol consumption necessarily crossing the constructed temporal boundaries between festival and fiesta.

At the festival, spectators, most of them Toropalqueños, stood or took seats on the benches that had been set up around the soccer field. With the exception of an invited delegation from Calcha and a few parish workers from Vitichi, I was one of the few outsiders present at the festival. Unlike other Toropalqueño fiesta contexts in which people always pulled me into collective dancing and singing, I, along with others of the audience, remained in the position of spectator. According to the printed brochure, in the "Grand Folkloric Festival" each community was to limit their participation to ten minutes. But over the microphone that had been hooked up for the occasion, the master of ceremonies, a Toropalqueño vecino, announced: "Please limit your presentations to seven minutes maximum." A sonorous hierarchy was already in place as the master of ceremonies had amplification while the performers had none. The announcer's voice boomed out of the speakers, and in comparison the musical sound of the performers seemed muffled and weak.

Each delegation entered in representation of a specific community, but the overall representation, to which the master of ceremonies constantly referred, was of "Toropalca" as a regional identity. He himself contributed to this representation through the use of familial analogies. He welcomed each delegation onto the stage with the phrase: "Here are the *hermanos* [brothers and sisters] of [X community]." To hurry them off the stage he would announce: "Let's applaud the brothers and sisters of [X community] as we say good-bye to them."

Audience members were demanding in terms of time limits. While Toropalqueños in the fiesta context would dance for hours to the same piece of music, they had no tolerance for lengthy *festival* presentations. No one looked at watches, but the moment a group seemed to lull in their performance, someone would yell "Time!" (*Hora!*). In fact, if the presentation seemed slightly uninteresting, someone would yell "time" after only a few minutes. The festival context shifted the role of time in competitive performance. In fiestas, the unofficial competition is often conducted in terms of who can play for the longest duration, but all competitors play simultaneously. Sonorous volume, combined with physical endurance and the ability to enter and remain in one's groove, determined winners in these unofficial competitions. The audience for Toropalca's festival consisted of other delegations of performers; with the Bishop gone, this was literally a show by Toropalqueños for Toropalqueños. A performer of a rival group could slip quietly into the position of spectator from one moment to the next. From that position the spectators could play a key role in limiting the time rival performers had to strut their stuff, by voicing dissatisfaction with the length of a performance. The length of performance was still key to the performers, but the festival context shifted the way performers competed; since they did not play simultaneously, rival performers, temporarily turned spectators, limited one another in time through the public display of impatience with whomever was performing at the moment. Festival time, like de Certeau's "place" (1984: 117), did not allow for the coexistence of multiple elements in a given time frame. In contrast, fiesta time, like de Certeau's "space" (1984: 117), allowed for the coexistence of multiple elements in a single time frame. In Toropalca's festival, sonorous volume took a back seat to the duration a group was visually on display. Within the amplification hierarchies of the festival, performing delegations could not hold the public's attention by getting into a sonorously driven groove. The space between the performers and the audience was vast; everyone could *see* the performers, but the setting was hardly conducive to *hearing* them. To hold the audience's attention, performers resorted to visually perceived details: costumes, and silent comic acting.

The spectators' calling of "time" was generalized, even for the guest delegation from Calcha. Although all the communities were "invited" to the village of Toropalca, the invitation for Calcha was directed at another village, another region (still within the Province of Nor Chichas), another local identity that made no claim to be Toropalqueño. In part, the presence of Calcheños gave Toropalqueños reason for presenting themselves in their typicalness, demonstrating to themselves and Calcheños their local identity. In this invitation from one local region to another the Calcheños were supposed to be treated as honored guests. In contrast to the other performing groups who were simply presented by the master of ceremonies, a member of the Calcheño delegation went to the microphone to explain their performance. While everyone in the audience recognized their instruments as flautas—a vertical flute that is also played in Toropalca—the Calcheño made the specification that these were special flautas played for the fiesta of Santa Barbara. But even the Calcheños's status of invited guests did not spare them spectator critique; after a short interval the spectators called "time" on the Calcheños. It had never been made clear if Calcha would be judged for the second tier of competitive prizes; many Toropalqueño organizers favored eliminating the Calcheños from the competition because they were "special guests." The definitive policy was never announced but the Calcheños did not win any of the competitive prizes.

The spectators' tolerance threshold was slightly higher for the performing groups who played ayarachis and Toropalqueña flautas—two instrument genres that are associated with particular kinds of Toropalqueño "typical dress." While the ayarachis were associated with ostrich-feathered headdresses, Toropalqueña flautas were associated with aymillas (indigenous dresses), unkus (men's knee-length pants), and ajsus (woven pieces worn over dresses and short pants). Women vecinos took this "typical dress" out of moth balls to wear for Toropalca's Carnival celebrations, but these clothes are not usually worn on a daily basis in Toropalca's communities. Like the flauta, ayarachis—a specific type of panpipes usually played in the Cachisla River Valley in southern Toropalca—held a special significance for a collective sense of being Toropalqueño.

The lowest spectator tolerance was demonstrated for the groups that performed zampoñas—panpipes performed with interlocking technique—and *anatas*—vertical duct flutes carved from a single piece of wood (elsewhere called *tarkas*). The performers in these groups were usually high school students and those who played anata dressed and played the part of Carnival, complete with firecrackers, flour on their faces, and streamers around their necks. Anata Carnival dance movement is best characterized as running wildly, usually traversing a tremendous amount of space, only occasionally circling back. Dancers would run in twosomes and threesomes, linking to each other through bent elbows, locking even reluctant dancers in this hold. The thrill of this dance movement is felt by the Carnival participant: a rush to the head, a shortness of breath, a breeze against the body. But a festival performance made spectators out of participants, and as a visual display the anata music and dance lost its thrill. The festival performance of anata lacked the sense of engagement necessary to the enjoyment of this genre, and anata groups were quickly "timed" off stage. The zampoña groups had no flashy costumes. The zampoñas, associated with the dry months on the opposite side of the calendar from Carnival, were not associated with any special dress; zampoña players and dancers wore their everyday attire of commercially manufactured pants, shirts, and dresses purchased in Potosi or other cities. During fiestas of the dry months, Toropalqueños danced for hours to the music of zampoñas. But in the festival, zampoña groups, like anata groups, were quickly "timed" off the stage.

Some groups managed to hold the interest of the audience through acting out rituals—not rituals as drama, but rather rituals as comedy. Some Toropalqueño community members parodied their own ritual celebration, comically feigning drunkenness, fights, and general havoc (Figure 3.1). Aurolyn Luykx analyzed, as a mode of cultural resistance, the folklore performances at a normal school (school for training teachers) in the Aymara area of La Paz (1999: 263–265). But unlike the Toropalqueño performances, students in the normal school only parodied the upper classes and, even more often, the upwardly mobile; performers found their own cultural expressions inappropriate material for satire (1999: 272). Toropalqueño festival performances were a mix of the serious with the satirical, but they were all conscious representations of their own cultural expressions. In the comic presentation of ritual, performers would project in a high falsetto voice, a voice I generally did not hear in actual ritual contexts.[5] It was the falsetto voice I have heard used by women as they greet each other from across a river valley. From the poor amplification of the festival, spectators could not hear the words spoken in these comedies, so the falsetto voice became a sign in and of itself, and as an exaggerated demonstration of communicative interaction, it always brought laughter from the spectators. The general theatricality in this festival context contradicted an identified tendency in which folkloric troupes are usually presented with very little theatricality and a heavy dose of ethnographic information (Kirshenblatt-Gimblett 1998: 216). When Toropalqueños performed their folklore for themselves, their

Figure 3.1   Toropalqueños act out a ritual in a folklore festival (photograph by author).

performances were filled with theatricality and were rather scant in culturally informative discourses.

The delegation from the village Toropalca performed last. The organizers had decided the order of appearance and they probably imagined this spot as the most advantageous for the vecinos. But after three hours in the afternoon sun, the final performance was exasperating, and some of the spectators began to leave as the vecinos performed. The vecinos chose to perform the flauta genre. Although the flauta could barely be heard, the women's voices rose as they dedicated a song to the Doctora. These performers broke the performer/audience wall, inviting the Doctora to dance with them. As the three-hour festival ended, spectators streamed away into fiesta activities, a celebration that would move throughout the village spaces, centering on the plaza for extended periods of music and dance. The plaza was under renovation at the time, but it was difficult to imagine this space used for the kind of performance/spectator division required of folklore festivals. In fact other folklore festivals I have seen in Calcha also used sporting spaces rather than the plaza. Plazas invited participation; soccer fields invited spectatorship. Even in its unfinished state, the plaza was the center of fiesta activities. Flautas were stored away; August was the wrong time of year for that instrument. The fiesta activities included endless dancing around an ensemble of zampoña players, precisely the genre that had been hastily "timed" off the festival stage.

The festival organization drained the vecinos' and the Doctora's energies and even before its finalization I had already heard the comment, "never again." This was said in reference to the festival, but not in reference to the fiesta. The *alferados* (sponsors) of the fiesta this year had arrived from Argentina to carry out the activities that would demonstrate both their faith in the Lord of the Poor and their dedication to Toropalca, even as they were living almost permanently in Argentina. Like the Doctora, they too killed a steer and made elaborate preparations for their multiple-course meal that was offered to all Toropalqueños, a ritual meal called "*mesa de once.*" In anticipation of her brother's sponsorship, Doña Prima, known to make some of the best distilled products of the region, had been refusing to sell any wine or *singani* (liquor of white grapes), even denying that she had any at all. Her reserves, along with corn beer, provided ample libations for her brother's mesa de once. Fiestas, unlike Toropalca's festival, were anything but "dry." During most nights of the fiesta week, several zampoña ensembles played in the sponsor's house. Unlike the festival performance, they played simultaneously and through the night, until the early morning hours.

A folklore festival in the middle of a village fiesta juxtaposes the different kinds of temporalities of these two performance contexts. The festival breaks out of the rules of the ritual calendar, as genres are performed outside of their specified contexts. No one expressed concern in breaking these "rules" for the festival but the practices within fiesta temporalities revealed a tacit return to those rules. Performance time of the festival was already subdivided, truncating the way people would actually sense the musical experience, and performance time of the fiesta was lengthy and without subdivision; fiesta time was about getting into a "groove" and staying there for a long time. Toropalqueños moved back and forth between these two kinds of performances, but in the festival context, time constraints as well as poor amplification led to a privileging of the visually displayed.

A CONCERT FOR THE INDIGENOUS PEOPLES: POSTCARD PERFECT

Picture a reed stage floating in the middle of Lake Titicaca, off the shore of Huajata, the mountains looming behind on the far shore. In front of the stage, in ponchos and *lluch'us* (a woven hat with ear-flaps), a few "indigenous" people paddled reed boats, responding to the Spanish-accented voice over the loudspeaker, a voice that asked for movement and action for the filming. Música de Maestros, *Altiplano* (a rock-jazz-Andean fusion band), and *Jach'a Mallku* (a Pan-Andean type ensemble similar to Kjarkas in their instrumentation, repertoire, and presentation) shared this idyllic stage with visiting Spanish artists. But more importantly for the Bolivian musicians, they were to share a television "stage" in the homes of people in 50 different countries.

This concert was an internationally televised folklore festival in which only one of the three Bolivian ensembles survived the final cut. The project, called "The Concert for the Indigenous Peoples," was promoted by the Spanish-based Foundation of Intellectuals and Artists for the Indigenous Peoples of Iberoamerica. The more encompassing identification to which the Spanish were referring for "solidarity" was a global community of citizens concerned about the plights of indigenous groups. This global identification around a perceived moral cause was similar to those of human rights and "save the rainforest;" they all claim to be beyond the local interests of nation-states. Laudable motives brought the Spanish foundation to Bolivia, but they were not sufficient to avoid problems that brought Bolivian musicians and the press behind them into a state of indignation. The performance of the "Concert," as well as the response of Bolivian musicians to the final cut of the "Concert," provided a window through which to view the claims made on the domain of Bolivian "national music." Once again, in this festival context, sensory preferences were reordered, but this time these transformations occurred through the temporal organization of the television medium.

The Concert for the Indigenous Peoples, televisually multiplied into millions of performances as experienced by individual television viewers, brought Música de Maestros's and other Bolivian musicians' conceptions of their music into direct conflict with the way a foreign country imagined them. Several opinion pieces in the local press decried the Spanish television's omission of Bolivian groups. Writers called for protecting the "sovereignty" of Bolivian music, pointed to the lack of formal contracts with the participating musicians, wrote of the "humiliating and discriminating cultural censorship," complained of "the paternalism and colonial airs of the Spanish," and critiqued "the great hegemony of the Spanish artists." While the discursive debate raged on the level of the still-colonized and the neo-colonial, a debate in which I played a role as musician and writer, the basic fact of the matter was that the Spanish *watched* the concert and edited it for television in accordance with this visual experience. I suspect that they edited according to the dictates of television time, a time akin to Benedict Anderson's homogeneous empty time of nation-states as marked by the daily newspaper (1991: 24)—a set of time frames that are finite, anticipated, subdivided, and mutually exclusive. The Spanish organizers seemed to adhere to one view of Bolivian authenticity that did not coincide with that of the Bolivian musicians. As a performing ensemble, Música de Maestros, in almost all performances, held at a conscious level the idea that they were representing a rendition of something authentically Bolivian. But in the Concert for the Indigenous Peoples, their performance was filtered through the dictates of television time, as well as through the Spanish organizers' criteria of what was authentically Bolivian.

Picture the musicians of Música de Maestros, standing on the floating reed platform in the middle of the water, as the fickle Lake Titicaca weather simultaneously boasted sun and threatened rain. The musicians were dressed in their usual concert garb: black pants, white shirt, black vest, and black fedora hat. On the reed stage, not a microphone was in sight yet the musicians swayed and moved; they seemed to be playing. They were playing along with the musical sound from the prerecorded, studio-mixed DAT tape; they were playing with playback—producing an image that was temporally split from performed sound. The sound of Música de Maestros rang loud over the speakers, as the group performed two themes for the Spanish television cameras.

Picture being a musician with the ensemble on stage. I had just stepped off of one of two small boats that carried all of the musicians of Música de Maestros to the floating stage. I had been holding onto my hat for fear the lake wind would take it for a flight. Since I was still dependent on the written music—visual supremacy still ruled my playing—I brought a music stand. In synchronizing with a prerecorded sound, the musician must still go through the motions of playing the piece that sounded. But you had to play softly; if you played too loudly, you would not hear the recording with which you were supposed to be synchronized. The wind pulled treacherously at the music stand; working like the sail on a boat, the stand almost blew over several times. I caught it with my foot and continued playing. I heard the instrumentalists who were in the recording but who could not make it for this performance and I wondered if anyone would notice that the score sounded fuller than the musicians seen on the stage. But nineteen musicians out of a group of twenty-four was a good representation. The director had told us that the Spanish had asked for three pieces or 15 minutes of performance time. But after the second piece the Spanish-accented director said, "That's all. Next." We packed up our instruments and boarded the small boat, which had just brought the next group of musicians to the stage.

The Spanish organizers brought Música de Maestros out from La Paz on a bus that left the city at noon. Upon arrival in Huajata, a lakefront village, the Spanish told the group that everything was running behind schedule. But after the group's nine-minute performance no one made any moves to take the group back to La Paz until 5:30 P.M. Although all the musicians knew this was a collaborative affair, there was an expectation of at least a modest invitation of food and drink, especially since they were all yanked from the city at the principal hour for eating a main meal (12:00 noon). Great trout meals were served in Huajata, but at prices measured to tourists' pocketbooks and beyond those of most Bolivian musicians involved in this performance. As the afternoon continued and the Spanish made no move to offer the musicians any kind of food or drink, the musicians were put in the uncomfortable position of asking them to invite them to something.

Knowing my colleagues in Música de Maestros, they had gotten on the bus in La Paz with little more than some loose change in their pockets, enough to take their transportation home after work, perhaps even enough to buy an evening *sandwich de chola*[6] and a cup of tea, but nowhere near enough to ingest something at Huajata's tourist prices. And if they were carrying cash, they were of no mind to pay such exorbitant prices during an activity for which they were already performing without remuneration. In collaborations and contracted jobs, musicians expected a gift of food and/or drink, even if they did not explicitly state the expectation. Even paid jobs in bars included a gift in some form of an alcoholic drink. In the social relations with musicians these "invitations" were often not discussed as part of a contract but they demonstrated the bar owner's generosity or lack of it, and this would color the frequency and nature of future contractual relations. While this gift is not like Mauss's primitive peace treaty—a substitute for war (1967 [1925])—according to many Bolivian musicians with whom I worked, it did determine answers to the questions: to play or not to play? and with what desire will one play? At a gig in the middle of the day—and a collaborative one at that, covering precisely the hours when Paceños eat their largest meal of the day—the musicians were expecting food. Upon direct request the Spanish finally provided sandwiches and sodas, but because the musicians had to ask for the invitation, the whole situation left a bad taste in everyone's mouth.

In their participation in this concert, Música de Maestros held no grand illusions about doing something for indigenous peoples. When the director of Música de Maestros, Rolando Encinas, told the group about this project, he was skeptical from the start—skeptical that any "indigenous peoples" would receive benefits from this enterprise. His skepticism was adamant: "We all know how these things work. The say 'oh, the indigenous people, the indigenous people.' Then the money disappears and no one knows anything about it. Or it pays for big cars to

travel around. Or it disappears into the salaries of functionaries."
Rolando was very aware of a sector of Bolivian society, educated professionals, who seemed to benefit endlessly from projects "for indigenous
people" as they were funneled through NGOs. While he never named
any specific organization, he expressed a general distrust and skepticism
of any such enterprise. His attitude toward NGOs seemed somewhat
analogous to the general attitude that individuals feel toward state bureaucrats—using a stereotype of unfair bureaucrats to explain personal
failures in bureaucratic interactions (Herzfeld 1992: 4). The similarity,
though limited, was not surprising, as NGOs in Bolivia increasingly
took on roles in spheres where the state has been absent or ineffective, a
topic to which I will return in chapters four, five, and six. But unlike the
work of state bureaucracy, the work of NGOs was often buttressed
within a perceived, stated or unstated, moral imperative. Rolando's distrust of a general enterprise to assist "indigenous peoples" was rooted in
the disillusionment around the perceived misuse of such moral imper-
atives. In spite of having seen this moral imperative abused, he still believed in the importance of assisting indigenous peoples, just as people
continue to believe in the imperative of the nation-state in spite of their
difficulties with its bureaucratic representatives.

For Música de Maestros the influential selling point of the Spanish
proposal was not the opportunity to assist indigenous peoples, but rather
the possibility of the group's television exposure in over 50 countries.
Música de Maestros's ongoing project had been to break out of the typical modes of what was nationally and internationally heard as "Bolivian
music"—to present something different, to surprise the listener. On the
basis of this potential television distribution, the group agreed to collab-
orate with the Spanish, and although Música de Maestros did not believe
that indigenous people would benefit from this enterprise, the group still
took seriously the task of representing to the world a different kind of Bolivian music and thus a different kind of "indigenous" Bolivian music. If
the world associated poncho-wearing five-person ensembles with Bolivian music, this was precisely the sound/image that the director of Música
de Maestros wanted to subvert. Through these criteria, Rolando chose to
perform the "Chovena del Beni" and "Trilogía India."

The "Chovena del Beni" harked to the warm lowland areas of Bolivia
that have more recently become the focus of official attention in relation
to indigenous rights. Beni is a lowland area in eastern Bolivia and the
chovena genre is particular to this area. While the choice of this lowland-
associated music was consistent with contemporary indigenous concerns
within Bolivia, it did not meet the Bolivian aesthetic ideal of "indigenous"
as seen from outside of Bolivia. While Bolivians may have rather recently

"discovered" their own lowland cultures, an international audience still lived with its stereotype of Bolivia as a highland Andean indigenous country that was then further stereotyped through the musical associations of panpipes, the quena, and the charango—both images of the instruments as well as their respective sounds. The "Chovena del Beni" used the oriental flute along with the rest of the ensemble's orchestra, but the chovena had neither images nor sounds of panpipes or quenas. The lowland indigenous reference of the chovena was lost on the Spanish eyes and ears because highland indigenousness has been the common international signifier of Bolivia.

The second piece Música de Maestros played, "Trilogía India" (Indian Trilogy), provided those indexical images and sounds that were absent in the chovena. "Trilogía India" is a composition by José Salmón Ballivián (1881–1963), organized in three short movements that musically move through different rural scenes in Bolivia. The composer himself wrote of this work in 1953:

> The first movement describes the arrival in Copacabana of an indigenous group which has come to pray in their ancient temple dedicated to the Pachamama (Mother Earth or Divine Mother) from which the priests of the Conquest much later derived the cult of the Virgin of Candalaria. When they finished with the worship and offerings, they leave content and happy, going to the measures of a musical motif taken from the panpipes. The group returns to their ayllu [own indigenous group]. On the way they meet with a rival group. In this part the theme is constituted by a "japapeo"[7] of jest and challenge. The fight is launched and the angry voices of the men are mixed with the frightful screams of the young women. When the battle is finished, to the measures of a warrior march, the group becomes lost on the highland horizon. [Música de Maestros, Vol. III 1993; Rivera de Stahlie 1995, my translation]

This composer's work and ideas can be situated within what are known as *indigenismo* movements of the early twentieth century. In chapter four, I will elaborate on this historical emphasis on Indian-ness and how it might be distinguished from the contemporary discursive return of the Indian. Many parallels can be drawn between this composer and Música de Maestros. "Trilogía India" is a piece by a master composer of yesteryear, a director of the National Symphony, a self-taught musician whose music was captured on the page by his daughters. He studied in Europe and returned to Bolivia as a pharmaceutical chemist and professor of medicine. From his travels in the countryside, he worked with indigenous themes that then became the basis for his musical "works." Similar to Ballivián, several members of the ensemble—self-taught, all with excellent ear and memory skills—earned their living in other professions while finding time to contribute to the activities of Música de Maestros. Música de Maestros usually placed their music under the labels of "mestizo" and "Creole," and if they represented indigenous music at a specific performance moment, they still did so from a collective identificatory position that leaned more toward mestizo than indigenous. Individual members of the ensemble identified to a greater or lesser degree with indigenous practices, and Música de Maestros could perform some excellent representations of indigenous music. But as an ensemble they did not claim to be indigenous performers, nor did they let anyone draw that conclusion from their self-imaging. Like Salmón Ballivián, members of Música de Maestros were mestizos and Creoles who drew on indigenous musical expressions in their attempts to performatively represent Bolivia, and "Trilogía India" was exemplary of this aesthetic project.

In its use of Andean instruments and sonorities "Trilogía India" had the potential to fulfill a foreign imaginary of Bolivian music. A wide variety of Andean instruments paraded through each movement. Going from one movement to the next involved quick changes of instruments—switching as rapidly and imperceptibly as possible from the last beat of one measure to the down-beat of the start of a new movement. In each performance of this piece I would see Rolando make this change between the first and second movements; the change was also one of meter (4/4 to 3/4) and tempo (slow to fast), so I always watched him as he stuffed one instrument under his arm, pointed another to the microphone, as he simultaneously gave the upbeat with his instrument.

At the close of the piece, we all changed instruments; the large drum (*bombo*) marked eight beats during which time we all grabbed a panpipe (*siku*) to begin the final march, played in standard interlocking technique—interlocking notes played by paired instruments (Figure 3.2). As previously mentioned, multiple authors have discussed interlocking technique as a performance practice that relates to a sense of community, interdependence, and a particular ethos.[8] But in a performance of Música de Maestros, the use of interlocking technique acquired a completely different meaning. Taken out of one context and inserted into another, interlocking technique in a stage performance of a professional ensemble that purported to play "Bolivian master composers" assumed greater meaning. Bringing interlocking technique to the stage filled a void that appeared when panpipes first moved into Pan-Andean performance ensembles, when it became a solo instrument to be performed by one musician. While interlocking technique as applied by Música de Maestros might still indicate the interdependence of a community of performing musicians, its significance went much further; this kind of performance

Figure 3.2   In the Concert for Indigenous Peoples, Música de Maestros performs panpipes on Lake Titicaca (photograph courtesy of Gonzalo Espinoza).

brought this style to a national stage and validated it as an "indigenous" musical presence within a repertoire of "Bolivian master composers"; for the Bolivian listener interlocking panpipe performance reintegrated the imagined performance ethos associated with panpipes—an ethos that somehow got lost in the decontextualization of the instrument as used by Kjarkas and other Pan-Andean groups. In this performance, Música de Maestros reconnected the panpipe with its performance ethos, while the panpipe genre also took a place among "master" compositions. But the use of interlocking technique may go completely unperceived by an international audience weaned on the Pan-Andean style in which panpipes are often played by a single musician, who displays virtuosity in the ability to single-handedly play what is usually played by pairs of musicians. Even in Bolivia, depending on the audience of each performance, this final panpipe march of "Trilogía India" either ended with a bang or a whimper; either the audience took to its feet, thrilled by the circle of musicians playing siku in this traditional performance style, or the audience had already felt the closure of the piece in the penultimate movement, applauded then, and could barely be moved to applaud after the final march. "Trilogía India" had enough indices of Andean musicality, but they were in unfamiliar form and played by musicians whose dress may have looked to some as more European than Bolivian. Dressed in what the charango player often jokingly called "our waiter uniform"—Música de Maestros played the part but did not dress it.

"Trilogía India" and "Chovena del Beni" were the only pieces Música de Maestros performed for the Spanish television cameras. To borrow from Derrida's critique of a metaphysics of presence (Balkin 1987: 746–751), I can also examine what was indigenous about Música de Maestros's participation in this concert by looking at the repertory that the group decided not to play. In this performance Música de Maestros did not give presence to their ample repertory of cuecas and bailecitos, genres that are more linked to a Creole and mestizo music tradition. While not denying their mestizo and Creole presentation as a music ensemble, the group privileged the pieces that, for them, would hold relevance within a Concert for Indigenous Peoples.

⁓⁓⁓

The inclusion of Música de Maestros came late in the organization of the Concert for the Indigenous Peoples. When the Spanish foundation first began planning the concert, they established ties with a local Bolivian institution called Multimedia and obtained further government support through the Subministry of Ethnic Affairs and the Secretariat of Tourism. One of the workers for Multimedia described in terms of reciprocity the original concert plans: Bolivia would provide its big name artists—Kjarkas and Altiplano—in exchange for the presence in Bolivia of other big names; the Spanish organizers had promised Paco Ibañez, Luis Eduardo Aute, Georges Moustaki, the Rodriguez, and José Manuel Soto (Aguilar Vásquez 1995). After ten months of doing fancy footwork in Bolivia for the Spanish foundation, responding to one change of date after another, swallowing one change of artist after another, and working without pay, Multimedia finally threw in the towel. The Subministry of Ethnic Affairs picked up the pieces from there, but the cast of musicians—both international and Bolivian—had already shifted several times. Only Altiplano lasted from the beginning of these plans through the actual filming, and the director of that ensemble came to work as an intermediary between the Spanish foundation and the other Bolivian participants. The invitation to Música de Maestros came from the director of Altiplano; if it had come from any of the other organizations involved, I doubt our director would have paid it much attention. By encouraging a decision by Música de Maestros to participate in the concert, Rolando was responding to a fellow musician from a group he held in high esteem.[9]

Altiplano took to the floating stage just before Música de Maestros. With only five musicians in the group, and almost all instruments with electronic pick-ups, Altiplano managed to use their own sound system. As a fusion band, Altiplano sought to combine Andean instrumentation (charango, panpipes, quena, and bombo) with modern musical sonorities of electric guitar, electric bass, saxophone, flute, and drum set. The musicians wore dark pants or jeans and colorful long-sleeve shirts or T-shirts. Some wore vests with pieces of Andean weavings sewn into them. One musician wore a round cap fashioned out of Andean weavings. In short, the musicians of this group each followed their own fashion, avoiding a uniformed look, but presenting a group image that modeled the sonorous mix of their musical styles. During 11 minutes of filming, Altiplano performed two pieces, "Aguas Sagradas" and "Caminando la Ciudad." But only a 30-second introduction to "Aguas Sagradas" made the final broadcast. Altiplano, along with Música de Maestros, were eliminated from the program.

In the final cut, Spanish television editors had to trim hours of footage to shape a two-hour televised concert that also included Colombian and Spanish artists, and of the Bolivian ensembles, only Jach'a Mallku survived the editing. As previously mentioned, Jach'a Mallku, as a six-person ensemble, followed the Pan-Andean model in dress and instrumentation. Of the three groups that played on the lake that day, they definitely dressed the most like "natives" to a foreign gaze; but colleagues pointed out that Jach'a Mallku seemed to wear striped ponchos from Tarabuco (Department of Chuquisaca) and white hats from Potosí, a mix of accessories that did not mesh with a Bolivian knowledge of the culturally authentic. While their instrumentation meets a foreign expectation of the Andean, their musical repertoire is actually as Creole and mestizo as that of Música de Maestros.

Most Bolivian musicians I knew did not have access to the cable television hook-ups that permitted a viewing of the Spanish television's broadcast, but word spread quickly about the content and omissions in the internationally televised performance. In fact, I only spoke to a couple of people who had actually seen the international broadcast, making all the more intriguing the ensuing indignation about the elimination of Bolivian performers. Many spoke and expressed opinions, not on the basis of seeing the performance, but on the basis of hearsay, myself included. In this case, hearing was believing, or at least what one heard was sufficient evidence to formulate an opinion.

As a musician in Música de Maestros I cared very much about what was not in the broadcast. In my anger about the omission of Música de Maestros, I wrote and signed a fiery article, conjuring up Said's Orientalism, neocolonialism, and the constructions of the Other. Though by no means the center of the piece, Jach'a Mallku took a strange beating along the way because they became the preferred image of Other as constructed by the Spanish television editors. Although I claimed to write as an anthropologist, I have to admit that my driving motivation to write the article was my position as a violinist in Música de Maestros. Not wanting to involve my colleagues of Música de Maestros in any backlash that might occur because of the article, I did not mention my connection with that specific group, but rather wrote as "one of the musicians involved in the concert" and as a musician who was temporarily donning the anthropologist's hat. After finishing the piece, I showed a draft of the article to the workshop's coordinator, who encouraged me to take it to a friend of his who worked with the cultural pages of the newspaper *Ultima hora*. I had expected they would make major changes in the editing process, including a toning-down of my suggested title to the piece. After correcting my grammatical mistakes, they did not edit a word; the next day the entire piece was published with two photos of the lake performance, all under my original title of "The Cultural Colonialism behind 'the Solidarity with Indigenous Peoples'" (Bigenho 1995).

I ended my article with an expression I had heard my colleagues say, "Después de 502 años los españoles nos siguen mamando." Although not completely untranslatable,[10] this expression, which I heard used in innumerable occasions in Bolivia, requires some explanation. Literally, I could translate it as "After 502 years, the Spanish keep nursing at our breast," but the meaning in Bolivia is more akin to "After 502 years, they keep tricking us" or "keep pulling the wool over our eyes," "keep sucking us dry" or "keep taking us in." But the literal meaning paints a picture that should not be ignored. To receive nourishment a baby nurses at its mother's breast. Past a certain age, the baby does not need the mother's milk, but may resist weaning. Deception is rooted behind the expression "está mamando," a mild deception, but a deception, nevertheless. It is a deception in which one knows and to a degree accepts the fact that one is being "taken in." The mother may give in and let the child nurse, but she knows that she has been coaxed into letting the child have his or her way. In this framework the colonized take on the role of a mother and the colonizers take on the role of the demanding infant. The deceived knows, and to a certain extent resigns herself to the deception, but not without expressing knowledge of the situation. When my colleagues told me the Spanish "nos está mamando," they admitted knowledge of being taken in by the promise of an international broadcast—a promise that was never fulfilled.

I was certainly not the only person to write about the fated broadcast. In fact so many protests were put into print that the Spanish organizers accused the director of Altiplano of orchestrating this kind of discord in what was supposed to be a generous cultural exchange—as if to suggest that individuals would not act alone in expressing such opinions. The Spanish foundation also expressed its dismay at the Bolivian reaction by referring to Colombian groups who had also been eliminated from the show, and who had not protested at all. These details did not sit well with my Bolivian colleagues. As one musician told me, "Just because the Colombian groups let themselves be walked over without making a peep doesn't mean we will do the same." An article in *La razón* on January 28 emphasized the Bolivian absences in the face of continuous uncut images of the Spanish artists who had participated; the author of the article ultimately questioned the motives of the Spanish: "our music is not all that commercial . . . The interest that was constructed around the intentions of the Foundation seemed to dissolve on television for completely commercial reasons (P. A. 1995)." In the cultural pages of *La razón* on January 31, 1995, Germán Araúz wrote that the whole affair seemed like an opportunity to show off relatively unknown Spanish artists without any respect for the musicians who simply did not have the luck of being born in that country.

On January 29 the entertainment guide of *El diario* published an interview with Altiplano under the title of "Cultural censorship: Participation of this excellent Andean fusion band suffered inexplicable mutilation in the Concert which was broadcast around the world." After a description of the omission, the article continued to document the fax communication that occurred between the Spanish foundation and the director of Altiplano. The Spanish foundation washed its hands of any responsibility by claiming that it had been present for the final editing before broadcast, and that "as agreed" with the Spanish television, a single piece from each group would be broadcast, and each group would have four minutes of airtime. In spite of limited temporal frameworks, the festival organizers attempted to promote a principle of equality among different groups in their representation. In this case, the planned equality of time frames went awry. The fax from Spain explained that one person had filmed in Bolivia and another had done the editing in Spain. Finally the fax said, "it seems that the Spanish Television reserved for the broadcast two hours instead of three. We [the foundation] apologize, but this was not our fault." The blame here was placed somewhat on the Spanish television workers, but more importantly the blame fell on television time itself. Even the director of Altiplano was quoted in the article as saying, "On the television, time is the principal enemy." Time was fetishized, imbued with its own spirit and personality; time was blamed for the omission of the Bolivian groups, thus masking other reasons for these omissions.

The director of Música de Maestros, did not accept this explanation and demanded a public accounting via the vice-presidency of Bolivia. On

February 5, 1995, the same day my article was published, the entertainment guide of *El diario* published an article/interview with Rolando. The article explained that the dress of Música de Maestros was a representation of the cultural mestizaje that occurred precisely when the Spanish and indigenous cultures met. Rolando was quoted as saying that most people in Europe do not know Bolivia, or what they know of it is by: "tarkas and sikus as interpreted by artists dressed in sandals and feathers. It seems the Spanish want to keep seeing . . . Bolivians as objects of postcards in spite of the fact that 500 years have passed." Although the article also detailed Rolando's logic for choosing the repertoire of "Trilogía" and "Chovena del Beni," the main point of contention, the elimination of Música de Maestros from the broadcast, was expressed in visual metaphors with a harkening back to the Conquest itself.

For at least a year after its filming, the image of the "Concert for the Indigenous Peoples" remained alive and well in Bolivia. The Bolivian television channels also taped the concert on the lake, and unlike the Spanish television channel, Bolivian television did not seem to be so short of time. At any particular moment, local television programming switched to the "Concert for the Indigenous Peoples," with complete coverage of the Bolivian groups performing on the lake. Time after time these repeated images reassured Bolivians of their participation in the concert but at the same time reminded the musicians of being taken in, of being "mamado" by this Spanish foundation. The images from the concert itself did not prove useless to Música de Maestros. The ensemble used a photo from the concert on the lake for the collectors re-edition of their first and second albums on compact disc. The Concert for the Indigenous Peoples was after all a great photo opportunity.

To Show Our Work

Although Rolando always fused dance and music in his own performance experiences, Música de Maestros generally played music for listening. At parties we would dance to our own recordings and we knew other people did too, but our staged performances included no dance outside of the usual enthusiastic body movements of performers. This condition of what I call schizokinesthesia—the splitting of music from dance—was turned around during the folklore festival tour in France. A Bolivian dance troupe by the name of Conadanz had choreographed an entire program from our previously recorded repertoire. Not unlike other dance performance experiences, our "music for listening" became the basis for choreographed dance. This reconstitution of music and dance in a folklore festival led to a foregrounding of the dance and an emphasis on the visually displayed; sonorous domains were secondary to visual appearances.

For a Bolivian music ensemble, a tour of France carried great significance. In spite of discourses about national sovereignty and cultural pollution, a trip to Europe provided a special validation to a performing group. Artists in Bolivia, like artists elsewhere, are often presented through a laundry list of internationally toured places—Europe and Japan heading the list in terms of prestige for a Bolivian musician. Half of the musicians who toured France with Música de Maestros had been to Europe several times. These musicians toured Europe during the summer months, often collecting significant earnings that would supplement their limited income the rest of the year in Bolivia. The novelty in the summer of 1996 was the tour of the specific ensemble, Música de Maestros.

When Rolando discussed the possibilities of touring as Música de Maestros, he was very clear about certain minimum requirements: the number of musicians who would travel and the "official" nature of the contract. Música de Maestros was one of the largest ensembles in Bolivia, outside of the symphony orchestra; the 24-member ensemble could not be reduced to 5 members and still be Música de Maestros.[11] Much of the sound of Música de Maestros depended on a quantity of instruments and a variety of instrumentation, without which the group simply did not sound like Música de Maestros. In Bolivia, Música de Maestros's minimum number of musicians fluctuated around 14; without this number Rolando would not accept a gig under the name of Música de Maestros. The French tour organizers set the number of musician spaces at 12 and Música de Maestros traveled with an instrumentation of 3 guitars, 2 mandolins, 2 quenas, 2 violins, a concertina, a charango, and percussion. Rolando's concerns about the official side of any touring possibilities were related, not to questions of prestige, but rather to survival. He told me a tale of a disastrous tour with another ensemble; the arrangements had been casually made, and when the tour commitments fell apart the musicians were literally on the streets. Rolando knew that members of Música de Maestros would travel with next to nothing in their pockets; if the tour did not provide the basic necessities of food and shelter, 12 musicians stood little chance of roughing it on the streets of France.

Conadanz was a dance troupe just getting on its own feet. In the late 1980s several dancers of a national folkloric dance troupe expressed dissatisfaction with the direction of this "official" ballet by dancing right out of it and into their own troupe. Since its foundation, Conadanz had been attempting to establish itself on a par with the ballet that its founding members had abandoned. An invitation to the folklore festival of Saintes, France was a coup in this respect. The rival dance troupe had always represented

Bolivia at this festival, and in fact, ten years ago several of the Conadanz per-formers had toured this same festival with the other group. Returning under their own troupe title moved them up a notch within Bolivian dance groups. Once at the Saintes Festival in France, we found out how deep these rivalries ran.

The planning for the Saintes Festival occurred with a two year lead time and I was told that standard invitations covered transportation and room and board in France, along with a small daily stipend. The Saintes Festival only lasted two weeks, but this festival then became a sponsoring organi-zation to link invited delegations to smaller festivals in the surrounding areas. Working directly with Saintes Festival organizers, small municipali-ties contracted Saintes Festival delegations for two or three-day village cel-ebrations. The folklore delegations were under separate contract to the Saintes Festival for stipulated consecutive calendar dates, whether they performed or not, and Saintes delegations were not supposed to accept gigs outside of the formal organization of the festivals. According to the stories I heard, the original invitation to the Conadanz/Música de Mae-stros delegation arrived with a statement of support for airfare, a daily stipend of 70 francs per person (approximately $14 at the time), and all housing and food expenses covered. But the offer was dropped eight months before the tour date, and a new offer was drafted that did not cover any airfare. Conadanz made the decision to do everything possible to go to this festival. All daily stipends immediately went to cover airfares. Conadanz agreed to cover the remainder of the musicians' airfares, but we would not be earning anything on this trip. Only when we were in France did we learn why the Saintes organizers had changed their original offer. When the director of the rival dance troupe had heard that Conadanz would be touring with Saintes and related festivals he sent a letter to all fes-tival organizers informing them that this group was not an "official repre-sentation of Bolivia." His letters caused one of the major co-sponsoring festivals to withdraw all offers to the Conadanz delegation. Only through the persuasion of the president of the Saintes Festival, a person who could vouch personally for the organizers of this new dance troupe, did Saintes emit a second financially tepid invitation. Thus members of Conadanz went into debt to establish themselves in France, and musicians who in three months of European summer performances usually filled their purses for the year, went to France to play without any remuneration.

Why did Música de Maestros go to France? Rolando was very straight-forward in explaining the finances of the trip; on the one hand, this would not be a trip to earn money and he wanted everyone to be very clear on that point. On the other hand he sold the trip as the possibility to "show our work" (*mostrar nuestro trabajo*), to perform a different kind of music than what the French were used to hearing as "Bolivian." He pushed the trip as a "demonstration"—as a secondary frame on top of a primary activity (Bauman and Sawin 1991: 299). Música de Maestros has never taken off as a commercial venture in Bolivia; the musicians do not make money playing in this ensemble. Thus the discourse about "showing one's work" was quite consistent with the mode of performances in Bolivia. What left some musicians in a difficult position was the commitment to work at no pay during the northern hemisphere's summer months, a work season on which Bolivian musicians often banked for their livelihoods.

Under these meager financial prospects the only means by which the dancers and musicians could make money during the festival tour was by selling Bolivian instruments and crafts to French spectators. The dance troupe sold Bolivian artisanal crafts and the musicians sold the ensemble's recordings and indigenous musical instruments. Neither the recordings nor the artisanal crafts sold extremely well. French spectators were reluctant to purchase compact discs of a recently heard foreign group, although they were more likely to invest in a cassette. The best-selling items were the musical instruments, and they were deftly sold by the musicians. When we were not on stage performing we were at the sales table, tooting away on various instruments. Bolivian musicians who would not be caught dead playing "El condor pasa" on a stage in Bolivia, lured French spectators to buy their instruments by playing this tune. While this tune was composed by the Peruvian, Daniel Alomía Robles, in 1913,[12] it was made famous worldwide through Simon and Garfunkel's interpretation of the melody set to with the opening lyric, "I'd rather be a hammer than a nail . . ." The disdain that Bolivian musicians felt for the tune was often expressed through the humorous renaming of the tune as "¿Qué te pasa condor?" ("What's happening to you, condor?" or "What's up, condor"). But toward the objective of selling musical instruments in France, Bolivian musicians took advantage of the global notoriety of the tune.

A cloud of debt followed the group through its festival tour and back home to Bolivia. The members of the dance group had left Bolivia with borrowed money and the proceeds of their sales were not significant. To complicate matters, the elderly French patron I mentioned at the opening of this chapter—I will call him Jean—put the delegation in an uncomfortable position. As a friend to some of the dancers since their French tour ten years ago, Jean had arranged loans for the group before they left Bolivia, but in France he acted as if he had loaned them the money himself. During the tour, the delegation would periodically receive extra snacks and drinks that would suddenly appear with the a statement of "This is thanks to Jean." His donated snacks left a bitter taste as the tour continued and the self-appointed patron exercised what he believed to be his right to critique and shape the Bolivian performance. Not only did he claim this right as a patron, but he also claimed it through his purported knowledge of Bolivia. His critiques set off an underlying discord between the dancers and the musicians over the perceived reasons for being in France in the first place.

WHAT YOU SEE IS WHAT YOU GET

On one of the first days in France our delegation was lined up along with delegations from other countries. I was dressed as the other musicians and my blonde hair was simply tied back to keep it off my neck. A young girl from a Belgian delegation approached me and said something to me in French. I did not understand French, so I asked the charango player to translate for me. As a student of tourism studies, the charango player, René Alinas, spoke English, French, and Spanish. He told me that as she pointed to me she said, "She's fake." Then she pointed to one of the Bolivian dancers dressed in her dancing costume with her long fake braids worked into her short dark brown hair. As she pointed she said, "She's real." René immediately tried to smooth over the situation by replying that while I was from the United States I was really "Bolivian at heart." And here begins the tale of two imagined authenticities, two imagined "reals" that were constantly parting ways. If the director of Música de Maestros ever considered the fact that I might not look Bolivian, I never heard about it. I was asked to join the tour because he needed a violinist and I had been playing and recording with this ensemble for the previous two years. In Música de Maestros I was never pushed into trying to pass for Bolivian. I was simply expected to follow the performance decisions about costuming and repertoire selection. When women in the dance troupe tried to wield influence over these decisions, I always felt out of place. The dancers had the idea that the two women musicians—myself and a German violinist, Christine Bergmann—should dress in highland indigenous straightline dresses and accompanying headdresses. This costume of the Bolivian indigenous woman would also require the use of fake braids—a fact that, because of my rather novice abilities in hair design, had me worried. We occasionally donned these dresses, but I was quite relieved when our musical director opted to have the women musicians simply dress "like the men" of the music group. For example, the highland woven hat with earflaps (lluch'u) that we wore when performing with Andean flutes in the streets of France, did much to cover up blonde hair and disguise femininity. Nevertheless, even "as men" Christine and I did not fit the mold of Bolivian native as imagined by Europeans, and during the tour more subtle divergences of imagined authenticities emerged—imaginaries that revolved around visually perceived representations.

The clash of authenticities fueled disagreement between the musicians and the dancers. Some members of Conadanz, under pressure from Jean, wanted to base their performance on a presentation that would guarantee them another ticket back to France in the next two years. This was an objective perceived, but not generally shared, by the musicians. The musicians held to their own objectives of "playing it like it is," under the conviction that faithfully presenting the musical diversity that existed in Bolivia was the best way to act as a Bolivian delegation. As I already mentioned, an underlying and sometimes explicitly stated objective of the musicians was to break some of the European stereotypes of Andean music. Although playing "El condor pasa" at the sales booth was good for business, the stage was the place to make a different statement, an artistic statement wrapped up with the way Música de Maestros viewed its music as "national."

Under this objective, Música de Maestros brought to France its usual repertoire, drawing from Bolivian mestizo-Creole, highland, and lowland sources. Only two general changes were made to performance practices. First, a traditional highland repertoire was developed specifically for the activities the French called "animations," parades of exotic musicians and dancers. When we arrived at a village for a festival, often our first task was to perform several animations, moving through a short parade route, in a major plaza, or along a beach. Animations advertised for the more formal festival performances, but since most of the festival performances did not charge admission for spectatorship, advertising seemed like a rather minor motivation of animations. Animations, parades of exotic musicians and dancers, seemed to be more about reminding the French villagers to feel good about summer, festivities, and a celebration of multiculturalism.

For this type of outdoor minstreling, the usual presentation of Música de Maestros, with orchestral arrangements and stringed instruments, would not work. In planning to meet the performance demand of animations, Rolando turned to the instruments and genres that were most appropriate: highland indigenous wind instruments played in troupe style, that is with 8 to 12 players, all playing the same instruments. These instruments and genres were designed for playing outdoors and in movement across space, a performance aesthetic found in many Bolivian performances, and one that I believe is crucial in establishing a relation between people, sound, and place.

The second performance change for Música de Maestros was a modification in costumes. Some modifications were based on the different climate of the performance context, and other changes were based on aesthetic choice in a representational situation. Black pants and black vests worked well in the cold temperatures of La Paz, but in the summer days of France, these costumes were intolerably warm. Rolando advised the musicians to bring several alternate costumes: white pants, white shirts, and Andean woven belts. As the group's show began to take shape in France, the musicians would alter the form of dress according to the origin of the music being played. One part of the program included a set of music and dance from the Chaco region of Bolivia and for this set, we would wear a brown poncho that was characteristic of the region. For the pieces from the highland areas we would often wear black pants, white shirts, and woven belts—a costume that, according to Jean's complaints, made the musicians "look like firemen." Those who had heavy wool ponchos—different from the lighter ponchos from the Chaco region—would wear them for some of the performances of highland music. When all ponchos came off for the playing of the pieces from Bolivia's lowlands, Música de Maestros received criticism from the self-appointed French patron. In response to critiques Rolando answered: "It is ridiculous to wear ponchos during the Suite Oriental [music from the warm eastern lowlands]! The one has nothing to do with the other." Clothing and dress, something taken for granted in Bolivia, with a standard costume worn for all performances, suddenly became the focus of argument in this international representation of Bolivia. Rolando imagined a cultural authenticity that linked sound and image while the French patron imagined Bolivian cultural authenticity through images alone, and the latter's image equated Bolivia with highland indigenous markers.

Rolando had prepared another set of special costumes to wear for the performances of the indigenous instrument genres. Before leaving Bolivia, he alone spent many sleepless nights making chicken-feather headdresses that were worn to play the Italaque panpipe genre: "No one will sell you these things. I tried to buy them. But they are very rare now. You see pictures of them in photos from the 1930s, 1940s, but they are rarely used now. I want to rescue this dress which goes with the Italaque music." The Italaque costume Rolando wanted to rescue looked identical to that documented by Thomas Turino, as worn by siku players from Conima, Puno (Peru) (1993a: Plate 14), and Rolando, like the Conimeños, called this dress a gala costume (*traje de gala*, Figure 3.3). This feather headdress and another purchased feather headdress called the *suri* (Figure 3.4) were only to be worn for the Italaque performance and only for special occasions on the tour. Jean and some of the dancers thought the musicians should wear these ponchos and feathers for all performances and all pieces, or if not the feathers, then at least the ponchos and woven hats with earflaps (lluch'us); for an international audience ponchos, feather

Figure 3.3   In France, Música de Maestros don their gala Italaque costumes with specially made headdresses (photograph by author).

headdresses, and Andean hats referenced "indigenous" and "Bolivian" in powerful ways. While Rolando wanted to rescue a certain look to go with a particular sonorous performance, the French festival context led to a clamoring for the "look" irrespective of the sound that was supposed to accompany it. Both sides of this debate over performance dress were equally concerned with an imagined cultural authenticity, but they were two different imagined authenticities, according to a different privileging of sensory experiences, which were ultimately shaped by different subject positions: the positions of Bolivian musicians, the positions of Bolivian dancers, and the position of a Frenchman who wanted to wield influence over the ways this delegation represented itself as Bolivian.

Limiting Synesthesia
and Learning to Dance

As in Toropalca's festival and the Spanish televised concert, temporal organization altered the performance experiences of Música de Maestros in France. During the tour of French folklore festivals the Bolivian delegation longed for a single, two-hour, continual performance. But the logic of temporal organization in the folklore festivals followed a division and

Figure 3.4   In France, Música de Maestros don their gala Italque costumes with suri headdresses (photograph by author).

partitioning of time which was enough to exasperate any performer who might be seeking that moment of groove that sometimes is found only after the first 15 to 30 minutes of a performance. In any given festival we usually shared the stage with at least two other foreign delegations and a local French delegation. A typical line-up of performances would feature brief segments, 15 to 30 minutes, of each of the four groups, each of whom returned to perform another brief segment after all of the delegations had performed. A fear of spectator boredom seemed to lurk behind this temporal cutting and pasting of cultural diversity. Or perhaps Guy Debord was correct in stating that the "society which eliminates geographical distance reproduces distance internally as spectacular separation," erasing history in the process (1983: 167, 192). It was not enough to show diversity; diversity had to be brief, equal, and multiple—an equality of nations indexed by equal time segments. An afternoon and evening of festival performances might look something like this: Poland 20 minutes, Bolivia 20 minutes, France 20 minutes, Ukraine 20 minutes, Poland 20 minutes, Bolivia 20 minutes, France 20 minutes, Ukraine 20 minutes, Poland 20 minutes, Bolivia 20 minutes, France 20 minutes, Ukraine 20 minutes. Although the order might vary between rounds, a strong group with athleticism and acrobatics usually closed the show (that is, Ukraine). These brief performances left truncated the potential pleasure of a synesthesiac experience. As performing musicians we felt this truncation, and I can hardly imagine the audience getting into much of a groove for these brief successive performances. Pleasure for the spectator then came from the visual spectacles and sonorities moved to a definitive back seat, a fact clearly reflected in the sound systems provided for our performances.

A sound system can make or break a performance. A poor sound system, or one not properly checked and adjusted, leaves next to no opportunity for the musician to feel a groove in performance. The feeling of playing with a poor sound system is not even like practicing alone; when musicians play through amplification systems, they depend on these systems to hear both themselves and the other musicians. During the tour, sound systems were generally of very poor quality; many local festival organizers were incredibly reluctant to do sound checks for any ensemble; and even though they knew Música de Maestros played with twelve musicians on this tour and needed twelve microphones, we often shared only two or three microphones. If the stage had a decent sound system, the sound technician struggled to find a balance during the brief performance intervals, only to have to change the entire board again.[13] In general, the French organizers gave very little priority to the sonorous side of these folklore festivals. These experiences rang true with Barbara Kirshenblatt-Gimblett's assertion of the European tendency "to split up the senses and parcel them out, one at a time, to the appropriate art form. One sense, one art form. We listen to music. We look at paintings. Dancers don't talk. Musicians don't dance. Sensory atrophy is coupled with close focus and sustained attention" (1991: 416). Rather than a particularly European tendency or something we can simply attribute to television, I would argue that this sensory reordering has to do with the organizational modes by which people consciously display their culture to themselves and to others. This display marks a shift in the kinds of authenticities that have value in a performance. In the folklore festival, visuality gains value over aurality, and clashing cultural authenticities leave no possibility for kinesthesic experiential authenticity.

This particular festival was about the French representing to themselves a spectacle of the other. Folklore festival contexts are generally ripe for contradictions between the audience's expectations and the folklore artist's presentational practices. The comments and critiques we received in France resonated with a statement made by one participant of the Festival of American Folklife: "[P]eople get mad when you ain't what they expect you to be" (Cantwell 1993: 154). The French patron and other critics who complained about the authenticity of the Bolivian musicians had an ideological stake in the maintenance of their concept of authenticity. Here is where the folklore festival performers cannot simply be seen as proudly representing their own cultures. When folklore performers do not act up to an international audience's expectations, a peculiar condition of these performances is often revealed: that the folklore performer is enacting a role *for the other* (see Žižek 1989: 106). To borrow from Slavoj Žižek, the performer can be seen as "already symbolically identified with the gaze for which he is playing his role" (1989: 106). While Žižek psychoanalyzes the result of this being-for-the-other, I want to underscore the instrumental reasons dancers had for clinging to a position of being authentically Bolivian for the French. Whenever the dancers complained about the lack of the Bolivian delegation's authenticity in representation, the complaints were usually couched in terms of the possible return trip to France. Members of Conadanz held various jobs in La Paz, dedicating themselves to dancing in their free time. They, like the musicians, worked in offices, banks, government bureaucracies, and NGOs. In choosing to accompany the group on the two-month tour of France, some dancers, as well as musicians, lost their jobs at home or had to resign from their positions before their departure. While members of Música de Maestros generally had many music performance possibilities in and outside of Bolivia, the dancers of Conadanz generally had fewer performance opportunities. While both dancers and musicians had much at stake in the French folklore tour, the dancers were even more likely to assume the "symbolic mandate" of being authentically Bolivian for the French.[14]

The French investment in the authenticity of the other was also linked to the ideologies and politics of multiculturalism. Within this multicultural spectacle of the French folklore festivals, a gesture toward world understanding was always part of the planned events. The Bolivian delegation was often asked to end their last performance by inviting the French audience to dance with them. These were explicit instructions from the French organizers and it was something the Bolivian delegation usually did quite well. But the dancers were not always pleased with these planned gestures of world understanding—attempts to move back to the all inclusive performance without performer-audience divides. As one dancer complained to a musician, "You don't know what it is like to dance the morenada for twenty minutes with someone who doesn't know how to dance. All you have to do is play." In other words the dancers could not find their groove because their adopted foreign partners did not know how to dance. Behind this statement was the idea that these dances, as recombined with the music from which they were once split, had to be explicitly learned to be enjoyed. Jane Desmond reminds us that as movement becomes codified as "dance," its production becomes highly controlled, and the parameters of acceptable movement narrow considerably (1997: 37). Dance then results from planned organized learning, which is more and more distant from its kinesthetic origins that stress the singular desire to move one's body to a compelling sound. In its recombined form, dance and music also occupy space in a different way. In the traditional rural music of Bolivia, the musicians always occupied the centerpoint of the movement with the non-musician dancers on the outside of the circle. But to accommodate a perspective toward the audience, the festival performance divided and shifted the spatial center; in the Bolivian delegation the dancers took the front of the stage and musicians took the back, and within an ethos of shared multicultural understanding, staged dancers were asked to close the show by crossing established performer-audience divisions and by drawing spectators into participatory dance.

Festivals subdivide performance time with an ethos of equality; they recombine music and dance in such a way that body movement must be learned to be enjoyed; they privilege the visual sensory experience over others; they limit the synesthesiac possibilities of music performance. Festival time favors sequentiality over simultaneity. Festival time goes hand in hand with Carol Greenhouse's concept of linear time—the time crucial to the discourses that construct and serve to uphold the legitimacy of nation-states (1996: 2). Linear time, born within the cultural history of mechanical clocks, printing presses, and the rise of capitalism, is a perception of temporality as an "irreversible progression of moments, yielding ordinal conceptions of past, present, and future as well as duration" (Greenhouse 1996: 20). Furthermore, the concept of linear time delineates difference through dichotomies of the oral and the literate (74); one is either inside linear time, inside history, or is perceived to be so other as to be outside of that time line (Fabian 1983). As an alternative to exclusion, festival time becomes another accommodation of difference, a taming of difference as it is squeezed under the strict dictates of a clock that privileges the ideals of equality and variety. Folklore festivals channel performative national patrimonies into sequential, orderly, observable time segments. This viewing of a nation's commitment to multiculturalism precludes a kind of listening that might be conducive to the production of experiential authenticity. But the festivals discussed in this chapter suggest that differently positioned Bolivians became active participants in these conscious performances of the multicultural nation and the multicultural world. Yet other Bolivian performers' concepts of cultural authenticity still clashed with those of international sponsors and spectators. The French patron imagined the authentic Bolivian as perpetually dressed in highland indigenous costumes. These imaginings clashed with Música de

Maestros's own imagining of a pluricultural Bolivian topography—an imagining that linked musical sound to visually perceived costumes from the lowlands, the highlands, and the Chaco.

The symbolic battle over these perceived authenticities is rooted in distinct modes of sense perception. Walter Benjamin reminded us that human sense perception is organized not only by nature, but also by historical circumstances, and that "changes in the medium of contemporary perception can be comprehended as decay of the aura" (1968: 222). While Benjamin began his discussion of aura in reference to original works of art and the decay of their auras or uniqueness, I want to bring this point to a discussion of imagined musical and cultural authenticities. There is a parallel between the perceived aura of an original painting and the perceived pulse or groove of an imagined original music performance. In folklore festivals the transformation in authenticities emerges from a privileging of the visual over the sonorous and through a particular organization of time. Benjamin wrote about a fading of ritualized logics in the age of mechanical reproduction, about a freeing of art from "its parasitical dependence on ritual" (1968: 224), but the loss of ritual within the logic of mechanical reproduction can also mean the loss of groove within sonorously driven experiences. As a participating musician I admittedly lamented the loss of groove in the festival context. But as an anthropologist I mention this loss, not to lament these changes, but in order to understand how Benjamin's visually focused argument might be read through sonorities of music performances. If the groove is the aura of the experientially authentic music performance, the aura has diminished in these festivals and the focus has moved away from an original music performance to the visually imagined authenticity of an indigenous image. Even as all these festivals produced rather willing participants in pageants of multiculturalism, the struggles that emerged over cultural authenticity often reproduced structures of domination and control—vecinos over indigenous communities, as in the Doctora's festival in Toropalca, and European organizers over Bolivian musicians, as in the Spanish and French organizations of the Concert for Indigenous Peoples and the Saintes Folklore Festival, respectively. As the struggle itself was often shaped through control of sonorous environments and a tyrannical insistence on equal sequential time segments, experiential authenticity was always secondary to cultural authenticity in these folklore festival performances. While this chapter has spanned music performances at local, national, and international venues, exploring the staged presentation of multiculturalism in these contexts, in the following chapter, I turn to the politics of culture and the politics of aesthetics within two Bolivian national music projects.

CHAPTER 4

INDIGENOUS COOL AND THE POLITICS OF AESTHETICS

While members of both the Bolivian Workshop of Popular Music, "Arawi" and Música de Maestros made references to indigenous cultures in their music performances, they were for the most part members of the mestizo-Creole culture of La Paz. The two musical projects followed a long historical pattern in which some Bolivians have represented other Bolivians—that is, Bolivia's mestizo-Creoles have represented Bolivia's indigenous peoples. These kinds of representational projects can be interpreted under the rubric of indigenismo, a political and cultural current found in many Latin American contexts in which mestizo-Creoles have used references to indigenous cultures to bolster a national or regional identity. But Bolivia has had its own flavor of indigenismo, marked by the Chaco War, the 1952 Revolution, and indigenous mobilizations particular to Bolivia. Through a closer examination of the cultural projects of the workshop and Música de Maestros, I will argue that particular changes in performance practices in the representation of the indigenous mark a shift from the early-twentieth-century politics of indigenismo to the more recent politics of what might be labeled as "the return of the Indian," to borrow the title phrase from an article by Xavier Albó (1991). By "return of the Indian" I refer to a resurgence of indigenous politics that has in turn shaped the ways elites, mestizos, and the state represent indigenous cultures within the national community.

Both indigenismo and "the return of the Indian" go to the heart of what is implied by the terms "politics of culture" and "cultural politics" (Williams 1991; Jordan and Weedon 1995; Alvarez, Dagnino, and Escobar

1998: 2–7). As Brett Williams succinctly put it, the politics of culture emerge when "some people have more power than others to shape who gets to say what" (1991: 3). In this chapter, I examine the politics of culture through a discussion of both aesthetics and authenticity: How do some people have more power to shape who gets to hear what; who defines the parameters of cultural-historical authenticity; and what then can enter a symbolic economy as alienable property? Both national music projects relate in distinct ways to what I have called cultural-historical authenticity and to unique authenticity, the latter referring to the new, the innovative, and that which is thought to emerge from the depths of individual creative genius. In this chapter these kinds of authenticities are revealed in their connections to particularist and universalist aesthetics. Even though in a French folklore festival Música de Maestros represented the particularist position of "Bolivian folklore," in Bolivia both this ensemble and the workshop strove for equal footing with the universalist positions of "Great music" and "Great composers." In this sense, Música de Maestros followed a cosmopolitan ideology whereby each nation is assumed to have its great composers who simply need to be recognized, recorded, and raised to the level of their European counterparts (see Turino 2000: 105–108). This chapter is about the balancing act of claiming cultural-historical authenticities—particularities about Bolivia, often metonymically represented through references to indigenous cultures—while also embracing the universalizing tendencies behind the ethos of the unique authenticity of artistic creation. Both of these musical projects make particularist and universalist claims in ways that are neither oppositional nor mutually exclusive. The classification of composers as "universal" or "particularist" is not foreign to Western classical music traditions (see Leyshon, Matless, and Revill 1998: 9), but a universalist claim has a distinct importance when it is made by composers in a country where social relations have been historically structured in subordination to the West.

In light of these two examples, it seems appropriate to return to David Whisnant's original discussion of the "politics of culture" in *All That is Native and Fine* (1983). Whisnant studied settlement schools in the southern Appalachian Mountains and their projects of cultural preservation and survival. Under the rubric of the "politics of culture," Whisnant emphasized both "systematic cultural intervention" and the function of fixating on a romanticized view of a culture that exists within a broader sociopolitical context (1983: 13). While neither the workshop nor Música de Maestros demonstrated any great affinity for the term "folklore," some of the differences between these two projects can be illuminated through what Barbara Kirshenblatt-Gimblett called the mistaken dichotomy between "applied folklore" and "pure folklore" (1992). While the workshop seemed to do more of the first and Música de Maestros did more of the latter, both projects were engaged with the nationalist discourses usually served by the study of folklore (see Kirshenblatt-Gimblett 1992: 35). While neither the workshop nor the ensemble Música de Maestros had official ties to the state, both musical projects involved research of ethnic or indigenous cultures within Bolivian territory, and both claimed to bolster, through their music, the position of Bolivian national identities. To varying degrees, both the workshop and Música de Maestros can be viewed through the "politics of culture," although the workshop was more engaged with "systematic cultural intervention," and Música de Maestros was more engaged with the romantic view of distinct cultures and historical memories. Through an ethnographic examination of these two mestizo-Creole musical projects, I want to showcase social actors and practices of a social group that is too often implicitly dismissed as uniform in its objectives and in its level of power and influence. I focus here on the musical work of mestizo-Creoles, on their musical representations of indigenous cultures, and on the ways these projects articulate with discourses of indigenous politics. While most members of Música de Maestros and the workshop did not identify themselves as "indigenous," many of them did ascribe themselves to the category of "musician." As this chapter explores the politics of culture, it must also address the economic base from which musicians wield their limited influences. First, I turn to the particular social geographies of the city of La Paz—the context in which members of the workshop and Música de Maestros made a space for themselves "as musicians."

VERTICALITY IN LA PAZ

At 11,910 feet (approximately 3,600 meters) above sea level, the city of La Paz sits in what Paceños describe as a cooking pot in the middle of the highland Andean plateau. Above the highland Andean plateau, sometimes visible from inside the cooking pot of La Paz, snow-capped peaks, like the photogenic and sacred Illimani, frame the spectacular geography of this city. At the rim of this pot, at almost 13,500 feet (approximately 4,100 meters) sits another city, El Alto, with a population that was about a half-million in 1995, and that continues to grow with the influx of rural migration. While La Paz and El Alto are two different cities, the spatial and economic practices of their inhabitants are inextricably linked as well as severely divided. In simplest terms, the poor live at the higher elevations and the rich live at the lower elevations, seeking lower venues in which to situate their homes, forever pursuing the remarkably warmer microclimate at these levels. Those of lower economic means, perching their homes on precarious foundations, live further up the sides of the urban pot and onto the high plateau. The divisions in these urban contexts mark a history of ethnic divides in La Paz, a city that has been described as two different cultural cities in one space, one Chukiyawu and the other La Paz, one indigenous Aymara, the other mestizo-Creole (Albó, Greaves, and Sandoval 1987, 1983, 1981). This was the context in which Música de Maestros and the workshop developed their activities. While the workshop drew in youth who might be part of Chukiyawu or who might live in the physically different space of El Alto, the institution's proposal writing practices and modes of operation were squarely situated in both the physical and the culturally mestizo-Creole city of La Paz. As will become evident below, Música de Maestros occupied more of a middle ground between the two cultural cities.

The center of town, divided in a horizontal fashion, occupied an intermediate space between the lowest and the highest levels of the metropolitan area. It was an area of the city that I came to know intimately through the musical activities of the workshop and Música de Maestros. The center of La Paz was a place for walking. While all forms of transportation in the city were relatively inexpensive, I soon discovered that on my own two feet I often could arrive at my destination more quickly than by taking a taxi or bus. This was particularly true at the noon hour, when people either flocked home for lunch or a union march stopped all traffic in the center of town. At any time of the day, traffic jams served as well-worn excuses for not making it to one's destination in a punctual manner.

The middle-class neighborhood of Sopocachi—located at the eastern end of the center of town, just before the drop-off to the warmer microclimates of below—was known for its nightlife that catered to middle- and upper-class imaginings of a bohemian life. In Sopocachi, NGO workers, politicians, intellectuals, and government ministry workers got a taste of bohemia on the weekends without having to live on the correspondingly scant wages of an artist. This was the Paceño neighborhood in which I lived, as did some of the workshop's organizers. But most of the musicians in both Música de Maestros and the workshop lived elsewhere. Sopocachi was the neighborhood in which working musicians spent many of their Thursday, Friday, and Saturday nights; if they were not working in Sopocachi on the weekend, they probably did not have a gig. The principal bars (*boliches*) of this neighborhood (Equinoccio, Mateus, Piano Jazz Bar, El Socavón) scheduled music groups to perform on the weekends, hoping to draw maximum crowds of middle- and upper-class consumers.

The Sopocachi neighborhood begins at the University of San Andrés, marked at the corner by the Plaza del Estudiante. Running in the opposite direction is the Prado, a street divided by a landscaped pedestrian island. The Prado officially ends after a few blocks, but the pedestrian island extends upward for several blocks, subtly climbing to the area of the Plaza San Francisco and the Pérez Velasco Street. The San Francisco Church, its plaza, and the market area around Pérez Velasco inscribe a symbolic line between the two cities of La Paz. On the north side of the street extending from the Prado are tall shiny buildings and shopping centers. On the same side, a few blocks up, one finds the Plaza Murillo, the government seat, and a colonial part of town with the most photographed street of La Paz: Jaén. On the other side of the divide, up through the neighborhood of Gran Poder, a commercial fervor spills over into the streets. Economic activity sprawls out of buildings into the streets, while cars and pedestrians struggle equally for a small space in which to maneuver. This is not a poor area of town. The fruits of this area's commercial activity are ritually displayed each year in the Fiesta del Gran Poder.[1] But a different logic dominates the organization of this side of town, a logic which is marked by the witches street (*calle de las brujas*), a part tourist-oriented, part locally oriented place where women sell amulets, llama fetuses, herbs, and anything one might need to complete ritual offerings, *k'oadas* (ritual burning of incense and other materials), and *ch'alladas* (ritual libations almost always performed when people acquire something new or begin to inhabit a new space). Those selling these materials have established stands in which they hock their wares. At dusk on Tuesdays and Fridays the Aymara shamans (*yatiris*) appear on the streets, offering to read coca leaves or cards, or to perform any rituals as needed by clients. On this side of town an Aymara and mestizo culture dominates the spatial organization and practices. This is not to say that the middle-class Creoles do not cross this divide. For example, prominent politicians have their own Aymara shamans of whom they are regular clients.

When I began my research, the workshop was located on the colonial-style street of Jaén. While the institution had to leave its original locale and was without a place of work for several months, it returned to Jaén when a new project gave the institution a new lease on life. The director of the workshop always talked about that street as "centrally located": close to the theaters for performances (the Municipal Theater two blocks away and the House of Culture perched on the Pérez divide), and close to the principal transportation routes to and from El Alto for students who came down to participate in the activities. When the workshop was passing through some of its most difficult times, I heard some instructors remark that the rent charged in any other area of town would have been less expensive than on Jaén Street; two blocks up on the other side of the Pérez divide seemed equally centrally located. But other ideologies were at work in clinging to Jaén as the place of the workshop. For the director, and for others involved in the decisions of locating the workshop, that narrow cobblestoned street, bordered by picture-perfect colonial balconies hanging from buildings, the adobe interiors of which harbored cold air in a place where heat is a coveted commodity, was the most appropriate place for a workshop that claimed to both create innovative musical projects for the future and root itself in indigenous traditions. For the director, the outward presentation of the workshop was just as important as the sum of its activities. Rather than an architectural disjuncture in this bohemian fantasy, the placement of the workshop on Jaén Street was consistent with the consciously "hybrid" nature of this project, the coexistence of the traditional and the modern and the perceived transformative potential of this mutual coexistence (see García Canclini 1995).

Near the witches street, on the other side of the Pérez divide, Rolando Encinas, the director of Música de Maestros, lived in a small room on a back alley, and these close quarters served as the rehearsal space for Música de Maestros. My ability to catch a taxi to the area of the workshop and my relative inability to catch one going to the other side of the divide were indicators of the differences I have already sketched. The Pérez divide indeed runs deep. Most taxi drivers did not want to fight the overflowing commercial activities for a space in the road on one side, but had no qualms about taking customers into the jammed traffic that inevitably clogged the more orderly streets on the other side of the Pérez divide.

The live performances and recording activities took musicians from both the workshop and Música de Maestros to the different areas of the city. Musicians spent weekend evenings in the bars of Sopocachi, playing for modest earnings, temporarily fulfilling the bohemian fantasies of middle- and upper-class Paceños. Recording studios were also vertically aligned. Música de Maestros recorded their third and fourth discs in Discolandia's analogue studio, which borders the Plaza San Francisco, just steps away from the Pérez Velasco. At this studio, recording sessions were often interrupted by fluctuations in the electric current. Rolando would throw up his hands at the frustration of this lost time, "Can you believe this? *The* major recording label in Bolivia, and they don't have a proper power stabilizer." While the recording process began at the San Francisco studio because Rolando preferred the analogue sound to that of digital,[2] the final mix was completed in Discolandia's digital studio, located in the warmer, wealthier, lower neighborhood of Obrajes.

Drinking practices also varied within these different urban spaces. The bars in Sopocachi filled with people drinking liquors: whiskey, rum, singani (the Bolivian liquor from distilled white grapes). Beer on draft was served sparingly and at exorbitant prices. As one moved toward the Pérez Velasco the bars still served liquors—more singani than anything else—but the customers often preferred bottled beer, which was cheaper, making their purchases auspiciously in even numbers of liter bottles or entire boxes of bottled beer. If instructors from the workshop or Música de Maestros had gigs in Sopocachi, they accepted the liquor-dominated scene's advantages as a part of the unofficial payment for their performances. But it was outside of the gig that I noticed differences in consumption patterns. Workshop organizers and instructors sought out the Sopocachi scene or created their own liquor-dominated party in someone's home. The musicians of Música de Maestros were more likely to seek out the less expensive beer-dominated bars. The spatialized practices of Música de Maestros and the workshop already reflected some of the social differences of these two groups, and members in both projects confronted in distinct ways the economic challenges of "being musicians" in Bolivia.

To Be a Musician in La Paz

Members of both the workshop and Música de Maestros self-identified with the occupational and artistic category of "musician." While few of them lived entirely from work in music, this identification—the statement, "I am a musician"—placed their musical activities in what, in the ideology of musicians, is presented as a realm constantly under threat from a drought of financial resources. At some level, this perceived threat of being unable to make music because of a lack of economic resources was not completely different from Toropalqueños' expressed need to receive outside support in order to present themselves in their typical dress. But differences emerge when making music stops being a ritual activity and begins to signify a condition of remunerated labor (see Attali 1985). While the complaint about the lack of support for musical activities may sound like a litany heard the world round, one also has to keep in mind that these musical activities were occurring in a country where social and economic indicators reflected conditions of extreme poverty for a large sector of the population. The musicians of these two projects fit into the national economic scheme in relatively advantaged ways, but their conditions of work should be seen in relation to the larger national economic picture. Many who called themselves musicians in Bolivia made significant sacrifices in pursuit of that position.

While most members of Música de Maestros had day jobs that were unrelated to music, many of them depended on La Paz's nocturnal musical life for part of their income. The musicians of Música de Maestros who also played with the Symphony Orchestra earned a modest salary from their work with this large ensemble, but orchestra directors held them to nightly rehearsals, Monday through Friday, and often refused to give them leave even to *perform,* let alone rehearse, with Música de Maestros. This inflexible rehearsal schedule created a tension between Música de Maestros in general and the musicians who had to strike a balance between the two performing groups. The director often expressed his frustrations, but he understood that between having their pay docked from the Symphony and missing part or all of rehearsals and even performances of Música de Maestros—an ensemble where earnings were scant at best—Symphony Orchestra members often had little choice but to attend their symphony rehearsals.

Instructors of the workshop as well as several members of Música de Maestros performed in *peñas* and boliches. Peñas are performance spaces for folkloric music that operate nightly in the center of town, draw on several different ensembles, and appeal to a tourist audience (for example, Los Escudos on El Prado street). I often heard musicians complain about having to perform every night in the peña, as nightly performances seemed to hold an ensemble's permanent place in the long line-up of competing groups. Musicians recognized the nightly peña performances as a sure way to burn out, and when musicians discussed having to play in peñas, they seemed to reflect on a stigma of mediocrity. "He is a peña musician," was an insult. Boliches or bars were a step up in the nocturnal performance scene. Single ensembles were contracted to play Thursday, Friday, and Saturday nights in Sopocachi, playing three sets between about 11:00 P.M. and 1:00 A.M. But some musicians ran into problems when they, as individual musicians, were double-booked through two different ensembles. Even though boliche owners tried to prohibit double-booking, many musicians held positions in more than one performing ensemble, and if two ensembles managed to secure a gig for the same weekend, musicians had little choice but to run back and forth between the two locales, trying to play sets in one boliche as the ensemble was taking a break in the other one. While Koji Hishimoto lived in Bolivia, he and Rolando Encinas, the director of Música de Maestros, formed an inseparable musical pair in these performance contexts. As a quena duo, Rolando on first and Koji on second, they performed and recorded with Wara, *Bolivian Jazz,* Jaime Junaro, Jenny Cárdenas, Henriqueta Ulloa, Zulma Yugar, and Yayo Jofré (*Los Jairas*). Many solo singers would call Rolando when they needed backup musicians for performances and recordings. He, along with several other musicians from Música de Maestros, would work with these soloists. One of the ensemble's guitar players jokingly commented on this widespread performance of Música de

Maestros's musicians with different Bolivian soloists: "And now we have [artist x] accompanied by *los de siempre* (the same old ones). Through these performances Rolando and Koji paid their bills, but for both of them their real musical commitment was in Música de Maestros. Koji relocated to Japan in 1996, but much like myself, he has maintained a transnational musical connection with the ensemble. He rejoined the group for their French tours in 1996 and 1998; he has continued to arrange some of the ensemble's new repertoire; some of his own compositions were recorded on the ensembles' VII recording, and his return trips to Bolivia have been coordinated with the tasks of final studio recording and mixing. Koji has also provided crucial contacts through which Rolando and a few other musicians have been able to complete four-month performing tours in Japan, making money to ease the lean earnings of music performance work in Bolivia. Koji has accompanied these Japanese tours as guide, translator, and musician.

A few of the musicians in Música de Maestros made the better part of their living in boliche performances, but these performances also had their burn-out factors, in both the saturation of audiences and the exhaustion of musicians. As an ensemble, Música de Maestros only played about once a year in a boliche, and the director always preferred to book these performances after a recent formal presentation in the municipal theater. The other source of income to which musicians turned came from the foreign tours mentioned previously, not folklore tours but small musical ensemble tours to European countries or Japan.

Organizers and instructors of the workshop were certainly part of the performance scene in La Paz, but much of the income on which they depended to "be musicians" came from pedagogical activities that were financed through international funding sources, the ministry of culture, and the municipality.[3] Workshop organizers were relatively adept at developing projects to tap these funds, framing their projects in terms of their knowledge of "traditional," "native," or "autochthonous" music. The organizers of the workshop saw the pedagogy of their institution and its corresponding projects as intellectual property, part of a process of knowledge production (see Schild 1998: 93). In a scramble to meet international funding agendas, such institutions are made and broken through the presentation of their ideas, a kind of discursive economy through which workshop organizers and instructors ultimately made ends meet as musicians. Their proposals spoke of the "consolidation of cultural identity as expressed through music." Their activities for students in the city of La Paz were aimed at "obtaining [for the students] a greater cultural identification and projection of their own musical expressions." Through the promotion of three types of music, "traditional," "popular" (or mesomusic), and "contemporary," the workshop's proposals presented a view of music identity in Bolivia, a view which was at the same time indigenous, multiple, hybrid, and avant-garde. But an apparent artistic attitude of openness was ultimately countered by the very processes of proposal writing and NGO institutionalization.

The workshop certainly did not begin with institutionalization as its objective. The founders of the workshop were intellectuals of the left who, along with other Latin American thinkers, were reconceptualizing the relation between culture and politics. Within the general Latin American return to democracy in the 1980s, a political approach to cultural and artistic expressions could not simply take aim at a repressive dictatorship. Workshop organizers turned to the writings of Antonio Gramsci to reflect on a new way of understanding the changing politics of their context. Evelina Dagnino discussed the influence of Antonio Gramsci's work in this general Latin American reconceptualization of culture and politics (1998: 36). With Gramsci's concept of hegemony, the dichotomy between state and civil society began to blur, and culture became viewed as a realm of political struggle and potential transformation (Dagnino 1998: 35–41).[4] The workshop's intellectual history balanced somewhere between Eco's semiotics of open works and a Gramscian "war of position" as fought through cultural forms; workshop organizers were vested in the idea that radical musical forms, like radical cultural forms, mattered in a politics that looked beyond traditional "political" spaces, and that these alternative political spaces worked as sites of "wars of position" in a democratic context in which a "war of maneuver" seemed out of the question (see Gramsci 1971: 229–239; Eco 1989).

The founding of the workshop in 1985 coincided with a general trend in the Latin American development apparatus: a focus on grassroots organizing and the creative use of local knowledge (Escobar 1995: 215; Starn 1999: 200). For Arturo Escobar, this shift allowed for a degree of optimism; within grassroots social movements, local groups could be imagined as breaking out of the otherwise all-determining developmentalist discourses that have controlled the politics of representation in Latin America and much of the Third World (1995: 214–216). Some people might question the "grassroots" nature of the workshop, especially if one associates grassroots directly with lower classes. Although the workshop was built on a multiple-class structure, its organizers were college educated and two of the organizers had graduate degrees from U.S. universities. But if one associated the term "grassroots" with the new interest placed on the realm of local cultural knowledge, the workshop could be viewed within this realm. As an explicitly cultural NGO, the workshop's ideologies also epitomized the turn toward a cultural view of politics. Unlike most NGOs that might engage directly with a legal or material issue,

the workshop made no claims to fight anyone's legal battle, nor to improve a material standard of living. While they claimed their projects
would help keep young people out of drugs and thievery, their stated objectives were explicitly and almost exclusively cultural and artistic; but for
the workshop organizers, the cultural was political. In his study of NGOs
and rap music projects in Cali, Colombia, Peter Wade suggested that state
agencies and some NGOs prefer to deal with oppressed minorities
through projects that seem to be purely "cultural," thus avoiding the more
controversial issues that might actually alter relations of power (1999:
453). In their public proposal writing, the workshop's organizers worked
within these "cultural" discourses, but the politics of the workshop were
not so easily dismissed. Even as organizers were from a more privileged
sector than either the instructors or the students of the workshop, they
maintained a discourse of a radical politics of aesthetics, even if those politics did not always enter the proposal-writing process. While NGOs and
other development organizations were reconceptualizing the relation between culture and politics, and perhaps attempting to maintain that division, the workshop completely inverted the relation; culture came first
and was the way to do politics.

Workshop organizers drew on multiple levels of symbolic capital
(Bourdieu 1977) in drafting, submitting, and promoting their projects;
they were well versed in "project culture" (see Wade 1999: 458). Their education and class positions allowed them direct access to the local political world and the circle of international funders. During part of my
fieldwork, the workshop's coordinator sat in a political position within La
Paz's municipal ministry of culture. All of these factors pointed to the numerous contacts and social networks that were crucial in getting any
NGO off the ground and running. Throughout Latin America, NGOs, for
better or worse, have become the intermediaries between grassroots organizations and the government (MacDonald 1995: 32). The workshop's
projects stressed cultural empowerment with specific reference to the participation of women in music. Although young women, under their own
initiative as students of the workshop, had formed all-women indigenous
troupes, the discursive addition of "women" in the proposal-writing, entered at the suggestion of a workshop organizer who had just been encouraged to do so by one of the officers of a funding agency. Another
proposal, which had not yet been fully fleshed-out, proposed to study the
music of the Chimane (an indigenous group in Bolivia's eastern lowlands), linking the project with environmental concerns. Through their
contacts, workshop organizers knew quite well how to respond to the
trends of international funding agendas, agendas that favored projects on
ethnic identity, women, and environmental concerns.

But "being musicians"—and politicized ones at that—through NGO funding of pedagogical projects was also wrought with complications, principal among them being the general trend toward professionalization in NGOs. In her work on the issues of Brazilian Indians, Alcida Rita Ramos detailed the shift in Brazilian NGOs "from political bricolage to technical professionalism" and likened this process to a Weberian bureaucratization in which the rules of bureaucracy are followed "at the expense of the goal to be achieved" (1998: 273–274). In the case presented by Ramos, this dominance of means over ends emerged as raw activism and was channeled into "rational" bureaucratized NGOs (1998: 277). Similarly, the workshop's organizers and instructors were pulled between maintaining their own politics of aesthetics, their own growing preoccupations with institutionalization and the stability of their projects, and the increasing demands for professionalization in the realm of NGOs. The workshop had its share of crises during the time I conducted fieldwork: they received a bad evaluation by a foundation that subsequently withdrew its support to the institution; and another NGO swindled their project ideas. The negative evaluation could easily be considered within the framework of increasing demands for professionalization and the inability of the workshop to respond to these demands. In recognition of their shortcomings in some organizational and managerial issues, workshop instructors often made comments like "well, we are only musicians."

During the crisis that followed the funder's negative evaluation, the workshop eventually had to close its locale and they reluctantly entered into an agreement with the very NGO believed to have plagiarized their project ideas. This NGO was created by a Bolivian economist—I will call her Pilar—to write and run her own projects for children and youth. I was told that Pilar was given a copy of a workshop proposal, and that with it she designed a project in music education that received funding through links with other educational projects in science and math. International funding organizations showed reluctance to fund projects that appeared to work only on "cultural" objectives. Through discussions with third parties of funding organizations, workshop organizers came to believe that the institution's name, know-how, and reputation had been used to obtain the funding for Pilar's project, while Pilar only wanted to hire individual instructors from the workshop. When the workshop suggested that she contract the institution as a whole to complete the music component of her project, she stalled even though that was what the grant seemed to require. "You see," she claimed, "I have no budget at all for administrative costs. I only have line items for music instructors." Pilar's NGO might be likened to Ramos's scenario of NGOs mushrooming off of each other: "The system in which NGOs are situated operates in such a way as to generate an increasing complexity that may eventually lead to its involution. It is symptomatic of this trend toward over-elaboration that NGOs are being created with the sole purpose of administering the finances of other NGOs, as in a corporate dream or science fiction nightmare" (Ramos 1998: 279). Pilar's NGO would use the knowledge of the workshop within a multifaceted project that, in its entirely, would be administered by an economist. Professionalism trumped politicized bohemian creativity. The workshop was a collective entity that had developed knowledge and pedagogy about teaching the playing of indigenous instruments, and this know-how was seen as property of the institution itself. This sense of the workshop as a whole made Pilar's piecework approach problematic for the workshop's organizers and instructors. At stake was the perceived proprietorship over the institution's collective name, knowledge, and project.

Much of the active life of the workshop had been conducted under the support of international funding sources. Their general discourse of reaffirming or consolidating different Bolivian identities through music research, composition, and dissemination may have a grassroots basis among middle- to upper-class intellectuals, but their discourse undeniably also responded to parameters set by international funding agendas. One of the most powerful and widely influential projects of the workshop was its dedication to the teaching of indigenous instrument genres, and in these activities, it made its claims to cultural authenticity.

THE TROUPE IS IT

One of the workshop's principal activities in La Paz, the "mass teaching" of indigenous instruments, was a pedagogical project that directly opposed the individualized virtuoso style of playing Andean instruments, the style popularized by Kjarkas and ensembles of a similar mode. Instructors held classes at the workshop locale on Jaén Street as well as in schools and neighborhood organizations throughout La Paz and El Alto. For example, the instructors would carry around La Paz an entire troupe of tarkas—the instrument of preference for teaching young people. As a six-hole duct flute, carved from a single piece of wood, anyone could easily produce a loud sound on these instruments, and the smaller tarkas were easily grasped by even the smallest of children's hands. Instructors taught tunes through a notation that reflected the fingered positions to be used in producing a pitch. Rhythm was generally not notated, and students depended entirely on ear and memory to pick up the rhythmic patterns of a tune, as played or sung by instructors. Not only was it easy to produce a loud sound on the tarka, but this instrument's timbre was rough and rich with overtones, a sonorous aesthetic often coveted in highland indigenous music traditions (see Stobart 1996a). At the workshop locale, a wide variety of other indigenous instruments and genres were taught. Workshop students would form their own troupes, rehearsing under the guidance of the workshop instructors and expanding their repertoire into the more difficult instrument genres from the surrounding areas of La Paz (that is, *kantus* and *italaques*—distinct panpipe traditions performed with interlocking technique—and *mohozeños*—cane duct flutes).

The students both at the workshop and in the workshop's outreach programs were usually children of Aymara migrants, and learning to play these instruments was a way of reconnecting with this indigenous heritage. Teaching indigenous music to sons and daughters of indigenous migrants was certainly a principal selling point behind the workshop's project proposals. The municipality of La Paz and the Inter-American Foundation—two entities that funded workshop activities on more than one occasion—found this cultural project particularly attractive. For example, Monica Medina de Palenque was the mayor of La Paz during part of my fieldwork, and her municipal government supported the workshop in mass teaching of indigenous instruments and genres. This project overlapped well with Medina's populist politics. At the time, Medina was still married to Carlos Palenque, the leader of the populist party, CONDEPA (Conciencia de Patria). As a political party, CONDEPA was born out of Palenque's control of television and radio channels (Radio y Televisión Popular [RTP] and Radio Metropolitana) on which he aired his signature program, *Tribuna libre del pueblo* (Free Tribune of the People). On this program, Palenque would listen sympathetically to personal emotional stories of the poor, sometimes offering immediate solutions to individual problems. Palenque was accompanied by Remedios Loza, a woman who dressed "de pollera," the wide gathered skirts that characterize the dress of Aymara women. Rafael Archondo (1991) analyzed how relations between these media figures and "the people" (el pueblo) were framed in terms of familial ties. Carlos Palenque and his wife Monica Medina de Palenque were idealized as the exemplar heterosexual matrimonial couple;[5] and, as a tradition of the program, everyone addressed each other through the titles of "comadre" and "compadre," literally the terms used to name the kin relation established between god parents and birth parents of a baptized child. The family model was a patriarchal one; even as Remedios Loza and Monica Medina moved into politics, they were consistently addressed as "Comadre Remedios" and "Comadre Monica." Only Carlos carried the appellative "Compadre Palenque." The political party of CONDEPA, what Hugo San Martin Arzabe analyzes as the social movement of "Palen-

Figure 4.1   Students of the workshop's indigenous instrument classes perform for the Mayor of La Paz, Monica Medina (photograph by author).

quismo" (1991), was born out of these mediatized relations. Widely supported by the poor and by people of Aymara identification, the party marked the politics of the 1990s: Remedios Loza became Bolivia's first elected representative "de pollera"; CONDEPA held the mayoralty of El Alto for most of the 1990s (see Gill 2000); and Monica Medina de Palenque was elected mayor of La Paz in 1993. Monica Medina's position within these populist politics illuminates the significance of her city government's support of teaching troupe-style performance of indigenous instruments. The workshop's mass teaching of indigenous instruments culminated in a tarka performance for Comadre Monica at the municipal building (Figure 4.1). The cultural capital engaged here was multiple. The workshop claimed an active role in reviving and teaching indigenous genres in an urban context, and Monica associated her municipal government with this cultural project. But before dismissing these projects of teaching troupe-style indigenous music performance as simply mestizos speaking for the indigenous, I am reminded of William Roseberry's assertion that cultural production is not limited to those who control the means of cultural production (1991: 33–36).

Around the rehearsal and performance of indigenous troupe-style music, the enthusiasm of the workshop's students was palpable. In particular, the students of adolescent age latched on to this music with a passion, drawing the identificatory associations to their indigenous roots in their public performances. Playing in a troupe was not just something their grandfathers did. It was cool and hip to play in an indigenous music troupe. Two groups of women, of their own initiative, formed all-women troupes in the workshop, and the members were well aware of the impossibility of this kind of ensemble in their grandfathers' villages of origin. Several of these young women reiterated in interviews the beliefs of their grandfathers: Women should not play musical instruments because "something bad might happen" and because, from the blowing on wind instruments, women are thought to lose their ability to nurse their infants. However, none of these beliefs kept these young women from forming their own indigenous music troupes in La Paz. They too entered in a kind of indigenous cool that was still a realm of social articulation, but one not completely dictated by the cultural mandates of the mestizos and international funding sources who in many ways controlled the resources of this project. Rafael Archondo, in consultation with German Guaygua, Mario Rodriguez, and Máximo Quisbert (2000) gave a commentary on the youth of El Alto and their seemingly equal passion for underground rock, rap, cumbia, salsa, *and* troupes of autochthonous panpipes (sikuris). Archondo discussed these musical practices with reference to Bourdieu's concept of "habitus," the way culture is transferred from one generation to another, not as a consciously learned set of rules, but rather as a set of embodied everyday practices in which cultural rules are implicit (Bourdieu 1977: 72–87). Archondo argued that these sons and daughters of Aymara migrants, while sometimes distancing themselves aesthetically from the patterns of their parents, still maintained an Aymara habitus, and unlike the more pessimistic reading of Bourdieu's habitus, as something that reproduces modalities of capitalism, Archondo suggested that this habitus works to reproduce the modalities of a group that has historically been oppressed (2000: 76).

While the workshop's organizers liked to claim responsibility for the surging popularity of troupe-style indigenous music, and this was certainly their strongest claim to an intersection with cultural authenticities, many factors contributed to this overall trend. The virtuoso playing of Andean instruments in small performance ensembles was the port of entry of Andean "folklore" into postrevolutionary Bolivian cities. In La Paz in the 1960s, this style was popularized by the group Los Jairas in their performances in the Peña Naira. Los Jairas included Ernesto Cavour on charango, Yayo Jofré on vocals and percussion, J. Godoy and then Alfredo Dominguez on guitar, and the Swiss man Gilbert Favre ("the gringo") on quena (see Wara Céspedes 1984). Gilka Wara Céspedes suggested that Favor's quena performance "laundered [the quena] of Indian connotations" and made it acceptable to upper and middle classes (1984: 225). While this was the kind of aesthetic that Kjarkas and other ensembles emulated, by at least the late 1960s, other musical proposals focused on the troupe performance. In direct contrast with the laundering of Indian connotations, these proposals sought to reconnect indigenous musical instruments with all those associations. For example, in 1975, the rock-Andean fusion band, Wara, naming its recordings through Aymara numberings (that is, "Maya" for first, "Paya" for second, and so on) broke new ground by sandwiching troupe-style playing of "sacred autochthonous" music between rock interludes played on Andean instruments (Wara, 1975). *Kollamarka,* an ensemble dedicated to traditional music of all Andean contexts, also included in their recording troupe-style performances on various genres of panpipes (sikuris and kantus) and on several genres of duct flutes (*pinquillos,* mohozeños, and tarkas, 1994 [1968]). For students of the workshop, these ensembles figured high among their musical heroes, providing examples of musical alternatives to the Kjarkasstyle ensemble. The troupe-style of indigenous music performance has been a central part of the Paceño context since at least the late 1960s. During the 1980s and 1990s—during the time of "the return of the Indian"— the troupe performance of indigenous instruments has experienced an increase in its symbolic value. The troupe has also occupied a prominent place in the multicultural aesthetics of Música de Maestros.

THE POLITICS AND AESTHETICS
OF THE PLURI-MULTI

In a press interview about Música de Maestros's fourth album, Rolando Encinas, the ensemble's director, expressed the following: "What we want to present is diversity through instruments and melodies. [We want] those airs of chovenas, bailecitos, etc. [to be] heard, the music of the different ethnic groups [*etnias*][6] of the country, those groups that many institutions talk about and show like anthropological objects from the museum; but in reality they do nothing to recuperate their music and culture" (*Presencia,* November 26, 1995).

In this statement Rolando took up the torch of cultural diversity and criticized those who had made a living on this discourse. Many Bolivian NGOs designed their projects—those on which many middle-class professionals manage to make a living in their own countries—within parameters set by international funding agencies that followed globally trendy agendas. One of these agendas was ethnicity within a celebratory framework of multiculturalism.

In Bolivia the shift toward a discussion of the pluricultural and multilingual—"the pluri-multi discourse,"—has included a shift away from class-based politics. I am borrowing the term from the book titled *Lo pluri-multi o el reino de la diversidad* (*The Pluri-Multi or the Reign of Diversity*), a collection of conference proceedings on this topic (ILDIS 1993). My use of the term goes beyond that expressed in that book; I argue that the pluri-multi is a major framework through which Bolivians are imagining their nation.[7] In recent years the pluri-multi discourse has formed a foundation for the national narrative of multiple nations within the Bolivian State. This narrative has become more prominent as the focus of indigenousness has expanded from the highlands to include the numerous indigenous groups living in the eastern lowlands. It was precisely these two sets of ethnicities—highland and lowland—that Música de Maestros was able to musically represent through selection of repertoire and self-presentation. They did not claim to be exclusively from either of these two regions, but their instruments, genres, and music performances artistically represented the indigenous realities of both the highlands and the lowlands.

Principal examples of highland/lowland representations are found on the fourth album, which included both the "Suite Aymara," a single work by an early twentieth-century composer, and the "Suite Oriental," a medley of eastern lowland tunes assembled by the director of Música de Maestros. The "Suite Aymara" was a four-movement work by José Salmón Ballivián (1881–1963). The composer described his work as follows:

> The Suite Aymara reconstructs the pre-Hispanic Andean social scene. The themes of the four parts have been carefully selected from among some of the most ancient [tunes], with the necessary [changes] to make [them] appropriate for orchestration. One of the intentions was to show that original music was virile, coarse when necessary, and soft to describe the bucolic landscapes, or tenuous and cloudy to paint their mystic ecstasies. It was not tearful nor mournful because those strong warriors had no reason to cry because they were well-fed and well-governed. The "*gamabundeces*"[8] came later, when the conquerors, or better said, the Arabs through them, moaned with the "[deep] song." This Arab music, injected with the Spanish, upon the

arrival of the Spanish in America, with time combined with that of the oppressed Indians, especially during the Colonial period, resulting in the three
of them starting to cry . . . all together. (from Rivera de Stahlie 1995: 73)

This early twentieth-century composer wrote music to represent the indigenous world before the Spanish Conquest—an idyllic romanticized view
of the pre-Conquest native. In his notes, the composer introduced each
movement of the composition with descriptive titles to set the musical
scene: "I: Warrior Dance," "II: Religious Dance," "III: Awki-Awki," "IV: When
the Broad Beans Bloom" (Rivera de Stahlie 1995: 74–75). According to
Salmón Ballivián's reading, the post-Conquest cultural mixing brought
grief to all. He displaced these negative results of the Conquest from Spanish to Arab influence. This paradoxical attitude toward the Indian—the romanticized pre-Conquest Indian and the unfortunate contemporary
Indian—was consistent with currents of indigenismo, a series of movements contemporary with Salmón Ballivián's compositions.

Bolivian indigenismo, like its Peruvian counterpart, had diverse, often
contradictory components, making it difficult to summarize in its political, ideological, and artistic facets. At a fundamental level, the various expressions of indigenismo represented the ways elites and middle classes,
Creoles and mestizos were expanding their conceptions of national communities to include the presence of indigenous cultures within them.
While Bolivian and Peruvian indigenismo followed similar paths in the
first half of the twentieth century, Bolivian indigenismo took significantly
different forms, as the position of indigenous peoples in the nation was
negotiated through the historical trajectories of the Chaco War, the 1952
Revolution, and indigenous movements particular to Bolivia.

Both Peruvian and Bolivian indigenismo included obsessions with issues of racial purity. Salmón Ballivián's commentary on his own composition reflected a belief in the unproblematic existence of the pure
pre-Columbian Indian who was forever corrupted upon Conquest. This
composer's reading, while more sympathetic to imagined indigenous
cultures, shared ideologies of racial purity with the writer, Alcides Arguedas. In 1909, Arguedas published *Pueblo enfermo,* a book in which he
argued that Bolivia was "sick" because of the racial mixing that had occurred with indigenous peoples. For Arguedas, progress, modernity, and
Bolivia's entrance into universal history would only occur through a
"whitening" and purification of the nation (see Salmón 1997: 61–76).
While the Indian assumes a more favorable position in the Cuzqueño Peruvian variety of indigenismo, Marisol de la Cadena's work has shown
that this indigenismo was also concerned with pure racial categories; the
pure Indian, as imagined to have ties to an Inca past, was the provincial

ideal category that directly countered the Lima-centered nationalist ideologies of mestizaje (de la Cadena 2000: 46, 84).

Beyond the questions of racial purity, Salmón Ballivián's notes about his own composition also reflected his belief in the intimate connection between the Indian and the environment—that the Indian was molded by his very interaction with a rural setting. This assumed connection was taken up by both artistic and political currents of indigenismo. In the Peruvian case, Mirko Lauer distinguished between two kinds of indigenismo: "indigenismo–2" referred to the Peruvian creative cultural artistic movements that interpreted "indigenous" as "autochthonous," while socio-political indigenismo read "indigenous" as campesino or peasant (1997: 11–13). The latter kind of indigenismo studied culture through the assumed objective sciences of ethnography and political economy, while indigenismo–2 relied on the subjectively produced artistic sensibilities in the representation of the indigenous (Lauer 1997: 39). Salmón Ballivián's sense of his own composition seemed to fall in the camp of indigenismo–2. Within artistic movements, the telluric connection to the Andean landscape was perceived as the source of natural indigenous talent (Poole 1997: 176). The *Misión Peruana de Arte Incaica* (Mission of Incaic Art), an indigenista theater troupe founded in 1923 under the direction of Luis Valcárcel, toured La Paz, Bolivia (Poole 1997: 191; de la Cadena 2000: 73), and it is difficult to believe that Salmón Ballivián and other composers of his generation were not influenced by these artistic manifestations.

The socio-political form of Bolivian indigenismo might begin with a reference to the writings of Franz Tamayo, a contemporary of Alcides Arguedas, but with fundamentally different ideas about the place of the Indian in the Bolivian nation. In his book, *Creación de una pedagogía nacional* (1944 [1910]), Tamayo placed the Indian as the cornerstone of an authentic Bolivian nation, as that which would make Bolivia distinct from European nations (Salmón 1997: 77–79). At the same time, Tamayo also drew strong connections between Indians and the natural environment, between peasants (campesinos) and the land (*la tierra*), and this connection was subsequently fleshed-out in the politics of the 1952 Revolution and the Agrarian Reform of 1953 (see Salmón 1997: 85–96). Peruvian socio-political indigenismo also played up the naturalized connection between Indians and the rural environment; the Indian outside of the rural community was thought to be a sign of decay (de la Cadena 2000: 63–65). Even José Carlos Mariategui, who looked to the socialist revolutionary potential of the Peruvian Indian in his own romanticized view of Incaic communism, saw the potential power of the Indian as inevitably linked to a world of agricultural production and the

Peruvian peasant "community" (Mariategui 1985 [1928]). In Bolivia, the leftist leader, Tristan Marof, who wrote *La justicia del Inca* (1926), also referenced an Inca past as the pure ideal to which the contemporary "degenerate" Indian should return; but this return would only be possible through revolutionary changes in land tenure, and this was seen as the only way that the Bolivian nation could be redeemed (Salmón 1997: 115–119). This is the point at which Bolivian indigenismo begins to stray from the similarities seen with its Peruvian counterparts. Indigenismo, in both contexts, engaged with ideologies of racial purity, telluric connections between Indians and the natural environment, and romanticized historical references to the lost time of the Incas. But political mobilizations by Bolivian indigenous peoples transformed in significant ways the subsequent politics of representing indigenous authenticity. This transformation is exemplified in a story told about one of the first performances of "Suite Aymara."

In 1926, Salmón Ballivián, organized a gala concert for the Fine Arts Circle in the Municipal Theater of La Paz. To close the concert with a bang, he performed "Suite Aymara," bringing a troupe of musicians from Italaque, in native dress and with native instruments. As the curtain opened on this performance, the audience left in disgust, holding their noses and complaining about the Municipal Theater bringing these "savages" to the theater (see Rivera de Stahlie 1995: 71). The master of ceremonies for Música de Maestros frequently used this story to introduce the Música de Maestros's interpretation of "Suite Aymara." In the telling of it, he underlined the incredible changes that have occurred since that time. Although few people would claim that racism has been eliminated in contemporary Bolivia, no one would leave a theater for the reasons they did in 1926. Yet most of the members of Música de Maestros were urban mestizos and their performance of indigenous music remained a representation. Música de Maestros's representation was based on their perception of cultural authenticity secured by reuniting indigenous instruments with their corresponding performance practices, making claims to represent authentic indigenous music performance on the basis of knowledge acquired in fieldwork research. But it was ultimately a representation of indigenous culture as filtered through the historical lenses of the Chaco War (1932–1935), the 1952 Revolution, and indigenous mobilizations.

The aftermath of the Chaco War sent Bolivian indigenismo in a very different direction from its Peruvian counterparts. The Chaco War underscored the crisis of the elite who held power in Bolivia, the large land holders (*latifundistas*) and the tin barons. Peasant and indigenous mobilizations began and a Bolivian bourgeoisie sought alliances with these movements in order to consolidate a revolutionary government in 1952.

While the 1952 Revolution has been labeled as "uncompleted" (Malloy 1989), because its more radical tendencies were brought under the control first by the recently empowered Bolivian middle class, and then under the control of a series of military dictatorships, the revolutionary ideology did place the Indian at the center of a nationalist discourse, even though the label "Indian" was substituted with "peasant" (campesino), and cultural differences were downplayed as union organizing was privileged over indigenous identities.

Postrevolutionary peasant and indigenous mobilizations continued to reshape the place of "Indian" in national discourse, and Katarismo was key among these movements. Tupac Katari was an Aymara leader who in 1781 led an indigenous uprising when the area known today as Bolivia was under Spanish colonial rule (see del Valle de Siles 1990). In the 1970s Aymara peasants began to articulate their union organizations with the long-term historical memory of these indigenous anticolonial struggles (see Rivera Cusicanqui 1986). While Katarismo grew out of peasant union organizing, the movement emphasized that peasant oppression was not only economic, but was also cultural and ideological (Ticona Alejo 2000; Rivera Cusicanqui 1986). As an indigenous political movement, Katarismo was accompanied by a renewed ethnic consciousness raised by Aymaras living and studying in the city of La Paz. Aymara intellectuals, through their "Indianist" research (Ticona Alejo 2000: 43), have continued to play crucial roles in the shaping and elaboration of cultural and ideological discourses about Indians in Bolivia (Mamani Condori 1991; Condori Chura and Ticona Alejo 1992; Arias 1994; Aruwiyiri 1992).

Even as Katarismo has since splintered in several factions and weakened in the process, this movement changed forever the face of indigenismo and indigenous politics in Bolivia, a change sometimes referred to as "Indianist" politics, and a trend Albó has labeled as "the return of the Indian" (1991). I use Albó's term to distinguish the contemporary place of "Indian" in Bolivian national discourse from its previous articulations with indigenismo at the beginning of the twentieth century. The return of the Indian in Bolivia marks a major difference from the Peruvian context, which has not undergone anything remotely resembling the indigenous mobilizations of Bolivia.

Bolivia's indigenous mobilizations have affected not only the place of indigenous peoples in national politics, but also the ways that mestizos and Creoles represent indigenous cultural forms. The "Suite Aymara" was a composition that emerged within the ideologies of indigenismo, but Música de Maestros's performance of it in the 1990s reflected the contemporary context. Their performance of "Suite Aymara" exemplified an attention to details as elaborated through a commitment to research.

Richard Bauman has suggested that researchers tend to place great authority in the text or score of a work, whereas performers emphasize their own contributions to the artistic performance (1992: 42). Música de Maestros straddled both of these approaches, placing great emphasis on scores and composers' intentions, while also putting their performance signature on these works. For example, between the first and second movements of the "Suite Aymara," the warrior dance and the religious dance, Música de Maestros included a brief interlude to represent music that is often played and sung in highland churches (*el q'uchu*). For instrumentation they used a violin accompanied by a man (José "Jach'a" Flores) and a woman (Juana Vásquez) singing prayers in Aymara. These two individuals were invited to sing this passage because of their knowledge of the Aymara language and culture. In performing this passage I was instructed to play with no vibrato and to follow the flexible tempo of the singers. This was the only passage I recorded with Música de Maestros that did not have a strict metronome in the background, and it was also the only recording I made with the simultaneous presence and performance of the other musicians, the singers.

The ensemble also put its signature on the third movement of this work: the "Awki-Awki" dance, which parodied the elderly Spanish man. In the countryside, this dance is accompanied by the *pífano* (a six-holed horizontally played cane flute). Música de Maestros performed this movement through a combined sound of a troupe of pífanos and the intricate orchestrations of the composer.

The group's other signature mark on this piece was the use of the mohozeño (vertically and horizontally played cane duct flutes) in the final movement titled "*Cuando florecen las habas*" (When the Broad Beans Bloom). According to the composer, this movement called for a particular siku panpipe. But as Rolando explained to me: "We did some research and the melody of that movement seems to have structures which are more like a mohozeñada then a sikureada. Besides, sikus are not played in the time of the year when the crops flower. This is the time of year for the instruments of the *pinquillu* family. So we decided to use mohozeños instead of sikus." In discussions of Andean music, an instrument's place in the agricultural calendar carries great significance, and Rolando used this argument to establish the cultural authenticity of his decision to use mohozeños instead of sikus from Italaque. Música de Maestros ended the "Suite Aymara" in a traditional style of playing indigenous music: the troupe of mohozeños, everyone playing the same class of instrument. We put away our other instruments, took up the mohozeño and moved out, away from the microphones, across the stage. In Música de Maestros's folklore festival tour in France, the mohozeño performance alone was

used for the Bolivian delegation's grand entrance in the opening ceremonies. The volume of the mohozeño troupe is very loud, and the performance of this instrument was chosen as a way to make a sonorous
impact in a context without amplification. In their performance of the entire "Suite Aymara" the ensemble interpreted the highly orchestrated work
of a mestizo master composer, a work based on indigenous inspirations
and romanticizations. But the orchestrated work ended with a performance of traditional highland music performance practices, a large
troupe playing a single kind of instrument. Through "Suite Aymara,"
Música de Maestros simultaneously paid tribute to a national composer
and revalued contemporary highland indigenous musical expressions. By
citing a contemporary indigenous performance, they resolved a contradiction between the composer's sense of cultural authenticity—a romanticized pre-Conquest Indian—and a more acceptable contemporary
performed representation of Indian-ness.

Música de Maestros also balanced these Bolivian highland representations with repertoire from the Bolivian lowlands, and the "Suite Oriental"
represented the lowland side of one of these balancing acts. The "Suite
Oriental" of the fourth album recording was a collection of several musical genres from the eastern lowlands of Bolivia. Rolando and Koji made
the production decision to unite these themes under the general title of
"Suite Oriental"—a decision that consciously balanced the highland references of the "Suite Aymara" with a comparable representation of lowland music. The official recording of "Suite Oriental," with ambient
sounds of a rainforest electronically produced in the recording studio,
took the listener to the exotic other place within Bolivia. In live performances these rainforest sounds were sometimes reproduced vocally by
the musicians of Música de Maestros. The "Suite Aymara" was an early-
twentieth-century composer's idea of highland indigenous music, while
the "Suite Oriental" represented Rolando's contemporary fieldwork and
musical collection; with the exception of the last pieces ("24 de Septiem-
bre" and "Alegre Carretero," carnavales by Orlando Riveros R.) none of
the themes in the "Suite Oriental" were listed with composers' names and
they are all described in the liner notes as part of local ethnic traditions.

Música de Maestros consistently recorded a varied repertoire that reflected the mestizo, highland indigenous, and lowland indigenous associations. Música de Maestros seemed to operate well within the pluri-multi
narrative of Bolivia. But how did this differ from the representations of
Indian-ness that emerged in the indigenismo movements of the early
twentieth century? Música de Maestros never pursued a pure pre-
Columbian indigenous performance. They sought an indigenous authenticity as a way of knowing and letting others know of the diverse cultural

manifestations that were performed by contemporary indigenous peoples in Bolivian territory. Indigenistas tended to romanticize the imagined native of a pristine past while ignoring the contemporary native or mourning the cultural demise of the co-temporal subject. Salmón Ballivián lamented the colonial influences that seemed to permanently sully the wonders of pristine Andean subjects and their musical productions. His lamentations were built entirely on his own imaginings of Andean cultures, as yet untouched by Spanish colonialism, and he imagined his music as reconstructing that lost moment of innocence. In contrast, in Música de Maestros's performances, the pluri-multi assumed the coevality of distinctly cultured peoples. The ensemble's inclusion of lowland indigenous genres also moved away from the associations made between indigenistas and an exclusively highland indigenous past.

Both Música de Maestros and the workshop pursued cultural authenticity in their representations of indigenous cultures, and these representational practices came under very different patterns of articulation than the early-twentieth-century patterns of indigenismo. While mestizo-Creoles controlled these two projects, they both were influenced by and articulated with the results of indigenous mobilizations of the second half of the twentieth century. In aesthetic terms, this translated into an emphasis on troupe-style performance, an inclusion of lowland indigenous representations, an emphasis on fieldwork and intentionally acquired cultural knowledge, and the pursuit of rough, highland indigenous genres rich in overtones. The indigenous instrument alone no longer held the aura of cultural authenticity; the instrument had to be played appropriately, in its genre, with its performance aesthetics. Through these aesthetics, the workshop and Música de Maestros marked the particular aspects of their music—what made their projects Bolivian. But their particularisms were accompanied by strong appeals to universalist ideologies, bringing a complex focus to any oppositional rendition of the universal and the particular. Música de Maestros made its universalist appeals through championing a history of great composers, while the workshop made its universalist appeals through the promotion of avant-garde compositions with indigenous instruments. Both projects intersected with the themes of unique authenticity.

RECORDING THE MASTERS, RECORDING TRADITION

As we sat through a long bus ride during the folklore festival tour in France, Rolando told me, once again, the story of Música de Maestros's first recording. Unlike previous tellings, this one, in the context of a foreign country, brought tears to his eyes as he remembered the struggles of independent recording. With the first recording, Música de Maestros was not yet an ensemble and the title of the album "Música de Maestros and Rolando Encinas" referred literally to the kind of music Rolando purported to record—music of Bolivia's master composers. This recording was made track by track, technologically producing an ensemble sound with individual recordings of musicians who had never played together as an ensemble. While the first recording was under production, Rolando was rather secretive about the project: "I would have [the musicians] come in one by one to record, but I didn't want anyone to know what I was doing. I was jealous about the whole project and I wanted to keep it a secret until we presented the recording. Many people who came to record knew next to nothing about what they were recording." In Spanish, this use of the term "jealous" (*celoso*) evokes an ownership of ideas, a concern that someone would steal the project idea before it had come to fruition. Through his general capacity to convoke people, Rolando pulled off this feat, convincing professional Bolivian musicians to record individual tracks in relative ignorance of what they were playing.[9]

Rolando Encinas always reminded people that the name of the ensemble, Música de Maestros, referred not to the musicians who played in the ensemble, but to the master composers represented in the ensemble's performances. Through the ideology of great composers and great works, Rolando expressed the project's appeal to the universal: those other countries in Europe have their great composers and Bolivia has great composers as well. Equivalency was important here. Rolando often critiqued the tendency of the National Symphony Orchestra to play primarily "foreign" great composers. Repertoire selection varied under different directors, but I did notice a general tendency of the symphony to rope in Bolivian music within a single concert program, while other programs were dedicated to a more general selection from master Western composers. One musician from Música de Maestros told me: "The younger generation of musicians in the symphony orchestra does not know national music. They do not know that the symphony used to play all kinds of pieces taken from national repertoire. Only recently the symphony has been playing nothing but foreign music. So they think *that* is the best there is, that everything that comes after that is easy to play and not worth studying. Not the older generation. The older generation knows national music because the symphony orchestra used to play it. They even used to accompany the National Folkloric Ballet." Many musicians of Música de Maestros commented on this reigning hierarchy—Western classical above Bolivian anything. The comment from the director was usually: "Why should the 'classical' always be foreign? Bolivia has its own classical music, its own classical composers." Rolando founded Música de Maestros on this alternative quest for an equivalency with universal great composers. Música de Maestros's beginnings underscore the emphasis on great composers and Rolando's belief that the recording medium was of the utmost importance in making this a musical project both of and for history.

As it worked with the universalist ideology of the great composers, Música de Maestros exploited a sense of nostalgia, drawing on particular claims to historical authenticity. In 1986 Rolando Encinas and Yolanda Mazuelos began to review archives of music—recordings and scores—in the department of ethnomusicology and folklore and the documentation center of the Bolivian Institute of Culture. Rolando often described the disorganized state of affairs in these institutions and the lack of concern for maintaining any of these materials: The materials were either on their way to a dusty death or were walking away in the hands of private individuals. Rolando proposed a contemporary recording of these materials in order to "save" this part of Bolivian musical history and to bring it alive for a new generation of listeners. This project may sound familiar to those who know the work of Ry Cooder with the Cuban musicians of the Buena Vista Social Club (1997) or Carlos Vives with the Colombian *ballenato* (Colombian song-dance genre; 1993), or even Juan Luis Guerra with *bachata* (song dance genre from the Dominican Republic; 1990). These musical projects of the 1990s located a currency in the revival, and sometimes even international popularization, of historically and geographically localized popular music traditions. Unlike the staged revival of the imagined Buena Vista Social Club, the impetus behind Música de Maestros came from within Bolivia, from the determination of Rolando Encinas to sonorously document Bolivia's master composers. Even though Música de Maestros's fifth album recording was made with Bolivian folklore singers who were famous in the 1950s, the principal project entailed a revival of works to be played by Bolivia's contemporary musicians.

Although Rolando had already recorded in Bolivia with many artists on principal Bolivian labels, in the recording industry, he initially found no support for what was tagged as a noncommercial project. Rolando produced this first album with money borrowed from a friend. The initial recordings were completed in a small Bolivian studio, but the final production was completed in Germany in a pay-as-you-go arrangement, and Rolando performed in Germany to make the money he needed to finish the production.

Música de Maestros as an ensemble did not form until the formal launch of the first album, with the performance of eight musicians. Only after the presentation of the record did the musicians begin to talk of formalizing a performing ensemble with the name "Música de Maestros."[10] The second album was again privately produced. It was not until Música de Maestros started working on a third album that negotiations began with Discolandia, a major recording label in Bolivia. Negotiations with this company did not begin unless Discolandia's executives saw potential commercial profits in a musical proposal.

The ensemble recorded its third (1993) and fourth (1995) albums with Discolandia, but the initial independence of the group remained amazingly intact. I often heard Rolando say, "I'm not going to give away our work." This comment usually came accompanied by some reference to the wealth of Discolandia, a wealth purportedly accumulated at the expense of recording musicians. Musicians of the ensemble would comment to me that the luxurious Hotel Presidente was constructed by Discolandia's owner with the abundant profits extracted from the poorly paid labor of musicians. The hotel, where every new Discolandia recording is formally launched, architecturally indexed what are perceived by the musicians as exploitative relations of music production.

With Discolandia's representatives, Rolando drove a hard bargain. He set a high price from which he did not budge. Musicians in Bolivia are usually paid a lump sum for which the recording company receives unlimited production rights over a limited time period. After that period, musicians may receive royalty payments, but Discolandia typically phases out production and distribution after this initial period. For Música de Maestros, that time period was set at five years. Rolando insisted on an inclusion of clauses which did not exist in other Discolandia recording contracts, a principal clause specifying the ensemble's control over international distribution. When Rolando pushed this point, the original response from Discolandia was that they had never drafted a contract with that condition. Discolandia had a form contract that was usually used for all recording artists. Rolando walked away from the negotiations because of disagreements over the exceptional contract he was demanding. He told me how, with low spirits, he returned home to begin an evening rehearsal and to communicate the impasse to the other members of the ensemble. Within 24 hours he received a phone call from Discolandia; they had accepted the stipulated conditions.

When Discolandia released the third album with several incomplete liner notes (they had left out several pages of the text in their binding process), the contract for the fourth album included a clause about Discolandia's accountability for a correct representation of the ensemble. I had been one of the unlucky consumers who bought one of the incomplete compact disc packages. When I took the disc to Discolandia's store they assumed no responsibility, insisting, "that's just the way it is," even as

I pointed out the missing content in a corresponding cassette brochure. The logic behind the new clause was that Música de Maestros was built on the idea of research and documentation, an idea that was conveyed through the liner notes of the ensemble's recordings. Liner notes on Música de Maestros's recordings often filled as many as fourteen pages and usually gave details of the composers' lives and of the particular compositions presented. If those liner notes were inadvertently cut from the production, Música de Maestros would be misrepresented to the Bolivian public because of Discolandia's poor quality control.

In his continued negotiations with Discolandia, Rolando has maintained a cushion of artistic independence. In 1995, he discussed the possibility of a re-release of the first and second albums in a collector's compact disc. Discolandia wanted the first album but did not want the second, at least at the price that Rolando asked. Undaunted, Rolando did the remix of the first and second albums in a private studio while the group was finishing the mix of the fourth album with Discolandia. He then traded with Discolandia some of the re-released albums for some of the commercially produced third and fourth albums. This gave the ensemble a jump on the distribution problems usually chronic to private productions, while also equipping the group with a repertory selection of compact discs for small-scale sale on international tours. The ensemble has continued to privately produce its recordings but the price for that independence has been a chronic problem of promotion and distribution.[11]

Listening to Nostalgia: "Arte y Trabajo" and the Chaco War

On the liner notes of Música de Maestros's first album Rolando Encinas wrote: "Music, like all art, belongs to the people; it is born from the people; the people provide inspiration for music; and finally music ends up influencing the people. Because of this our task is not only to create but to popularize the music of our greatest masters, masters who with a profound aesthetic sensibility produced works of a high musical level and made of our music the 'superior art' of Bolivians" (Notes by Rolando Encinas on Música de Maestros, Album I 1988). In this statement "the people" and "music" are bound in a mutually affecting relation and the mention of great masters and their "works of high musical level" reads as a clear reference to a Eurocentric measure of individually inspired composers whose aesthetic sensibilities come to represent the people of a nation. In his study of the reception of Beethoven's music in Germany, David Dennis drew connections between Germany's unification in the nineteenth century and the manipulation of aesthetics that sought to draw multiple sectors of the population into a new nationalist project (1996: 2). While Música de Maestros was not associated with any official state politics, its emphasis on Bolivia's master composers as a kind of musical sounding of "the people," worked within similar nationalist constructs. The task of this project was also stated as one of popularizing this music. In the process of moving from a disembodied recording project to a fully embodied performing ensemble, the group itself also underwent transformations.

Between 1988 and 1995, the ensemble of Música de Maestros slowly shifted from an 8-person group to a 24-piece orchestra. For some music performances, especially those done without remuneration, out of "good will" (*buena voluntad*), the group would be reduced again to about 10 people. Música de Maestros voluntarily performed at events to honor Chaco War veterans, in prisons, and for youth activity centers (for example, Cafe Semilla Juvenil). The financial demands of extended travel—the cost of sending each musician, as well as the personal earnings the musicians would lose while away from their home jobs—also reduced the group to 12 for the French folklore festival tour in 1996. Musicians of the group called this smaller ensemble an *estudiantina,* a Spanish word meaning literally a student music group. Estudiantina refers to a style of ensemble, found throughout Latin American countries, in which plucked stringed instruments represent a better part of the group, and most instruments are doubled or tripled in performance. For Música de Maestros, playing in estudiantina form immediately eliminated several pieces from the repertoire, the compositions with complex orchestrations: "Trilogía India," "Albórada Andina," "Suite Aymara," "Suspiros," "Noche Tempstuosa." In a gala theater performance, Música de Maestros always played with its orchestral size of approximately 24 musicians. In these performances the actual number of musicians varied from 21 to 28, but as long as it hovered around 22, the ensemble could produce Música de Maestros's sound.

The unique sound of Música de Maestros developed out of several different influences that remained unstated in the formal presentation of the ensemble, but that emerged in conversations with the director of the group. The director's father played guitar in the *Trio Cochabamba,* and the trio's recording of Simeón Roncal's "El Olvido" was, according to group lore, the seed that inspired Rolando to begin this project. Recordings of the group *Cuarteto Sucre,* a quartet of guitars and mandolins, also inspired Rolando in his choices of repertoire; Rolando was particularly inspired by their interpretations of the cueca "Gloria," a tune that entered Música de Maestros's second recording. Música de Maestros imitated this ensemble's interpretations of cuecas and bailecitos at stately tempi, particularly when interpreting the cuecas from Sucre (a city in the Department of Chuquisaca).

Beyond these small ensembles and specifically named pieces, Rolando sought a sound that was somewhere between an estudiantina and an orchestra. Estudiantinas are not a particularly prevalent ensemble in contemporary Bolivia; Rolando took his cue from historical documentation of these groups, which were more popular from the nineteenth century through the 1950s. In contrast with five-person Pan-Andean ensembles of the contemporary "national music," estudiantinas do not highlight solo performances. In the arrangements for estudiantina most of the musicians play a first or second line of melody, with the guitars following a moving bass line (*el bajeo*). In Thomas Turino's studies of Peruvian music, he situates estudiantinas as vehicles of mestizo identity carried through romanticized adaptations of indigenous motifs (1993a: 126). Turino compared the performance styles of estudiantinas and indigenous groups: estudiantinas have an active bass line that is balanced with high-pitched instruments; estudiantinas sound "less strident" than indigenous performance styles. Unlike most indigenous performance styles, estudiantinas work with genres of "closed forms"—with set structures and a fixed number of repetitions (Turino 1993a:126). Turino's description of estudiantinas fits Música de Maestros's earliest recordings. Only in the third and fourth albums did the group move toward more elaborate arrangements and orchestrations, as well as toward a clear attempt to bridge romanticized indigenous motifs with the indigenous troupe-style performance.

To move from estudiantina to orchestra, Rolando once again turned to historic photographs and documentation. He told me that one of the most significant influences on his work with Música de Maestros was a group in Potosí called *Sociedad Arte y Trabajo* (Society Art and Work), a group that performed at various times between 1931 and 1967. Rolando described the group as follows: "I've seen photographs of the group. Incredible! Some 70 musicians. And they had some of the strangest instruments, like clarinet, trombone, saxophone, cello, violin, all together with mandolins, charangos, quenas, guitars. What would they have sounded like? We don't have any way of knowing; we have no recordings. That's why I think it is so important to record our work. . . . And they would have played all of their performances acoustically. No amplification systems. I dream about the day that Música de Maestros might play with 70 musicians! What would we sound like!" Rolando was intrigued by the variety of instrumentation as well as by the size of the ensemble and these two elements have influenced the way he has conceptualized Música de Maestros. His statement also reflected a self-consciousness about the process of recording these materials—the urgency he felt about leaving a sonorous trace for another generation.

Sociedad Arte y Trabajo gave both theatrical and musical perfor-mances. Rolando showed me photographs of and articles about the group, published in a magazine, *Homenaje a Potosi* (1980). The magazine article assigned the label "folk symphony" to Sociedad Arte y Trabajo. I was intrigued by the women musicians in the photographs of Sociedad Arte y Trabajo; these pictures were taken in 1938 and 1945. There were not many women, but that there were women at all was significant to me because I was one of three women who played in Música de Maestros in the 1990s. On my many trips through the city of Potosi, on the way to the areas of Toropalca and Yura, I began to seek out those musicians who had played in Sociedad Arte y Trabajo. Rolando had told me so much about the group that I felt it was in some way intimately connected to the work of Música de Maestros. I too was becoming obsessed with historical au-thenticity, the imaginative origins of Música de Maestros.

In Potosi I contacted two musicians from Sociedad Arte y Trabajo: a vio-linist (José [Pepe] Rivera) and a guitarist (Edmundo Bellido). As I explained my position as a musician with Música de Maestros, the conversations with both musicians took off from old printed concert programs and yellowed newspaper clippings. They had no recordings of Sociedad Arte y Trabajo. Neither of them had heard of Música de Maestros, but their own tangible pieces of history worked as visible brag sheets and memory-joggers as they began to tell me about Sociedad Arte y Trabajo. Pepe Rivera had kept metic-ulous records of his participation in the group, saving all printed concert programs and relevant press releases. Edmundo Bellido, in contrast, had more mementos from his participation in a guitar-charango duo (*Duo Lopez-Bellido*). As Edmundo Bellido explained to me, "Sociedad Arte y Tra-bajo brought together musicians of many then renowned groups, like Duo Lopez-Bellido, *Kollur, Serranitos, Cuarteto Potosí*." Similarly, musicians in Música de Maestros doubled between numerous contemporary music en-sembles: Kollamarka, Wara, Bolivian Jazz, Yayo Joffre y los Jairas, *Jaime Ju-naro y su Grupo Tierra*, and the National Symphony Orchestra.

I had originally planned to construct an oral history of Sociedad Arte y Trabajo, but when Pepe Rivera perceived my interest in the subject, he himself took on the task of writing the group's history, a story that was published in the local Potosino newspaper, *El siglo*. His story, published in six installments, focused primarily on the group's performances, the repertory played at these performances, and endless lists of participating artists for each different performance. The inclusion of names was ex-tremely important for Pepe Rivera, "I want our young people to read the names of their grandfathers and to realize that they are connected to all this." While neither Edmundo Bellido nor Pepe Rivera had heard of

Música de Maestros, a colleague of theirs had heard us perform for the Third International Festival of Culture (November 1994), and had commented to Pepe, "I heard a group called Música de Maestros and they are doing something like what Sociedad Arte y Trabajo used to do." Sociedad Arte y Trabajo, as a group documented in photos and print, was highly influential in the projected imaginings that transformed Música de Maestros from estudiantina to orchestra.

The debate over the cueca in two or the cueca in three, discussed in chapter two, exemplified the divergent ways "empiricals"—*empíricos,* the term used to refer to those who learn music by watching and listening to someone play—and sight readers feel a music performance. To get the swing, groove, or pulse of a cueca, one has to go beyond counting in two or three. For the musician not reading from a score, the two or three debate is irrelevant. In my own quest for cultural-historical authenticity, I asked Pepe Rivera of Sociedad Arte y Trabajo how they had counted their cuecas. After a long thoughtful pause he responded with uncertainty, "I think we counted them in two."

While *written* distinctions between a cueca in two and a cueca in three were irrelevant for many of Música de Maestros's musicians, the general project of the group put great store in going back to original written scores. Three musicians of the ensemble have been involved in transforming these originals into orchestrations for Música de Maestros: Rolando Encinas, Koji Hishimoto, and Alfonso Bustamante (a French horn player). Both Koji and Alfonso have had formal training in orchestration and their mode of work produced written musical parts for each instrument. Koji also worked with a computer program through which he could listen to his proposed arrangements, but without the distinct timbres of the various instruments in the arrangement. Rehearsals of new repertoire always began with the written parts, as reading musicians helped musicians just learning to read memorize their parts. While the empiricals and sight readers ultimately reached an equilibrium in performance, written documentation was heavily weighted in the orchestration process and in the research behind the group, research that constructed connections between written original musical scores, Música de Maestros's repertoire, and a principal narrative of Bolivian national origins.

Música de Maestros drew upon national history in its presentations. The program notes for their concert at the International Festival of Culture in Sucre (1994) read as follows:

> The works that were produced have a point of reference, meeting, and identification with the tragic and heroic events that were produced in the Chaco War and its effect in the '52 Revolution.

> Music, dance, painting, sculpture, and architecture proposed aesthetic values which achieved, for the moment, unification of the Bolivian spirit; economic ordering did not follow a parallel development and has not been resolved even today; the inequalities and marginalization of cultures continue, cultures that have the right to decide and take responsibility for the construction of their future.

Música de Maestros's program notes, varying little from the cited example, usually evoked a connection with the Chaco War, its historical aftermath, and the incomplete project of a unified Bolivian nation. In the Chaco War a Bolivian feeling of nation began, but according to the view expressed in the program notes, Bolivia as a nation has never taken full shape because of continuing socioeconomic inequalities. Aesthetic unity was achieved at this mythic birth moment, but a social unity has remained short of its imagined potential. To understand Música de Maestros one must remember what the Chaco War means in contemporary Bolivian historiography.

Bolivia fought and lost to Paraguay in the Chaco War (1932–1935). Although this confrontation occurred between the two states, some hundred years after Bolivia's formal independence from colonial rule, Bolivia was still a state without a "nation." Bolivia was run by an oligarchy, an elite who produced their fortunes through the export-oriented mining of tin, a business that was concentrated in the hands of a few "tin barons." Members of the oligarchy saw in the Chaco War a chance to reinvent their fantasy of nation-ness through a territorial confrontation with the neighboring state of Paraguay. The Bolivians who met in the trenches and actually fought the war refashioned the oligarchy's territorial conceptualization of nation through a common experience; Bolivians of different subordinate positions met in the trenches, and became aware of their shared position of inequality. This collective experience made multiple post–Chaco War Bolivian Others imaginable to each other in the subsequent relative isolation. An incipient "imagined community" (Anderson 1991) emerged from Bolivia's Chaco War experiences (see Arze Aguirre 1987; Montenegro 1943: 235–239; Rivera Cusicanqui 1986: 45–48) and provided the groundwork for the peasant and labor mobilizations that came to a critical juncture in the 1952 Revolution (see Ranaboldo 1987: 75). The significance of the Chaco War is key to understanding the nostalgic associations of Música de Maestros; a large part of their repertoire is from the 1930s and has direct associative links to this war.

With reference to these historical junctures and through a selection of pieces composed during the Chaco War era, Música de Maestros musically evoked the national narrative of a potentially unified Bolivia. It did so by

evoking both death and love. The third album had a high concentration of
these Chaco War themes: "Brigada Fantasma," "Alas," "Boquerón," "Despedida," and "Carandaytí." Many ensembles have interpreted the song, "Boquerón," but during my fieldwork period this piece, with music by Antonio
Montes Calderón and lyrics by Humberto Palza Soliz, inadvertently became the sonorous emblem of Música de Maestros. The lyrics, sung from
the perspective of a soldier going to war for Bolivia, brought together romantic love, possible death, and nationalism. The soldier begins by telling
his love not to cry if death should separate them forever ("*No me llores si
la muerte cava un abismo entre los dos*"; "Don't cry for me if death should
dig an abyss between us"). The soldier imagines the suffering of his own
death in solitude and the rebirth of his romantic love as a garden flower.
But the song concludes with a reference to Bolivian nationalism and the
sacrifice of death that is made in its name ("*Bolivia ha de ganar, después
morir, morir*"; "Bolivia should win, afterwards to die, to die").[12] Música de
Maestros never ended a program without playing "Boquerón." At times,
when the reduced ensemble played a collaborative performance, the director would hesitate to play this intricately orchestrated piece, but the public
seldom let the ensemble off the stage without at least one rendition of this
composition. For a time, "Boquerón" was Música de Maestros and Música
de Maestros was "Boquerón." It was one of those songs that seemed heavy
with memory—memory of a war fought and memory of stories of this
war, told by surviving relatives.

According to the liner notes of Música de Maestros's third recording,
the composer of "Boquerón," Antonio Montes Calderón, a conservatory-
trained clarinetist, joined the army during the Chaco War, and for 33
years remained in their ranks as an army band director. "Boquerón" was a
well-known tune in Bolivia, but in the 1990s, many Bolivians knew it by
the title "Boquerón Abandonado" (Abandoned Boquerón). The liner
notes of this recording cited a 1990 radio interview with the composer in
which Montes Calderón criticized the error of this popularly known title
that emphasized the abandonment of battle and the defeat of Bolivia. Boquerón was the site of a costly battle that Bolivians lost to Paraguayans. Yet
Música de Maestros's liner notes indicated a "commitment to popularizing the original piece" as the composer had titled it. Música de Maestros
cited the composer's intentions in setting the record straight about "Boquerón," and during radio interviews, I often heard Rolando make references to these original intentions of Montes Calderón.

The songs that referenced the Chaco War on the third album drew on
themes of duty to a nation, a soldier separated from his lover, and luck or
destiny that might take the soldier to death rather than home. On this
recording, the cueca "Despedida" was followed by the sound of a departing

train, a sound that then led into "Brigada Fantasma," the nine-minute cavalry bolero that evoked, through its genre structure, a remembered or an imagined experience of the Chaco War. As I already mentioned in chapter two, this stately genre was performed by military bands as they marched to battle sites. The studio-recorded version of this cavalry bolero was punctuated by the sound of rifle shots.

Música de Maestros was not alone in its fascination with the music from the Chaco War era. The singer/songwriter, Jenny Cárdenas, had taken a great interest in this period of musical creativity. Her father had fought in the Chaco War, and on the music of this era she completed a sociological thesis at the Universidad Mayor de San Andrés (UMSA) in La Paz. Her research eventually led to a recording titled *Homenaje a una generación histórica* 1932–1952 (Homage to a Historical Generation, 1932–1952; 1999), which featured recordings with Música de Maestros and with the Symphonic Military Band. Many themes included in the repertoire of her recording overlapped with those of Música de Maestros ("Alas," "Despedida," "Khuniskiwa," "Carandaití," "Por un minuto de amor"), creating at times a delicate tension between her project and theirs. From several different sources I heard varying stories as to how some of these musical gems were extracted from historical obscurity and as to who really "discovered" them. Rather than retell these conflicting stories and draw supposedly definitive conclusions about the "real origins" of the idea of focussing on music from the Chaco War, I want to emphasize the collective focus on this era by musicians and artists who at least throughout the 1980s and 1990s, were key musical performers in Bolivia. Jenny Cárdenas and Música de Maestros seemed to smooth over potential tensions through collaborative work, and Rolando Encinas made sure that Jenny was cited on Música de Maestros's third recording as the "collector" of both "Alas" and "Despedida." In chapter seven, I return to problems of collecting music and assuming proprietorship over music, but of significance here is that the idea of performing music from the era of the Chaco War, as a musical project, was one over which many musicians made claims. As a national music project, playing themes from the Chaco War era had a value in a local Bolivian symbolic and nostalgic economy.

Through the decisions to develop a repertoire from what was considered a golden age of Bolivian mestizo-Creole music, the 1930s, Música de Maestros became associated with Bolivia's popular origin narrative. While the Chaco War did not mark Bolivia's official narrative of nation, which had to place national origins at the moment of independence from Spain, the Chaco War became the trope through which Bolivians imagined themselves to be part of the nation. Música de Maestros's third album, the first to be recorded with Discolandia, emphasized music from the Chaco

War. Its liner notes stated: "The concern for collecting and restoring the compositions which represent a special and specific moment of Creole music has allowed us to identify the '30s as the point of encounter and discovery of the poor [of this] country, and for the first time [they stood] naked before themselves, face to face in a war which was fratricidal and alien to their interests" (1993).

In these narratives, popular sectors of both Bolivia and Paraguay were imagined as meeting in the trenches and through this experience coming to a consciousness of shared inequalities. These interpretations permeate contemporary historiography about the War. With war veterans still living, multiple generations participated in a collective experience of remembering this founding moment. A newspaper commentary by Carlos Toranzo Roca captured the sense of this popular memory as it crossed generations:

> At home they said that I was half crazy because I loved to listen to "that music of dead people." So especially since I got married, I have had to elude my wife or my children so that I can furtively listen to my cavalry boleros. As time passes I realize more and more that it is not death which attracts me, but rather it is the Chaco War which intrigues and impassions me. Because of this I am happy when I am transported to the Chaco sands, through the beautiful performances of the group Música de Maestros. They do not know it, but it is because of their mastery of interpretation that now my children, my family, my friends, or my social gatherings converse, 'nostalgiate,' and dialogue about the same thing, that is to say about the Chaco and what has been the source of so much passion and pain.
>
> There was a moment when sons and fathers could finally dialogue about the same thing, mutually tell each other "Let it be," speak of the same topics and like the same music. That magic was reached by the Beatles . . . in a more national space, Música de Maestros made it possible for our children to understand why tears fall from [our eyes] when we listen to "Boquerón Abandonado." (*La razón,* December 18, 1994)

In comparison to English, the Spanish language does not easily accommodate invented words. Looking beyond the apparent mistile of "Boquerón Abandonado," it was with surprise that I read in this opinion piece a Spanish verb *nostalgiar* (nostalgiate). While the noun and adjective forms (*nostalgia* and *nostálgica*) are common enough, the verb form "to nostalgiate," is a linguistic innovation. With this word the author satisfied his need to discuss nostalgia as an action. Nostalgia is not just something people feel; it is also something that people *do*. Furthermore, the expression "that music of dead people," so often used to refer to the supposedly universal classical music composers, has been brought into direct association with the music of specifically Bolivian composers.

When Rolando Encinas first explained to me the ensemble's objectives, I imagined looking out at the ensemble's audience—a sea of graying elderly Chaco War veterans and others of their generation. I imagined incorrectly. Audiences of multiple generations, social classes, and ethnic backgrounds came to nostalgiate at Música de Maestros's performances. Young musicians from the city of El Alto would approach us after a performance and profess their adulation of the group. Audience members would tell me of their emotional reactions to our concerts. The Bolivian historian, Silvia Rivera, told me she and her father attended one of our concerts, and both of them were in tears through parts of the performance.[13] Young, middle-aged, and elderly people listened to a nine-minute cavalry bolero in absolute theatrical silence—that silence of a mesmerized audience, broken only with a final burst of applause. Música de Maestros brought cavalry boleros and their listeners out of the closet, and formed a new generation of listeners for the music from that era.

As Toranzo Roca wrote of his nostalgiating, it was not death that attracted him but the Chaco War itself. He thought of the Chaco War, but not with a longing to return to that face-off with death. Like most nostalgia, one does not really want to return to the period for which one longs. The attraction was to the Chaco War, not as a war but as an era—an era that has taken on mythic proportions in the contemporary Bolivian imagination. While Bolivians felt little personal connection to the independence era and its heroes, most Bolivians could make a connection to the Chaco War, through personal experience or through stories told by or about their grandfathers. Jonathan Boyarin has suggested "identity and memory are virtually the same concept" but memory is never superorganic because of its necessary embodiment in individuals (1994: 23–26). Many Bolivians have this embodied connection to the Chaco War, as veterans, sons and daughters of veterans, or grandsons and granddaughters of veterans. Anderson claims that death is linked with the nation through "a secular transformation of fatality into continuity, contingency into meaning" (1991: 11). In Bolivia it was not the death involved in the nineteenth-century war for independence that achieved this transformation, but the death—or threat of it—involved in the twentieth-century Chaco War.

As Música de Maestros's program notes suggested, the Bolivian nation was born in the Chaco War, but the nation-making process was stunted along the way. Música de Maestros played on this popular narrative of national origins through research agendas that focused on original scores and the original intentions of composers as deduced through interviews with composers, or with their surviving relatives. While Música de Maestros fed national nostalgia as it trumpeted Bolivia's great composers, the workshop could not have been further from this "nostalgiating" process.

ANTI-NOSTALGIA

Workshop organizers and instructors maintained a strong rhetoric against museumizing, in favor of constant artistic creativity. While the "traditional" wing of the workshop's activities included a pursuit of culturally authentic music performances, the avant-garde wing of their activities toyed with unique authenticity, a focus on the innovative compositions of individuals that spoke to aesthetic principles that could be appreciated beyond the borders of the Bolivian nation-state. The institution's avant-garde activities placed this project within universalist discourses, and paradoxically, workshop organizers would emphasize this connection through reference to the very particularities of Bolivia's indigenous instruments. To create a Bolivian contemporary music, the workshop used as their principal medium of expression the Contemporary Orchestra of Native Instruments (OCIN), an ensemble that used "native" instruments from the Bolivian countryside. They presented their compositions in the forum of the Bolivian Festival of Contemporary Music, an event in which the workshop had played a key role as organizers since the festival's initial year in 1992. Many of the workshop's compositions for the OCIN had no meter or tonality, incorporated techniques of over- and underblowing wind instruments, exaggerated the rich overtone series of the instruments from Bolivia's indigenous cultures, and applied open and aleatory methods of organization (the intentional incorporation of chance and unpredictability in a work). In the context of the Contemporary Music Festival, workshop instructors were encouraged, sometimes even gently pushed into composing new works to be performed by the OCIN; it was a performance context that operated under the motor of innovation. The festival was also the medium through which the workshop made connections with the universal and internationalized music world. As an event, the festival attracted sponsors and support from the National Conservatory, the Goethe Institute, the U.S. cultural unit (USIS), as well as participation by national conservatory musicians and international performers. The program title of the 1993 festival gave a sense of this project's hybridity: "Sonorous Objects and Organizations from the Bolivian Musical Tradition in the Creation of Our Time." Festival program listings resembled the liner notes of Música de Maestros's recordings, with extensive entries for each individual composer and each individual work.

One particular work underscores the contrasting aesthetics at work here: Paúl López's "Imaraycu" ("Why" in Quechua). This work was included on the OCIN's recording *La doctrina de los ciclos* (1990). López was a workshop instructor and his work called for three troupes of mohozeños, the instrument for which the troupe genre was performed in Música de Maestros's performance of the last movement of "Suite Aymara." According to the liner notes, the piece questioned the entire process of the conquest and colonization of the Americas. López's piece began with cluster chords (imagine simultaneously playing a series of consecutive notes on the piano), further enhanced by the natural overtone series of the instruments. Sections of the ensemble then played a fluttering pattern that seemed to be moving back and forth between two semi-tones at different registers, contrasting high and low. Then the larger ensemble played the same flutter pattern at these different registers. This was followed by a different sound texture, something like the sound of moaning animals. This is the kind of sound produced from a mohozeño when the instrument is underblown.

Workshop compositions like this one did not evoke cultural authenticity. Nor did they move anyone to feel nostalgic for the past. The aesthetics at work here followed a logic similar to the anti-ethnographic approach to the 1990 Los Angeles Festival of the Arts, where avant-garde performances were scheduled alongside performances of cultural difference, but with an intentional absence of ethnographic explanatory discourse accompanying the latter performances (Kirshenblatt-Gimblett 1998: 238). Los Angeles festival organizers worked under the idea that the avant-garde listening experience trains an audience to value any performance that comes from a position of difference (1998: 234–235). Festival organizers defined the "authentic experience as one in which audiences confront the incomprehensible" (1998: 203). This perspective of authenticity in facing the new and startling provides a different take on the experiential authenticities discussed in chapter two, and it helps locate a different perspective on the pleasures of music. If one kind of pleasure in music listening emerges in a groove, a driving repetition of elements with microlevel tensions and discrepancies, another kind of pleasure is encountered in the consistently new and different. This "confusing pleasure" (Kirshenblatt-Gimblett 1998) operates in ways that are quite distinct from the cultural performance criteria employed by Música de Maestros, in which cultural authenticity refers to a national community with which Bolivians, to varying degrees, identify; cultural authenticity in Música de Maestros was shaped through performing and listening to one's own sonorous representations of a national community.

When Música de Maestros played mohozeños in the "Suite Aymara," they brought audiences to their feet, but they did so by playing the instruments in a troupe, in their perceived culturally authentic performance style and genre. López was more interested in exploiting the sonorous capabilities of the instrument than in replicating indigenous authenticity; in López's work, members of the workshop played mohozeños without playing a mohozeñada; they played the instruments without their genre. For all of its rhetoric against Kjarkas music, in its contemporary music activities, the workshop shared a similar strategy of making a music "national" by decontextualizing and transforming the way an indigenous *instrument* was played. With very different results, both Kjarkas and the avant-garde wing of the workshop played indigenous instruments without their respective performance genres. But unlike the Kjarkas's ambitions to represent an essentially Bolivian national music, the workshop preferred to blur the national associations, which cling to the aura of the indigenous instrument, with a universalizing aesthetic of the avant-garde. The workshop's compositions also alluded to the diverse Bolivian cultural geographies of the pluri-multi, but their compositions worked within avant-garde principles, held complete irreverence for the repetition of other works, and brought a mock death to the very idea of trying to represent a previously established, culturally or historically authentic work.

In this chapter I have addressed primarily mestizo musical representations of indigenous cultures, and both of these musical projects discussed here engaged in distinct ways with the politics of aesthetics. Javier Sanjinés's has suggested that the contemporary Bolivian context is characterized, not so much by Benjamin's politicization of aesthetics, nor by the aestheticization of the political, but by the "aestheticization of the Real" (1998: 95). In explaining this term, he refers to three characteristics of postmodernity through which the "aestheticization of the Real" operates: the collapse of the distinction between elite and mass culture, the end of master narratives, and the waning of the art work's aura. While Sanjinés's assessment fits well with the workshop's attempts to popularize a Bolivian avant-garde music, it is far less congruent with two characteristics of these musical projects: the urban rebirth of the troupe performance of indigenous instruments, and the appeals to a narrative of universal aesthetics. In spite of it all, cultural authenticity and unique authenticity still hold value in this symbolic economy.

The next chapters turn to indigenous music performances in ritual context, a comfortable old groove of anthropological inquiry. While the previous two chapters have focused on conscious representational practices, the next chapters turn to a primary frame of music performances (see Goffman 1974), and shift somewhat away from the process of conscious representation. But representational issues return in full force as Yureños had to prove themselves to the Bolivian state as real "indigenous" people and as Toropalqueños expressed nostalgia for the culture they felt they had lost.

CHAPTER 5

—⤳⛭⤶—

THE BURDEN AND LIGHTNESS
OF AUTHENTICITY

When I began my fieldwork in 1993, I remember a brief conversation with a woman in a remote community of Toropalca. As I explained to her that I wanted to study the music of the area she quickly responded, "Oh, you want to study folklore and culture. But there is no culture here. If you *really* want to study culture you should go to Northern Potosi." I was intrigued by this statement, which summarily negated the existence of culture in Toropalca and referred me to the place in Bolivia where many anthropologists have had a "field day." The anthropologist, Olivia Harris, whose work has focused precisely on Northern Potosi, was advised by her British colleagues not to do any of her research in the highland Andes—an area believed to be too subject to external forces for a "distinctive" anthropological study (2000: 1). In his study of Peruvian peasant patrols in northern Peru, anthropologist Orin Starn was similarly advised by a Peruvian to shift his study to Cuzco, Machu Picchu, or Lake Titicaca, where peasants "had culture" (1999: 24). The assumed "purity" of the anthropologist's fieldsite has certainly been buttressed from within the discipline. The discipline's hang-ups over cultural purity, even as these hang-ups have generally moved to anthropological history, still remain present in the places where anthropologists have worked. The comments I heard reflected the degree to which people of the Andean region have incorporated the assumption that anthropologists arrive to study the visibly exotic, a description that did not match the visible presentation of most Toropalqueños.

In the context of Toropalca, the comment about having no culture reminded me of Renato Rosaldo's point of who has and does not have culture: simply stated, the weak have culture and the powerful don't (1989a). But Rosaldo's assessment did not fit this situation. Toropalqueños could not be considered particularly powerful, and they certainly were not any more powerful than their northern neighbors who *did* "have culture." This encounter brought me to questions of the way people perceive the presence or absence of their own culture. Here the debate centers around cultural authenticity of collective traditions as they are perceived to be rooted in an imagined eternity, untouched by historical forces. While the national music projects discussed in chapter four also underscore the way musicians consciously construct a culturally historically authentic national music, self perception of cultural authenticity in Toropalca or Yura is particularly charged. Within these Bolivian national spaces, rural folk are still expected to embody some essential part of the Bolivian nation. In some sense, "national" natives are expected to remain rooted to their physical places of origin (see Malkki 1992: 30) and steeped in their traditional ways. Here is where "cultural" and "historical" authenticity take separate paths, as the first is framed within a stage supposedly untouched by history, while the second supposedly builds on historical moments. Through an analysis of songs lyrics, performance context, and discourse, I will explore the contrasting ways that Toropalqueños and Yureños carried this burden of cultural authenticity.

Cultural authenticity may be about roots, but these songs are about being uprooted, on the move. The lyrics of these songs express, in distinct ways, how Toropalqueños and Yureños related to translocal places. Toropalqueños and Yureños, particularly men and single women, migrated annually to other areas of Bolivia (Cochabamba, Beni, Santa Cruz, and Tarija), as well as to Argentina—leaving home after the April harvest and returning for the October planting season. Away from home Toropalqueños and Yureños sought temporary employment in agriculture and construction, thus supplementing their subsistence on maize production at home. These migration patterns were widespread throughout the Department of Potosi; temporary migration was the rule rather than the exception. The songs I analyze here provide a window into the ways Toropalqueños and Yureños experienced these processes of migration, from the perspectives of those who left, as well as from the perspectives of those who remained at home.

While both Yureños and Toropalqueños participated in these migrations, the song lyrics from these two places had two very different tenors. The songs from Toropalca and the discourses about them expressed nostalgia for many things, while the songs from Yura, and the discourses about them, generally lacked any sense of nostalgia. Song lyrics in Toropalca made vague references to translocal places, while those of Yura named specific translocal places, details, personas, and phenomena. In spite of the hum about globalization and the erasure of place, these songs were all about places. Toropalqueños and Yureños were often financially obligated to enter temporarily the labor force in a place distant from their homes. But Toropalqueños and Yureños reacted very differently to these processes. Toropalqueños were ultimately weighed down with a tragic sense of their perceived loss of cultural authenticity, while Yureños hardly seemed to feel this burden.

I often heard Bolivian social scientists and NGO workers lamenting the processes of seasonal migration occurring in Potosi. The attitude was generally that something was terribly wrong if people had to migrate from their homes. While I do not want to ignore the obvious strains that migration can put on the social fabric at home,[1] I would suggest avoiding a completely negative view of migration. The anthropologist, Allyn MacLean Stearman, in her study of migrants in the lowland region of Santa Cruz, Bolivia, reminds us that "it is interesting how middle-class Americans 'move,' while the less affluent, particularly those in the Third World, 'migrate' . . ." (1985: 2). Stearman suggests a more measured view of migration as one of many economic strategies (1985: 2). Taking a more neutral position on migration, puts into greater relief the differences between Toropalca and Yura.

In Yura, the specificity of expression about translocality was directly related to the terms under which locality was produced; a stronger local identity in Yura was related to the specificity with which Yureños sang about translocal phenomena and a relatively weaker local identity in Toropalca was related to the vagueness with which Toropalqueños sang about translocal phenomena. These contrasting cases—one in which nostalgia pervaded the songs and cultural discourse (Toropalca) and one in which nostalgia is conspicuously absent (Yura)—call for a reexamination of the alleged link between nostalgia and the processes of modernity. I do not want to make a causal argument about what does and does not constitute modernity. Rather, my objective is to open a set of questions related to commonsense expectations of modernity. Following Mary Louise Pratt (1999), I view modernity as an ideological story that the West tells about itself, to itself and to others. The story—one of progress, enlightenment, and rationality—is presented as universal and naturalized as inevitable. As the philosopher Enrique Dussel argued, the underside to this story is the conquest and colonization of Others that began in 1492, and this domination over an other has been foundational to the identity narrative of the West (1993). For Dussel, the story is a discourse of Western identity, built on the foundational violence of Spanish conquest and colonization. While it is a story the West tells about itself, it is also a story that has been imposed on the rest of the world; we cannot deny the "imposed receptivity" of this story, but it has meandered down millions of different paths of meaning in the contexts of "peripheral modernities" (Pratt 1999).[2] My analysis of songs in Toropalca and Yura will highlight two different peripheral modernities that geographically and, to a degree, culturally, sit side by side.

Simply stated, a commonsense approach to modernity assumes that an increased interconnectedness of the world leads to a loss of local culture. Of course, only salvage anthropologists would agree to that interpretation. But this commonsense view pervades much of Bolivian discourse and implicitly lurks within many Bolivian anthropological projects.[3] These projects often emerge within the nostalgia felt for the worlds that are assumed to inevitably disappear with the forward march of modernity. The material I present here will suggest a tempting alternative model: that increased interconnectedness generates and sharpens the view of local culture. This model is not new to contemporary anthropology; it is the model whereby people become consciously aware of their own identity through increased contact with others (see Barth 1969; Turner 1991; Ramos 1998),[4] and this model is founded on the relational characteristic of all identities (see Laclau and Mouffe 1985: 113). But rather than suggest this as a definitive way to approach modernity, I want to insist that these processes defy a single interpretive model because people do not experience modernity in the same ways. Therefore we should not expect any single coherent connection between modernity and cultural transformation.

COMPARING TOROPALCA AND YURA

While both Toropalqueños and Yureños shared a common history as the pre-Conquest ethnic group called the Wisijsas, and even shared the colonial history of the reduction policies of Toledo, I observed many points of contrast between these two groups. These people lived in places that were shaped by distinct connections with external agents and influences. A well-traveled road passed through the canton of Yura in route to the salt flats of Uyuni, a major tourist site. On their way to Uyuni the tourist buses regularly stopped for lunch in the Yureño community of Pelqa. In contrast, the road to Toropalca was more remote and during the rainy season trucks had to travel by lengthy alternate routes to reach the village. In the case of Yura a bus company with other routes in the Province of Quijarro ran a daily route between the village of Yura and the city of Potosí, a trip on which travelers could purchase assigned seats. In contrast truck owners in Toropalca made sporadic trips to Potosi, carrying as many passengers as had the need to travel and as could be uncomfortably accommodated among the personal supplies purchased by the vehicle's owner. In the case of Yura, the Punutuma hydroelectric plant, built by the now-waning national mining company COMIBOL, provided electricity for the village of Yura and a few neighboring communities. In Toropalca only two privileged houses had electricity, which they received from solar panels. While Toropalqueños in the village and in the communities hauled drinking water from the river, Yureños had water piped into the village and many Yureño communities had their own potable water systems from nearby springs.

In Yura, potable water projects were often undertaken through ISALP (Social Investigation and Legal Advising Potosi; *Investigación Social y Asesoramiento Legal Potosi*), the small non-governmental organization working in the area. But with few exceptions,[5] no NGOs had been working in Toropalca. Nevertheless, for the last twenty years a Belgian woman had been volunteering in Toropalca as a doctor and lay worker. While her pastoral work in Toropalca focused on traditional Catholic catechism, the pastoral work in Yura, conducted in relative association with the NGO there, applied concepts of liberation theology. In the 1970s, two anthropologists from Cornell University conducted fieldwork in Yura and one eventually published his ethnography in Bolivia in Spanish (Rasnake 1989). Although one anthropologist recently did survey work in Toropalca for the FAO-sponsored drawing of the Potosi indigenous territories map, the area had been rather untouched by the ethnographic gaze. While Rasnake's ethnography provided a basis for contemporary collective self-reflective work among Yureños, which has strengthened indigenous authorities and organizations, no parallel process had occurred in Toropalca, where the ayllu structures whipped in the contemporary political winds like empty shells of symbolic power imagined to have existed in some previous age.

While unequal relations continued to exist between vecinos and comunarios (ayllu members) in both Toropalca and Yura, vecinos in Toropalca played a defining role in the expression of local identity. In contrast, Yura as a local place was ritually recreated through a predominance of Yura's comunarios, the vecinos there providing little more than sideline commentary, usually complaining that it just wasn't like it used to be. The relatively weak position of vecinos in Yura may be related to the organization of communal stores under the sponsorship of the local NGO; communal stores challenged one of the economic means by which vecinos established their dominance over comunarios. Local rituals in Yura focused on the ayllu's authorities and gave prominence to these organizational forms, while local rituals in Toropalca focused on individual sponsorship of fiestas—drawing upon interpersonal relations of exchange. I continually asked Toropalqueños about their ayllus, and their answers were vague and filled with uncertainty. Toropalqueños maintained the semblance of two large ayllus, but many people could not name the current indigenous authorities (kuraqas), and no ritual forms reinforced these indigenous structures. In contrast, Yura's ritual cycles annually recreated the ayllu structures, bringing Yureños together to a ritual center. Toropalca's rituals tended to be singular isolated events in different communities, fiestas that drew together a few neighboring hamlets, but that never ritually united all Toropalqueños.

In the lyrics of Yureña songs, the masculine perspective on migration predominated, while those of Toropalqueña songs took a feminine perspective. While young, single women did migrate for part of the year, men of all ages migrated in more significant numbers. I suggest that these divergent ways that Yureños and Toropalqueños express translocal experiences are inextricably linked to the way these people conceive of their local places, and that a specificity or vagueness about other places emerges directly in relation to a specificity or vagueness at home.[6] While Karsten Paerregaard, in an ethnographic study of the migrants from Tapay, a Peruvian Quechua community, emphasized the fact that not living in Tapay gave these people a very different sense of being Tapeño (1997: 45), the situation of temporary out-migration from Toropalca, seemed to shape similarly the way one felt Toropalqueño in Toropalca. The vague references to translocal experiences in Toropalca's songs parallel a local nostalgia for a home place and an accompanying sense of cultural loss. In contrast, the specific references to translocal experiences in Yura's songs parallel a sense of home place that is not plagued by nostalgia.

Song Text and Music Performance

The focus on lyrics in this chapter necessitates a few comments on the relation between song text and song performance. Charles Seeger wrote: "It cannot be too strongly emphasized that what is sung and the singing of it are not, musically speaking, two things, but one. Abstraction of the song from its singing is a necessary procedure in talking about music which makes two things out of the original one" (1977:278). I focus on the content of a song text, even though strong evidence suggests that lyrics are secondary in importance to the nonlinguistic expressions within song performance contexts. To situate Andean cultures in alternative positions within an otherwise logocentric letter-dominated world, Denise Arnold and Juan de Dios Yapita proposed an intertextuality of Andean cultures, emphasizing the Andean textual practices (weaving, song, stories) that intersect with the lettered world (2000). In a similar vein, Regina Harrison has emphasized the Andean sign systems at work, particularly those that do not constitute language but that communicate through indexicality and iconicity (1989). In making song lyrics part of my analysis, I do not want to reduce these multiple textualities and sign systems to a few lines of written words, but an analysis of the lyrics belongs alongside an interpretation of these social and performative contexts.

My approach to song lyrics necessarily differs from other studies. For Toropalqueños and Yureños, song cannot be seen as an oblique way of venting feelings about forbidden subjects. Unlike Lila Abu-Lughod's case of the Bedouins (1986) or Susan Rasmussen's case of the Tuareg (1991), the themes of Toropalqueño and Yureño song texts are the acceptable themes of daily talk. Song in Toropalca and Yura is also not a form of personal or collective protest. Song text has often been analyzed as a critique of a particular status quo, the songs' entire meaning changing when a government shift occurs.[7] Contemporary Bolivian history sports a long list of dictatorships and repressive government measures, particularly in the 1960s and 1970s. But since 1982, Bolivia has enjoyed peaceful transfers of power from one democratic, at least nominally, government to another. During my fieldwork the most intense place of government repression occurred in the coca-growing region of the Chapare, and one song from Yura poignantly referenced this "war." Nevertheless, most of the song texts analyzed here express individual hardships and joys.

The sense of loneliness expressed in Toropalca's song texts might be read as another example of the sociocultural orphanhood expressed in other Quechua song texts: not a real orphanhood, but a cultural one that pervades since the Conquest. Martin Lienhard makes this point in reference to Peruvian songs that always include references to lost parents. He argues that the texts do not refer to concrete social situations, but rather to post-Conquest historically structured social relations (1996: 361–362). But precisely through the comparison with Yura's songs—songs that do not generally express these sentiments of loneliness—I propose an alternative interpretation for these cases. Songs in Yura and Toropalca represent two different gendered perspectives on the real social situations of temporary out-migration.

Nor do Yureño and Toropalqueño song texts alone reveal an organization of emotional experience (see Yano 1995). Within performance contexts, with music, dance, and inebriation, Toropalqueños and Yureños shed tears as they sing, but the song texts themselves are tangential to these emotional responses, as the singers often lapse into a mere humming of the song. Song text, song performance, and discourse about song reveal a plethora of different emotional experiences. Doña Norma, a woman in the village Toropalca, explained that to lift up her spirits, she sang at home all the time. "The neighbors sometimes think I'm drunk. But I'm not. When I'm drunk I cry as I sing." And there is the rub: She sings at home in contentment; she (as well as many other singers) sings through tears in the inebriated state common to ritual; and the lyrical content of the songs she sings includes both pleasurable and painful references. In their ritual context, these songs access deep emotions, a kind of "sentimental education" (see Rosaldo, M. 1980: 25). The affect of these performances is more closely tied to musical sound, physical movement, and ritual context than to the content of the lyrics.

Even as I approach an analysis of song lyrics, I follow other studies of song that posit the importance of the music performance through which the text is expressed (Keil 1979; Seeger 1987; Titon 1988; Frith 1996: 166). I used similar methods to those that Charles Keil used in his analysis of Tiv song (1979: 170–173). Specifically, I sought to find out: Could performers reproduce the tune without the words of the song? The endless humming of song tunes indicated that indeed they could produce the music without the text. But an even more revealing method emerged when I asked women and men, outside of the ritual context, to confirm the textual content of the lyrics. Words sung in any language are often difficult to discern. To document the lyrics of songs I often had to interview singers outside of the ritual context, re-recording the song, writing the words, and having the singers confirm that I had gotten the song "right." As a referential written song text emerged in my notes, I found that singers had difficulty confirming this text without singing the song. I would read back the song text with questions or gaps, but the singer could not fill those gaps through speech; the singer had to sing the words to remember them. It was something akin to memorizing a piece of music on an instrument and then having someone ask you to repeat a passage in the middle of it. What rolls off the fingers when played together with the surrounding passages suddenly becomes strange and awkward. Memorization of song lyrics works in a similar performative fashion; one does not memorize song lyrics as semantic meaning but rather as sung words, words connected to a perception of pitch and rhythm. In spite of what seems to be an argument for the primacy of music and movement in the performance of Toropalqueño and Yureño songs, I insist on a concomitant study of song text because of the aforementioned contrast between Toropalca and Yura. These contrasts may shed light on the different ways that Toropalqueños and Yureños experienced being part of local places within a modern nation-state.

Furthermore, the documentation of song texts was important to Toropalqueños themselves, important enough that when they knew I was studying the music of the area, they suggested that I compile a book of their songs. Song text was important to the singers as they foresaw the possibility of not remembering in the future. Toropalqueños imagined this book in the hands of the village school children; in Toropalca the song book project went hand in hand with nostalgia and a defensive strategy against a perceived loss of cultural authenticity. Song text may be analyzed as symbolic representation (the meaning within the text itself), but as a songbook, or even as liner notes on a cassette, the song text works indexically to represent the incomplete whole: the song performance and the cultural context from which the performance is perceived to emerge.

The music transcriptions of these songs, both from Toropalca and Yura, indicate a close link between rhythmic and syllabic articulations. With few exceptions, these songs have few melismas—where more than one note is sung to one syllable—and few cases where two syllables are sung on a single articulated note. Each syllable tends to have its own rhythmic articulation and rhythmic patterns tend to be slightly altered, at the level of individual measures, in order to accommodate individually articulated syllabic utterances. These tendencies underline the necessity of studying as a unit the music, the lyrics, and the context of each performance.

The Threatened Source of Authenticity

Toropalqueña women talked and sang about the absence of men, a lack that was acutely felt and widely discussed during Toropalca's carnival. Carnival in Toropalca provided a clear contrast with Yura's Carnival music performance dynamics, which I will discuss in the next chapter. Unlike Yureños' united rituals that reproduced the structures and spaces of the indigenous organizations, Toropalqueños' Carnival consisted of several different celebrations, each locally situated, none meeting in confluence with others. Carnival began with Comadres (the Thursday before Carnival) in Sarapalca, a community north of the village of Toropalca. The village of Toropalca then celebrated the Saturday and the Sunday of Carnival, some activities spilling over into the Tuesday of Ch'alla, the day when all houses and automobiles, especially new constructions and purchases, received ample ritual libations. In 1994, Carnival ended south of the village, as the community of Kollpiri celebrated on the Sunday of Temptations, with music of the anata or tarka instrument. While I followed these three different celebrations, no one else made the same travels. Each group remained within the area of their own local celebration, each place celebrating their own Carnival.[8]

As I previously noted in chapter two, the fiesta of Comadres in Sarapalca was renown as the time and place where musicians of an entire region "*sacan sus huayños*" (compose, or literally "pull out" their songs).[9] I confess that I was rather disappointed with the music performances I documented in Sarapalca. It became clear to me that despite its grand reputation as a transregional meeting timespace, this was a very local celebration.

The localness of Comadres in Sarapalca was also reflected in its organization and sponsorship, structures that reflected a consciousness and explicit discourse of maintaining traditions in the face of change. Principal among the threats to tradition, as mentioned by Sarapalqueños themselves, was the presence of evangelical Protestantism and the out-migration to Argentina. While Yureños were also experiencing out-migration to Argentina and the presence of evangelical Protestant groups, these factors were discussed in ayllu meetings, not within the context of music performance celebrations. Sarapalqueños explicitly linked their traditions to the institution of the indigenous authority or *kuraqa* of the *ayllu chico* or small indigenous organization, and to the music performance of the flauta instrument. In 1994, Sarapalca's kuraqa of the ayllu chico was a community level authority, but one that was assigned by a system of rotation within the families of the community. This system of rotation, as well as the kuraqa's fiesta of Comadres was perceived as doubly threatened by out-migration and evangelical Protestantism.

When I arrived in Sarapalca I asked a boy where the kuraqa lived and he responded in a heavy Argentine drawl, "*¿Qué sé jo?*" (What do I know?), the "*yo*" pronounced with a "j" sound. With one phrase I was yanked out of Bolivia's localities and transferred across the border to Argentina, and a particular way of speaking Spanish. As more young people were leaving for Argentina, returning only to visit, a kuraqa system in Sarapalca counted on fewer and fewer families through which to rotate the burden of authority. In 1994, Sarapalqueños were notably concerned with the desertion of their community, and the topic crept into our discussions at every turn.

During Carnival of 1994, I heard the Sarapalqueños' discourses that were directed at me in my study of the music of Toropalca. I sensed a desperation with which Sarapalqueños were clinging to the kuraqa's fiesta and the music of the flauta, a continual invocation of following what the ancestors used to do, in the hopes of maintaining a thread to the past, as a community was vacated by all but its elderly inhabitants. The school-aged population in Sarapalca was so limited that the community was fighting to keep its locally assigned schoolteacher. With a perception that no future generation was living in Sarapalca, the community was fighting to keep a history, a tradition.

As the principal day of the fiesta of Comadres passed, I asked why the Sarapalqueños had no plans to go to Toropalca. "We weren't invited," said one man. "We have a band coming here from Potosi tomorrow. Why don't you just stay here? Nothing will happen in Toropalca," said another, dismissing the Carnival celebrations of Toropalca. The crowning glory for a fiesta sponsor in Sarapalca, as well as in Toropalca, was the ability to pay for a band from Potosi. As Sarapalqueños commenced their dance band activities, I continued my Carnival travels alone to the village of Toropalca.

Carnival in the village of Toropalca focused on the activities of the sponsor (*carnavalero*), the village dance troupe (*comparsa*), and the household ritual libations (*ch'allas*), which occurred on Tuesday. The carnavalero or alferez officially sponsored the village celebrations; this single sponsorship was voluntarily assumed by a family for the prestige it conferred. Drawing from these activities the vecinos, through dress, song, and music, assumed as their own a Toropalqueña comunario identity. At the same time, they participated in activities that were easily identifiable as "vecino." What in Yura was a relatively transparent dichotomy of vecinos and comunarios, had to be viewed differently in Toropalca. In 1994, although a few authorities arrived in the village of Toropalca with their staves of authority, the presence of comunarios was minimal. This was the fiesta of vecinos, but paternalistically it was also the fiesta of vecinos for the annual reconstruction of "indigenous" Toropalqueño displays. For example the village dance troupe or comparsa had specific days on which they were supposed to dress in ajsus and aymillas, and other days on which they were to dress de pollera (which was associated with mestizo influence). Many of the women who were part of the comparsa dressed *de vestido* (Western dress) in their quotidian activities, but for Carnival, ajsus were taken out of moth-ball storage and polleras of matching colors were made for the occasion. When the women dressed de ajsu, the comparsa danced principally with the flauta music, and when the comparsa changed to polleras they danced to the band music. These costume changes during Carnival were undertaken by women of Toropalca, but not by the men. For women of Toropalca, dancing and singing to the music of the flauta marked a tradition that they explicitly identified as threatened. In this way, Sarapalca had been symptomatic of the kinds of attitudes I encountered throughout Toropalca: an expressed fear of losing culture and a placing of blame for the loss on outward migration and Protestant churches. Although Yureños experience similar migration patterns and relations with

Protestant churches, I never heard them express the same kind of nostalgia for lost culture.

In Toropalca the perceived loss of culture was associated with an absence of men. As one woman told me: "There are no men here. They have all gone to Argentina, at least our young men. That's why we have no flauta players. Maybe women should learn to play the flauta. We think they should learn to play the flauta, otherwise we will lose this music." A woman vecino told me this, as we watched three flauta players who struggled to connect a few notes into melodies during the Carnival music performances of Toropalca. What they did not talk about was the way women, and usually women vecinos, through their song lyrics, were carrying-on the tradition of the flauta genre. I watched as the women danced in a circle around the flauta players, forcefully singing songs, primarily in Quechua, and leaving the floundering flauta players somewhere between the song and a well-performed melody. The women were directing these musical performances: They composed the songs; they sang them; and they passed them on to daughters. Hand in hand with the spoken theme of cultural loss, the principal lyrical themes of the songs were personal absence, being left alone, and missing loved ones.

THE ABSENT AND THE VAGUE

The following flauta genre song was sung by women in Toropalca's Carnival in 1994 (see Figure 5.1).

Sonqetuypi	Inside my heart
Mamaypa palabrasnenqa	My mother's words
Sumaq grabasqa	Are well engraved
Kunan jina	Like now
Waqanaypaq	To make me cry
[repeat]	[repeat]
Mamitaypis	My dear mother too
Jallp'aq sonqonpi	Is in the earth's heart,
Ñañitáy	My dear sister
Papitaypis	My father too
Karu llaqtapi	Is in a far away village,
Ñañitáy	My dear sister
Tukuypuni	Everyone
Munakuwanku	Loves me
Kay llaqtapeqa	In this village
[repeat][10]	[repeat]

Figure 5.1   The music transcription of "Sonquetuypi," Toropalca Carnival flauta
huayño, 1994 (transcription by author).

Doña Norma, a vecino of Toropalca, sang this song during Carnival.
Many people sang this song, but it was Doña Norma's voice that stood out
from the others. On many penultimate syllables her voice curved up in
pitch, momentarily sounding more like a spoken word than a sung pitch.
The music transcription of the song, shows the closeness of syllabic expression and musical articulation. With other women of Toropalca Doña
Norma would grab my hand to encircle the musicians with dance. Dust
rose around the moving circle as the dancing women barely lifted their
feet. The inward and outward steps of the dance punctuated Doña
Norma's phrasing. She threw her head slightly back as her voice rose
above the sound of a few struggling flauta players. There was no doubt
that Doña Norma was leading this song.

The lyrics of the song recount personal loss. The Quechua term ñañita
(a woman's sister) reveals the female gender of the addressed as well as the
addressee. The singer addresses her laments to "my dear sister," a term of

endearment used between women. It is a song performed by a woman and sung to a woman. The singer's mother is buried in the earth and her father is in a far away village. Death and migration equally carry away a loved one. The song ends on an ironic note, "Everyone loves me in this village." In other performances of this song *munakuwanku* (everyone loves me) was sometimes substituted by *cheqnikuwanku* (everyone hates me).

This song performance was representative of many I heard in Toropalca: women leading songs with a lyrical content about longing and loss,[11] women singers accompanied by a few men playing the flauta. Song lyrics typically referenced a "far away village" without naming any specific places. The accompanying spoken discourses about Carnival in Toropalca were equally nostalgic. In the village Toropalca, as well as in the surrounding communities I sensed a desperation with which Toropalqueños were clinging to the music of their "ancestors." For their cultural losses Toropalqueños blamed migration and local Protestant churches. Evangelical Protestant groups in the area prohibited the celebration of fiestas, the playing of instruments, the chewing of coca, and the making of corn beer (*chicha*)—all crucial activities in a cycle of cultural reproduction. Nevertheless, it was not completely impossible for an evangelical Protestant to fulfill community responsibilities. In 1995, I heard that the kuraqa of Sarapalca was a *hermano* (the term used to refer to someone who has joined a Protestant church). In this case the kuraqa's brother and sister-in-law sponsored the fiesta of Comadres in the name of the kuraqa, the latter covering the consumption expenses but remaining distanced from the production and consumption of chicha and alcohol.

In the following anata carnival song the fear of being forgotten is associated with clear indices of modernization and a tempting alternative way of life.

Saucilloronchu kasqani	Could I be a weeping willow
Noqa waqanaypaq	To cry so much
[repeat]	[repeat]
Chaypaq tiyan	For that I have
camionetitay	My little truck
Chaypaq tiyan	For that I have
Avionetay	My little airplane
Phawarispa ripunaypaq	So I can go flying
[repeat]	[repeat]
Karu llaqtapiña kaspa	Being in a far away village
Piña yuyasonqa	Who will remember you?
[repeat]	[repeat]

Chaypaq tiyan	For that I have
Chaki maki	Feet and hands,
Trabajuytapis yachayllani	And of my work I only know
Sonsamantachus sufriyman[12]	Maybe I suffer from being stupid
[repeat]	[repeat]

Doña Máxima, a single mother of two sons and two daughters, sang this anata song in Sinandoma during the final moments of the 1994 Carnival season. I met Doña Máxima on my first trip to Sinandoma, a hamlet south of the village Toropalca; I was told that she had a "store" and that there I could probably find shelter for the night. A "store" in these communities usually meant a family storeroom of products that could not otherwise be obtained without traveling to the village of Toropalca: soft drinks, cane alcohol, and cooking oil. After my long walks to and from surrounding communities, she would offer me food and shelter. Doña Máxima spoke only Quechua, although her children were fluent in both Quechua and Spanish. She never accepted payment for my stay, but she always requested that on my next trip I bring her coca from La Paz. An ongoing joke, perhaps part wish on her part, was that I would become her daughter-in-law. Using the Spanish term for son-in-law (*yerno*), and making it feminine, she introduced me to the community as her *yerna* (the Spanish term for daughter-in-law is actually *nuera*). At the time, her son was 15 years old, but she boasted that she had sent him off to Argentina and that he would return a man. Her eldest daughter clarified the lyrics of this song as I copied them into my notes.

The lyrics encompass an internal reflection on the process of migration, the exposure to a different standard of life, and the inclusion in a different way of laboring. Although sung by a woman, I read these lyrics as a dialogue, perhaps between a man and a woman or between a man and his own conscience. The initial sadness in the song ("Could I be a weeping willow") is countered with modern implements (a truck and an airplane "so I can go flying"). Material items, and ones that heavily index modernity, are suggested as consolation for one's suffering away from home. But the subject of the song returns to sadness in realizing that no one will remember him in "a far away village." He labors with hand and foot for the money to buy accoutrements of a different life and yet his life remains empty. He may have a truck and an airplane but in the process he will be forgotten.

The following flauta genre song was recorded in Toropalca's 1994 Carnival celebrations.

Unay tiemposta yurarini	I remember old times
Soltera kashaspa chayamuni	I arrive as a single woman
Carnavalesta yuyarispa chaya-muni	I arrive remembering Carnival
[repeat]	[repeat]
Kunan tuta tusurisun	"Tonight let's dance
Q'aya día takirisun	Tomorrow let's sing
Watakunapaq	For years
Niñapis kutimusaqchu	I won't return"
Ay, jovencito	Oh, young man
[repeat]	[repeat]

Nostalgia for lost youth pervades this song as a woman remembers when she too was young, single, and potentially able to travel—in seasonal migrations or even to neighboring regions for Carnival celebrations. But within this nostalgia, the song text does not mention specific places. People circulate, and temporarily meet in unnamed places.

In focussing on nostalgia I heed Debbora Battaglia's warning about assigning a negative judgement to indigenous expressions of nostalgia (1995). Rather than criticizing Toropalqueños for their nostalgic discourses, my question focuses on nostalgia's predominance in one place and its relative absence in another. People can feel nostalgia for many different foci: for a geographical place; for an absent loved one; for one's youth; and for one's cultural traditions, which are perceived as waning. In Toropalca all of these kinds of nostalgia—memory trips across different temporalities—crosscut speech, lyrical content, and music performance. But it was precisely the last kind of nostalgia, the longing for a lost culture, that connected the different temporalities involved in these remembrances. This metanostalgia stretched as an umbrella over individual nostalgias, linking the individual experience to a Durkheimian view of Society. Song texts as read within a performance context revealed a conflation of nostalgias—longing for lost/absent youth, lost/absent loved ones, lost/absent lovers, and lost/absent culture—as Toropalqueños imagined their local place and culture in relation to unnamed translocal places, a kind of lament for what was lost as Toropalqueños seasonally, and sometimes permanently, migrated to other places.

The theme of nostalgia commonly emerges in relation to the movement of people and perceived cultural change. According to Alice Bullard, in the nineteenth century nostalgia, identified as a medical disease, was experienced by uprooted individuals living in rapidly changing societies, places on their way to "civilization" (1997: 186–187). Bullard traces the disease of nostalgia to the seventeenth century, but it was in the nineteenth century that the malady became associated with modernization and the increasingly rapid circulation of people through different places; in the dislocatedness of an individual's existence, a lost sense of self brought on the symptoms of nostalgia (1997: 187, 189). According to some authors the present-day sense of nostalgia, while not medically labeled, remains entwined with a sense of what has been lost in the process of modernity. As Malcom Chase and Christopher Shaw claim, "The home we miss is no longer a geographically defined place but rather a state of mind" (1989: 1). As Toropalqueños entered labor situations that required at least temporary movement, their song texts marked the nostalgia for home places, nostalgia for lost youth, and nostalgia for absent loved ones. This nostalgia, unlike Toranzo Roca's nostalgizing for a historical connection to the Chaco War, was carried as a burden by Toropalqueños.

As I already mentioned, the text alone does not make the song. Through informal interviews with women in Toropalca, I recorded songs outside of their ritual context and pursued a clarification of lyrics and their translation. Within these interview contexts the women insisted that these songs, as recorded without the flauta instrument, were not "music." According to speech about these songs, the element that made these genres "music" was the playing of musical instruments apart from the human voice. These flautas were played only by men, many of whom were described as absent from the region. Furthermore, the flauta genre sharply pointed to that local "culture" that was perceived to be involved in an unfortunate disappearing act. Nostalgia in Toroplaca, through its connection to absent kin, provides a strong case for what Marilyn Strathern calls "substantive nostalgia" (1995). "Substantive nostalgia" is based on actual relationships that "constitute the past in the present, the enacting of obligations because a prior relationship exists . . ." (Strathern 1995: 112). According to Strathern, "synthetic nostalgia" more clearly separates the traditional past from the modern present—a separation made possible by an ironic break (1995:111–112). In Toropalca a tragic—rather than ironic—break forms a "substantive nostalgia" for certain personal relationships, as well as a nostalgia for collective cultural representations. Absent fathers, absent sons, absent lovers, absent flauta players, absent social reproducers, and a fear of a vanishing cultural authenticity were all referenced through Toropalca's song performances.

How one experiences nostalgia differs according to where one stands—one's social position, one's power (Stewart 1988: 228). These song performances conjoined diverse nostalgias as felt by all Toropalqueños, vecinos as well as comunarios. A longing for lost culture, if attributed only to vecinos, might be read in terms of Renato Rosaldo's "imperialist nostalgia": colonial officials who long for "the very forms of life they have intentionally altered or destroyed." (1989b: 107). Vecinos have been linked—and often rightly so—with projects of progress and modernization within which indigenous ways of life are perceived as obstacles to such advances. The resulting approach of researchers has often included an implicit value judgement and a tendency to focus on the "good" indigenous cultures, as easily separable from the "bad" vecinos. Many contemporary anthropologists of the Andes have moved away from these dichotomies, some even making the expressions of people in these interstitial categories the very focus of their research.[13] Focussing only on the most "indigenous" cultures and ignoring vecinos' cultural expressions would imply complicity with imperialist nostalgia (see Rosaldo 1989b: 120). To write against this complicity, vecino and comunario cultural expressions should be viewed as a unit—a unit in which unequal power relations have been historically structured, but also a unit in which each individual's position is defined in relation to others who occupy the same geographical space. In the case of Toropalca, I would not apply an interpretation of imperialist nostalgia because during my fieldwork, both comunarios and vecinos expressed nostalgia for lost culture.

In comparison with Yureños, Toropalqueños had relatively fewer connections with the outside world; they made vague references to translocal spaces; they had a relatively weak sense of local indigenous identity; and they expressed nostalgia for lost culture. In the following section I turn to the contrasting case of Yura—where nostalgia was conspicuously absent and where song lyrics referenced specific places of migration.

YUREÑOS' SONGS IN COMPARATIVE PERSPECTIVE

In the next chapter, I will describe in detail Yureño Carnival performances. To briefly summarize, Yureño Carnival music was performed by 4 different troupes of 20 to 30 flauta players, each troupe representing one of Yura's ayllus and each player dressed "as a good Yureño." The imperative here was to sound off through all the spaces of the ayllu. But of significance in this comparative project is the fact that Yura's Carnival music had no lyrics. The notched flute (quena) music of the planting season is one of the few Yureño genres that has lyrics.

In the comparisons I am making in this paper, I am using songs that are performed in two different seasons of the year, two different temporalities in relation to the experience of migration: Carnival, when people are just leaving the area, and the planting season, when people are just arriving from their travels. This seasonal variation alone might explain the difference in lyrical content: the Carnival lyrics about longing and loss, the planting season lyrics about the migration experience itself. A directly parallel comparison of lyrical content is impossible in these contexts because Yureños' Carnival music has no lyrics and Toropalqueños have no planting season songs. Nevertheless, Toropalqueños do have song genres that are performed throughout the winter months—the months of migration and return—and the lyrics of these songs are similarly nostalgic and vague about translocality. I point to the following Toropalqueño song, which was recorded within the ayarachis genre.

Para jina yaku jina	Like rain like water
Sonaririspa	Sounding
Chhika karu llaqtamanta	From a village very far away
Chayakamuyku	We have arrived
[repeat]	[repeat]
Mayustapis, puntastapis	Rivers and hillsides
Wasakurispa	Crossing
Qanta munasqayrayku	Because I love you
Linda cholita[14]	Pretty cholita
[repeat]	[repeat]

Not only do the lyrics of this Toropalqueño song reflect a masculine perspective, but also the performance context of this genre was far more marked by the participation of men, both playing the instruments and singing the songs. But within this masculine perspective the lyrics are equally vague about the translocal: "From a village very far away, we have arrived." I suggest the ayarachis genre as the closest parallel genre with Yura's planting season songs, in terms of both seasonal context and gendered perspective. With this clarification I continue my analysis of Yureños' songs.

The planting season songs of Yura—unlike the song repertoire of Toropalca—described in great specificity people, places, and events beyond the scope of Yureño territory. While they expressed a sense of suffering through travels, Yureño songs were not steeped in nostalgia and their references to absent loved ones were minimal. In Yura those "far away villages" took on specific names in association with detailed references to geographical highpoints, native fauna, coca eradication, international borders, and Bolivia's 1994 World Cup Soccer participation.

Yureños sang these songs within the context of the large planting season in the latter half of October. Those who migrated for the off-season usually returned in August or September to begin preparing the land for planting. Those two weeks in October represented a period of intense agricultural labor, and the heavy workload of this period was managed through a system of labor exchange or *mink'as*. Mink'as were organized by individual families with the goal of sowing all a family's lands in a single day's work. Work during the planting season in Yura operated under the principle of "I work for you, so you in turn will work for me." The family sponsoring the mink'a was expected to provide all workers with corn beer, alcohol, a midday meal, a dinner, and a morning meal the following day. After these immediate obligations, the sponsoring family was then expected to work at the mink'as of the people who worked for them.

Planting tasks were divided by gender: in general, the men plowed and furrowed the fields with oxen; women scattered and covered the seeds. The *dañanes* (men who plowed the fields with oxen) were the composers and musicians of the planting songs—performances that the dañan sang as well as played on a notched flute, with the accompaniment of a small drum.[15] During Carnival, Yureños performed their music in constant movement. In contrast, Yureños' planting season songs were performed from a seated position. Usually one dañan took the lead as the composer of a song, and only a few other dañanes would accompany him. Although this music did not move performatively through space, its lyrics sent imaginations to places far beyond the locale of Yura.

The following Yureña song told of a return from Trinidad, a city in the Department of Beni, a lowland area to the east of La Paz and to the north of Cochabamba (see Figure 5.2).

Trinidad llaqtitaymanta	From the village of Trinidad,
Dañansituy	My dear dañan
Q'ayasilla ? lloqserqamuni	[?] I have left,
Dañansituy	My dear dañan
[repeat]	[repeat]
Leupardu chawpillanta	In between the leopards
Leupardu chawpillanta	In between the leopards,
Dañansituy	My dear dañan
Kay pasaylla pasarqamuni	I passed quickly and stealthily,
Dañansituy	My dear dañan
[repeat][16]	[repeat]

The singer shifted the listener to the lowland environment by mentioning an encounter with leopards, rare dangers through which he "passes quickly and stealthily." The song harked to a male bravado—going out in the world, conquering danger, and returning home triumphant. The

Figure 5.2   The music transcription of "Trinidad," Yura planting season quena huayño, 1995 (transcription by author).

song also suggested the highlanders' perspective of the lowlands. One dañan explained another song about a singing parrot; he made references to these birds of the lowlands and immediately associated the song with forms of dress—past and present, there in the lowlands and here in Yura: "We used to wear unkus [17] here, but now we almost always wear pants. We have become civilized." These references were consistent with a sense of nation that was imagined across a highland/lowland fault line. Stearman discussed the highland/lowland hostilities created around mutual assignation of stereotypes between *kollas* (highlanders, the word "kolla" is from Kollasuyo, the part of the Inca Empire which is today highland Bolivia) and *cambas* (lowlanders) (1985: 20–39). While Stearman's work in Santa Cruz found the contemporary use of the term "camba" to refer primarily to mestizos (1985: 20), an imagining of the lowland indigenous Bolivian was at work in these songs. Yureños, as highlanders, situated themselves vis-à-vis a difference with the lowlands; they perceived the lowlands as wild, untamed, and somehow associated with a "precivilized" state of affairs through which they saw themselves as having already passed. This imagined precivilized state of affairs associated Yureños' past and present with a geographical link between lowland and highland; otherness to being Yureño was expressed both temporally and spatially.[18] The highland/lowland fault line marks

a difference, but one across which Bolivians both designate local differences and narrativize translocal unities.

"In Bolivia, Everything is Etcheverry"

Yureños' planting season songs also took up the subject of national sport.
Bolivia's participation in the 1994 World Soccer Cup Championship held
great significance for Bolivians of different classes, ethnicities, and locations. As an exception, Toropalqueños were the only Bolivians I found to
be rather distanced from the entire affair. Yureños, even a year after the
championship, were still singing about Bolivia's participation; beyond
sports heroes and references to specific games, Bolivia's participation became a temporal reference against which to measure passing time. For example in one Yura planting season song the two lines "After a whole year"
and "Since the World Cup" became interchangeable as temporal points
against which one measured the passing of time. Another Yura planting
season song, toted out again in 1995, referenced the challenge of Bolivia's
first championship match with Germany. They sang: "Mundialmantari
lloqserqakaykU Alemaniawan tinkorqashayku, Dañansitu" (From the
World Cup we left, with Germany we competed, Dear dañan).

Bolivia's first match at the World Cup was against Germany and in relation to this match Bolivians lived and dreamed soccer. With chalk, people in Potosi wrote on their cars imagined scores for the first Bolivian
match (Bolivia 2, Germany 1). Although Bolivia officially lost this soccer
match (1–0), Bolivians claimed the game should have been tied. In iden-
tifying their team as victims of unfair referee's decisions, Bolivians gave
two reasons why the game should have had a different outcome. First,
their team star, Antonio Etcheverry, unjustly received a red card, an extreme assessment of foul play that requires a player to be suspended from
a soccer game. Second, the goal made by Germany was, according to Bolivians, shot from an off-side (*posición adelantada*), and should not have
been counted. In the Bolivian telling, their team could have claimed a victory over Germany if it were not for unfair refereeing. Thus, in spite of official defeat, urban Bolivians celebrated victory in city streets, chanting
"Bolivia campeón, árbitro cabrón" (Bolivia champion, referee cuckold),
and Yureños, even a year later, sang a song about this memorable match
with Germany.

Bolivian pride in World Cup participation was inextricably linked to
their soccer star, Etcheverry. The following Yureño planting season song,
sung again in 1995, honored that hero and linked him to a river in Bolivian territory.

Dale dale	Go! Go!
Etcheverry	Etcheverry
En las orillas	On the banks
Del Río Guadalquivir	Of the Guadalquivir River
[repeat]	[repeat]
Cantaremos bailaremos	We will sing we will dance
En estos días	In these days
De la siembra	Of planting
Todos nos alegraremos	We will all be happy
Al año una vez	At least once a year
[repeat]	[repeat]

Etcheverry as a national soccer hero, symbolically straddled the high-land/lowland fault line. He is from Santa Cruz (in the lowlands), but Bolivian soccer in international competition is, in an ironic way, all about the highlands. That is, Bolivian high altitudes have been used as a comparative advantage when playing foreign teams.[19] But the Yureño explanation of this song brought reference to good work animals and the confluence of Bolivian rivers. As one Yureño explained to me, Etcheverry was equated with someone who did his work well: "One of the dañanes named his work animal 'Etcheverry.' He compared the animal with Etcheverry. One played well, the other worked well." This person has identified this as a song to a work animal, and another planting season Yureño song, not included here, was dedicated to a burro. These songs add another dimension to an entire corpus of songs to animals, as studied by Denise Arnold and Juan de Dios Yapita in the Aymara community of Qaqachaca; they interpreted these songs of the pastoral world as a direct view of the feminine world of work (1998: 25). In contrast, these songs about animals seem to emerge from the male perspective on out-migration and the return to planting season tasks of ploughing and furrowing fields.

In an interview, another Yureño explained: "So all Cochabambinos, Santa Cruceños, Potosinos, all, Paceños, all of us lauded [Etcheverry]. Because he became famous at a world level. . . . So together with this World Cup everything has been Etcheverry; in Bolivia everything is Etcheverry." In this song Yureños also united the soccer star with references to Bolivian river systems. Yura's waters are part of the larger river basin of the Pilcomayo River, which eventually flows into the Plata River. But in the Yureño explanation of the Guadalquivir River reference (a river in Tarija, southeast of Yura), Yureños mentioned the Bermejo and Paraná Rivers and discussed a confluence of these rivers with the waters of Yura. Metaphorically speaking the Yureño singers linked the national soccer star with large connecting river systems, perhaps ones with which Yureños had personal reference through temporary labor migrations, but ones that stood for the unification of many different Bolivian waters. Besides highland/lowland differences and references to Bolivia's World Cup participation, the corpus of Yureño planting songs also included a reference to the Chapare, a major coca-growing region in the department of Cochabamba.

The Politics of Coca in Yura

For Yureños coca leaves are part of daily life. They are chewed on a daily basis in work and meeting contexts and ritually offered to the Pachamama or Mother Earth. While coca is lived in Yura, these daily chewing and ritual uses of coca bring Bolivians in general to reject the international criminalization of the leaf. Since a 1961 international convention, the coca leaf has been classified as a narcotic along with cocaine, thus reaffirming the position of the U.S. government since the 1914 Harrison Act. Through the coca-cocaine entanglement,[20] the war on drugs has consistently been linked to U.S. aid received by Bolivia, putting Bolivian governments between Uncle Sam's pocketbook and the domestic demands of coca growers.

While Yureños live with coca, other Bolivians demonstrate for coca. Foreign pressure creates the context in which coca is demonstrated, most visibly by urban Bolivians, politicians, and coca growers. In 1992, Jaime Paz Zamora, then President of Bolivia, who had been capitulating for some time to the eradication directives of the United States, arrived at a conference in Madrid with a coca leaf on his lapel. Thus Paz Zamora opened his policy of "Coca Diplomacy" with a statement that cocaine was bad, but coca as used traditionally for centuries in the Andes was good. The date of this conference coincided with my first fieldtrip to Bolivia and I immediately noticed the urban fashion of wearing a coca leaf on one's lapel—a lacquered real leaf or a ceramic representation of it. The coca leaf worn on the lapel of a resident of La Paz came to index the ethnic defense of coca, its millenarian tradition, which stood as sufficient reason to strip the plant of its negative connotations, to legalize it in the international sphere. The defense of the coca leaf was constructed through its associations with cultural authenticity. Paz Zamora also declared that the coca leaf was a "national patrimony" of Bolivia, and then it was reasoned: how could *national* patrimony be *internationally illegal?* Coca politics established this line between the internationally illegal and the nationally legal, a line that provided a common point of national identification, as defiant victims stood up to the pressures of a superpower.

In front of television news cameras, coca growers also demonstrated against U.S. eradication pressures. At conferences and dialogues of the coca growers' trade union, participants had cheeks bulging with coca leaves, foregrounding coca through a visible demonstration of its quotidian use; while flagrantly doing the *internationally illegal* in Bolivian national territory, it was shown that coca could not possibly be equivalent to cocaine. These flauntings of coca, based on a defense of respect for cultural differences, outwardly reaffirmed a Bolivian national sovereignty that consistently faced a real threat in the tangled knot of coca-cocaine politics.

Through the performance of this song in Yura, the politics of coca reached far beyond the coca-growing region of the Chapare:

Oh, Chapare llaqtaypi	Oh, in my village of Chapare
Huelgalla guerralla kashan	There is a strike, a war
Chayllaqa munaypaq	I just wanted to be
Maylla kashan	Anywhere but there
[repeat]	[repeat]
Oh, melgaykoqtinku	Oh, when they make furrows
Sonqoy nanarin	My heart aches
Surkaykoqtinku	When they plow
Tinkurqorisun	Let's meet them,
Dañansitu	Dear dañan
[repeat]	[repeat]

The Chapare is approximately a three-day trip from Yura—a trip down in altitude to the warmer regions of Bolivia's varied landscape. The "war" in the Chapare is about eradication of the coca leaf under pressure of the U.S. government, but the song from Yura ends with references to local planting practices. Migration travels brought Yureños into direct contact with the coca-cocaine debate and its demonstration politics in their most overt form: the strike.

The song speaks of the war or strike in "my town" of the Chapare. In Quechua the "y" after "*llaqta*" (village) shows personal possession. Although the singer is from Yura he has already taken on the Chapare as his own village, almost in a sense of endearment. The second phrase speaks of the planting activities during which the singer will remember the conflict he has encountered in the Chapare. But the planting season is also a time to reunite with other Yureños; the planting season also means homecoming, meeting family, friends, and earth deities in the fields. The song itself embodies this ambiguity of remembered suffering and the present joy of coming home.

When I asked the composer of this song to explain his composition, I received a very deliberate speech, a performance in and of itself. I had turned off my tape recorder and as I pushed "record" he asked "¿Ya estoy comunicando?" ("Am I communicating yet?"). He knew he was not simply explaining this song to a curious *gringa* anthropologist in Yura; he was conscious of communicating to a much wider audience through an anthropologist, who also happened to be from the United States.

He explained his song in Spanish, pausing almost in a way that one might read poetry. "I have suffered so long in Chapare in Cochabamba. When we were in the Chapare, in Cochabamba, a strike was made with the United States. The United States had come to the [coca growers] with an eradication. But now, for so long we have done [it] and nothing has happened, but we are—we are just peacefully here . . . in Bolivia." He added the "in Bolivia" after a long pause. The recorded interlude ended with a community member shouting "Union Chullpa," a reference to the local community of the particular planting party in Yura. Through their translocal movements Yureños constructed an idea of being Bolivian and at the same time they reaffirmed themselves in their local identity. The local and translocal identities juxtaposed themselves in this speech as the singer clearly identified the external power against which an idea of "Bolivia" was locally performed. As Bolivians contested U.S.–imposed eradication policies, the politics of coca continued to occupy a central position in nationalist perceptions.

MODERNITY, NOSTALGIA, AND IMAGINED COMMUNITIES

The corpus of songs from both Yura and Toropalca reflected interiorized relations with the natural environment, ties not unlike what Denise Arnold and Juan de Dios Yapita, in their analysis of songs from Qaqachaka, identify through the term *terreno* (terrain), something known from the position of insider, as opposed to *paisaje* (landscape), something that is appreciated by an outsider (1998: 30). Sounding rain, weeping willows, hills, rivers, and mountain peaks mark the interiorized relation to a natural environment in both Yureño and Toropalqueño songs. The similarities end with the songs' references to translocal places, places to which Yureños and Toropalqueños refer from the position of outsiders. Why are Yura's song texts so specific about translocal places while Toropalca's song texts are so vague? In Toropalca vagueness, like an emptiness, is filled with nostalgia while nostalgia is conspicuously absent in Yura. The differences may stem in part from the distinctly gendered perspectives of the songs:

masculine and feminine takes on the experience of temporary out-migration. This divergence in lyrical content and gendered perspectives is related to the different ways in which Toropalqueños and Yureños have been traversed by modernization, modernity, and the modern.

Néstor García Canclini, like Habermas (1987) and Harvey (1989), has distinguished between modernity, modernization, and modernisms: modernity is a historical period; modernization consists of the socioeconomic processes that construct modernity; and modernisms are the experimentally renovating cultural projects that accompany modernization (García Canclini 1992a: 19). García Canclini proposes the hypothesis that, "the *uncertainty* about the meaning and value of modernity derives not only from what separates nations, ethnic groups, and classes, but also from the sociocultural hybrids in which the traditional and the modern are mixed" (1995: 2, emphasis in original).[21] In reference to the cases of Yura and Toropalca the very categories of "modern" and "traditional" are productions of modernity, leading to seemingly paradoxical statements like: Yureños act more traditional because they live in a place more profoundly traversed by the modern. Anthony Giddens constructs an argument about modernity in terms of space and place: "The advent of modernity increasingly tears space away from place by fostering relations between 'absent' others, locationally distant from any given situation of face-to-face interaction. In conditions of modernity, place becomes increasingly *phantasmagoric:* that is to say, locales are thoroughly penetrated by and shaped in terms of social influences quite distant from them" (1990: 18, emphasis in original). Giddens names three processes of modernity that result from this dynamic separation of space and place: "disembedding" (uprooting and replanting of social relations after a space/time movement), "gearing mechanisms" for "rationalized organization" (nation-states, bureaucracies, etc.), and a reflexivity made possible by radical historicity (historical consciousness that shapes present and future actions) (1990: 20–38). While these three characteristics pervade modernity, the cases of Yura and Toropalca indicate two alternative modern dynamics of space and place. Yura, as a place more profoundly marked by external influences and modern conveniences, is far from phantasmagoric. External penetration, rather than erasing local differences, seems to have heightened resolution on views of local and translocal places. In contrast Toropalca seems more phantasmagoric and has been subject to relatively less external penetration.

These comparative cases underline the paradoxes of modernity, the ways in which the "traditional" takes on a profile precisely in relation to the "modern." We might say that Yureños are more touched by modernization, more self-reflectively indigenous—*a la* Giddens' "radical historicity"—and less likely to express nostalgia for lost cultural authenticity, while Toropalqueños are less touched by modernization, less self-reflectively indigenous, and very likely to have multiple ways of expressing nostalgia for their loss of cultural authenticity. With this comparison it becomes problematic to view nostalgia as a symptom of what is lost through the processes of modernity. Toropalqueños attributed their loss of culture to labor migrations and competing religious communities, but Yureños, who have limited expressions of nostalgia, have been subjected to the same labor migrations and competing religious communities, plus a few other processes (ethnographic gazes, NGO interventions, modern conveniences). Yureños experienced these processes without expressing feelings of cultural loss. Much like the marked *lack* of anguish over cultural loss that Olivia Harris describes in her work on Northern Potosi (1995: 106), in Yura nostalgia was relatively rare in local discourse. These two cases, both within the realm of modernity, demonstrate at least two different local identification styles produced within a single nation-state: romantic, tragic, and rigidly defined in Toropalca; ironic and flexible in Yura. Irony prevails when Yureños dress "as good Yureños" during Carnival and refer to this form of dress as "precivilized" in another context. Tragedy prevails when Toropalqueños perceive that there are no men to make "the music."

Toropalqueños imagined their present local place through—to borrow from Michael Herzfeld—"structural nostalgia," as lacking from some pristine original state (1997: 22, 109); their imagined community was based on longing for what was perceived as irreversibly sullied. Toropalqueños' expressions of nostalgia paralleled the Australian Aboriginal melancholic subject as described by the anthropologist, Elizabeth Povenelli (1999). The authentic Australian aboriginal is defined by non-Aboriginal Australians such that this authenticity should be pursued even though it can never be fully restored. This leaves "non-Aboriginal Australians [to] enjoy ancient traditions while suspecting the authenticity of the Aboriginal subject, [and] Aboriginal Australians enjoy[ing] their traditions while suspecting the authenticity of themselves" (Povenelli 1999: 31). Toropalqueños suspected the authenticity of themselves and participated in the narrative that painted them as melancholic subjects. Yureños, on the other hand, did not long for their own lost authenticity; instead they manipulated this narrative with a touch of irony—consciously moving in and out of being dressed "as good Yureños."

Yureños imagined their local community through references to translocality and otherness, specificity at home leading to specificity about otherness. Toropalqueños vaguely sang about being in a far away village while Yureños named those far away villages, mentioning their characteristics of otherness. Here we have an implosion of Marshall

Sahlin's model of the island culture reproducing itself in translocal places (lecture at Cornell University anthropology colloquium 1997); Yureños came home having ingested translocal experiences into their bodies and practices. The otherness through which Yureños reflected on their own local identity was also the means by which they identified with more encompassing communities beyond Yura—imagined communities through which highland/lowland divides, soccer stars, and coca politics provided master tropes by which Yureños identified themselves as part of a Bolivian national community.

Taking song in its totality has opened up questions of different gendered views of temporary out-migration, and in the case of Toropalca, it has placed women at the center of music performance. Women played a predominant role in the composition and singing of Toropalca's Carnival music, even if they did not consider their song to be "music" without the presence of men to play the flautas. In contrast, the women in Yura seemed to be involved in performance at the level of dance movement, leaving the production of sound and lyrics as an entirely masculine sphere. I prefer not to read into these gendered differences the trite narratives of women maintaining tradition in the face of modernity. The gendered dynamics of music performance and modernity are far too complex to be encompassed by this romantic narrative of the soon-to-disappear native. Besides, one of my points is precisely to view both cases as distinct examples of peripheral modernities.

The contrasts between Toropalca and Yura suggest that the nation-state as an organizational form produces contrasting, even contradictory, forms of modernity. In spite of the evidence that points to a neat model, I still argue that no single interpretive model will suffice to explain the various ways that modernity is locally experienced. Modernity, ever fragmentary, does not even respect its own history (Harvey 1989). Nostalgia for any kind of authenticity is a repetitive theme in questions of modernity. Rey Chow remarks on Benjamin's nostalgia within the dawning of the Age of Mechanical Reproduction: "Benjamin is at once nostalgic about the aura and enchanted by its loss. While aura represents art's close relation with the community that generates it, the loss of aura is the sign of art's emancipation into mass culture, a new collective culture of 'collectibles'" (Chow 1994: 139). In chapter seven, I will explore my own complicity in a mechanically produced project that moved the music of these cultures toward a "collectible" status, and in the process, authorship, creatorship, and ultimately ownership, took center stage. In closing, I mention a trip to Bolivia in the summer of 1997. A Bolivian applied anthropologist, working with an NGO, had taken up residence in the village of Toropalca. On this trip Toropalqueños talked to me more about ayllus than they ever had when I was previously working there. When I asked how they knew these things about the ayllus, a woman—one of the best singers in Toropalca—said, "The anthropologist told us, but I also remember it all from when I was a child. Maybe now with the ayllus Toropalca can go forward [*salir adelante*]."

In the next chapter, I will explore the ritual reproduction of Yura's ayllus through the music of Carnival and through the bureaucracy of the state. Yureños did not assume their cultural authenticity as a burden, but neither was this authenticity served up easily to the state in credible forms. At certain stages of this process, Yureños carried the burden of proof.

CHAPTER 6

SONOROUS SOVEREIGNTY

During the Carnival tour Yureños never hurried.[1] When people told me about the tour, I had originally feared physical exhaustion from walking. But my own exhaustion stemmed more from the apparently slow progress toward the village of Yura. The flauta troupe might spend two or three hours in a single house before continuing the tour to another house. In the morning hours, the tour moved along, but as the level of inebriation rose throughout the day, the length of time spent in each house increased. The importance of time dwindled when faced with the task of sonorously filling space. Our only spacetime (Munn 1986: 10) obligation was to be in the village of Yura for Ash Wednesday, but any unvisited area of the ayllu could also be toured after that day. Carnival season in Yura extended from the Thursday before Carnival, *Jueves de Comadres* (Thursday of Comothers), to *Domingo de Tentaciones* (Sunday of Temptations) and beyond, in all about a two-week period beginning the Thursday before Ash Wednesday and continuing until the Sunday after Ash Wednesday. Yureños told me that Carnival only ends when the corn beer, or chicha, is gone; chicha cannot be stored and must be consumed within about a week after it is made.

During the entire tour, whenever the musicians moved through space they were playing the flauta. As I hobbled along the edges of hillsides, trying to maintain what felt like a precarious balance between my heavy backpack and the pull of gravity toward the river below, everyone else in the troupe insisted on playing the flauta as they walked. If a silence crept into the tour in a moment of exhaustion, someone protested, "We can't *just walk* to the next community. This is Carnival. Even if we are tired we have to *play as we walk.*" The preferred performance practice of playing as one moved through space[2] connected people dwelling in disparate places to a common social space. The flauta music of Yura was never played standing still, but rather was played, as well as danced, in constant movement. Playing as one walked, marking the social space of the ayllu through sonorous and kinesthetic dance performance—this was the Yureño groove, the experientially authentic moment. While this experiential authenticity established ties between Yureños and the places they considered to be part of their ayllus, this sonorous sovereignty, as I call it, eluded representational forms, which were necessary as Yureños resituated themselves as an indigenous group under the Law of Popular Participation (1994). This law was supposed to recognize existing indigenous organizations, and was an initiative to decentralize municipal decision-making processes. Carnival rituals established one relation to Yureño places, but bureaucratic interactions in the application of this law, what Michael Herzfeld calls "rituals of state" (1992),[3] established a relation to Yureño places that depended on a representation of cultural and historical authenticity.

While the rituals associated with the Law of Popular Participation sought to map ethnic identities within discrete territories, the ethnic identities that emerged from the rituals of Carnival had more to do with moving music and people—sounds as well as those who produced and heard them—through meaningful spaces. Domain over place in the case of Carnival depends on performing and listening individuals, a dependence on subjectivities that prioritized people and centerpoints over margins or limits of territory. The rituals of state, as viewed through the implementation of this law, attempted to establish domain over the same place through mapping activities that emphasized visually represented contiguous territorial unities and the limits of those territories. Rather than positioning these two sets of rituals as Andean (Carnival) and Western (state bureaucracy), with the tired series of dualisms that implicitly follows (indigenous/Spanish, resisting/dominating), I underline the way Yureños, within different temporal frameworks, were involved in both sets of rituals. Through this ethnographic material, the existence of multiple belongings emerges as a problematic condition for implementing any model of representative democracy. While the rituals of Carnival more successfully worked through the ambiguities of multiple belongings, both the music of Carnival and the language of bureaucracy attempted to tie down fluid processes of identification.[4] When local bureaucrats challenged Yureño claims as an indigenous group, demanding an official statement of their cultural authenticity, Yureños recurred to the new Ministry of Ethnic, Gender, and Generational Affairs. When bureaucrats of this centralized entity justified their support for the Yureño claim, they cited the book of anthropologist Roger Rasnake (1989). Yureños participated in both sets of rituals—of Carnival and of the Bolivian state—and in their relationship to the state, Yureños were drawn into the representational practices necessitated by the pursuit of cultural authenticity.

A PLACE CALLED "YURA"

"Yura," as many "practiced places" (de Certeau 1984: 117), is a canton, a village, a set of ayllus, a set of communities, and a *reducción* (resettlement). For the benefit of colonial taxation and control, in the second half of the sixteenth century the Viceroy Toledo reorganized Andean indigenous settlements into reducciones. Ethnohistorians identify Yura as one of three Wisiqsa reducciones (Yura, Toropalca, and Caiza), and the Wisiqsas were thought to have comprised one of several pre-conquest indigenous groups organized under the rubric of the "Charcas Confederation" (see Rasnake 1989: 92–99). Today the identification of Yura as a Wisiqsa reducción or as part of the ancient Charcas Confederation represents a discourse of anthropologists and ethnohistorians, rather than a discourse of Yureños. I might suggest that these are the "fictions" of ethnohistorians in the Geertzian sense of something made or something fashioned (1973: 15), but this word still carries an accusation of falsity that Geertz so much wanted to avoid. To evade the essentializing nature of presenting this as "pure fiction" (see Herzfeld 1992: 49), I simply suggest that Wisiqsa reducciones are discussed by ethnohistorians, but they remain absent from the daily discussions of Yureños. If Yureños talk at all about being "Wisiqsas"—which I have not yet heard them do—it may be a direct result of the ethnohistorical teachings that a local nongovernmental organization (NGO) is conducting in the area, with the use of Roger Rasnake's ethnography (1989).[5]

The senses of belonging experienced by Yureños must be viewed in conjunction with a discussion of the activities of the local NGO, ISALP (Social Research and Legal Assistance, Potosí, *Investigación Social y Asesoramiento Legal Potosí*). ISALP, active in Yura for over 12 years, has been committed to improving Yureños' standard of living by strengthening local indigenous organizations (ayllus). Composed of a multidisciplinary technical team of engineers and social scientists, ISALP organized and sponsored ayllu meetings, and within these contexts ISALP played a key role in interpreting for Yureños the potential power granted to indigenous organizations through the Law of Popular Participation. Predating the work of ISALP, a group of Catholic priests worked in Yura under principles of liberation theology. The work of ISALP was rooted in these Catholic origins of social commitment and, in 1995, the parish continued to coordinate activities with the technical team. As part of its activities, ISALP used Rasnake's ethnohistory and ethnography of Yura—published in Spanish in Bolivia—to encourage Yureños in a process of reappropriating their own history from the archival and interpretive work of this anthropologist.[6] The politically committed work of this NGO cannot be overlooked when considering how Yureños felt themselves to be part of an ayllu and how they negotiated their position in relation to this new legislation.

The work of ISALP should also be considered within the general mushrooming of NGOs in Bolivia. According to Thomas Kruse (1994), this phenomenon in Bolivia was associated with several national shifts of the 1980s: structural adjustment, privatization, and return to democratic rule. The increasing number of NGOs was symptomatic of changes occurring in nation-states throughout Latin America: downsizing of the state apparatus, emphasis on participatory citizenship, blurring the boundaries between state and non-state entities, and a discursive promotion of citizenship via constituencies (indigenous, gendered, etc.; see also Alvarez, Dagnino, and Escobar 1998). While the NGO world used to be more clearly defined as a leftist field of political action and as against repressive states, NGOs now come in all political flavors. In the midst of the motley politics of NGOs, ISALP continued to locate its politics on the left, even rejecting suggestions of particular funding sources on the basis of their own politics, and not without a touch of anti-Yankee imperialism. For example, I once suggested the possibility of submitting a grant proposal to the Inter-American Foundation (IAF) which had funded the music workshop. The idea was politely dismissed by members of ISALP because the IAF received part of its funding directly from the U.S. government. Alternatively, Danish international cooperation had recently entered Bolivia in a big way, and ISALP's mode of work in Yura was held up as the model that the Danish cooperation wanted to support. While they worried about the problems of increasing the scale of their activities, ISALP did not reject the Danish funds, which were to support the Yureño model of work in other areas of Potosi.

While ISALP's work in Yura focused on Yura-as-ayllu, for Yureños the term "Yura" referred simultaneously to a village, a canton, and an ayllu. The canton Yura is a political division of the Bolivian state with legal recognition since 1863 and borders that approximate the *mojones* (boundary stones) of the large ayllu Yura. "Yura" is also the capital village of the canton Yura, as well as the ritual centerpoint of the large ayllu Yura. The ayllu, as a basic social structure in the Andes, is classically described as a nested set of moieties (moiety referring generally to a system of dual descent groups). But other characteristics of this organizational form prove more salient in a discussion of local-state interactions. As

Frank Salomon has emphasized with reference to Karen Spalding's work, an ayllu is "a concept of relatedness" and it "has no inherent limits of scale" (Salomon 1991: 22). Thus, reference to ayllu identification often shifts according to a speaker's context and audience (Allen 1988; Urton 1984: 39). For example, in the city of Potosi a woman from Yura may say she is from the ayllu Yura, but within Yura she may specify that she is from the ayllu Chiquchi. The large ayllu Yura is segmented into four principal ayllus—two of *Anansaya* (the upper half), named Qullana and Wisiqsa, and two of *Urinsaya* (the lower half), named Qhurqa and Chiquchi.[7] Within a meeting of the ayllu Chiquchi, she may make reference to the minor ayllu of which she is a member. Ayllus often do not form discrete territorial groups (see Platt 1986: 231). Membership in one of the four principal ayllus was determined by membership in minor ayllus, and membership in these was determined by where one owned land, with the distinct possibility that individuals might own land in more than one ayllu. The duties required of ayllu membership centered around a system of authorities that rotated responsibilities among its members. The kuraqas were the principal indigenous authorities of the ayllu, one representing each of the four ayllus. In 1995, the large ayllu Yura had no overarching authority beyond these kuraqas, a fact that became relevant during one stage of the initial implementation of the Law of Popular Participation.

Outside of the contexts of Carnival and the Fiesta of Kings (January 6)—the two rituals of ayllu authorities—the ayllu authorities and organizations, although discursively exalted, often occupied positions of secondary importance to the more immediate issues of the community. Through organizations in their place of residence—the community—Yureños addressed irrigation canal maintenance, loose animals, potable water, annual planting, and water distribution. Although the technical team of ISALP attempted to push the apparently symbolic role of the ayllus' kuraqas into a more active position, projects generally were undertaken at the community level, and this was generally the practical level at which a consensus had to be reached for Yureños to work on a project.

ISALP worked at a community level but their process of intervention began at the ayllu level. With funding from Oxfam America, ISALP sponsored at least one annual ayllu meeting each year—one for each of the four principal ayllus—as well as trimonthly meetings of the large ayllu Yura. In these meetings the kuraqas, to varying degrees depending on their leadership skills, assumed an authority that extended beyond merely the symbolic. While some activities at these meetings were self-reflective in nature—about the ayllus, the kuraqas, and Yureño culture in general—the assessment of needs and the targeting of specific projects to specific communities were standing agenda items of all meetings. These projects, though discussed under the authority of the ayllu's kuraqa, were generally implemented at the level of individual communities.[8] Kuraqas were assuming greater roles, but the community level remained vital in addressing local problems.

Members of the ayllu Yura interacted with authorities of the canton Yura and the village Yura, but outside of ritual moments, when such exchanges were symbolically negotiated, hierarchical distinctions on the basis of racial and ethnic categories often left the ayllu members in subordinate positions vis-à-vis vecinos. Vecinos in Yura did not identify with the ayllu; they usually engaged in commerce and entertained aspirations of "urbanization" and "modernization" for the village (also see Rasnake 1989: 44). Vecinos usually held local appointed and political positions in Yura. The *corregidor,* appointed by the state with the support of the vecino population in the village Yura, was the principal authority of the canton. His duties encompassed dispute settlement in the entire canton. But his authority over Yureños was mediated by two other authorities: *kamachis* and assistant corregidores. The kamachis or *alcaldes* of the ayllus, chosen by the kuraqas, were supposed to work with both the corregidor and kuraqas to symbolically mediate between state and ayllu authorities (also see Rasnake 1989: 66–87). In the context of community assemblies, an assistant corregidor was elected to serve as the voice of the community in interactions with the corregidor of the canton.

It is important to remember that Yureños moved through the space of these different socialized entities—ayllus, communities, villages, and cantons—and conducted significant interactions with the institutional representatives of ISALP.

The Tour:
Sonorously Practiced Space

A Yureño locality as constructed in Carnival rituals depended on the people, the centers, and the multiple sensory experiences of that ritual "spacetime" (Munn 1986). Anthropological research has frequently dealt with the socialization of space in terms of specific places through which an individual moves during a lifetime (Rosaldo, R. 1980: 136), as well as in terms of moving in processes of exchange (Munn 1986: 268). In interpreting Yureño senses of place as experienced through Carnival, Nancy Munn's concept of "spacetime" proves useful in its incorporation of the temporal and intersubjective nature of all social practices: People do not simply move through time and space, rather in the process of moving they constitute a spacetime that articulates a relation between people and a relation between people and places (1986: 8–11). A significant organizing agent in constructing the spacetime of Carnival was the kuraqa's tour. When Carnival became a topic of conversation, someone always made reference to the kuraqa's tour with a series of comments about what was supposed to occur. The Carnival tour is supposed to take the kuraqa through the space of his entire ayllu, reaching the furthest boundary stones of this socialized space. He is supposed to be accompanied by his alcalde or kamachi, the ayllu authority chosen by the kuraqa, and the "commissioned one," an individual who is assigned the task of safely transporting the kinsa rey or wooden staff of authority. Both the kuraqa and kamachi are supposed to be positions fulfilled by a man and woman together (qhari/warmi). These authorities are supposed to travel with a troupe of ten to twenty young men, playing the flauta. During the tour the kuraqa is supposed to visit all households considered to be within the ayllu, gathering these people into his entourage as he continues toward the village Yura. The kuraqa is supposed to arrive in the village of Yura on Ash Wednesday for the entrada (ritual entrance). On Friday the kuraqa is supposed to leave with his troupe, continuing to visit the rest of his ayllu before returning home.

Scholarship on the Andes has often used the pilgrimage as illustrative of the way local, regional, and national spaces are connected through ritual practices. Authors may read the ritually constructed space of pilgrimage as recovered sacred space, somewhat beyond state control (Sallnow 1987: 269), or as a space that, through pilgrims' movements, becomes more integrated within larger regional systems (Poole 1991: 334). Nevertheless, the pilgrimage generally aims to go beyond the limits of a locality while the Carnival rituals of Yura aim only to go as far as the limits of a locality, and to then turn around and focus inward—the centerpoint, in practice, taking priority over the limits. Sarah Radcliffe's description of a Carnival limit-marking tour in a Peruvian community provides a more suitable contrasting case; in this case the boundary markers, visited and sacralized with formal speeches, are definitely the focus of this tour (1990). But common to both this Peruvian Carnival tour and the Yureño one is the focus on the subjectivities within that space.[9]

When one considers the settlement patterns of Yureños, the kuraqa's Carnival tour looms large in its physical and temporal demands. The people who considered themselves part of the ayllu Yura (approximately 7,200 inhabitants) lived in communities spread out over approximately 2,000 square kilometers in four river valleys (Yura, Tika Tika, Taru, and San Juan). Within single communities, Yureños might identify with two or more of Yura's four principal ayllus. When I asked people to which ayllu they belonged, I received complex responses. Some would say they were from the ayllu of Yura. When I asked them to specify with which of the principal ayllus—Wisiqsa, Qullana, Chiquchi, or Qhurqa—they identified, some Yureños evaded the question. Others responded with details of one parent belonging to one ayllu, the other to another. They usually ended up talking about their land: that they had a piece of land in this river valley and another piece in the valley over the hill, and so on. At the root of this ambiguity are concepts of space and identity. Yureño residence is not necessarily isomorphic with the geographical space of their respective ayllu. Beyond quotidian ambivalence in an individual's ayllu identification, this relation to space created links between people who lived in dispersed places. Nevertheless, some of this discursive ambivalence of daily ayllu identification vanished during the 1995 ritual performances of Carnival.

On Ash Wednesday and the following Carnival days spent in the village Yura, during the day women danced into the village plaza with a particular ayllu, even if at night these distinctions faded as women danced circles around the competing flauta troupes. In contrast there was little doubt about the respective ayllu identifications of the four troupes of musicians and their kuraqas. The music performed, the kuraqas, as well as the troupes of flauta players, represented the four different ayllus within Yura, divisions that blended into each other during the remainder of the year. The bigendered authority system usually sent wives to accompany their kuraqa or kamachi husbands, but the kuraqa's musical Carnival tour was principally a male domain. While Yureños talked about positions of authority being jointly held by a man and his wife (qhari/warmi), during Carnival the kuraqa and the symbolic elements related to the musical tour were male gendered in association: the staff of authority (only permitted to be carried by men), the kuraqa's musicians, and the flauta instrument. The female gendered domain was also present at Carnival, most prominently in the making of chicha, the display of a woman's woven productions, and the dancing around the competing flauta players. Nevertheless, while the women of the four ayllus danced together around the *rollo*—a single wide pillar in the center of the main plaza[10]—it was precisely the male gendered domains that musically fixed the four different ayllu identities, even if they succeeded in doing so only for a temporary period. Musical pieces and the kuraqas they were to accompany marked and differentiated the four ayllus of Yura during Carnival.

As a general rule women did not play the flauta in Yura. In 1995, few women accompanied the kuraqa's Carnival tour, although they certainly were present in the households that received the travelers. As a gringa in Yura, I was already an anomaly and my attempts at playing the flauta with ayllu Chiquchi extended from this irregular position. My anomalous situation as a gringa, outsider, and woman playing flauta added an element of prestige for the troupe I accompanied, and members of other ayllus disappointedly asked me why I did not play the flauta with their ayllu. Similar to the experiences that Thomas Turino noted in his work in Peru with Puneños (1993a: 73), when I entered Yura on Ash Wednesday, playing the flauta with ayllu Chiquchi, my participation seemed to be considered an added advantage for that ayllu, overlooking my position as woman, and ignoring any considerations of my actual music performance skills. Nevertheless, musical movement through the space of the ayllu during Carnival was an activity of male gendered domains and I had crossed over to that domain for the duration of the ritual.

As I have remarked, what caught my attention during the kuraqa's Carnival tour was the way everyone moved through these spaces *while playing the flauta.* Even inside each house the musicians would dance in a circle as they played. An earthen jar of chicha and a glass bottle of cane alcohol, offered by the house hosts, became the centerpoint of the circle in which the musicians played and danced. To the dismay of any women present, the musicians almost always mixed the chicha and alcohol together. Women spent two to three days making chicha, and their efforts seemed to vanish before their eyes as they watched the musicians combine it with cane alcohol. The musicians preferred the more intoxicating mixture, and under its influence musicians only stopped moving when they stopped playing.

Few were the moments of silence in Yureño Carnival. Upon entering a house a moment of silence was observed, with hats off, as the kuraqa offered coca leaves and libations to the ritual table, which was usually covered with corn stalks—auspicious signs of the coming harvest. During this silence the kuraqa and his kamachi also conducted a *ch'alla* (the ritual sprinkling of alcohol) at the corners and doorways of the house. Each member of the troupe gave the same ritual offerings before beginning to play again. Yureños stopped playing music to eat whenever a house would offer soup and *ch'arki* (dried meat)—something usually only expected in the morning hours. As the last light of day vanished, the sonorous tour continued in the dark until we arrived at a house that could receive some 25 people for a restless night of sleep. Outside of these selective moments of relative silence, continuous music performance was a valued part of the kuraqa's tour.

COMPETING REFRAINS

The boundary stones of the ayllu were a focus of concern at several non-ritualized moments during 1995, and to settle disputes the kuraqas had to travel to these limit markers. Nevertheless, in the Carnival tour I accompanied, the kuraqa did not visit the ayllu's boundary stones, a fact that did not seem to concern the members of the tour. In a prioritization of "supposed tos," this activity fell after those of visiting each household and meeting the other ayllus in Yura on Ash Wednesday. During this temporary privileging of the center over the limits, the four ayllus of Yura did not harmoniously unite, each identity ceding space and time to the performance of the other. Yureño identities as performed in Carnival were produced through competition—not over borders, but over music as focused on hearing subjects and the ritual center of the ayllus. Fierce competitions boiled between the four ayllus of Yura as well as beneath the recognizable unity of these four troupes.

The competition between the four ayllus began with the ritual entrance on Ash Wednesday. The ayllus arrived in the village of Yura, everyone dressed "as a good Yureño" (*como buen yureño*)—an expression Yureños used to refer to the wearing of native dress. During most of the Chiquchi tour, young men wore jeans and T-shirts; but before entering the village Yura they all changed into their "good Yureño" clothes. Each of the four ayllus entered the village plaza from "their" respective corners. A few men put away the flauta to dance as condors, pumas, or condor *umas*. A condor uma was a hollow wood-framed obelisk, about three times as tall as the man who danced with it. Bright-colored yarn and fabric appliqués decorated the sides of the obelisk and the effigy of a condor's head perched on its highest point. In spite of its weight and odd shape, men danced with these phallic structures, moving them up and down, stabbing the air. The men who danced as condors attached condor wings to their arms and donned sunglasses to affect the beady eyes of a bird. The puma dancers draped the animal's skin over their backs. Both the condor and puma dancers carried colorful appliquéd cloth banners over their backs. The appliqués of all these figures included *ñawis* (eye-motifs), snakes, lions, Argentine flags, Bolivian flags, condors, mirrors, and jungle scenes. Sometimes the appliqué consisted of a colorful beach towel, pasted to a section of the condor uma. These male dancers led the ayllu into the village, followed by young women dancing with flags. As each troupe proceeded around the plaza to finish at the centerpoint of the rollo, the dance movements were understated, and the more significant movement was the connection between dancers as they moved in a braided pattern.

At night the visually stimulating condors, pumas, and condor umas were put to rest. Evenings in Yura were all about competing sounds. Around the rollo all four ayllus played at once, each ayllu trying to outplay the others. The result was a cacophony of flauta sounds. In encompassing circles, moving in the opposite direction as the flauta troupes,

women danced in tiny side steps while holding hands. Their dance movements were entirely through the feet, with hips, head, and shoulders facing the center of the circle. Unlike the flauta troupes, at night the women
did not distinguish themselves as being from one of the competing ayllus.
In fact, they had to dance to the music of all of the ayllus, each troupe fading in and out as they worked their way around the rollo. The sonorous
and kinesthetic experience might be likened to dancing to a radio, tuned
to a frequency that was simultaneously picking up the broadcasts of four
different, yet similar, pieces of music.

While many flauta players drifted off to dance cumbias in house parties, the musical competition at the rollo continued until one ayllu was left
alone, playing its emblematic tune or *huayño*. The next day people would
talk about which ayllus had the best music, usually commenting on which
ayllu they had heard playing alone during the early morning hours. Since
the plaza was relatively empty at this time, people usually spoke about this
from an auditory rather than a visual memory. The practice of ritual competitions in the Andes, with no official winners (see Platt 1986: 240;
Turino 1993a: 66), allows discursive room to maneuver when commenting on the competition. Anyone can claim victory and one can declare different winners in different contexts, depending on the audience.

Just as the unity of Yura was ritually reenacted each year through a competitive musical process, the four principal ayllus internally underwent similar processes of musical competition. In 1995 the musical unity of ayllu
Chiquchi was anything but a given. Two troupes of flauta players had
formed in representation of ayllu Chiquchi: one that accompanied the kuraqa and one that accompanied the kamachi. A fight broke out between the
two groups of musicians because one group refused to play the huayños of
the other group. The two groups began to play against each other, each
group performing a different huayño. Although an ayllu has many different
huayños, each with an individual composer, only one huayño is used as the
emblematic piece of the ayllu when they enter Yura to play against the other
ayllus. As one young composer told me: "If you want your huayño played in
the entrada in [the village] Yura, you have to be in the tour from its start.
You have to teach everyone else your huayño. You have to make sure it gets
played over and over again, so it sounds strong." During the tour, the composer would await the hint of a pause after innumerable repetitions of one
huayño. He pounced on the suggestion of silence with the opening notes of
his own tune, stressing every note in exaggeration, hoping the other musicians would join him. They usually did. Although the choice of one huayño
over another brought no official fame to the composer, he was quietly acknowledged in post-Carnival discussions. The musicians nonverbally chose
the emblematic piece to represent the ayllu; no official vote was taken, but

rather the piece was chosen through music performance—what sounded strongest for the entire ensemble. What sounded the strongest after several days of celebration was usually the piece that had been played most frequently. In 1995, ayllu Chiquchi chose the huayño that even I, in my novice status, had been able to learn in its entirety.

The earlier dispute among Chiquchi musicians led to the exclusion of one group's pieces from possible consideration as the ayllu's emblematic piece. The excluded group consisted of those musicians who had originally accompanied the kuraqa; they lived near the community in which the kuraqa resided while the other musicians lived near Thauro, the residence of the kamachi. The schism ran deep during the entire tour, to the extent that in the initial entrance to Yura, the kuraqas of Chiquchi and Qhurqa had exchanged places, and some of Chiquchi's musicians were playing with ayllu Qhurqa. The volatility of ayllu identity seemed to exemplify the risk involved in all performances (see Schieffelin 1998: 198).

Depending on the context, ayllu identification might be ambiguous for many, but it was far from ambiguous for the kuraqas. The switch of the kuraqas was disapprovingly noted by many people. Only in the relative sobriety of the next morning did the kuraqas return to the flauta troupes of their respective ayllus. In contrast, the musicians who had shifted ayllus simply played upon ambiguous ayllu identifications, some remaining with Qhurqa and others continuing with Chiquchi. The kuraqa, as the principal authority of the ayllu, remained a fixed sign of the ayllu, with ambiguity only entering over time when the individual was no longer kuraqa.

The kuraqa and his music were involved in fixing ayllu identities. When I first heard the huayños of the four ayllus of Yura, they all sounded the same. But through careful listening I consciously learned to identify particular huayños with their respective ayllus. These pieces have no lyrics. Furthermore, Yureños tend to individually purchase their flauta instruments from a single artisan. This eliminates sonorous distinctions we might attribute to different instrument makers or to the distinct sound of a group of instruments purchased as a collective troupe.[11] The huayños were thus linked to a particular ayllu through melodic structure and motifs. During Carnival, in the presence of contextual and multisensorial clues, I heard several Yureños identify and label a huayño as being from one of the four ayllus: Qullana, Wisiqsa, Qhurqa, or Chiquchi. But in listening to cassette recordings of these same huayños, at another time of the year, outside the context of Carnival, the Yureños I informally interviewed could not or would not make these distinctions. Most people said the huayños were from the large ayllu Yura, and made no further differentiations.[12] While more musicological as well as ethnographic data is needed to confirm the reasons for the different ways this music is heard and identified, I would suggest two preliminary explanations, which I do not see as mutually exclusive. Heightened sense experiences of the ritual context may be working through a process of synesthesia to make these sonorous differences distinguishable. A focus on synesthesia follows Billie Jean Isbell's work on Ricoeur's model of metaphor and Isbell's claim that we cannot separate intellectual and emotional aspects of the metaphoric process (1985: 287). Here I refer to "synesthesia" not in reference to its significance as a psychological condition, but rather in its relationship to theoretical approaches to performance and meaning construction. As outlined by Edward Schieffelin, performance involves the creation of presences that "alter moods, social relations, bodily dispositions, and states of mind" (1998: 194). Synesthesia is one of the distinguishing characteristics of "performance" as opposed to "behavior" (Sullivan 1985: 6), and it refers to a generalized process of meaning construction whereby one sense experience evokes the modality of another in the formation of personal and collective symbols (see Shore 1991). We might simply state that in their decontextualized forms the four different huayños were indistinguishable. But more specifically, I want to suggest that listening to this music through a recording outside of the ritual context fractures the "unity of the senses" (Sullivan 1985: 6) and thus blurs the distinctions that are easily made during Carnival. A second explanation might point to "the contingency of time" that regulates systems of segmentation (Herzfeld 1992: 108). Distinguishing between the four ayllus of Yura was important during Carnival, but it became relatively less important at other times of the year when the large ayllu Yura became the principal level of ayllu identification. Within the ritual moment, the differences that marked a music as being from one or another of the four ayllus were recognized and seen as worth fighting for, but outside of the ritual moment, the music was more often labeled as "Yureña" with no further differentiations.

The music of Carnival rituals provides an analytical lens that magnifies the multisensorial nature of the way individuals experience a relationship to locality. Through Yureño Carnival music, a "refrain" was heard, the sounding-off through space in order to mark "my" or "our" territory versus "your" or "their" territory (Deleuze and Guattari 1987: 311–312). The sonorous power of these Carnival rituals depended on repeated performances, worked through a process of synesthesia, and defied the clearly delineated borders required of visual representations. The emphasis in this domain over place was on auditory and kinesthetic sense experiences; it was a power established through synesthesia—a cornucopia of sense experiences, each sense experience potentially evoking the modality of another. The "work of metaphor as synesthesiac correspondences across distant realms of sensory experience, [formed] an important basis for musical communication [and allowed] us to know one thing in terms of another" (Waterman 1990: 218). The borders of the resulting sonorously constructed locality remained fuzzy, depending entirely on performing and listening subjects.

While these competing refrains constituted the experientially authentic way of being Yureño and of being sonorously connected to Yureño places, the new decentralizing law necessitated other ways of expressing a Yureño identity. I want to emphasize the intersections between a locally defined spacetime during Carnival in Yura and a spacetime as imagined through state law and as experienced by local citizens. For these intersections I borrow the concepts of space and place from Michel de Certeau, viewing space as "practiced place" or the "intersections of mobile elements," while place "implies an indication of stability" and "excludes the possibility of two things being in the same location" (1984: 117). These conceptual distinctions of space and place will be used to illuminate a difference between Yureño space as felt through Carnival ritual and Yureño place as represented in Bolivian rituals of state. Rituals of state were aimed at bringing legibility to the illegibility of social practices (see Scott 1998: 2). In Bolivia, the implementation of the Law of Popular Participation provided a window into this difference.

NEW NARRATIVES OF NATION,
NEW RITUALS OF STATE

The Law of Popular Participation aimed to achieve several shifts within the nation-state's organization. It decentralized fiscal spending decisions—"corruption" according to some people[13]—to the level of municipalities. In its initial implementation, each municipal section was to receive funds according to a national census taken in 1992.[14] These funds were to be administered through annual spending plans, supposedly developed with an input of ideas from the entire municipal section.[15] The input on spending decisions for the municipality was to occur through Territorial Base Organizations (OTBs, *Organizaciones Territoriales de Base*). These organizations were supposed to represent the most prominent form of local organization *already in existence*: that is, a neighborhood organization, a union local, a community, an indigenous group. The registration of an OTB required a statement of its statutes, a mapping of its territory, and other documents; the process was complicated by the high degree of discretion on the part of local municipal authorities. Upon successful registration, an OTB would receive its "juridical personality," a legal confirmation of existence in documentary form.

In its recognition of indigenous organizations, the Law of Popular Participation was consistent with the discourse of the pluricultural. In spite of this legislative salute to cultural difference, and to the dismay of many—especially those working in Ethnic Affairs—the highland indigenous organizations or ayllus in general were not registering as OTBs. In a diagnostic study conducted throughout the Department of Potosí in July 1995, the overwhelming tendency for registration of OTBs was at the level of *comunidad campesina* (loosely translated as peasant community). Municipal authorities, and to an extent the state-backed Municipal Strengthening Unit (Unidad de Fortalecimiento Muncipal, UFM) encouraged the registration of OTB-as-community as one of the less complicated forms of registration that could lead quickly to rosy statistics on "participation" in "projects" and a show of the successes of the new law (Bigenho and Cajías 1995). In many cases campesino syndicates seemed to be the popular catalyst around which to form OTBs at the community level, leading some anthropologists to blame peasant unionizing for the disappearance of ayllus. While conflicts between unions and indigenous organizations should not be underestimated in many areas of Bolivia's countryside (see Arias 1994), this was not a prevalent concern in the context of Yura.

Language further complicated new bureaucratic rituals. Many local collectivities learned of the new law and assumed that they needed *to form* an OTB rather than register an already existing organization as an OTB. Words made things; the very language used in implementing the law was structuring new bureaucratic procedures (see Herzfeld 1992: 114–116), but in a way that, according to COB (*Central Obrero Boliviano*, the principal Bolivian workers' union) and Ethnic Affairs, was contrary to the letter of the law. The nomenclature used in the law soon became the site of debate between the government and the COB, leading to the official elimination of the OTB abbreviation. News of this COB-government pact was slow in trickling down to those it was supposed to affect, and when I left the countryside of Potosi in November of 1995, the term "OTB" was still in use. The other tendency among government institutions and NGOs was the coining of new, equally problematic acronyms and abbreviations. If the bureaucratic procedures of the nation-state can be likened to the rituals of a religion (Herzfeld 1992: 10), the Law of Popular Participation can be viewed as a moment of transformation in Bolivia's state rituals. The new rituals were not yet established, not yet routinized, and in the fray to define those rituals, language played a curious role. The new signifier, "OTB" was supposed to signify something that already existed, but instead the acronym was read as an empty signifier to be stuffed with a newly created signified. Instead of Derrida's formulation of the signifier supplementing that which it signifies (quoted in Balkin 1987: 759), the OTB signifier was motivating Bolivians to create its signified. Bureaucratic practices, like the rituals of a religious system, invoke a community—a national one in this case—in which "members' individual sins cannot undermine the ultimate perfection of the ideal they all share" (Herzfeld 1992: 9–10). The taxonomic activities of bureaucracies are ultimately about organizing identity within a sacralized national order that, in its founding principles, is beyond criticism (Herzfeld 1992: 35, 39, 67). The Law of Popular Participation was by no means beyond dispute by sectors of Bolivian society, but the content of these debates never questioned the existence of the Bolivian nation-state as a common community, the unstated shared ideal.

Behind the registration of OTBs, or whatever one wants to call them, lurked a project of mapping national spaces. The nation became a grid, with each organization isomorphic with a specific territory. No two organizations could make a claim over the same territory. Popular literature to educate people about the law stated that a request to register an OTB would be rejected if two organizations sought to represent the same territory. One picture in a brochure showed two individuals, each with their feet planted inside a hypothetically mapped territory, both adamantly claiming to be the "real OTB" for that territory (Figure 6.1 [Ministerio de Comunicación Social 1995: 11]). Disputed claims, like those illustrated, would bring rejection to petitioners. According to the law, corresponding territories were considered spatially contiguous within specific border lines.[16] Such mapping by the Bolivian state proves consistent with a "panoptic practice" (de Certeau 1984: 36) or a "carceral texture" of society that divides, fixes, and records in order to exert control over spaces (Foucault 1977: 305). In this way the Law of Popular Participation extended a spatial logic—that used to differentiate nation-states from each other—to the internal dominion over Bolivian territory. Official discourses were in the process of reifying a pluricultural model of Bolivia, but the Law of Popular Participation brought to the internal reorganization of Bolivia the familiar model of nation-states—one people, one territory, one nation (see Anderson 1991; Appadurai 1996; Borneman 1992; Falk 1985; Hobsbawm 1990; Malkki 1992; Radcliffe and Westwood 1996).

Two assumptions implicit to the law were consistent with a logic of nation-states: the assumed isomorphism between one social group, a "nation," and one territory, and exclusive membership in a single social organization that is attached to a particular territory. This model extended the logic of the sovereign territorial states into the foundational logic of representative democracy within states. Working within the concepts of borderlines and contiguous territories with their exclusive iso-

Figure 6.1   Government literature explained the OTB. Left: "But the petition will also be rejected when: there are two organizations for the same territory. 'I am the real OTB.' 'No, I am the real OTB.'" Right: "'It's me!' 'No, it's me!' When two people want to represent the same OTB; when the documentation is not complete." (Ministerio de Comunicación Social 1995).

morphic organizations, bureaucrats who implemented the new law mapped, identified, classified, and registered citizens within the Bolivian nation.

This mapping project is rooted in perspectivism, which prioritizes the visual sense experience and the ability to truthfully represent what is seen; mapping extends from perspectivism in its attempts to reify and control diverse cultural phenomena by assigning an "unambiguous" and "secure" place to cultural differences (Harvey 1989: 245–250). The mapping project—ultimately colonizing in its erasure of the practices that produce social space (de Certeau 1984: 121), yet inherent to the Law of Popular Participation—proved contradictory to Yureño logic of spatial organization in Carnival rituals. Here I want to distance my position from essentializing Yureño spatial logic as uniquely Andean. Through emphasizing the on-the-ground practices of Yureños and a variety of sensory experiences, I identify contradiction between logics of spatial organization as locally practiced and as translocally structured in a framework of representative democracy. Rather than a dilemma that springs from something "essentially" Andean, the contradiction is likely to be found in many other localities within nation-states. I also do not want to suggest that Yureños necessarily note as problematic this contradiction of Yureño space through Carnival rituals and Yureño place through rituals of state. Yureños participated in both sets of rituals, and the difference is more important in terms of grasping the distinction between experiential authenticity and cultural-historical authenticity. The latter became the realm of operation as Yureños represented themselves to the state as an indigenous organization.

REHEARSING NEW RITUALS OF STATE: POPULAR PARTICIPATION IN YURA

Yura's Carnival rituals invoke a common community—members of the large ayllu Yura—as they also demarcate classificatory lines within the community—ayllu segmentations and gendered groups. Bureaucratic practices, viewed as rituals of state, also invoke a larger shared community—a Bolivian nation—and they also accomplish classificatory tasks. In 1995, Yureños were full participants in both sets of rituals. In Yura, the process of defining and registering Territorial Base Organizations (OTBs) was a story in and of itself—an on-going story that I will limit to the events of 1995. In their interactions Yureños placed a certain amount of faith—albeit with a healthy degree of skepticism—in that intangible entity, the state, more often called *el gobierno* (the government). On this level of faith in the unseen, the state might be mapped as God (Taussig 1992: 114) and the bureaucrats as sorcerers (Herzfeld 1992: 62). When the magic of local bureaucrats failed to bring results, one sorcerer was exchanged for another. Failure was blamed on individual bureaucrats without seriously challenging the law itself or the order of the state that had produced it. Members of ISALP critiqued the Law of Popular Participation, claiming that its logic led to the parceling and division of any potential broad coalition among popular sectors of Bolivian society. While members of ISALP expressed these concerns to Yureños, they also took it upon themselves to interpret and explain the law to Yureños in the way that would be most beneficial to the indigenous organizations of Yura. Through new bureaucratic rituals of state, a local region negotiated its position as an indigenous group within Bolivia, but this process was far from straightforward or self-evident. In explaining the law, the technical team of ISALP encouraged the Yureños to present themselves through their ayllu organizations and kuraqas. But the ayllus of Yura met with several obstacles in their OTB registration.

Under the new law, Yura became part of the second municipal section of the Province of Quijarro, and its municipal capital was Tomave—a village nowhere near Yura, nor anywhere close to the routes Yureños usually traveled. Upon the first attempt to register their ayllus as OTBs, the municipal authorities in Tomave requested the statutes of the ayllus, a requirement that was consistent with the letter of the law. In several meetings and with the assistance of ISALP, each ayllu of Yura produced its statutes in written form, a process of formalizing in writing the contemporary practices of Yura's ayllus.[17] Each ayllu listed its kuraqa as its representative to the municipality, but the authorities in Tomave required that the ayllus present their authorities as elected officials under the titles of "president," "vice-president," "secretary," and "directors." Again language itself seemed to obstruct the intent of the law. The law was supposed to recognize existing indigenous authorities and yet the language used by local bureaucrats demanded conformity to a single norm. For a kuraqa to be recognized by local bureaucrats in Tomave, he had to be called "president." The decision to name kuraqas as "presidents" was made at an ISALP-sponsored ayllu meeting in the village Yura.

At this meeting, the ayllus agreed to call their kuraqas "presidents" in order to satisfy bureaucratic requirements, but the ayllus followed "ayllu democracy" in their selection of these authorities. Silvia Rivera and THOA (Andean Oral History Workshop, *Taller de Historia Oral Andina*) make the conceptual distinction between "ayllu democracy" and "Western democracy" highlighting the fact that the latter views individuals as unlinked from corporate or kinship ties, while ayllu democracy regulates the rights and obligations of families in relationship to the ayllu by requiring a taking of turns, by family, in assuming the responsibilities of their authority systems (1992: 118). Each family of the ayllu, in turn, had an obligation to assume the costly burdens of the organization's authority positions. In the meeting, Yura's ayllus decided to call their kuraqas "presidents," but these positions as well as those of "vice-president," "secretary," and "directors" remained assigned through this system of rotation and turns.

Once again Tomave's authorities denied juridical personalities to Yura's ayllus. This time the local authorities in Tomave asked for the founding act of the ayllus. With this demand for documentation of primordial origins, proof of cultural-historical authenticity, the story could have taken a complicated turn. Unlike the Cumbal Colombian tradition described by Joanne Rappaport, in which residents maintain a consciousness of their own local identity through references to documents that detail land repossession battles that they have undertaken over the last four centuries

(1994), and unlike the *Apoderados Espiritualistas* (Empowered Spiritualists) of Chuquisaca as studied by Juan Felix Arias, for whom indigenous people have used an early colonial document called the *Ley de Indios* (Law of Indians) in their resistance to the post-hacienda, Agrarian Reform's push for individual land titles (1994), Yureños, who have had direct access to their land, do not base their identity on references to written documents. How does one explain that Yura was one of three resettlements formed by the Viceroy Toledo in the sixteenth century as a forced reorganization of a preexisting group called the Wisiqsas? How does one explain that the "indigenous" authorities today have very different roles than they had in the colonial period, or even the early republican period (see Rasnake 1989: 127–138)? ISALP was using Rasnake's book, *Autoridad y poder en los Andes,* as a source text to teach Yureños about these interpretations of their own history, but in the face of local bureaucratic demands for transparent documentation of origins, history had the potential to confuse rather than clarify (see Clifford 1988: 277–346).

To the defense of Yura's ayllus as indigenous organizations, the new La Paz–based bureaucratic authority stepped in: the Ministry of Ethnic, Gender, and Generational Affairs. Along with members of ISALP, I visited the office of Ethnic Affairs to discuss the case of Yura's ayllus. The officials of this bureaucracy made a few statements of outrage about "local bureaucrats not understanding the law," and lost no time in drafting a certification of the long-term existence of the four ayllus of Yura (Wisiqsa, Qullana, Qhurqa, and Chiquchi), and a letter to the mayor of Tomave, admonishing him for his failure to comply with the new law's recognition of indigenous organizations. The discussion took place in the morning and by the afternoon these documents were ready to send—record time for any bureaucracy.

The letter to the mayor and the certification of the existence of Yura's ayllus were drafted by lawyers of the Ministry of Ethnic Affairs and were written in a Spanish "legalese." Both documents had an initial paragraph that addressed the specific locality and ayllus in question, but the bulk of the texts consisted of citations to the different articles of the law that supported the registration of indigenous organizations as OTBs. The weight of these documents rested less on their semantic content—for the most part a restatement of the new law's specific articles—than on the naming of the four ayllus of Yura in relation to this law and on the presentation of this material on ministry letterhead, complete with the Bolivian coat of arms and the denominations "Republic of Bolivia, Ministry of Human Development, National Ministry of Ethnic, Gender, and Generational Affairs." The power of the documents rested on the relations of contiguity drawn between Yura's ayllus and signs of the Bolivian state. Attempting to fix Yura's origins within Bolivia's contested "monumental time" (see Herzfeld 1991: 14), the certification was prepared with all appropriate seals and signatures—indexical signs of state authority that would have to weather the hazards of any future "historical" identity claims. While preparing the documents, several officials working in the Ministry, anthropologists among them, mentioned knowledge of the existence of the ayllus of Yura not by some official national register or from practical experience, but rather *in relation to* Roger Rasnake's book published in Spanish in Bolivia.

The Law of Popular Participation aimed to decentralize, but in the case of Yura, the defense of local difference was obtained at the most centralized, and geographically distant, bureaucratic institution. The Ministry of Ethnic, Gender, and Generational Affairs could make official documents about the existence of Yura's ayllus but only the local authorities could grant juridical personality to these entities as OTBs. Furthermore, in spite of good intentions, the new Ministry was in no way able to deal with all that was under its newly established jurisdiction. The Ministry had been concentrating its efforts in the lowland rather than highland areas of Bolivia—a designation defined to an extent by the earmarking of international contributions to salary items for the purpose of working in those areas. Furthermore, Bolivian "ethnic affairs" were not the same in the lowlands as they were in the highlands, a fact of which many Ministry officials seemed painfully aware. In comparison with highland groups, lowland groups define their cultural difference and their relationship to territory in very different ways.[18]

Yura's ayllus then had their official documents of existence as indigenous organizations, but before any new resolution was issued from Tomave, a juridical personality for an OTB arrived with the simple name of "Yura." With this document in his hands the corregidor publicly stated that Yura now had its juridical personality, as if these were the definitive documents of regional identification. The ambiguity of this document greatly annoyed Yura's ayllu members because "Yura" could mean the village of Yura, which to an extent was controlled by vecinos, the canton of Yura, which was under the authority of the corregidor who was usually a vecino, or the large ayllu of Yura, which, although existing as an organization of the four ayllus, had no over-arching authority at that level. While the ministry's magic brought results and in November 1995 the four ayllus of Yura received their juridical personalities, mystery continued to surround the original ambiguous OTB of "Yura," especially in light of the law's explicit wording, which stated that "In each territorial unity only one OTB will be recognized . . ." (Chapter II, Article 6). Some Yureños speculated that it remained as the village Yura OTB, formed by the vecinos, whose interests would not be represented by the ayllus' OTBs. An OTB to represent village interests brought to the forefront crosscutting issues that could not be singularly tagged as "racial," "ethnic," or "class-based." Even though in another context Yura's vecinos might be labeled as mestizo or even Indian, based upon appearances and rural origins, these vecinos did not define themselves within the organizational structures of the ayllu. The issues behind this ambiguous OTB of "Yura" thus differed from those behind potentially ambiguous ayllu spaces.

Beyond the external obstacles to the registration of Yura's ayllus as OTBs, there were local disputes as well. Phajcha, the southernmost region of Yura, belonged to the ayllu of Qullana but many of the communities there had historically been considered as "*agregados.*" "Agregados" literally means "added ones" and the term makes its appearance among other tributary and census data from eighteenth-century Yura (Rasnake 1989: 130).[19] In contemporary Yura "agregados" names one of the minor ayllus within the ayllu Qullana and its members live in Phajcha, far from the ritual center of the village Yura. During my fieldwork Phajcheños often referred to the fact that they were "agregados" but they did not exploit this historically rooted term as evidence to support a separate OTB. The local schoolteacher in Phajcha had his eyes focused on a project to construct a new school and saw the funds of the Law of Popular Participation, in conjunction with already-promised funds, as a means of completing this objective.[20] It was not difficult to convince the community members in Phajcha of the need for the new infrastructure, and in order to access the necessary funds, they enthusiastically supported the registration of their OTB at the level of their community. Apparently Tomave placed fewer obstacles to this more straightforward registration of community-as-OTB, and Phajcha quickly obtained a juridical personality.

The case of Phajcha presented another contradiction in the policy of one OTB per territorial unit. Ayllu identity, based on land ownership and ritual reproduction of social spaces, did not preclude a concern for the community in which one resided. Not surprisingly, in the next few months representatives from a few other Yureño communities arrived at ayllu meetings with OTB juridical personalities in hand for their respective communities. What becomes of these overlapping registrations will be an on-going story in this new alignment of state-Yura relations and in the establishment of norms for these new rituals of state.[21]

Finally, some Yureños toyed with the possibility of changing municipal sections. At a Thauro community meeting to discuss the Law of Popular Participation with ISALP, the ayllu members expressed an interest in becoming part of another municipal section altogether—Porco, which has its capital on the main road between Yura and Potosi. Yureños constantly traveled to Potosi on a standard transportation route that, on a daily basis, arrived at and departed from the village Yura. Tomave, from a Yureña perspective, was en route to nowhere; Yureños had to take two forms of transportation to arrive at this municipal section capital. Although the possibility of Yura joining Porco seemed quite logical, municipal section switching was not permitted during the first years of the new law, something that was not taken into account by the local schoolteachers who originally promoted the idea. But another general concern expressed by the Yureños at the meeting in Thauro was that through this law, power would simply become centered, as it always had in the past, in the hands of the vecinos in the village of Yura. Upon leaving that meeting I was not at all sure that the Yureños were convinced that this would not occur, even with the presentation of the four ayllus as OTBs.

Contrary to the letter of the law, the initial implementation of the Law of Popular Participation did not bring about the registration of territorially discrete units linked to single collectivities. Although bureaucratic language structured and often obstructed the law's implementation, in 1995 many local entities in Yura did receive their juridical personalities. In this process the "peasant community," as the unit that on a small scale most closely embodied the form of the nation-state (see Herzfeld 1992: 104), more quickly flew across the ritual tables of local bureaucrats. In contrast the ayllus had to seek the magic of more powerful sorcerers to make their case.[22]

Sensing Ayllu Spaces Through Music and Language

In 1995, Yureños participated in their annual Carnival rituals and in the new state rituals as administered through the Law of Popular Participation. Both sets of rituals implied the shared ideal of a community—of Yureños in the first case, of Bolivians in the latter. Both rituals accomplished taxonomic activities in the name of that greater community, the first through music performance practices, the latter through written language and visually perceived indices. In Carnival rituals Yureños constructed social spaces by moving and performing through dispersed places, by sounding off their music through space. The movement of people and music created the spatial connections of their territory and allowed for ambiguities of individual practice. Yura's ayllu identities—as experientially authentic—were reproduced through the performance of musical competition—competitions to musically represent an ayllu. Next to these multiple processes of subject-centered identification, the Law of

Popular Participation assumed a transparency of local identities based on proof of cultural-historical authenticity and mappable territories, a question of where (not with whom or when) one identity ended and another began. The law aimed to classify people within unambiguous "places" (de Certeau 1984: 117), thus ignoring the temporal component of individual subjectivities in relation to localities (Munn 1986: 10). Sonorously marked spaces, in contrast, are necessarily subject-centered and temporally sensitive. The person producing the sound becomes the point of departure in marking a space and the extension of the sound waves beyond the sounding subject is fuzzy and ambiguous, ultimately depending on the volatile ears of another listening subject to hear "the call" (Basso 1985: 67). Not surprisingly, the sonorously marked ayllu space of Carnival focused on centers rather than on the limiting borders emphasized by the nation-state's bureaucracy.

During Yura's Carnival, the symbolic center of the ayllus—the rollo—was far more important than the boundary stones.[23] Even if the kuraqas did not make it to the outer limits of their ayllu, they had to be at their respective corners of Yura's plaza for the entrance on Ash Wednesday and for the ultimate centerpoint meeting around the rollo. A kuraqa may claim to have visited the boundary stones and few ayllu members could question that claim, while a presence or absence of a kuraqa at the musical face-off in Yura's plaza would be known by all others drawn together at that ritual centerpoint. At other moments of the year, boundary stones became important within the framework of disputes with neighboring non-Yureño communities, but during Carnival they remained of secondary importance to a spatial center. Even if Yura's boundary stones were used as sight lines (see Guillet 1998), something I have not been able to confirm or deny for the case of Yura, the three-dimensional marking of a line by sighting between two boundary markers was not transferred to a two-dimensional mapped representation for Yura's OTB petitions. The maps that accompanied the ayllus' petitions were a series of communities, or points, marked as belonging to one ayllu or another. According to an anthropologist working in the Ministry of Ethnic Affairs, this institution often recommended this form of mapping indigenous territories for OTB petitions, even though they recognized the inadequacy of this representation of ayllu spaces. In spite of the fact that Yura's ayllus could not be mapped according to the law's specification—as discrete territories—this was not one of the major points of contention with the local bureaucrats in Tomave. Instead, the state's ritual language provided major stumbling blocks to the representations of Yura's ayllus.

Maurice Bloch argued that within ritual song and dance forms, language becomes so formalized that it stands as an extreme form of traditional authority (1974). But Bloch is silent on two points that are of relevance to this analysis: the sonorous and kinesthetic experiences that encompass these purportedly fossilized forms of language and the tyranny of language within apparently new ritual forms. The bureaucratic practices surrounding the Law of Popular Participation, as new forms of state ritual, still fell victim to inflexible uses of language (i.e., "presidents," "vice-presidents," and "territorial base organizations"). An innovation in ritual forms did not avoid the tyranny of traditional language use. However, the traditional forms of Yureño Carnival music were far from tyrannical. With its absence of lyrics, Yureño Carnival music forces our attention on sonorous practices that allow for considerable maneuverability in individual identification processes.

In spite of the contrasts, both the ayllus' music and bureaucratic language were used to establish domain over the specific locality of Yura. The kuraqa was key to this process both in and outside the ritual of Carnival. The fixed nature of the kuraqa, as a sign of the ayllu, extended to this authority's physical movement. At a 1995 meeting of one of the ayllus, I listened to the kuraqa solicit permission to leave for a month in order to seek temporary employment—something which a majority of the male Yureño population does between May and August—between the harvest and the next planting season. The kuraqa's request was denied. The answer was definitive; the kuraqa had to remain in Yura, especially with the new demands of the Law of Popular Participation. All other Yureños could move and shift—physically and in their ayllu identification—but the kuraqa, during his tenure (usually of one year) had to geographically and ideologically, remain fixed to a particular ayllu. Consistent with Billie Jean Isbell's contention that in the Andes the feminine is an unmarked category while the masculine is marked (1997), symbolically male-gendered elements—kuraqas, staves, flautas, musicians, a Carnival ayllu tour—are involved in ritually fixing ayllu identities.

Like the kuraqa's music, the state's bureaucratic language—OTBs, statutes, territorial maps, official certifications, presidents, vice-presidents, and so on—although multifariously applied through many personal interactions, still performed the function of fixing local identities. Bureaucratic language, particularly as applied under this new law, was employed in a performative way that sought to "self-constitute" (Sullivan 1985: 6) the objects of its reference. Rather than following the tendency to fence off the performance-centered study from the text-centered study (Sullivan 1985: 3), this ethnographic material forces a look at the ways order is performatively established through significant sonorities and significant bureaucratic texts.

Although the Law of Popular Participation recognized indigenous organizations, local bureaucracy was slow in adopting the spirit of the new legislation. In the face of legislative inclusion of difference, the explanations of this exclusion were numerous: local misunderstanding of the law; bureaucracy seeking the least common denominators and greatest demonstrative results; internal disputes of supposedly unified indigenous groups; and even the possibility of ayllu organizations, in the interest of their own self-preservation, preferring to maintain a distance from such explicit state relations and potentially divisive monetary matters. Each of these explanations holds some water.

I have suggested another explanation, which stems from an analysis of Yureño music performance practice: the logic of spatial organization inherent to the Law of Popular Participation contradicted the ayllus' sonorously practiced space of Carnival. In Carnival rituals Yureños recreated the social space of their ayllus in a movement through the discontiguous places where people lived. It was a movement continuously accompanied by music, and the ritual performance of music had to move, much like the fluid nature of the four ayllus of Yura. The musical process was fraught with competition: competition for which huayño would represent the ayllu and competition of endurance among the four ayllus of Yura. Winners of such competitions were not formally declared. Competition was a means of being Yureño rather than a means of determining who was and was not Yureño. Such processes defied the isomorphism of single identities linked to single territories. Under the discourse of recognizing Bolivia's cultural diversity, the logic behind the Law of Popular Participation sought this isomorphism for easy classification of specific populations with mappable territories. Unlike the project of promoting a general national character to which all segments of the society conform (see Herzfeld 1992: 3), inherent in the Law of Popular Participation was a national ideal constructed on the principle of unity in diversity. Nevertheless, bureaucratic practices as applied through the law reflected a national project of fixing, on single terms, the nation's diverse range of populations—revealing a logical contradiction of representative democracies in general.

In spite of the contradictions between spatial organization through state ritual and spatial organization through Carnival ritual, I have identified a similarity in these rituals that brings bureaucratic language into functional equivalence with music performance practice. Bureaucracies of all kinds conduct taxonomic activities (Herzfeld 1992: 39). The impulse to classify and attach people and myths to specific places is widespread among state structures, even those predating the Westphalian order.[24] Just as the language of the new bureaucratic rituals sought to fix and establish domain over specific Bolivian places, the music of Yureño Carnival temporarily fixed the four different ayllu identities, creating a sonorous sovereignty by sounding off while moving through the spaces of the ayllu. During Carnival the securing of identity was associated with male gendered domains: the male musicians who performed and the kuraqa's ayllu tour. But these attempts to fix ayllu specificities depended on temporalities—the social temporalities of ritual and non-ritual periods and the subjective temporalities of the kuraqas who were temporarily fastened to their ayllu. Although in the defining of social space bureaucratic language may work like music, the latter never strives for the timeless iconicity sought by the language of the state (see Herzfeld 1992: 108). The huayños of Carnival are supposed to be new to each annual celebration. Furthermore, the distinctions between the four ayllus (Qullana, Wisiqsa, Qhurqa, Chiquchi) depended on the moment of Carnival, and when this moment passed Yureños often privileged other levels of identification.

In fact, Yureños, like most people, have multiple identifications and belong to multiple communities. Their participation as ayllu members does not preclude important interactions at the community level or necessary interactions with village and canton authorities. In this sense the tale of Yura's registration with the Bolivian state could be a tale of any locality within a representative democracy. I cannot suggest a better alternative to this form of local-state organization, but the inherent contradictions between a decentralizing law of representative democracy and a nation-state discourse of the pluri-multi brings us back to Herzfeld's paradox of the state's dependence on "concealed segmentation" (1992: 104). While the Law of Popular Participation claimed to recognize, even champion, local difference defined through indigenous identifications, the law ultimately required a selection and fixing of multiple identifications as single identities. In the contemporary Bolivian case segmentation is not concealed but rather reified in an exalted state, even if this reification ultimately brings the same subordination of local differences to a common state.

Heeding the warnings against resistance frameworks, which while morally compelling are all too tidy (see Brown 1996), I have avoided interpreting this ethnographic material as the imposing Bolivian state versus the resisting Yureños. Thinking about "sonorous sovereignty"—two words that uneasily sit together as a single term, the adjective depending on performing and listening subjectivities and the noun striving for dominating permanence—provides a way of conceptualizing the elusive nature of identification processes in relation to local and national spaces. Within theories of nation-states "sovereignty" has referred to the idea that there was "a final and absolute political authority in the political community . . . and no final or absolute authority exist[ed] elsewhere" (Hinsley 1986: 26). But this realist vision of sovereignty has been questioned. Theorists of "sovereignty" have increasingly emphasized the historically and culturally contingent nature of sovereignty (Doty 1996: 123; Bartelson 1995: 2; Biersteker and Weber 1996: 11). As theorists turn away from the essentialist question of "what is sovereignty?" (Doty 1996: 142; Bartelson 1995: 2), sovereignty becomes viewed as "not the location of the foundational entity of international relations theory but a site of political struggle" (Weber 1995: 3). Cynthia Weber associates sovereignty with the failure of representation, and she proposes an approach to sovereignty through Baudrillard's logic of simulation "in which there are no ultimate foundations but instead a chain of interchangeable signifiers" (1995: xi, 126).

Within the spirit of Cynthia Weber's contested signs of sovereignty, and within the spirit of theorizing cultural authenticity that assumes foundational claims to origins, I propose the concept of sonorous sovereignty to view the way groups within nation-states feel and negotiate their relationship to a particular territory. Some readings of modernization theory assume that people will give up their ethnic loyalties as they become part of a national project, but ethnonationalist projects with territorial claims have clearly challenged this assumption (Murphy 1996: 103, 109). Furthermore, the nation-state's recognition of ethnic groups within its territory has also been read as a means of incorporating difference within a continued hierarchy of domination and subordination (see Comaroff 1987). While Yureños did not challenge the principles of the Bolivian nation-state, their way of sonorously constructing a territory followed a very different logic than that applied through bureaucratic practices that called for clear representations of cultural authenticity. Sonorous sovereignty suggests the flexible, subject-centered approach to the way territory is experienced and remains important in peoples' lives, and I propose this concept as a counter to the more widely touted processes of deterritorialization.

In these processes, Yureños have had room to maneuver. Within the fervor of the discourses of the pluricultural, to favor ayllu identification over others was a political move. In Yura, with the exception of the kuraqa and his music, ambiguity reigned as ayllu organization resisted the map and grid logic of nation-states and representative democracies. Like the kuraqa's music that sonorously marked a territory, bureaucratic language, as it attempted to fix an ayllu identity, similarly strove to establish an order over specific places within the state. Just as the ayllu identities

within the state remained difficult to taxonomically represent, the musical differentiation of the four ayllus within the large ayllu of Yura faded
away; it was not heard outside of the fiesta.

In the following chapter, I explore the implications of capturing these
sounds on cassette recordings, of turning experiential authenticity into
tangible, culturally authentic, and potentially alienable objects.

CHAPTER 7

THE INDIGENOUS WORK
AND ITS AUTHORSHIP

It would be as wrong to equate the author with the real writer as to equate him with the fictitious speaker; the author function is carried out and operates in the scission itself, in this division and this distance.

—Foucault 1984:112

ANTHROPOLOGIST: "What names or organizations should be listed on the liner notes of the cassette?"

YUREÑO: "Everything should be officially registered in La Paz, everything."

YUREÑO: "Put the ayllu names on the cassette, all of them should be there"

YUREÑO: "The names of the kuraqas should also be there."

YUREÑO: "That's it, the ayllus and their kuraqas."

The Yureño ayllu of Wisiqsa had gathered in Pelqa for their annual meeting under the auspices of the local NGO, ISALP (Investigación Social y Asesoramiento Legal, Potosí, Social Research and Legal Advising, Potosi). The agenda of the meeting was filled with discussions of specific projects—potable water, land recuperation, canal construction, and so on. The discussion of a cassette production was added to the agenda at my request. I had produced a cassette of Toropalca's music for Toropalqueños and I intended to do the same in Yura. I posed the above question within a broad discussion of the entire Yureño cassette production. Although my fieldwork in both Yureño and Toropalqueño contexts indeed revealed an association of individual composers with specific compositions, Yureños and Toropalqueños seemed to favor the presentation of these materials under the name of a collectivity.

As Yureño and Toropalqueño music was captured on tape and refigured within a sixty-minute audio cassette representation of that experience, the questions of unique authenticity, individual creatorship, and ownership over these creations took center stage. Within the ideological framework of modernity, the individual creator of a uniquely authentic work is assumed to hold proprietorship over the idea of that work. But the same framework of modernity denies such individual creatorship, and corresponding ownership, to those who produce cultural works. To state the prevailing logic in its blunt and admittedly oversimplified terms, Western individuals produce art and collective Others produce culture. In this art-culture system (Clifford 1988: 215), the concept of individual creatorship is out of place next to the Western view of the "primitive" or exotic (see Napier 1992: 24). One simply does not look for individual authorship within the exotic, and part of the attraction to these aesthetics emerges from the romantic concept of collective creations in which the individual has been forever subsumed (see Napier 1992: 26).[1] The production of these cassettes brings to the fore issues of ownership, but the relevant question is not who owns the music on these cassettes, but rather how things that index a cultural authenticity become entangled in the logics of property, individual ownership, and patrimony of the modern nation-state. The issues of unique authenticity prove irremediably intertwined with those of cultural authenticity. Following the "social life" (Appadurai 1986) of these cassettes and the "author function" (Foucault 1984) of the originals within them illuminates a site of negotiation and symbolic exchange between the anthropologist, indigenous peoples, and the Bolivian state.

THE ANTHROPOLOGIST'S EXCHANGES

During my first visit to Toropalca in 1994, I had a difficult time finding any collective body that claimed to represent Toropalqueños. I was facing a vast territory with communities spread throughout it, and I was still clinging to the idea that this area all coalesced as an ayllu. An anthropological team working with FAO-Holanda had recently completed a mapping of the ayllus in the Department of Potosí and their findings revealed a reference to two ayllus in Toropalca—Urinsaya and Anansaya—in a classic moiety model. From the beginning of my research in Toropalca I was plagued by two concerns: how to conduct research throughout the ayllus of Toropalca, and how to give something in return for my presence there as a researcher. Of course several of my own imaginings cluttered my thinking on the matter—points that only become clear to me in hindsight and with the comparative reference to my research in Yura. I began my method of moving through places in Toropalca with a walking tour that took me first south of the village Toropalca and then north along the river. Hamlet residents were often amazed at my arrival on foot. As one Toropalqueño commented to me, "We have lost the custom of walking places." The import of this statement did not become evident to me until I saw how much Yureños did walk! While roads south of the village of Toropalca would bring an occasional vehicle, often headed for a junction with the trunk road to the Argentine border, no such roads stretched north along the Toropalca River. In fact the river came to a narrows through which not even the locals liked to travel alone. I passed back and forth through these narrows twice in my work, each time seeking out a resident guide from one of the hamlets on either side of the narrows. During the rainy season, when the river swells, people simply do not travel through the narrows, taking instead lengthy alternate routes. For me these narrows formed a geographical metaphor for the disjointed nature of the relations between the different communities that were supposedly part of the two ayllus of Toropalca. The ayllus of Toropalca never seemed to cohere as such, and each community received me in distinct ways. Sometimes my interactions were limited to individuals within the community; in other cases community meetings were called in which I would discuss my wish to research the music of the area. At the same time, I proposed the project of producing a cassette of their music—my consciously intended object of exchange. In some communities, the people nodded in agreement with the project; in others the community demanded things I was unable to provide. For example, upon my arrival in San Jorge (between the village Toropalca and the narrows to the north), the local schoolteacher called a meeting and suggested that the community should only approve of my research if I agreed to buy a new roof for the school. The community easily agreed to this proposal. While I could probably afford one such roof, I would not be able to buy new roofs for all the schools throughout Toropalca. I was operating under my own illusions of equity and fairness. I did not return to San Jorge for their fiesta, and this community's music was not represented on Toropalca's cassette. San Jorge was emblematic of my dilemma in Toropalca: I was looking for the indigenous collectivity of the ayllu and this was the entity with which I imagined exchanging a cassette production of their music. But during my fieldwork the concept of ayllus in Toropalca was ephemeral and fleeting. The disjointed nature of Toropalca's communities left me awash in doubts and questions as to the social boundaries of this imagined entity and how to interact with any collectivity of Toropalqueños. After facing these frustrations in Toropalca, working with Yura's ayllus was deceivingly straightforward. Beyond ritual and walking practices that brought a coalescence to the ayllu forms, ISALP sponsored meetings of Yura's ayllus, and it was in the context of these meetings that I discussed the production of a cassette of Yureña music.

I intended these cassettes as objects of exchange between myself as an anthropologist and the people with whom I worked. Most anthropologists, even if they do not write bestsellers, construct careers out of discourses that emerge from fieldwork experiences, and many anthropologists engage in a project of giving-back to the people with whom they work. Academic discussions of these delicate fieldwork relationships are sometimes mired in a sense of guilt, self-doubt, and—to borrow a term from my colleague, Henry Stobart—"post-colonial angst" (personal communication 1998). Postcolonial angst has forced anthropologists to reconsider their general enterprise, a reassessment that has its own merits. Nevertheless, the discussion of our own ethics often blinds us to alternative forms of analyses that might otherwise emerge through these reassessments. I prefer to highlight how this ethnographic situation illuminates the local, national, and global factors that structure and place value on cultural representations of indigenous authenticity within the Bolivian nation-state.

The relationship between anthropologists and indigenous people has never been transparent, but in recent years it has increasingly come under scrutiny. Our ethnographic practices and the texts that we produce circle back, with or without our conscious knowledge, to the people with whom we have worked—what Abu-Lughod has called "the Rushdie effect" (1991: 142; also see Warren 1998). In many cases this circle of products proves crucial to the self-identification of a group as indigenous. As anthropologists research indigenous histories and put cultural practices into explanatory discourse, these researchers and their texts, for better or worse, have played a role in the author function of indigenous authenticity. For example the ethnographic text of Roger Rasnake was key in the development of Yureños' consciousness of their own subject position as indigenous peoples. According to one member of ISALP, Rasnake had brought multiple copies of his translated book to Yura, in hopes that it might be used in local schools. Whether or not his book has been used in local schools remained a point of debate, but members of ISALP decided to use the book in a series of informal meetings or alternative schools they called *Yachaywasis*—the Quechua word for "schools."

Through Yachaywasis, ISALP's objective was to create alternative educational contexts through which Yureños could systematize their own knowledge of the world, as well as have access to other relevant knowledge sources. By bringing Yureño knowledge to a conscious level, Yachaywasis were intended to foster a judicious use of multiple knowledge bases and to discourage a simple discarding of the traditional and replacement by the modern. While many Yachaywasis revolved around themes of agricultural production, animal husbandry, and medicinal plant use, I attended one Yachaywasi that centered on Yureño history. A member of ISALP gave a lecture on Yureño history, situating it within the more generally known framework of "Bolivian history" as taught in public schools. As the lecture ended a Yureño asked the lecturer: "How do you know this?" The lecturer answered that this information came from Roger Rasnake's book. During my fieldwork many Yureños expressed memory of Roger Rasnake's and Inge Harmon's presence during their fieldwork in the 1970s, but Yureños were less aware of Rasnake's visits to archives and the subsequent "Yureño history" constructed within his book. As I have already suggested, this historical narrative also played a crucial role in validating within Bolivian state structures Yura's ayllus as culturally historically authentic. Anthropological texts, through the presentation of cultural practices and the elaboration of local histories, have the potential to make an indigenous group conscious of themselves as indigenous, a consciousness that can be used in political ways (Turner 1991; Jackson 1995; Ramos 1998). As Yureños discover they have or own culture, that culture also acquires the potential to be expressed as alienable property.

In my analysis of these productions, I am not concerned with specifically distinguishing these cassettes as gifts or commodities—a dichotomy that has too often been reified in anthropological theories of exchange (Appadurai 1986: 12). In this dismissal, I also refer to Olivia Harris's reflections on her fieldwork experiences in which she made clear distinctions between gift exchange and commerce while her Andean hosts did not make the same distinctions (1989: 247). I adopt Arjun Appadurai's suggestion that exchange itself, rather than the form or function of that exchange, is the site of value creation and thus of politics (1986: 3). Furthermore, exchange is precisely where I want to explore that Foucauldian division between writers and the author function (1984: 112) or—as may be better suited to the cultural medium of music—between composers and the composer function.

WHOSE CASSETTES ARE THESE?

A simple answer to this question is "Yureños'" or "Toropalqueños.'" But the answer is deceptive because the attribution of these musical works to a collective group brings out the contradiction between intellectual and cultural property. In previous chapters, in an attempt to debunk romantic notions of communal Andean music making, I have underlined the individual creation of these compositions. Nevertheless there is a plurality of authorship inherent to any author function (Foucault 1984: 112). Keeping in mind a distinction between plural and communal authorship, let me begin with the details of the production itself since these can only be delinked artificially from the author function.

For both Yura and Toropalca, I paid for the production of 700 copies of an edited cassette, each production costing approximately $1000, not including equipment and travel expenses. The music came from my field recordings at ritual fiestas during the years 1994 and 1995. The funds to cover these productions came from my individual research grants (Fulbright IIE and Fulbright Hays), although in the liner notes of the cassettes I also credited the funding sources of the institutions that in some nonfinancial way backed these endeavors: the Inter-American Foundation, which funded the music workshop in La Paz, an institution that assisted in the production of Toropalca's cassette; and Oxfam America, which funded Yura's ayllu meetings through ISALP. The cassette productions for Yura and Toropalca were noncommercial productions of adequate, but far from superior sound quality. Steven Feld has discussed the drawbacks of noncommercial recordings of "world music" and has also lamented the relatively poor quality of these recordings (1994a: 284). Feld was responding to academic, poor quality recordings with *Voices of the Rainforest,* a commercial recording that experimented with the most advanced recording technology available (1994a). My recording projects in both Toropalca and Yura varied on at least two points: technology and audience. The field recordings in Toropalca were made on a simple 100-dollar analogue cassette recorder and the Yureño recordings were made on a 350-dollar professional analogue cassette recorder. The production of these cassettes was intended for an audience of Yureños and Toropalqueños. Feld's general critique of ethnomusicological recordings assumes an audience of outsiders—academics and researchers who will prefer "exotic content . . . indexically signalled by muffled grooves" (1994a: 284). Feld's commercial recording, although more popularly distributed, still aimed at an audience of outsiders. I mention these differences not to justify the sound quality of my productions, nor to criticize Feld's commercial approach, but to mark this significant difference in the intentions behind these productions. Given the choice, I too might opt for the "technoaesthetics" and "hyperreal" results of Feld's recording (1994a: 283–284).

In the two editing processes, I worked with two different sound engineers. My knowledge of recording studios was limited, and because of this, both engineers asserted their limited spheres of power through the manipulation of the studio sound board. The Toropalqueño cassette was edited without any special effects because the engineer opposed this type of sound manipulation of traditional music. In contrast, the Yureño recording has effects because the sound engineer wanted to give the music some of the depth that would be felt if one listened to it as a live performance. The first engineer seemed to be working from an idea of capturing the traditional music in a pristine state, a logic that goes hand in hand with collection and preservation projects, an archiving of music through recording, a sound likened to what Feld has described as "documentary realism" (1994a: 283). The second engineer's response was more consistent with the intentions of my project: to produce a recording that would sound good to the Yureños themselves. I believe the resulting sound of this production was closer to what Feld has called "hyperrealism" (1994a: 283). The first production had a sound aimed at researchers; the second production had a sound aimed at the pleasure of a Yureño listening audience. The results were a rather flat sound on the Toropalqueño cassette, and almost too much echo on the Yureño cassette. These cassettes appealed to two different aesthetics of authenticity. The fashioning of the Toropalqueño cassette strove to represent a culturally authentic sound as collected and heard by an outsider, while the fashioning of the Yureño cassette attempted to recreate the pleasure of the experientially authentic moment—the feeling of listening to and grooving with the live Yureño performance, even if the pursuit of this kind of authenticity necessitated sonorous manipulation in the studio.

In the two cassette productions I made different economic trade-offs between audio and visual quality. The studio I used for the production of Toropalca's cassette charged one lump sum for studio editing time, cassette purchase, and duplication ($900). They did their duplication in real time (700 hours). In the case of the Yureño cassette, I completed the production through piecework. After making the master in a different studio, I took it to a business that did cassette duplication for small record labels in Bolivia. Up on a hill, in the commercially vibrant areas of the Gran Poder neighborhood, I bought 700 blank cassettes, and with some of my colleagues from Música de Maestros, we carried the cassettes down the hill to the duplicators who used machines that copied simultaneously both sides of the cassettes. In this second production, I decided to save time and money and to risk a difference in sound quality; I knew the kinds of cassette players on which Yureños would listen to this cassette, equipment through which one could not distinguish between real-time and speed-dubbed recordings. Such distinctions are difficult to perceive on mediocre cassette players with chronically low batteries. "Better quality" under these conditions had more to do with the combined audio-visual presentation of the cassette. I had already received complaints from Toropalqueños about not having photographs in their black and white brochure. From their initial discussions Yureños assumed that their cassette brochure would have color photographs. In the Yureño production, with the money saved on duplication, I was able to utilize a full separation of colors and include color photography. But beyond budget concerns, the contrasting contexts of the productions were reflected in the final product. While the Toropalqueño cassette had a drawing of a flauta on the cover—a drawing by one of the music workshop's organizers—the Yureño cassette brochure was filled with drawings by Yureños themselves, drawings that emerged during meetings to discuss the production of their cassette.

In the case of Toropalca, production decisions were made on the basis of my interactions with many individuals, while in the case of Yura, production decisions were made through the ayllu meetings. I spoke individually with many Toropalqueños about this project, but I was unable to find a collectivity of Toropalqueños, a forum beyond the level of individual communities, or the individual village of Toropalca. The cassette for Yura, in contrast, emerged from a set of participatory meetings of ayllus in which Yureños discussed their music, the cassette production, and the general presence of researchers in their region.

Nevertheless, in both cases, the final decisions about what to include, and the length of each musical interlude were mine alone. The combined criteria of brevity and variety dominated my editing choices, creating an aesthetic quite different from that which exists in ritual performances of Toropalqueño and Yureño music. The interludes on the edited cassette, with fade-ins and fade-outs, last from one to five minutes, while a ritually contextualized performance of any one of these pieces may last twenty minutes to an hour. As the analysis of folklore festivals suggests, the temporal logic of brevity and variety is not foreign to Toropalqueños and Yureños, but is applied in performance frameworks that are removed from the assumed original ritual context, from its "primary framework" (Goffman 1974: 47)—those contexts in which Toropalqueños and Yureños are conscious of their performances as *representations* of their culture.

The organization of the cassettes between sides A and B was guided in the case of Toropalca by my own perspective as researcher and in the case of Yura by the collective discussions of Yura's ayllus. The Toropalqueño cassette sonorously and visually takes on the voice of the omniscient ethnographer, while the Yureño cassette speaks from the Yureño perspective, the Yureño "we." In the case of Toropalca, side A was dedicated to the genres of the wet season and side B was dedicated to the genres of the dry season. Wet-season/dry-season distinctions pervade the literature on Andean music (Baumann 1996: 21; Stobart 1996a: 67–68; 1996b:474; Turino

1993a: 41), and I followed this lead in spite of the fact that Toropalqueños or Yureños did not talk about this seasonal divide of music. As part of their own discourse Toropalqueños and Yureños temporally linked musical genres to the dates of specific fiestas or rituals. These fiesta dates do fall in wet and dry season divisions, but this division seemed secondary to the more explicitly expressed ritual associations. The organization of the Yureño cassette reflects these ritual associations of the musical genres.

The textual content of the cassette brochures also marks the contrasting ways in which these productions were undertaken. In the case of Toropalca, I composed the text from my observations, using third person perspective and passive voice. The introductory paragraph reads as follows:

> If music represents one of the most lasting indicators of an identity, the ayllu of Toropalca (Department of Potosi, Province of Nor Chichas, Canton Toropalca) can be an exemplary case. In spite of the increase in migration to Argentina and the influence of non-Catholic religions, music continues to be a common starting point for the communities of the ayllu Toropalca. The genres corresponding to each instrument are maintained, in some cases even with the absence of men to play the instruments. With migration to Argentina, sometimes the women are left alone to maintain, through song, the collective memory of their music. (*Canciones de Toropalca* 1994)

My text echoed the general nostalgia expressed by Toropalqueños themselves, but the emphasis on the role of women's song performance was my interpretation. During the Toropalqueño Carnival, women sang songs as men played the flauta, but during the 1994 carnival few men played flautas and the genre appeared more driven by the women's lyrics, even if women did not perceive song alone as "music." Rather than a reflection of Toropalqueña women's claims to musical prowess, the comment about women's participation in song reflected my own amazement at, even celebration of, women's roles in music—a sphere so often presented as an all-male realm.

Toropalqueños critiqued the cassette production on another point. In the liner notes I refer to "the ayllu Toropalca," but in a subsequent visit, Toropalqueños told me I had made a mistake; according to them it should have read "Canton Toropalca" rather than "Ayllu Toropalca." These were the same Toropalqueños who later expressed optimism for Toropalca's future "now that [they] have the ayllus." Toropalqueños have demonstrated an ambivalence toward the organizational unit of the ayllu, and this ambivalence could not be explained through a line-up of vecinos' desires versus the desires of surrounding indigenous communities. Although Toropalqueños often expressed nostalgia for lost culture, in 1994, such symbolic material did not seem to be attached to nostalgia for an ayllu organization.

Finally, the Toropalqueño cassette has a message that reads *prohibida la venta* (sale prohibited). I was concerned about the possibility of individuals within Toropalca selling the cassettes to other Toropalqueños. While I decided to put the "sale prohibited" message on the Toropalqueño cassette, the Yureño cassette does not have this label because Yureños themselves, at their ayllu meetings, decided to sell their own cassettes—inside Yura for one price and outside Yura for another.

———

ANTHROPOLOGIST: What do researchers learn from Yureños?
YUREÑO: They come here to learn the Yureña culture. They try and try, but they can't learn it.

This was one of the questions I posed and one of the responses I received at one of Yura's ayllu meetings. The Yureño answer drew a sharp insider-outsider division; researchers learn about but do not learn to be Yureño. The ayllu meetings themselves were social spaces of internal collective reflection combined with insider-outsider interaction. These meetings were giving organizational form to the ayllus, but the ayllu meetings were sponsored by ISALP. For ISALP, the meetings were a forum for strengthening Yura's ayllus, but they also provided a venue through which Yureños could collectively interact with outsiders. The existence of these meetings provided the context, outside of ritual and daily interactions, through which I discussed with Yureños a cassette production of their music.

The ayllu meetings, as an interactive timespace, existed prior to my arrival in Yura, but these meetings were still not exactly a part of Yureño *habitus* (Bourdieu 1977: 72–95); they still depended on the impetus of ISALP. ISALP sponsored a meeting of the large ayllu Yura every three months and at least one annual ayllu meeting with each of the four ayllus of Yura. The participatory methodology of these meetings emerged from 19 years of pastoral work in Yura. The meetings of the large ayllu of Yura were held on two days in the parish of the village of Yura: the first day—under the direction of a priest—was dedicated to guided reflections on Yureña culture with a theological point of closure, the second day—under the direction of the technical team of ISALP—was dedicated to a discussion of needs, problems, and projects at the community level. The priest was enthusiastic about the present ayllu meetings, but he told me about their first attempts to hold such meetings: "When I first came to Yura we had meetings and only a few people came. When we gave them questions to discuss, the room was silent. No one said a word. We just sat there in silence. It took us a very long time to get people to talk, to get people to participate. Now the people are used to talking about their way of life. More people come to the meetings. They talk among themselves. We are all learning in this." In ayllu meetings, ISALP pushed Yureños to develop discourse about their life practices, to make explicit those lifeways that are usually buried in the nondiscursive depths of "second nature" (see Bourdieu 1977), and to situate those practices within a politically conscious awareness of their own position in Bolivian society. Meetings began with a set of pre-prepared questions designed around a general theme. Although ISALP designed the questions, the kuraqas, the principal authority of the ayllus, officiated the meetings and the themes in general sprang from concerns expressed at previous ayllu meetings. After the introduction of the theme, the participants would break into small groups to discuss a related series of questions. Each small group prepared posters that, through the written word as well as through drawings, conveyed their principal reflections. The meeting would reconvene and each small group would present their ideas through reference to these posters. Then the floor opened for general discussion. Yureños were quite accustomed to this participatory methodology, and I adapted it to the theme of music and a discussion about a cassette production.

The first set of questions dealt with music practices, compositions, and instruments, and the answers to these questions provided the textual content for the cassette brochure:

1. What instruments do Yureños play?
2. When is Yureño music played?
3. How is Yureño music composed? Who composes it?
4. What Yureño music is no longer played. Why isn't it played? What do you think about that?
5. What is special about Yureño music?
6. Is Yureño music important? Why?
7. On paper express what is special about Yureño music.

In response to these questions, one drawing (Figure 7.1) shows a man, dressed "as a good Yureño," playing a flauta. He is surrounded by depictions of the instruments considered to be part of Yureño traditions. Below the man it says, "Yureña music is an invention. Those who have interest in it pull it out [or compose] it." The use of the word "invention" seems to refer to the original nature of this material; it is viewed as an indigenous original characterized by a distance from electronic instruments and modes of reproduction. Below these statements the uniqueness of Yureña

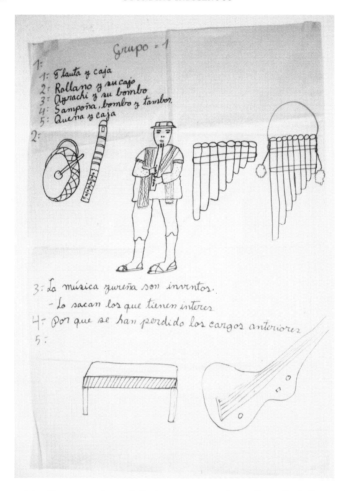

Figure 7.1   Yureños write and depict answers to the anthropologist's questions about their music. About music composition they write: "3. Yureña music [is an invention]. Those who are interested compose it." In answer to the question of why some music is no longer played in Yura, they write: "4. Because the previous authority systems have been lost." They depict their own musical instruments as well as electronic instruments, which are today a part of their sonorous environment (drawings by the ayllus of Yura).

music is contrasted with electronic music, the drawings of a keyboard and an electric guitar.

Another drawing (Figure 7.2) is divided into several horizontal layers. The people on the top layer are playing many different instruments: flauta (wooden duct flute), caja (small drum), zampoña (panpipes played with

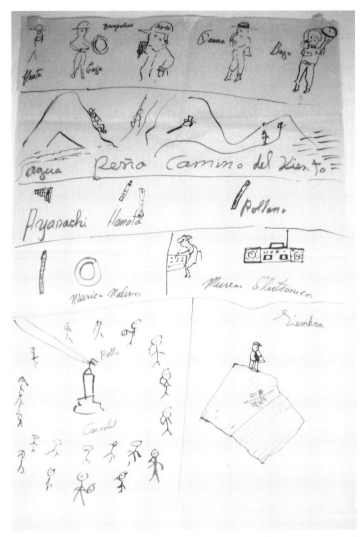

Figure 7.2   Yureños depict answers to the anthropologist's questions about their music: the instruments played in Yura; the process of music composition in the mountains, "water," "rock," and "path of the wind"; the instruments no longer played in Yura; the distinction between native and electronic music; and the difference between music of Carnival and music of the planting season (drawings by the ayllus of Yura).

interlocking technique), and quena (notched flute). With a tuba player in the upper right hand corner, these artists also included the brass band in their representations of Yureña music. The second layer from the top shows Yureños composing music. The words "water," "rock," and "path of the wind" are written across the bottom of this layer and the sketches seem to move across the page. This drawing depicts Yureño music composition as a solitary activity; isolated individuals sit on slopes, play instruments, and draw inspiration from the natural and supernatural elements. I rarely heard musicians play or "practice" instruments alone, as I might practice my violin, a studied repetition of pieces with an aim at some level of technical mastery.[2] While Yureños did not practice music alone, the act of composing, at least as it was depicted, was an activity of human solitude, but one in which the composer might interact with spiritual beings of the earth.

The third level from the top depicts those instruments no longer played in Yura: ayarachis (panpipes not played with interlocking technique), anata (duct flute carved of a single piece of wood), and *rollano* (an instrument that is similar to the flauta). The next level draws a sharp distinction between Yureña music that is "native" and "electronic" music as heard on a keyboard or on a portable double cassette player. The bottom level of the poster, again divided in two sections, shows spatialized representations of Carnival music and planting season music. The sheer numbers of people in the depiction of Carnival sharply contrast with the single quena player, playing on the edge of his plot of planted land. Carnival emphasized the space of the ayllu, ultimately represented in the ayllu's symbolic center—the rollo, a pillar in the center of Yura's plaza—and sonorously represented through masses of flauta players. In contrast, the planting season was more about reciprocal relations between individuals and the quena playing of this season followed a parallel aesthetic that featured individual performers.

In general, the answers to questions four and five again revealed a lack of nostalgia and a matter-of-fact attitude about the coexistence of different kinds of musics. The music of ayarachis was no longer played in Yura, and Yureños go straight to the point in explaining why. As one participant in an ayllu meeting explained, "We don't play ayarachis anymore because they were played in Corpus [Christi] for the fiesta of the *jilaqata*. We don't have jilaqatas anymore. So that fiesta and the ayarachis are gone." The jilaqata was the indigenous authority who collected a tax (*tasa*) twice a year, which was then turned over to government officials. Some ayllus have continued to pay the tax although it was officially eliminated after the 1953 Agrarian Reform (see Harris 1989). These ayllus have viewed the tax as a means of maintaining an ayllu-state reciprocal pact that secures indigenous rights over productive lands. This reciprocal pact has been repeatedly threatened by the 1874 Law of *Exvinculación* and the 1953 Agrarian Reform (see Platt 1982). Yureños were still collecting this tax in the 1970s, when Rasnake did his fieldwork (1989), but they were no longer doing so in the 1990s when I conducted fieldwork. When the question of ayarachis and jilaqatas surfaced in the ayllu meetings, one of the members of ISALP planted the idea of reestablishing the jilaqata and the possible collection of an internal tax, just for use in Yura. In reference to the 1953 Agrarian Reform that abolished the tax, the member of ISALP said: "Why should Yureños let the government determine their own life and culture. They pass a law and a Yureño authority disappears along with the music which was played at that authority's fiesta." Yureños briefly voiced agreement, but the discussion about reviving the jilaqata quickly evaporated as the meeting turned to other concerns. Perhaps an internal tax made less sense because the jilaqata, and what he was about, was the means for a symbolic reciprocal relation between Yureños and the state. If the state did not receive the tax, the circles of reciprocity were broken. Although members of ISALP never hesitated in making suggestions like these, they did not press a point that Yureños themselves did not show an interest in pursuing. Yureños agreed that cultural loss had occurred, but they responded to that perceived loss neither with emotional attachment nor nostalgic longing.

In a similar vein, the uniqueness of Yureño music was expressed through the adjectives "native" and "autochthonous." Native music was verbally or pictorially set in contrast to electronic, band, radio, and cassette music. While Yureños admitted an influence from these other musics, their influence over "native" music was never expressed in negative terms.

The second set of questions I developed for the ayllu meetings explored notions about Yureño-researcher interactions as well as possible schizophonic situations (see Schaefer 1977), the possibility of their music being in places outside of Yura:

1. Why do anthropologists and sociologists come to study the Yureña culture?
2. What do the researchers learn from Yureños?
3. Can researchers do something for Yureños? What? Or why not?
4. What do you think about the possibility of your music being in places of study (libraries, archives, national museums, international museums)?
5. Outside of Yura, where do you want your music to be heard? Where would you prefer it not be heard?
6. On paper express what anthropologists learn from Yureños.

In discussing these questions, Yureños expressed a clear sense that they were the "owners" of something called Yureña culture and that outsiders should not be permitted to study this culture without first seeking permission from Yura's ayllus. But the attitude toward researchers was far from closed. During the time I was conducting research, an archaeologist

Figure 7.3   Yureños write and depict answers to the anthropologist's questions about researchers in Yura. While a red jeep and its driver wait in the background, the woman researcher films llamas and ducks (drawings by the ayllus of Yura).

entered the region and in reference to his presence, I heard several concerned comments from Yureños about the disappearance of their *chullpas,* a term they use to refer to artifacts that connect Yureños to their mythic ancestors. While chullpas seemed to refer to inalienable things,[3] not to be separated from Yureños and Yureño places, musical productions held a different status. Without hesitation Yureños expressed a desire to have their music heard *en todo el mundo* (throughout the whole world). No schizophonaphobia here!

A conflation of several different outsiders emerged in response to the first question: Why do anthropologists and sociologists come to study the Yureña

Figure 7.4   Yureños depict answers to the anthropologist's questions about re-searchers in Yura. The "anthropologist" with tooth-clad boots films pottery, mu-sical instruments, and rituals (represented by a church and a Yureño hat) (drawings by the ayllus of Yura).

culture? Anthropologists, NGO workers, and tourists were all mixed together as people who learned about Yureña culture without ever *being* Yureño. One drawing (Figure 7.3) shows "the researcher," a woman with red hair, a video camera, and a backpack. A red jeep has brought her to this place, and a dri-ver waits patiently while she films llamas and ducks, focussing on natural scenery rather than on any human context. Yureños titled another drawing as "Anthropologists" (Figure 7.4). This drawing shows a man holding a video camera that is pointed toward three sets of items: pottery and weaving, mu-sical instruments, and ritual life (represented by the church and a typical Yureño hat). Tourists, anthropologists, and researchers were drawn and dis-cussed as having the same accoutrements: video cameras, tooth-clad boots, and cars. The man with the video camera showed a striking resemblance to an agronomist who was working with ISALP. Everyone laughed as the sub-ject of this drawing futilely protested, "Hey I'm an agronomist, not an an-thropologist." For Yureños, there were more similarities than differences between tourists, anthropologists, and agronomists.

Yureños did not attend ayllu meetings with the intention of discussing their music and the presence of researchers. The separate ayllu meetings, usually held in one of the communities of the ayllu, were aimed at assessing needs and planning projects for the following year. My questions on music and the cassette production opened these meetings, as the ayllus delayed discussion of other projects until latecomers arrived. The meeting began with a discussion of the proposed cassette production, a request for permission to produce the cassette, and a debate about how it should be distributed. Then the meeting broke into small groups to discuss the above questions. An open discussion about the cassette title and cassette cover design followed the presentation of each group's ideas, the latecomers usually arriving in time for the final discussions.

In terms of distribution decisions, the first ayllu to hold its meeting set a standard that the others followed with little variation. When the other ayllus heard that Ayllu Wisiqsa would sell its cassettes within the ayllu, they all decided to do the same. Each ayllu designated the kuraqa as the person in charge of selling the cassettes and accounting for the proceeds. Each ayllu set an internal price of 5 bolivianos (Bs.) ($1), and agreed to an external price of Bs. 15 ($3). The external sales were to be handled through ISALP with the argument that members of this institution had more connections to possible outside markets. Each ayllu would decide what to do with the proceeds from their internal sales.

Proceeds generated from external sales would form a special fund to cover travel expenses of the kuraqas. Kuraqas did not receive any remuneration, a theme that was thoroughly discussed at one of Yura's ayllu meetings. Yureños were asked to put a price on the activities of the kuraqa, and they discussed whether the kuraqas should receive some form of payment. The Law of Popular Participation as progressively interpreted was demanding that kuraqas assume a more active role if the local people chose to register as indigenous organizations. The very registration with the state transformed the nature of the kuraqa's authority and the expectations of this authority's position. In 1995, Yureños gave a resounding negative response to the possibility of kuraqas receiving remuneration, adding the comment that Yureños would continue to pay their kuraqas "with respect." As the kuraqas assumed more active roles through the Law of Popular Participation, they needed to travel more frequently to the municipal section capital. Respect does not pay transportation prices and Yureños had demonstrated themselves reluctant to let their kuraqas leave the area in search of temporary paid labor in Santa Cruz, Cochabamba, and Argentina. From these discussions the idea to form a travel fund from the external sale of cassettes emerged. In December 1995, I left 690 cassettes in Yura, to be distributed to the kuraqas at the next meeting of the ayllu Yura.

The beginning of 1996 brought a change in the kuraqas, and the plans for distribution went awry. "Ayllu democracy" works on the basis of rotation whereby assuming a position of authority is an obligation of membership in the ayllu rather than a competitive electoral process (see Rivera Cusicanqui and THOA 1992). As usual, each ayllu rotated to new kuraqas, but not all of the supposed kuraqas had accepted their obligations to hold these positions of authority. During a visit in 1996, I found some ayllus temporarily in doubt as to whether or not they even had kuraqas. With the uncertainty surrounding the existing kuraqas, most of the cassettes were still collecting dust in the village Yura. During subsequent visits to Yura I heard that the cassettes were being raffled off at Yura's ayllu meetings. The power, assumed to be vested in the kuraqa's position of authority, was temporarily volatile. With the uncertainty of Yura's kuraqas the cassettes entered circulation in an improvised fashion. I later heard that those who were kuraqas at the time of the production were claiming an ownership of the cassettes. After all, the kuraqas were the only Yureño individuals named on the cassette brochure, and I had listed their names under the heading of "production organization." The theme of ownership of these cassettes ultimately brings with it a discussion of the Bolivian state, its laws, and the paradoxes of owning culture.

Owning Culture

Yureños wanted to make sure that their cassette was properly registered through the official channels in La Paz. They were conscious of their music as a cultural product with rights of ownership. I offered to document composers' names on the cassette brochure, but even though Yureños locally recognized their musical creations as compositions of individuals, they did not want these names listed on the cassette. The ownership was viewed as collective even if the delineation of that collectivity remained ambiguous—sometimes an ayllu, sometimes a community, but never an individual. The context in which these decisions were publicly made—the ayllu meetings—was obviously conducive to this collective, rather than individual, attribution of authorship. In publicly opting for collective ownership in the representation of this music, Yureños shifted from the realm of intellectual property to the realm of cultural property; individual Yureños lost potential ownership over what could be considered as uniquely authentic compositions. Instead, Yureños claimed collective ownership of a culturally authentic representation. The differences between the realms of cultural and artistic originals, between cultural and intellectual property, are marked by law, custom, and power relations. One of the significant differences Rosemary Coombe noted is that copyright law, which defends intellectual property, allows authors to make claims over all reproductions of their original works, whereas cultural property laws only allow possessive claims to be made over "original objects or authentic artifacts" (1998: 225). While this distinction may appear straightforward when applied to seemingly palpable, tangible originals, it remains clouded in reference to musical originals. How does one distinguish the single authentic musical performance over which an indigenous group might hold control, especially if one hears the live musical performance, and all possibilities of representing this experiential authenticity must assume some medium of mechanical reproduction?

As Rosemary Coombe suggested, with reference to cultural property laws affecting Native peoples of Canada, intellectual property assumes individual authors speak through universal reason, whereas "those who have culture speak only on behalf of a cultural tradition that must be unified and homogeneous before we accord it any respect" (1998: 243). Any attempt to champion the collective rights of a group over its musical creations must buy into the same logic of property, ownership, and "possessive individualism" that holds for individual author's rights. Possessive individualism is rooted philosophically in Locke's labor theory of value whereby individuals are assumed to have ownership of their own bodies as well as over those products that result from an interaction of one's own body with natural objects (Locke 1960 [1689]; also see Handler 1985: 210). Richard Handler has remarked on the "worn out" yet still dominant metaphors that emerge from possessive individualism: metaphors of collectivities as individuals and culture as property (1991: 68–70). As the kuraqas' claims over "their" cassette so clearly exemplified, there is nothing straightforward or transparent about collective or individual ownership of original compositions.

Yet the Yureños' public decision to collectively claim the materials of this cassette as cultural property added to Yureños' symbolic capital in representing themselves as an indigenous group. In mid-1990s Bolivia, such symbolic sources had real potential to be converted into material capital, by tapping sources from international foundations that favored indigenous peoples as target populations. Art or culture, intellectual or cultural property—these were not issues Yureños discussed, but their decision in favor of cultural property had unintended consequences for the author function of these cassettes. Yureños did not make these production decisions with a knowledge of Bolivian copyright law, nor did they subsequently have institutional encounters—as they did regarding the Law of Popular Participation—that would exert the limits of Bolivian copyright law. Although the results of relinquishing individual authorship were not consciously perceived nor necessarily intended by Yureños, I believe these results to be important for several reasons. When the law operates hegemonically it operates "not only when it is institutionally encountered, but when it is consciously and unconsciously apprehended" (Coombe 1998: 9). Yureños did not know of copyright laws but they did perceive this cassette as cultural property over which they could claim ownership. Secondly, according to J. Balkin's reading of Derrida, studies of meaning and signification should be just as concerned with the unintended meanings as with the intended (Balkin 1987: 777). Yureños did not want their authorship removed from this cassette; they simply wanted it presented as a collectivity. The unintended consequence was a kind of disappearance or shift of the author function. Rather than simply accept a supposed disappearance of an author, "we must locate the space left empty by the author's disappearance, follow the distribution of gaps and breaches, and watch for the openings that this disappearance uncovers" (Foucault 1984: 105). The tale of gaps, breaches, and unintended consequences continues with my attempts to officially register these cassettes.

When I began asking musician colleagues in La Paz about official registration procedures, I received helpful advice along with a good dose of skepticism about the effectiveness of these processes. Ineffectiveness was clearly illustrated in the recent Kjarkas-Kaoma disputes over the rights to the lambada song "Llorando se fue" (see Wara Céspedes 1993). One musician mentioned this case, but he still viewed official registration as an important step in any music production. Another musician dismissed the whole idea of official registration as a waste of time. His perspective was based on skepticism of these bureaucratic procedures.

Considering the history behind copyright law, there is no reason to expect that official copyright registration will bolster any claims to ownership by Yureños. Mark Rose reminds us that in eighteenth-century England, copyright law as related to "literary property" emerged through a commercial struggle between booksellers; within this commercial struggle the author as proprietor was elaborated in law long before authors sensed themselves as owners of their creations (1993: 3–5). As a contemporary example, Jacqueline Seignette underlines the fact that "the primary objective of U.S. copyright law is not to reward the labour of authors, but to 'promote the Progress of Science and useful Arts'"; this law places progress ahead of the creator doctrine (1994: 22). Rather than being an eternal, natural, or universal idea, the modern concept of author has historical and cultural specificity. The marks of the modern author include internal rather than divine inspiration and a sense of ownership over one's own works (see Rose 1993: 1; Woodmansee 1994: 42). Before the modern author, patrons were proprietors over artistic works. The modern author emerged within the development of capitalist markets in the late seventeenth and eighteenth centuries (Rose 1993: 16; also see Attali 1985).

When this individual authorship is transferred to the collectivity of an indigenous group, copyright law does not simply remain inadequate in addressing the rights of indigenous communities (see Seeger 1996: 90). There are major contradictions in the very notion of proprietorship that copyright law assumes. Michael Brown has addressed the crucial issues of this debate in an article titled "Can Culture Be Copyrighted?" (1998). Brown critiqued the impassioned advocacy for indigenous groups, often assumed by anthropologists and activists, that in the name of cultural protection often pushes the expansion of copyright laws. While well intentioned, these politics of advocacy rarely critically examine the implications of turning culture into property: the encroachment on public domain, the threat to open political dialogue, and the fact that a realm of culture as colonized by copyright law will ultimately work to the advantage of those who are in a financial position to litigate the enforcement of copyright laws as applied to an endlessly expanding realm of cultural property (Brown 1998: 196, 204). For Brown, the expansion of copyright is disturbing precisely because the endless chatter about culture as commodity has drowned out the crucial discussions about the real moral and ethical issues related to the position of indigenous peoples in the world of global capitalism (1998: 199). In line with Brown's argument, I am suggesting that the kernel of contention in these cassette productions is not on the plane about which we usually hear—indigenous groups being swindled out of their own culture—but rather in the very notion of *proprietorship* over art and culture. In smoothing over these contradictions, Bolivian law and bureaucratic institutions that work in copyright registration foster patronizing practices in the collecting of culture.

As I attempted to complete the official procedures of registration, I encountered the standard contradiction of copyright law: the inability to register these cassettes as the creative property of collectivities. The forms I completed could not be filed without *my name* as the compiler (*recopiladora*), and the entities of "Yura" and "Toropalca" were forced into a secondary position to my individual identity as a researcher. In many cases, those who record a traditional music have been claiming rights over these productions, even though they are not the performing musicians. This is a trend that, according to Anthony Seeger, is now shifting toward the allocation of rights and a payment to the original performers (1991: 296). According to bureaucratic perceptions, in Bolivia compilers have rights. As one bureaucrat explained: "This policy began in a time when the government wanted to encourage more research of Bolivia's cultures. So the compiler was given part of the commercial rights over anything they registered with us." I recalled heated debates in the 1994 meetings of the National Museum of Ethnography and Folklore (MUSEF, *Museo Nacional de*

Etnografía y Folklore, La Paz), in which musicians/researchers felt that their rights as compilers or "discoverers" had been usurped by other artists. I remembered hushed critical comments about music ensembles not recognizing a compiler in the notes of their recorded interpretations. These policies that require official recognition of a compiler are constructed through a colonizing logic and recall the systems of patronage that existed prior to modern authorship. A government wants to know more about the cultures in its territory, presences that are usually expressed in terms of "patrimony." Researchers of these cultural treasures are considered as discoverers and much like the crown's assignment of encomiendas to Spanish conquerors, compilers are rewarded with a claim to commercial rights over symbolic creations that are not their own (also see Seeger 1996: 87). Even though I did not want to operate within a "my-people" framework of anthropological research, I was suddenly pushed into that framework as I tried to comply with the publicly stated wishes of Yureños. Whether I wanted it or not, I became the "compiler" of the music on these cassettes. But the tale of authorship does not end there.

Patrimony: The Nation-State as Author

The bureaucrat who told me about compilers' rights did not specify which law had given such entitlements, and I have found none in the books that correspond. But this overall attitude was expressed as recently as 1995 in a Conference on Cultural Politics and State Promotion of Culture: "[The protection of our patrimony] implies the development of research that backs the defense of our folkloric works—anonymous and of public domain—as national patrimony. So there should be a strong support of centers dedicated to ethnographic [and] folkloric research . . . (Velarde 1995: 6).

In 1909, Bolivia's Intellectual Property Law made no mention of collective productions or of "folklore." But the 1992 Author's Rights Law (1322) places musical expressions like those I recorded in Toropalca and Yura under the rubric of "National Patrimony." In Title XI Article 58 the law states that "folkloric works and those in traditional culture by an unknown author" constitute "National Patrimony." Title V Article 21 defines folklore as: "the set of literary and artistic works created in national territory by unknown authors or *by authors who do not identify themselves* and are presumed to be nationals of the country, or of its ethnic communities, and that are transmitted from generation to generation, constituting one of the fundamental elements of traditional cultural patrimony of the nation" (emphasis added). Collective authorship is not recognized under the law, but rather is read as "unknown" or unspecified authorship. Any description of Toropalqueño or Yureño authorship as strictly individual or strictly collective would be misguided. Beyond the Toropalqueño example of collective composition in Sarapalca, further examples can be drawn from the production process of the Toropalqueño song book. In collecting and documenting these songs, I often intentionally pushed the question of authorship, even asking the singer for approximate dates of composition. I found that more recent compositions were easily assigned to specific creators, but Toropalqueños were unsure of the creatorship of what they perceived as older songs. I also found singers more quickly assigned creatorship of other people's compositions and were reluctant to say, "I composed that song." Toropalqueños recognized individual authorship, but within a limited temporal framework, close to the experiential moment of the present. Furthermore, I never heard the concept of individual creatorship accompanied by a claim to individual ownership over that material. Even if it was never clear if Toropalqueños represented themselves principally as an ayllu, a canton, or simply as a group of communities, the song book was always discussed in terms of a collectivity of Toropalqueños.

Some of the musical compositions from Yura did appear to have individual authorship, to the extent that young men entered fist fights to assure the playing of their tunes in Carnival. Yureños depicted composing as an activity of the solitary individual engaged with inspirations and spirits of the natural world. Nevertheless, in the public debate about the cassette production, Yureños favored a collective presentation of the music as belonging to the ayllus of Yura. The choice of collective rather than individual recognition left the nation-state as author, and to borrow from Louis Dumont's argument, the nationalism symbolically served by such a consequence still worked within the values of individualism (1986: 10). The logic of patrimony operates through these principles of "national culture as property and the nation as a property owning 'collective individual'" (Handler 1985: 194). Through laws of national patrimony the Bolivian nation-state posed as the proprietor of the collectively authored originals, all created in its territory.

Another section of Bolivian law, which does not specifically mention folklore, is no more conducive to transferring this proprietorship to another collective entity. Title III, Article 8 states, "Only a natural person can be an author; nevertheless the State, the entities of public law, and juridical and moral persons can exercise author's rights as derived bearers [of those rights]." Under the law only individuals, or an individual who has been "derived" from the group, are recognized as authors. The "derived bearer" of these rights holds the rights of commercial exploitation (Title

III, Article 13). In light of this law, it was in vain that I put on each cassette, "The rights of all the huayños of this cassette belong to the respective ayllus of the large ayllu Yura." By law these expressions belonged to the State as "National Patrimony" or to some "derived bearer" of these collective rights, but it is doubtful whether this law does much more than sit on the books. While Bolivian newspapers often run stories on the ongoing feud with Chile about the true origins of the devil dance (*diablada*), policies related to national patrimony and folklore remain circumscribed in the details of law and rhetoric. Institutions of the Bolivian state have taken no drastic measures toward controlling folklore.[4]

In practice, copyright processes run rather fast and loose in Bolivia.[5] Musician colleagues in La Paz attested to the fact that no one regularly receives royalties within Bolivian systems of copyright registration. So even disgruntled compilers are clamoring for little more than symbolic recognition. Nevertheless, it is worth noting that the patronizing copyright policies hardly seemed consistent with other contemporary Bolivian government discourses that emphasized indigenous recognition and entitlement. The logic of copyright over folklore, establishing state power over cultural expressions, is similar to the logic of registering indigenous organizations under the Law of Popular Participation. Through both logics the state establishes domain over national places. But the artistic registration policies remain in a more paternalistic mode of accommodating Bolivia's differences; the State's language in relation to national folklore is couched in terms of "protection" and protection legally means a transference of authorship to the state itself.[6] What remains unclear is the status of the indigenous organizations that have received juridical personality through the Law of Popular Participation. Will the state recognize indigenous organizations with juridical personalities as full authors of their own cultural expressions? How does this authorship potentially transform the indigenous organization and its relationship to the state?

Even state authorship over this material remained muddled as the wheels of bureaucracy lived down to our usual expectations. With the intention of returning this official paperwork to both Yura and Toropalca, I attempted and failed to obtain papers for the registration of these cassettes. My departure date was imminent and my frustration increased as I returned to the office, day after day, and the bureaucrat, seated behind mountains of paper, said, "Can you return tomorrow? I'm sure we will have it for you tomorrow." I asked friends if I should offer a bribe, but they seemed to think that this was not a stalling behavior, rather it was just business as usual. Papers that enter this process are often simply lost. When I left Bolivia I asked a colleague in La Paz to continue pursuing this bureaucratic task. A year later, he had been equally unsuccessful. In 1996, we both went to the office and received the same answer of "Can you return tomorrow?" I have since given up my attempt to return this official paperwork to Yura and Toropalca. The paperwork for the cassettes of Yura and Toropalca sits buried in a bureaucrat's office. Even if I had wanted to assert commercial rights as a compiler, or the Bolivian state had wanted to assert authorship rights over patrimony, the bureaucratic process itself has forestalled any possibility of acting on those rights.

Music performances that established domain over places entered a process of schizophonia as an anthropologist attempted to give something back to the people with whom she worked. In each stage of producing a culturally authentic music performance on a packaged cassette, different individuals asserted power within limited spheres of influence, and circumstances alone diffused the author function. By law, the state held the author's rights for these cassettes. Through law, the performative relation to place shifted from Toropalca and Yura to Bolivian national territory. The anthropologist entered a fuzzy category of "compiler." The hard evidence of all this was lost in a bureaucratic shuffle.

But I would suggest that in the case of Yura, opting for collective representation brought another unintended consequence: a reshaping of the relation of exchange that has existed between the ayllus of Potosi and the Bolivian state. The nature of this state-ayllu exchange was most recently a symbolic sum of money in return for guaranteed rights over land. But the state will no longer accept this sum. The global economy today has placed a high value on cultural difference itself, differences that are spotted through customs, music, and folklore. Nations have consistently manipulated these cultural expressions as "national patrimony," but perhaps today these expressions have de facto become part of a new state-ayllu reciprocal pact: The ayllus leave unspecified the authorship of their cultural expressions; the nation-state has its source of patrimony in "unauthored" creations; the ayllus—through their effectiveness in presenting themselves as collective indigenous groups—are in a privileged position to receive projects through nongovernmental organizations funded by state and international sources. In opting for collective representation of their music, Yureños unknowingly relinquished the author function to the state, but this sacrifice generated other economic values for Yureños.[7]

This new exchange emerged within a global fashion of respecting cultural diversity. The cry for respect of cultural differences is certainly a discourse to which anthropologists, for better or worse, have contributed. In the guise of multiculturalism, this discourse displaces other disputes and becomes a comfortable realm of politics that appears to operate in a less-polarized environment.[8] But the politics of multiculturalism may be deceiving in that they overlook the nefarious side of ethnic politics and mask social inequalities that persist below this global pageant of folklore. Within global multiculturalism the structures of the Bolivian nation-state continue to subordinate indigenous people to its jurisdiction.

Nevertheless, as seen from this particular ethnographic example, pre-structured relations of inequality do not necessarily predetermine how power is asserted in cultural productions. Neither the anthropologist, nor the state, nor the indigenous people seemed to be completely in control of these productions. If we continue to follow Michael Herzfeld's assertion that bureaucratic practices are rituals of state (1992), these rituals seem to be effective in both dispersing a sense of where power lies and in making believers out of citizens in all different social positions—believers in the state's potential of justly ordering reality despite individual experiences to the contrary. The author function behind these cassettes remained in a plurality and no definitive author emerged within a clear position of ownership. The modern narrative of authorship tells a Romantic tale of individual strokes of genius from which works of art emerge. But equally modern and Romantic is the narrative of a collective creation characterized by peaceful cooperation, from which cultural artifacts and expressions pour forth. Both narratives of authorship leave auras around their creations—the aura of art linked to the individual and the aura of culture linked to a rooted community or nation imagined as Dumont's collective individual (see also Clifford 1988: 225; Benjamin 1968; Chow 1994). The auras of both art and culture mediate a sense of value in and proprietorship over creations. In the production of these cassettes Yureños publicly opted for collective authorship with a general sense of their own culture as something alienable. As described here and in previous chapters, the musical struggles behind this collective front were multiple. According to Bolivian law, the ownership of this cultural material belonged to the nation-state as national patrimony. Peter Jaszi suggests that works that do not fit the model of individual authorship become invisible within copyright logic (1994: 38). Perhaps this explains the disappearing act that seems to have occurred with the registration of these cassettes. But in the case of Yureños, I suggest that one kind of visibility was traded for another. In publicly opting for "culture" over "art" Yureños gained symbolic capital and visibility as a collective indigenous entity, even if in the process Yureños' authorship became invisible. Unique authenticity was traded for a reassertion of cultural authenticity, as Yureños gambled in favor of the advantages to be gained through this form of collective representation.

CHAPTER 8

CODAS, *DESPEDIDAS*, AND *KACHARPAYAS*

coda: "a concluding section or passage, extraneous to the basic structure of the composition but added in order to confirm the impression of finality
—*Harvard Concise Dictionary of Music,* Randel 1978.

despedida: a Spanish word for a farewell song, dance, or celebration.

kacharpaya: a Quechua word for the closing music and celebrations
of a fiesta.

In 1995, the ensemble Kjarkas underwent a significant makeover:
Kjarkas became *Pacha.* While the name "Kjarkas" invoked pre-Conquest fortresses built by the Incas to protect against invasions (Wara Céspedes 1993), the name "Pacha" invoked all the expansiveness of both
space and time of the Andean world. The makeover consisted of more
than a change of names. In their transformation, the ensemble went to
Los Angeles and recorded a CD of their classic themes, but with the
backup of a full symphony orchestra. They went to Mexico, where, with
another full symphony orchestra and Mexican dancers, they filmed videos
of themes from their repertoire. They kept their standard repertoire and
their own Andean instruments, but they took off their ponchos. While the
addition of the symphony orchestra transformed the sonorous presentations of Kjarkas-Pacha, many of the other transformations seemed driven
by the attention to visual cues that accompanies the music video genre,

perhaps "the art form par excellence of late capitalism" (Jameson 1991: 76). The Kjarkas-Pacha transformation was part of a marketing pitch "to the world" according to local Bolivian news reports, but the resulting sound image looked more like a specific pitch to Latino/Latin American audiences who might thrive on the ballads of Luis Miguel or the romantic songs of the late Selena. Several members of Música de Maestros applauded the Kjarkas-Pacha transformation, claiming that the ensemble had found its proper niche, that they had always been performing romantic ballads under the guise of indigenous dress, and that they had finally revealed their "true" musical selves.

The Kjarkas-Pacha transformation posed a classification question. What kind of music was this? What kind of music had it become? While many Bolivians felt unsettled by the emergence of Pacha, Kjarkas did continue to perform in their previous style, and Bolivians continued to find a groove in this music. The question of classification deserves attention, not because I want to properly catalogue this new performance expression of Kjarkas, but because issues of classification have haunted this entire book. Is that music avant-garde, popular, or traditional? Are those musical expressions more modern or traditional? Is that rural music or urban music? Is that mestizo-Creole music or indigenous music? Is that music composed by an individual or by a collective group? Is that music art or is it culture? Anthropologists have long puzzled over the tendency of human beings to classify the elements of their world (Radcliffe Brown 1965 [1929]; Levi-Strauss 1963; Levi-Strauss 1966), and their writings have revealed the political and ideological underpinnings of these classification systems (Comaroff 1987; Borneman 1988). While I have addressed these kinds of classifications as expressed by Bolivians in relation to their music performances, I have also spent a good deal of time presenting these ethnographic materials on Bolivian music performances, and feelings of belonging, in an intentional project against classification. My anticlassification project has been one of revealing and dislodging from their comfortable positions systems of classification that often remain implicit within studies of social life. This kind of project, in reference to anthropology's terms of analysis, is the most useful application of the currently popular concept of "hybridity" (García Canclini 1992a). My terms of analysis in this book have been intentionally hybrid, refusing to replicate the standard dualisms that often emerge from the get-go, in the way we frame our studies. Someone might argue that I have simply substituted for the old classifications of rural-urban, traditional-modern, indigenous-Spanish, and culture-art another system of classification of three conceptualizations of authenticity. But I have applied these concepts as a fluid and flexible way of making sense out of articulations that occur precisely between these dichotomies.

As a theoretical framework, these three ideologies of authenticity are significant through their relations to each other. Through an analysis of experiential, cultural-historical, and unique authenticities, I have addressed the corresponding issues of pleasure, representation, and commodification within a multiclass and multiethnic analysis. The pleasures of experiential authenticity clash with the representational demands of cultural-historical authenticity, and these contradictions may play out in a policing of indigenous authenticity by mestizo-Creoles who occupy a relatively more privileged position. But within folklore festival contexts that strive for cultural authenticity, the temporal organization of these multicultural panoramas moves all subjects into representational logics that curtail the multisensorial experiences of ritual and of the groove. If Yureños ritually mark their territory through a sonorous experience, they also enter into the representational practices of state bureaucracies when they must prove themselves as "truly" indigenous. As indigenous peoples in Bolivia occupy a special position in the contemporary imagining of a multicultural nation, indigenous subjects in Toropalca and Yura assumed this burden in very different ways. Toropalqueños who were more isolated from the kinds of interactions that might raise a consciousness of indigenous identity mourned their perceived loss of culture. Yureños, long in contact with anthropologists and NGOs, negotiated their own representational practices as an indigenous group, without the expressions of nostalgia for lost culture.

In both cases, Yureños and Toropalqueños demonstrated an awareness of the value, in an economy of national and global funding opportunities, of a thing called indigenous culture, and this awareness revealed the logic of what I have called unique authenticity. Two principal elements characterize unique authenticity: 1) a Romantic ideology of inspired artists who produce unique works that speak to universal human questions, and 2) the corresponding ideology of proprietorship over such creations. These ideologies may be more commonly associated with Western classical music traditions and the idea of great composers was certainly a part of the mestizo-Creole project of Música de Maestros. But unique authenticity is also the logic at work in a claim to ownership over the cassette productions in Yura and Toropalca, the concept of these cultural expressions as property, and their symbolic transformation into national patrimony.

Furthermore, indigenous peoples' ritual contexts are not the only domain of experiential authenticity. The current trend of mestizo-Creole national music projects to play indigenous instruments in their troupe styles is an attempt to reconnect with an experiential authenticity of these particular genres. In addition, the mestizo-Creole genres like cuecas and bailecitos have their grooves as well, and these are also affected by representational practices—everything from the writing of music to the performance of this music in international folklore festivals. I have used experiential, cultural-historical, and unique authenticites to explicate the cultural politics of Bolivian music performances in local, national, and international contexts.

To provide an ethnographic window into Bolivian music performances and their connections to national and ethnic affiliations, I "moved through places" and rejected traditional divisions, explicitly placing side by side what is often relegated to oppositional categories and even separate books. As I suggested in the introduction, "hybridity" as a "strategic essentialism" (Spivak 1988) is a useful concept in melting down what have been our own rigid terms of analysis, but the concept becomes problematic in at least two ways: when an enthusiasm for hybridity undermines the "strategic essentialism" that minority groups themselves apply in order to strengthen their already subordinate positions (Wade 1999: 460; Warren 1998: 78; Albó 1999: 80–83) and when the concept of hybridity becomes identified with a celebration of cultural mixing, which is seen as easily transposed to any social context. This paradox parallels Paul Gilroy's seemingly contradictory position both against ethnic absolutism and for an anti–antiessentialist position in analyses of black Atlantic culture (1993: 2, 101). While we need to stop looking for the pure and unchanging Andean cultures, we also need to recognize the import of cultural politics of oppressed groups that may invoke the very essentialisms that academics have discarded as the refuse of modernity.

In the Bolivian context, cultural mixing might be read through an understanding of "mestizaje," a term with varied historical connotations, but with a general reference to a mixing of Spanish and indigenous cultures. The contemporary concept of mestizaje in Bolivia carries the heavy symbolic load of the homogenizing narrative of the 1952 Revolution, a narrative of erasing indigenous differences under the uniform recognition of the category of "peasant," and of the 1953 Agrarian Reform's attempt to transform indigenous lands into individually held private properties. Thus it becomes difficult to simply apply mestizaje or hybridity to a reconceptualization of knowledge production, especially within a political context in which demonstrating the authenticity of one's position as indigenous has real value in economic and political terms. Counter to the grand narrative of the end of grand narratives (Lyotard 1984; Harvey 1989), the associated end of "works" (Jameson 1991: 77), and the end of the need to identify the culturally authentic—or "culturally pure"—I have shown that quests for cultural authenticity and the historical authenticity of "works" are still very much alive, not only in the politics within Bolivian territory, but also in the international politics that often set the parameters through which Bolivians negotiate their representational practices. The Bolivian examples I have presented also have reflected a strong persistence of the ethos of great "works." If hybridity helps to take apart problematic terms of analysis, it becomes a hindrance when blindly applied to processes of mestizaje in Bolivia, when terms of analysis are mistaken for social life itself.

Critiques of mestizaje in Bolivia bring the political back to what can easily become a sanitized field of celebrated hybridity. R. Radhakrishnan, from the subject position of an academic immigrant from India to the United States, made a parallel distinction through a discussion of metropolitan hybridity that sits comfortably within national and transnational citizenships and postcolonial hybridity that still seeks a legitimate political identity. "When metropolitan hybridity begins to speak for postcolonial hybridity, it inevitably depoliticizes the latter and renders its rebellion virtually causeless" (1996: 159). Radhakrishnan's concerns are not unlike those of Bolivian analysts. For example, Silvia Rivera critiques the 1952 celebration of mestizaje as one more form of internal colonialism, one more attempt by a dominant class to impose its will on subordinate Bolivians (1993), and Xavier Albó finds suspect the discussion of a national mestiza identity that potentially undercuts the radical edge of indigenous politics, that presents an either-or proposition in which a uniform national identity, constructed around a premise of shared cultural mixing, precludes the continued maintenance of cultural differences (1999: 83). In Bolivia, mestizaje is entwined with a contentious national historical project, and it is difficult to imagine an application of hybridity, as read onto the Bolivian cultural context, that could be completely decoupled from this history. Hybridity is not the only conceptual proposal placed on the table, as academics attempt to move beyond analytical essentialisms. Thomas Abercrombie has referred to "cultural interfaces" or "cultural frontiers" (1991: 95; 1998: 83–86). Mary Louise Pratt has written about "contact zones" (1991). Guillermo Mariaca and Xavier Albó have engaged with the term "intercultural" (Mariaca, Rivera, Quisbert 1999: 212; Albó 1999: 84–87).[1] But even the concept of the "intercultural" has come under sharp critique, as it became the buzz word of Bolivia's Law of Educational Reform. Denise Arnold and Juan de Dios Yapita have critiqued the Educational Reform's politics of interculturality because they assign a kind of primordial orality to Andean cultures, next to the unmarked Western textual traditions, while ignoring the alternative textualities of Andean cultures, those expressed through song, music, and weaving (2000). Instead of "interculturality," Arnold and Yapita propose "intertextuality" (2000: 419–420).[2] In spite of their differences, all of these alternatives demonstrate a concern with the presentation of an inter-relational position in the study of cultural practices in Bolivia, and all of these approaches seek to underscore, rather than sweep under the rug, the contentious positions and unequal power relations that shape these politics. Hybridity's conceptual usefulness wanes as we try to understand the shift in Bolivian national narratives from the mestizaje of 1952 to the return of the Indian in the contemporary narrative of nation. With this return have come a plethora of activities in which groups pursue perceived cultural authenticity, and a celebration of hybridity risks overlooking the critical politics of this pursuit. When used as a descriptive adjective for a particular social or cultural context, "hybrid" sounds too much like the Bolivian national ideology of homogeneity, and this ideology has been strongly resisted by Bolivia's indigenous peoples.

In relation to the themes I have developed in this book, the Kjarkas-Pacha transformation was indicative of a shift in the politics of authenticity, a shift in the way indigenousness stands in for the culturally historically authentic. The aesthetics of Kjarkas—taking indigenous instruments from the countryside and inserting them into a stylized urban performance context—followed the Bolivian 1952 revolutionary narrative of revaluating the generic "peasant," and was a radical move in its time. Musicians today still talk about the kind of stigma that was attached to these peasant instruments in the era before the 1952 Revolution. But the contemporary narrative of nation, counter to the revolutionary ideology of mestizaje and cultural homogenization, called for a different musical aesthetic, consistent with the return of the Indian. It no longer sufficed to simply play the indigenous instrument, but the instrument had to be reconnected with its perceived original performance aesthetic with a troupe style performance of specific genres as associated with particular instruments. This reuniting of indigenous instruments with their performance aesthetics was precisely what Música de Maestros did in the mohoceñada at the close of the "Suite Aymara," or in the first themes of the "Suite Oriental." It is also what the workshop did in its wing of traditional music activities.

While I agree with Gilka Wara Céspedes that Kjarkas's music did have national associations in Bolivia beyond mere labeling, and that Kjarkas and ensembles like them were at one time linked to a prominent narrative of nation rooted in Bolivia's 1952 Revolution (1993), those national associations have since shifted. Members of Música de Maestros perceived their own project as the production of an alternative "national music," but beyond self-perception, their musical project heralded narratives of nation that differed from those implicit within performing groups like Kjarkas. If one listens to musical soundscapes, not only as a herald of changing modes of music production (Attali 1985), but also as a herald of changing narratives of nation, one can hear in Música de Maestros's performances, as well as in the performances of other contemporary Bolivian musical projects, an attempt to reestablish the authenticity of indigenous music performance. While Música de Maestros may have made reference to cultural mestizaje in their outcry against the Spanish television's representation of Bolivia as an imagined highland Indian, members of this ensemble were obsessed with historical and cultural authenticity. The terms "master composer" and "works" intentionally echoed a European ethos of musical creation, but Música de Maestros extended this ethos to indigenous works. While the authenticity of the "works" from the 1930s was pursued through archival work and interviews with composers or their families, the authenticity of indigenous works was pursued through fieldwork and an attempt to reconstruct the performance aesthetics believed to belong to particular indigenous instruments. For the workshop, this fieldwork had to end not in a dust-collecting archival project, but in music performances that would bring alive these traditions for sons and daughters of Aymara migrants in the city of La Paz.

The shift from indigenous instruments to include indigenous performance aesthetics placed higher stakes on the representation of cultural authenticity. Cultural authenticity demanded a reenacted embodiment—a stab at someone else's experiential authenticity that a musician might claim to achieve after long stints of arduous fieldwork—as well as an attention to the details of differences within indigenous genres. The return of the Indian was the appearance of "Indians" in plural form. Indians of the highlands and lowlands were recognized in all their distinctiveness, and an emphasis on authentic performance aesthetics underscored that recognition. In the context of these new demands in national music aesthetics, Kjarkas went Romantic-Latin, and aimed at a completely different audience.

The return to culturally authentic performance aesthetics harkens to the ritual use-value of music, from which, according to Walter Benjamin, art was to be emancipated within the age of mechanical reproduction (1968: 224). While Benjamin may have felt nostalgia for the waning of art's ritual use-value, as well as optimism in the freeing-up of art for politics, Rey Chow and others have already signalled the dangers of celebrating this transformation (Chow 1994). The politicization of aesthetics slips dangerously into the aestheticization of politics, and, as Benjamin suggested of Nazi Germany's use of art, this mode of politics can turn in any direction. The workshop's avant-garde compositions using indigenous instruments may break out of the tyranny of tonality while indexing a rootedness to the traditional indigenous, but ultimately, the political meaning of these open works is up for grabs. Música de Maestros's performances provided a point of multigenerational bonding in relation to personal memories of the Chaco War, but the ensemble's video-taped performances and audio recordings are tossed precariously into the sea of signifiers that seemed to remain outside of both the control of the artists and the copyright laws that might entitle these musicians.

As music performances become collectable in the forms of videos and recordings, they take on a "life of things" (Appadurai 1986). The resulting schizophonia is more than an issue of changing technologies. Recordings make indigenous music collectable and often form a crucial part of studies about music and culture. As the music performances on the cassette productions in Toropalca and Yura moved from the realm of direct experience to the realms of representation and potential commodification, the question of ownership became central. Even though recent Bolivian legislation like the Law of Popular Participation provided opportunities for the recognition of indigenous ways of life, copyright law, based on the myth of the individual creator of unique works, could not accommodate indigenous compositions in a straightforward way. Rather than placing collective versus individual authorship at the crux of my argument, I have preferred to highlight the very ambiguity of creatorship and examine who attributes collective and individual authorship to others, and why. While the Western concept of the modern author romanticizes the uniquely authentic work, the Western concept of the indigenous composition equally romances collective harmonious modes of creation. While I have presented material from Toropalca and Yura that casts doubt on any essentialized notion of the collective cooperative mode of indigenous composing, I would argue that neither collective nor individual creatorship goes to the heart of this matter. The central issue is the transformation of cultural symbolic material into property—into something to be possessed. Yureños unwittingly, entered this logic of property, exchanging individual possession of their music performances for a stronger representation of themselves as a collective indigenous group. In the exchange, the Bolivian state banked more symbolic capital in the form of national patrimony, and Yureños gained symbolic capital through the ideology of cultural-historical authenticity.

Yura's exchange of symbolic capital was consistent with Bolivia's contemporary configurations in which culturally authentic indigenousness, of both highland and lowland references, has taken center stage. The people living in the territory now referred to as Bolivia have a long tradition of indigenous uprisings—Tupac Katari and the circling of La Paz in 1781, Zárate Willka in the late nineteenth century (see Zavaleta Mercado 1986: 96–179), and the Kataristas of the twentieth century. The historian Silvia Rivera has shown how these movements work through long- and short-term historical memory of those who have been oppressed (1986). Oppressed, yes. But vanquished? Never.[3] The more recent return of the Indian in state and popular politics, the substitution of the pluri-multi model for the universalizing model of citizenship, is part of a global trend, consistent with neoliberal currents of the 1990s. While Goni's exit from the presidency and the entrance of a previous dictator, Hugo Banzer Suárez, led to the closure of the Ministry of Ethnic, Gender, and Generational Affairs, the world of foundation politics and Bolivian NGOs still closely follows these trends in formulating their projects around questions of indigenous and gendered categories.

If the unpredictable path of modernity's narrative has now turned to a celebration of cultural differences, those who experience modernity on the periphery are not simply passive victims of this process, nor are their experiences by any means uniform. Yureños felt a relation to their land through the experience of sounding off through space, of establishing a sonorous sovereignty that depended on listening subjects, and on hitting a Yureño groove. But this experiential authenticity meant little in the battle to establish themselves as a culturally authentic indigenous group in relation to the Bolivian state. This latter kind of authenticity required representational practices and a manipulation of the visually perceived—that which could be documented and read by state bureaucrats now and in the future. In the flurry of the pluri-multi, Toropalqueños felt themselves at a disadvantage, expressing nostalgia for their lost culture and stating hope in their freshly remembered affiliations to their local indigenous organizations. Both the Yureño ironic approach and the Toropalqueño tragic nostalgic approach to indigenous authenticity exemplify distinct ways that the traditional becomes defined—as a presence or a lack—within the processes of modernity. In very different ways, Toropalqueños and Yureños experienced the subject position of "indigenous" within the Bolivian nation.

While textual representations play a key role in the bolstering of both national imagined communities (Anderson 1991) and ethnic imagined communities within nations, I have explored how representational practices in general intersect with an embodied sound, feeling, pleasure, or affect of imagined communities. During Carnival celebrations, Yureños had to fill their territory with sound. In their ritual music performances outside of the rigid time frame of the folklore festival context, Toropalqueños could dance to the same tune for an hour or more. To *feel* like they were performing Bolivian music in France, Música de Maestros had to play music as they moved along a parade route. Bolivian audiences of Música de Maestros felt a groove in this ensemble's music through the embodied memories of surviving Chaco War veterans and the families who have heard their tales, and through the performance of indigenous genres of music in their perceived original performance style. In this sense, the performances and recordings of Música de Maestros have worked within both an experiential authenticity and a cultural-historical authenticity for urban sectors of different classes and ethnicities. I would venture to say that this combination is unusual, and that the more common occurrence is to have experiential authenticity pitted against cultural-historical authenticity. Members of both Música de Maestros and the workshop were somewhat disdainful of the general popularity of Kjarkas's music and all the polluting cumbias. One person's groove is another person's inauthentic music, but it is often from a position of relative power over another that such a judgement is made.

Throughout my analysis of experiential authenticity, I have been wary of essentializing the embodied. Through a critique of the Enlightenment and a discourse that has slighted the body and the sensuous experience of knowing the world (Stoller 1997), the academy has called for a more embodied form of cultural analysis. While I certainly see the strengths of a scholarship that brings bodily experience back into the plethora of discourse analyses inundating the academy, I have not wanted simply to invert the mind-body hierarchy implicit to the discourse/embodiment opposition. In my exploration of the ideologies of experiential, cultural-historical, and unique authenticity I have spent a good deal of time in the middle ground between experience and representation, and between representation and ownership. In these interstitial conceptual spaces people distinguish their groove, cultural heritage, and proprietorship from that of someone else. These interstices constitute the space of cultural politics.

NOTES

NOTES TO CHAPTER 1

1. Here I am concerned with bridging more phenomenological approaches with the political (also see Desjarlais 1997).
2. John Borneman analyzes this framework of nation-state and its breakdown in contemporary Germany (1992). Many other authors have explored the challenges of this nation-state model (see Appadurai 1996; Bhabha 1990; Malkki 1992; Radcliffe and Westwood 1996).
3. This was the topic of a paper as presented by Elizabeth Krause at the 2001 meeting of the American Ethnological Society in Montreal.
4. I take these exceptional characteristics as particularly revealing because the study of exceptional or contradictory cases helps define the limits of rules (Bourdieu 1977: 105).
5. Local inhabitants, at least in the case of Yura, contest official 1992 census statistics that were taken precisely when a significant section of the population was away from the area on seasonal labor migrations.
6. Charles Keil distinguishes "embodied meaning" from "engendered feeling." This is perhaps a confusing selection of terms, as one might expect to find the human body in "embodied meaning." Instead the human body emerges within the concept of "engendered meaning"—the signification that depends on the chance and process of specific performance moments—and "embodied meaning" refers to signification through already existing elements of the musical form's body (Keil 1994a: 55). Keil rejects the simplistic mapping of these two ideas on a mind-body dualism, but admits that music that emphasizes engendered feeling is more likely to be linked to dance (1994a: 55–56).
7. Desjarlais analyzed the constructedness of "experience" in the context of a homeless shelter in Boston, where mentally ill residents consistently failed to engage with the life-narrativizing practices that are implicit within U.S. models of individual "experience" (1997: 10–17).
8. As a tool of anthropologists and historians alike, the narrative form lends meaning to otherwise disparate events or empty bits of information (Brooks 1984: 10; Bruner 1986: 147). Through the emplotment of events,

narrative creates a story, a metaphoric referencing to an imagined whole, when we only have access to knowledge of the parts (see White 1987: 9; White 1978: 81–100; Fernandez 1986: 50).

9. The philosopher Peter Kivy, with reference to early music in Europe, distinguished between historic authenticity and authenticity that referred to something that is not a copy, something that was true to the work and performance of a particular composer (1995: 6). This latter kind of authenticity is akin to what I am calling unique authenticity.

10. Gayatri Spivak's discussion of strategic essentialism is set within a debate about retrieving "the subaltern consciousness," while I am referring to terms of analysis in general.

11. The Agrarian Reform, like the 1874 Law of *Exvinculación,* which attempted to break-up indigenous landholdings, was not warmly received in areas where indigenous structures continued to function (Rivera Cusicanqui 1993: 74–89).

12. For further analysis of these texts see Bigenho, 1996.

13. To trace the trajectory from a 1952 national ideology of *mestizaje* to one of the pluricultural, I also reference two texts of the Bolivian intellectual René Zavaleta Mercado: *La formación de la conciencia nacional* (The Formation of the National Conscience; 1990 [1967]) and *Lo nacional-popular en Bolivia* (The National-Popular in Bolivia; 1986). While Zavaleta's *La formación* fashioned a nation built on an orthodox Marxist model led by the mining proletariat (1990 [1967]: 121), in his last work, *Lo nacional-popular,* Zavaleta recognized the "motley" (*abigarrada)* nature of Bolivian society and saw this as an obstacle to Bolivia ever consolidating as a nation-state under a system of representative democracy (1986: 19–20). Between these two works, marking the beginning and end of an intellectual career, Zavaleta's focus of nation shifted from class to cultural difference. The life-story of the campesino leader Antonio Alvarez also provides insights into this shift, as Alvarez' adversaries would accuse him of being a "dangerous mestizo" if they wanted to cast aspersions on his position as an "indigenous" peasant leader (Ranaboldo 1987: 87).

NOTES TO CHAPTER 2

1. Charles Keil used the term "feelingful" to refer to that aspect of the musical performance that could not be interpreted simply as signs, nor read as "meaningful" text (1994a).

2. "Cultural irrigation" provides an all-too-bland metaphor for the process of conquest and colonization in the Americas. Perhaps more appropriate to a debate on cultural transformations in the Latin American context is Mary Louise Pratt's discussion of the imposed reception of modernity on the non-Western world (1999).

3. Henry Stobart studied these instruments through one of their principal artisans in Vitichi (1988). Stobart encountered the terms "*saripalka*" and "*malichu*" to refer respectively to the large and small flautas (1988). The

two instruments, pitched an octave apart, follow a single melody line in parallel octaves. In another article, Stobart proposed an interesting hypothesis about the possible influence of European recorders and duct flute technology on Andean flutes (1996b).

4. In Carnival of 1995, I purchased a Yureña flauta in the city of Potosí, sold by the wife of the artisan of Vitichi (see Stobart 1988). This instrument measures 26 inches in length.

5. These refer to the best clothes, which are donned during fiestas. The *unkus*, knee-length pants, are considered traditional dress for the men of Yura. The traditional dress for women in Yura consists of the *aymilla*—a longsleeve blue or green dress with a straight skirt—and the *ajsu*—a handwoven garment worn over the aymilla. The width of the decorative weaving, or *pallay*, along the border of the ajsu, serves as an indicator of a woman's prowess as a weaver. Men rarely wear unkus outside of the context of the fiesta, whereas some women wear aymillas and ajsus on a daily basis, even though their best woven ajsus are always flaunted during the fiestas.

6. For a detailed description of how this instrument "works" acoustically and within different contexts, see the work of Arnaud Gerard and Marcos Clemente (1996).

7. For confirmation of the absence of interlocking technique in ayarachis performances of other areas of Potosí, see Arnaud Gerard and Marcos Clemente (1996). Other authors, specifically those who aim to write general pieces on Bolivian or Andean panpipes without any performance analysis, continue to lump ayarachis together with other panpipes, insisting on the use of interlocking technique in their performance (Baumann 1996: 30; Sanchez Canedo 1996: 85). Obviously these claims need to be confirmed through a performance analysis, on a case-by-case basis.

8. Although this song was composed by the Paceño Manuel Monroy, the group *Norte Potosí* made this song into such a hit that it was adapted by many bands playing for the Entrada del Gran Poder in 1995.

9. "Llorando se fue" was the disputed composition which the French/transnational group, *Kaoma*, converted into a lambada hit, causing authorship and plagiarism disputes which in Bolivia continue to intersect with popular nationalist discourse (see Wara Céspedes 1993).

10. For some of his preliminary analyses, see Templeman (1996).

11. The saya craze was also documented in Cusco, Peru, by Zoila Mendoza, in her study of the tuntuna dance, which is similar to the caporales; Mendoza found that many young Cusqueños danced to sayas as popularized by the group Proyección Kjarkas, and the author interpreted this musical identification as a way through which Cusqueños felt united with other youth of the southern Andes (2000: 211–212).

12. For an analysis of Oruro's entrada and its multiple meanings in relation to miners, see June Nash's *We Eat the Mines and the Mines Eat Us* (1979).

13. Lesley Gill explores the participation of indigenous recruits in the Bolivian military and the way this experience shapes masculine as well as national identities of subaltern subjects (1997).

14. In one case, I heard that a dance troupe gave the association a telephone line in order to advance several positions in the entrance order.
15. Financial necessities have reshaped this aesthetic as Música de Maestros has entered international touring contracts.
16. For example, many of the cuecas of the composer and pianist Simeón Roncal (1872–1953) make this key change in the quimba.
17. In 1987, I began to study Peruvian violin with Máximo Damián, a migrant from Ayacucho who resided in Lima. This was my first attempt to learn a musical tradition by ear.
18. Charles Seeger made the classic distinction between transcriptions that prescribe anticipated performances and those that describe performances that have already occurred; the first kind of transcription is for performance and the latter is for analysis (1977). But Bruno Nettl argued that these distinctions are not always as clear as Seeger implies (Nettl 1983: 68–70).
19. For example, violin is played in the Peruvian Andes (see Gushiken 1979) as well as in the Bolivian musical traditions of Tarija and the Chaco (see Cavour Aramayo 1994).

Notes to Chapter 3

1. *Abarcas* are the sandals often worn by people in the countryside of Bolivia.
2. For similar discussions of representations as founded on the presence of something absent, see the work of Ernest Laclau and Chantal Mouffe (1985: 119) and Slavoj Žižek (1989).
3. Andrew Orta has conducted research with Aymara catechists and the missionaries who train them. He found that missionaries believe the catechists lead double religious lives, part Aymara and part Christian, while catechists themselves bring an embodied coherence to this doubleness attributed to them by the pastoral workers (Orta 2000).
4. Robert Albro has examined how the municipality of Quillacolla (Cochabamba) sought to control the celebration of local fiestas by folklorizing them and thereby reaping rewards from what had become a lucrative celebration (1999). While Toropalca has not yet moved in that direction, of significance in this comparison is the way power is articulated through this transformation of fiesta performances into folklorized festivals.
5. An exception to this would be the *khusillo* figure that I observed in a fiesta in Concepción—a community south of canton Toropalca but still within the Province of Nor Chichas. In general the person who takes on the role of khusillo, literally "monkey," jests, makes overt sexual references, and wreaks boisterous havoc in the fiesta context. The khusillos in Concepción talked endlessly in a high falsetto voice.
6. Members of Música de Maestros regularly frequented a vendor of these sandwiches in the Rodriguez Market of the San Pedro neighborhood. From evening until 5:00 or 6:00 A.M., women prepared sandwiches in outside stalls, catering to those who, for work or pleasure, were part of La

Paz's nocturnal life. The sandwich usually included a *maraqueta* (traditional Paceño roll), cooked beef, sautéed onions and tomatoes, and a local herb (*quirquiña*).

7. I have not yet found an adequate translation for this word. Root words in Quechua may include: jap'inakuy = to rival; jap'isqa = grabbed; jap'ay = burp.

8. Many authors have extensively discussed interlocking technique in the performance of panpipes in the Andean region: among the Chipayas (Baumann 1981), among Puneños (Turino 1993a; Turino 1993b) in the Charazani region (Baumann 1985; Langevin 1992).

9. Among his many musical activities, Rolando had been playing for over ten years with a rock-Andean fusion band called *Wara*. Altiplano, next to Wara, represented a rival musical project. But in his comments, I never heard Rolando fuel the flame of these potential rivalries. On the contrary, he had tremendous respect for the group Altiplano, as well as for the musicianship of its individual players.

10. Svetlana Boym suggests that every cross-cultural study should include a dictionary of untranslatables in order to "prevent the transformation of a culture into mere exotic movie backdrop or kitsch object" (1994: 3).

11. A sextet from Música de Maestros has toured Japan and in these tours the director had to resituate both repertoire and orchestration. Even as Rolando realized that some tours just do not work with the large ensemble, he always expresses hope for the possibility of returning to tour as a complete ensemble.

12. Robles's works were widely performed in and outside of Peru. Robles himself lived in both Cuba and the United States for several years (Lloréns Amico 1983: 100–104).

13. Conadanz and Música de Maestros returned to France for the 1998 and 2000 Festival tours, and on these trips the ensemble carried its own microphones, cables, and sound board. With the flashy costumes of the morenada dance, they also became the closing group in many of the performances. As one musician told me, "It was because of the incredible costumes that Bolivia ended up closing some of the shows, and the more acrobatic dance troupe would look at us rather disapprovingly."

14. Slavoj Žižek links this symbolic mandate to the performative: "The subject is always fastened, pinned to a signifier which represents him for the other, and through this pinning he is loaded with a symbolic mandate, he is given a place in the intersubjective network of symbolic relations. The point is that this mandate is ultimately always arbitrary: since its nature is performative, it cannot be accounted for by reference to the 'real' properties and capacities of the subject" (1989: 113).

Notes to Chapter 4

1. Xavier Albó and Matías Preiswerk detail the economy behind this urban fiesta, a fiesta in which money is lavishly spent in ritual, combining religious

devotion to the Señor del Gran Poder with the demonstration of one's devotion through a show of political and economic power (1986).

2. One might consider Rolando's preference for the analogue sound as part
of an underlying quest for experiential authenticity. Many authors have
commented on the cold, hard, analytical sound of digital recording (see
Frith 1996: 235). But when I asked Rolando why he preferred analogue,
he simply replied that the Andean wind instruments sounded better
through this recording technology.

3. Homi Bhabha made the distinction between the nation as a pedagogical
object whose authority is based on a tradition as represented outside of
but visible to oneself, and the performative aspect of nation that inserts
an interstitial temporality between the unified self-generating nation and
the outside world (1994: 147–148). The distinctions I make between the
performative and pedagogical activities of Música de Maestros and the
workshop do not follow Bhabha's distinction. Both cases fall within the
performative and the two cases differ in the material strategies they em-
ploy in order to improve their performative positions.

4. In looking at "development projects" in Bolivia, we cannot follow Ferguson's suggestion to explore "non-state forces" (1990: 276, 286). The
boundary between state and the nongovernmental has blurred beyond
distinction as both fields respond equally and even in collaboration to an
international funding agenda (see Starn 1999: 222).

5. In a soap operatic style, not unlike that often displayed on the Tribuna
Libre, the very public Palenque marriage did subsequently falter, and
Carlos Palenque's sudden death in 1997 left party romantics pointing ac-
cusatory fingers at Monica Medina and suggesting the possibilities of
death from a broken heart.

6. The Spanish noun "*etnia*"—in common usage in contemporary Bolivia—
avoids the two word phrase "ethnic group." I have not found an English
equivalent noun to match "etnia."

7. For arguments related to what is presented in *Lo pluri-multi* and other examples of this reigning narrative, see *Por una Bolivia diferente: aportes para
un proyecto histórico popular* (CIPCA 1991) and *La revuelta de las nacionalidades* (UNITAS and Cuadros 1991). Elsewhere I link this Bolivian
class-to-ethnicity shift to David Harvey's and Frederic Jameson's discussions of postmodernity (Harvey 1989: 341; Jameson 1991: 318); I argue
that the Bolivian popularity of the "pluri-multi," rather than a locally defined phenomenon, actually is consistent with the cultural logic of late
capitalism (Bigenho 1996: 490–494).

8. With this term, the author may be referring to numerous transformations
within the musical scales (*gamas*) being used.

9. The list of invited musicians on the first recording included: Rafael Arias
(of *Duo Sentimiento*) Oscar Corihuanca (of Kollamarka) on Mandolin, Eduardo Cuarita on concertina, Carlos Daza (of Wara) on guitar, Donato Espinoza (of *Naira, Savia Andina,* and Altiplano) on charango, Oscar García

(of the workshop Arawi) on bass, Fernando Jiménez (of Naira) on siku, Takaatsu Kinoshita (of Naira) on guitar, Clarken Orozco on charango, Cintia de Pareja on violin, Freddy Santos on guitar, David Santalla on animation, Omar Valdivieso (of *Canarios del Chaco*) on violin, and Rolando Encinas on quena and oriental flute. The associations I have noted in parenthesis to other musical endeavors in Bolivia may not be complete.

10. The possibility of recording music and never performing it on a stage reveals how recording technology transforms the way we experience music. This phenomenon is not new in recording history. Manuel Peña documents the work of a famous Mexican-American orchestra (*orquesta*) of the 1930s and 1940s, under the direction of Manuel Acuña; this ensemble never performed in public and their fame was derived entirely from their recordings (Peña 1999b: 84). Other authors have discussed the existence of rock primarily as recorded music, that its aesthetics have been driven by recordings and the presentation of recordings (for example, see Auslander 1999; 61–111). On the other hand, pianist Glenn Gould was so enthralled by the possibilities of perfection offered by the studio recording that he retired from concert life in 1964 (see Bazzana 1997; 238–240). Most recordings of Bolivian national music are made through the recordings of individual tracks, and all of Música de Maestros's recordings were done this way until the eighth recording in 2001. Unlike the aesthetics of rock, I do not see the aesthetics of Bolivian music driven by recordings. In their eighth recording, Música de Maestros's desire to record in the studio as a performing ensemble still reflected an aesthetics of experiential authenticity, rooted in the concept of a special spark that ignites a fire with the simultaneous presence of all performers.

11. As of 2001, the ensemble had made eight recordings, and all but the third and fourth were independent productions. On the fifth recording, "Recantando" (1998), the ensemble accompanied several women folklore singers who were famous in the 1940s and 1950s. The sixth recording, "Supay" (1999) is a work of Rolando Encinas, composed for choreographic presentation with the dance troupe Conadanz. The other recordings followed the standard format of previous albums.

12. The suggestions of Pamela Calla were useful in the translation of this song (personal communication 1997).

13. Silvia Rivera's own interests in the music of Adrian Patiño (1895–1951) led to her production of a docudrama of this composer's life (videocassette 1990), and her enthusiasm for Música de Maestros's interpretation of Patiño's "Qhunuskiwa."

NOTES TO CHAPTER 5

1. For a discussion of the way indigenous Otavleños in Ecuador maintain their social ties in spite of the migration involved in their transnational

textile trade, see Rudi Colloredo-Mansfeld's *The Native Leisure Class* (1999).

2. Pratt revives the core-periphery model because it maintains a marked center and a geographic locus of power while many theories of globalization seem to leave unmarked any place of power (1999).

3. In the Mexican context, the Zapatistas' cry for "dignity" is a prime example of the rejection of this premise that modernity and cultural difference are mutually exclusive categories (see Gilly 1998).

4. For example, Terence Turner in the Brazilian Amazonian case clearly demonstrates how the contact of the Kayapó with anthropologists was key in the realization of Kayapó "culture" as a political tool (1991). Indigenous peoples do not necessarily welcome the academic message of constructed identities, particularly if it detracts from the forcefulness of their politics (see Warren 1998).

5. The Project San Juan del Oro has conducted campaigns in Toropalca to exterminate the chagas-carrying beetle (*vinchuca*).

6. According to Marilyn Ivy, movement, travel, and translocality only come into focus in relation to a home place (1995: 31).

7. Pablo Vila discusses the changing significance of Argentine tango lyrics between pre-Perón and Perón periods. While pre-Perón tango lyrics often included critiques of government, critiques that were to a great degree tolerated under a hegemonic agreement between the ruling and popular classes, when Perón came to power tango lyricists no longer viewed the government as opposition and some tango composers even left tango to enter official government politics (Vila 1991). Similarly, the New Song (*Nueva Canción*) movement, developed in the contexts of repressive military dictatorships throughout Latin America in the 1960s and 1970s, lost some of its punch as many countries turned to regimes that had at least a semblance of democratic rule.

8. I can only speculate on the Carnival celebrations further north in Toropalca. With the high river of the rainy season, it was impossible to reach the areas beyond the narrows (Chiquchi and surrounding communities). As an exception the kuraqa who lived on this side of the narrows in Sanagati did come to the village of Toropalca for Carnival.

9. "*Sacar sus huayños*" literally means "to pull out huayños." According to Charles Keil, these are the same words that the Tiv use to describe their music composition process (1979: 159).

10. Toropalca's songs of all genres (flauta, anata, zampoña, ayarachis) follow the form of AABB and a single song is usually repeated continuously during a performance period of about 20 minutes. While women dominate the performance of Carnival flauta songs, men and women will sing the songs of other instrument genres: anata, ayarachis, and zampoñas.

11. Some Toropalqueño songs not included in this chapter turn the sense of loss in another direction—toward losing oneself, remembering, and forgetting. Forms of the words *chinkay* (to lose), *yuyariy* (to remember), and

qonqay (to forget) may work together to form extended cultural metaphors that parallel the sense of *purina* (to walk, travel, wander) in Quichua song texts (see Schechter 1996). Michael Thomas, working from the ethnographic context of Cuzco (Peru), has conducted a semantic analysis of *chinkana* ("the place of getting lost"); Thomas highlights the ambiguity of what it means in Andean culture to "lose oneself": "Losing oneself" can mean both the disorientation of losing a sense of ethnic identity, as well as the willingness to enter social interactions that must occur to reaffirm such identities (Thomas 1991).

12. This anata song was recorded in Sinandoma, February 1994.
13. In the case of Peru, mestizo cultures have formed the basis of two recent studies (de la Cadena 2000; Mendoza 2000).
14. This ayarachis song was recorded in Lamachi, June 24, 1994
15. Denise Arnold, Domingo Jiménez Aruquipa and Juan de Dios Yapita document a tradition of seed-planting songs from Qaqachaka, a region in the present-day Department of Oruro, but that has cultural links to the ethnic groups of Northern Potosí. According to their work, women sang these songs or, alternatively, men sang them in a falsetto voice, a vocal imitation of a woman's voice. The women do not remember the lyrics or melodies of these songs and it is a man, a co-author of the material, who remembers and details the songs and their contexts (Arnold, Jiménez, and Yapita 1992: 109–173).
16. Planting season quena huayños follow an AABB pattern of organization with multiple repetitions of a single song. The dañan will usually play the melody of the song a few times before singing the lyrics. Although not always the case, the second phrase often refers to planting season activities [that is, *surcar* (to plough, to furrow) *melgar* (to furrow), and the inevitable *dañansituy* (my dear agricultural laborer), which is used throughout parts A and B]. Part B often has the feel of formulaic language, easily substituted from one song to another (see Lord 1964).
17. Unkus are the knee-length pants considered an important part of masculine "good Yureño" clothes.
18. Sarah Radcliffe and Sally Westwood also found that the lowlands play a similar role in Ecuadorian imaginings of nation (1996). In the story of the highland *Kallawaya,* peasant leader Antonio Alvarez, one finds further evidence of the way highlanders imagine the lowlanders as "behind them" in a rubric of social developmental. Alvarez referred to his wife, a woman from the lowlands, whom he met at an Indigenous Congress in La Paz, as his "tribe savage woman." According to Alvarez, upon this woman's arrival in La Paz, they gave her a pollera and a name (Ranaboldo 1987: 106), thus bringing her into "civilization." Alvarez still expressed concern for the children he had with this "tribe woman," fearing that they would grow up to be "savages" under their mother's care (Ranaboldo 1987: 137).
19. When Bolivia was to host the 1997 America's Cup, soccer officials met in 1996 to decide if matches would be permitted in cities at high altitudes.

During the debate, Bolivians used the slogan "Say 'no' to the veto of the [high] altitude" (*No al veto a la altura*)." The much-celebrated decision was that Bolivia would be permitted to hold its matches at high altitudes.

20. Thorough discussions of this problematic can be found in the works of CEDIB (1993), Eduardo Gamarra (1994), and Madeline Barbara Léons and Harry Sanabria (1997) and Eusebio Gironda C. (2001).

21. "[L]a *incertidumbre* acerca del sentido y el valor de la modernidad deriva no sólo de lo que separa a naciones, etnias, y clases, sino de los cruces socioculturales en que lo tradicional y lo moderno se mezclan" (1992a:14).

NOTES TO CHAPTER 6

1. In contrast, in her study of place in Robeson County, North Carolina, Karen Blu states that movement through space, while a sign of well being, should be completed directly, and in pursuit of a particular goal; one "should not spend all their time sheerly in motion" (1996: 215). The real difference here may be rooted in the distinctions between movement in ritual and non-ritual moments, for I can hardly imagine Yureños, outside of carnival, taking long walks without a specific goal and an immediate purpose to their travel.

2. This movement practice is paralleled in the Entrada del Gran Poder (see chapter two).

3. Michael Herzfeld is not alone in transferring the study of religion to the study of the state; Michael Taussig does precisely this to explain State fetishism (1992). The genealogy of both arguments explicitly harks back to Emile Durkheim's *The Elementary Forms of Religious Life* (1915). Bruce Kapferer implemented a similar twist by comparing Sinhalese Buddhist nationalism and Australian nationalism as religions (1988). In this case I am not dealing with popular nationalism, but rather with that problematic hyphenated form, the nation-state—the way that the Bolivian nation-state incorporates its multiple "nations" under a single state.

4. This proposal leads to the question "Is language music?"—an inversion of the more commonplace question of "Is music language?" I have an intellectual debt to Stefan Senders for suggesting this twist on the more obvious question (personal communication, January 1997; see also Feld and Fox 1994).

5. In the contemporary milieu of NGOs and international funding sources, Yureños are not alone in rediscovering and consciously reinforcing their Indian-ness. Jean Jackson documents a similar process in a long-term evaluation of her work with the Vaupés of Colombia (1995).

6. Anthropologists are forever reminded of their lack of control over the use of their ethnographic texts. While in Yura the reappropriation of a history—the demonstrated continuity of a particular cultural group—has thus far had favorable results, we are consistently warned about the vio-

lence that can be unleashed through texts that tend to reify ethnic identity through foundations of cultural essentialism (Herzfeld 1997: 88;
Malkki 1995: 14).

7. As Paul Gelles has argued, such moieties should not be viewed as pre-
Conquest structures, but rather as models that proved conducive to the
extractive and administrative activities of the Inka Empire, the Spanish
colony, and the early Republican periods (1995: 718). In contrast to
Gelles's contemporary Peruvian case in Cabanaconde, in Yura the
Anansaya and Urinsaya divisions were acknowledged, but ritual differentiation and competition operated at the level of the four ayllus—precisely
the level at which the kuraqas, the highest Yureño indigenous authorities,
held jurisdiction.

8. Some projects represented exceptions to this norm. For example, when I
left Yura, comunarios were discussing a project to construct a dam that
would affect an entire river valley. Projects of potable water sometimes included more than one community if the source was located relatively close
to two or three communities.

9. According to Radcliffe's description, male inhabitants and mountain spirits of the region are formally named in these boundary-marking speeches
(1990: 581–582).

10. Rasnake discusses several symbolic meanings of the rollo. As the central
meeting point of the ayllus' ritual travels, it represented the unity of the
four ayllus of Yura. But he also suggested that Yureños associated the rollo
with the domination of the colonial period; Yureños claimed that it was
the site where the authorities of the time (hereditary indigenous authorities who purportedly worked more with the Spanish crown than with
their ayllus) meted out punishments (1989: 228). Twenty years after Rasnake I was not able to confirm the oral tradition attributing colonial origins to the rollo. Nevertheless, Helen Nader detailed the presence of
stone columns, also called rollos, in Habsburg Spanish royal towns of the
sixteenth century; these columns represented previous sites of punish-
ment, and the town's independence from other municipalities (1990:
135–137). Rollos dot the landscape of other villages in the region of Potosi, Bolivia (Tomave, Tacobamba, Atocha Vieja), although in some cases
these columns have been moved from their position in the center of the
plaza and in one case even transformed into a pedestal for statuary.

11. I owe much of this point to conversations with Henry Stobart (personal
communication 1998).

12. With few exceptions these interviewees were not the flauta players, individuals who would be more likely to recognize these distinctions because
they have played the huayños. Nevertheless, my point is related to how
this music is heard by Yureños in general, not only by those who are involved in performing these huayños.

13. In Bolivia, categorically accusing government functionaries of corruption
goes hand in hand with derogatory remarks about bureaucrats—those

remarks that, according to Herzfeld, serve the ends of the state while explaining away one's own personal failures in specific bureaucratic interactions (1992: 9, 37). Structural problems of the state are attributed to individual moral shortcomings. General complaints about corruption do not propose any alternative bureaucratic organization of the state, but rather assume that by eliminating this bad spirit, other failings of the state will magically vanish.

14. Yureños contested the accuracy of this census because it was taken during the period of the year when many people, in search of salaried employment, leave for Argentina, Cochabamba, and Santa Cruz. The census figured Yura's population at 4,823; Yureños estimated their population at 7,200.

15. Not more than 10% of the designated funds were to be spent on salaries and administration of the municipality; 90% of funds were to be spent on projects. The budget for "projects" included specific constructions, *obras* or works, as well as the price to be paid to the consultants for the required preconstruction studies.

16. Article 4,I of the law references the official recognition of OTBs as representing "the entire urban or rural population of a particular territory." Article 6,I underlines the exclusive recognition of only one OTB within "a territorial unity."

17. In this case writing once again proves crucial to the workings of the bureaucratic state (see Goody 1986: 92).

18. In relation to contemporary political movements, Xavier Albó details some of these differences in "El retorno del indio" (1991). Lowland groups are more likely to use the self-reference of "indigenous peoples" while some highland groups, especially the Kataristas of Aymara distinction, are more likely to use the more challenging self-reference of "nation." Indigenous claims to discrete territories originally stemmed from lowland experiences, although after the 1990 March for Territory and Dignity, they then expanded to include highland claims. But the Kataristas, through a use of history, symbolism, and language, had already proven themselves effective in politically mobilizing an Aymara identity that was not necessarily linked to claims upon discrete territorial units (see Albó 1991: 316–318).

19. The common categories included in the colonial tributary system were *originarios* (originally from that place), *forasteros* (strangers to that place), and *yanakunas* (a floating population, considered delinked from the ayllus). In eighteenth-century documents, Rasnake finds "agregados" of Yura mentioned in conjunction with "forasteros" (1989: 131–132). For several ethno-historical discussions of these fluid categories and the use of the "forastero" category as a way to avoid paying colonial tribute, see Carlos Sempat Assadourian (1987), Thierry Saignes (1987), and Ann Zulawski (1987).

20. Many Bolivian funding sources immediately began a policy of matching funds with local municipal sources from the Law of Popular Participation.

21. Benjamin Orlove, using a series of maps to discuss a local peasant-Peruvian state conflict over a reed-growing area of Lake Titicaca, shows that the different sides in this conflict drew mutually contradictory lines of domain as they also claimed that the opposing party agreed to their own claims (1991). I doubt the overlapping registrations in Yura would reach the same levels of polarization since for the moment they are not about disputed land claims between Yureños and the state, but rather about different overlapping collectivities as they officially register with the state. The parallel I draw is between the above discussion of music competition styles, where there are no officially named winners, and Orlove's discussion of a local-state conflict without a referee to call the game (1991: 31). Yura's overlapping registrations may have contradicted the letter of the Law of Popular Participation, but this may never be discussed as a problem as long as all parties can in some way make their own claim to victory.

22. In a visit to Yura in 1999, I found Yureños even more proactive in negotiating their position within the Law of Popular Participation. With the assistance of ISALP, they had obtained the designation of "indigenous district" as a submunicipality with their own mayor. The Law of Popular Participation provided this form of further recognizing indigenous organizations, but it did not accompany this recognition with any fiscal backing. Funds for the submunicipality had to be negotiated with the mayor in Tomave. As a result, Yura's ayllus were considering putting forward a candidate in the elections for mayor of Tomave.

23. In an analysis of the spatial concepts of the Lumbees in North Carolina, Karen Blu reads the relative importance of centerpoints in combination with visually blurred boundaries as a way of "resisting or evading attempts by those with greater economic and political power to locate and control Indian people and their lands" (1996: 198).

24. Since the Treaty of Westphalia in 1648 the world has been organized through nation-states as based on the principle of territorial sovereignty, with this territorial principle underlying systems of international relations (Falk 1985: 116–121). The Inka state's need to link their origin myth with a specific place (see Urton 1990: 12), exemplifies a pre-Westphalian state obsession with fixing places.

Notes to Chapter 7

1. These logics have been propped up through academic discourses that reify these art/culture distinctions (see Dissanayake 1988).

2. Thomas Turino discusses how he puzzled Puneños (in Peru) when he practiced instruments alone (1993a: 58).

3. Annette Weiner's discussion of "inalienable possessions" illuminates my thinking on this point (1992).

4. In contrast John Collins (1993) documents the way the government of Ghana has attempted to implement a system of permissions and fees for the use of Ghanaian folklore. According to Collins the system was intended to give Ghana an advantage when First World countries cashed in on Ghanaian folklore, but the regulations became burdensome for Ghanaians themselves (1993: 151).

5. In a recent sociological study of recording and publishing in La Paz, Erick Torrico Villanueva, Karina Herrera Miller, and Antonio Gómez Mallea confirmed this trend in the music business (1999: 155).

6. This patronizing logic parallels the way the Brazilian state has treated its Indians. As Alcida Rita Ramos explains, the Brazilian state has viewed Indians as needing protection but as simultaneously on the road to assimilation; however, if Indians became full Brazilian citizens in the process of assimilation—something likened to a civil coming of age—the Indians would lose their status as Indians and the rights adherent to that special status (1998).

7. Here I am using Arjun Appadurai's reiteration of Simmel: that economic value is generated through an exchange of sacrifices (Appadurai 1986: 4).

8. In reference to Cold War and post–Cold War historical moments, Néstor García Canclini discusses this shift from polarized to unpolarized politics within the concept of "transnational deterritorialization" (1992b: 42).

NOTES TO CHAPTER 8

1. Albó and Mariaca differ in their references to the intercultural. Mariaca uses the reference of "cholo" interchangeably with "the intercultural" (Mariaca, Rivera, Quisbert 1999: 212), whereas Albó discards "cholo" as a pejorative term, almost always applied by an other, and almost never used in a self-ascribing way (1999: 82). There is nothing straightforward about defining the term "cholo," but it might be used to refer to a person who seems not quite indigenous, but not quite mestizo either.

2. This proposal is quite interesting next to Frederic Jameson's claim that the language of "texts and textuality" has replaced the language of "work" (1991: 77).

3. Although Silvia Rivera and Nathan Wachtel have two different projects in their respective books, the title of Rivera's book, *Oppressed but not Vanquished* (1986) rings out against Nathan Wachtel's *Vision of the Vanquished* (1977).

GLOSSARY

abarcas: Sandals often worn by people in the countryside of Bolivia.

ajsu: Woven wool garment with a design along the bottom border, usually worn over the aymilla dress; this attire has taken on the most indigenous associations in Bolivia and women who dress "de ajsu" are distinguished from others who dress "de pollera" (more mestizo), or "de vestido" (more Western).

alcalde: Also called "kamachi," this authority in Yura, chosen by the kuraqa, acts as an assistant to the kuraqa and as an intermediary between the kuraqa and local elected officials.

alferes/alferado: Sponsor/sponsorship of a fiesta, usually responsible for caring for the religious image, sponsoring musicians, and serving the mesa de once, food, and chicha during the fiesta.

anata: Also called "tarka," a six-holed duct flute made from a single piece of wood and played in carnival celebrations in Toropalca.

awki-awki: The dance of the old men; dancers dressed as old men and carrying canes poke fun at elderly Spanish gentelemen; this dance is usually accompanied by the music of the pífano.

ayarachis: Reed panpipes with two rows of seven tubes; the row of tubes that are blown are open at the top and closed at the bottom; only one row of tubes is played; Toropalqueños play these instruments in a unison style.

ayllu: Organizational structure found throughout the Andes; although classically defined as a dual system of moieties, in everyday practice it is a shifting point of identification.

aymilla: A dress with a straight-line skirt, worn by highland indigenous women in Bolivia; women wear this when they are dressed "as good Yureñas."

bailecito: A song-dance genre of Creole/mestizo association; it follows a standard structure of introduction, theme, repetition of theme, quimba, jaleo; it is played at a faster tempo than the cueca, thus requiring different dance steps; the same bailecito piece is repeated three times, or alternatively, three different bailecitos are consecutively performed.

bajeo: Moving bass line often played by the guitars in performances of cuecas and bailecitos.

boliche: A bar or pub.

bombo: Large skin drum used in many Andean music genres.

caja: Small skin drum, held vertically and struck with a stick or mallet.

camba: Person from Bolivia's eastern lowlands.

campesino: Loosely translated as "peasant;" the Revolution of 1952 brought the use of this term as a substitute for "Indian."

canton: A state-defined subdivision of local regions.

capataz: Slave foreman.

caporales: Music-dance genre of Bolivian entrance parades, in which male dancers represent slave foremen; see also *capataz.*

carnavalero: Principal sponsor of village celebrations in Carnival.

carnavales: Musical genres associaed with Carnival season.

charango: "A hybrid stringed instrument of the central Andean region," fashioned after the Spanish guitar but with the high-pitched sound quality as favored by an Andean indigenous aesthetic (Turino 1983: 115).

chicha: A corn beer made and consumed during fiestas, the planting season, and special activities.

chovena: Song-dance genre associated with the Bolivian lowlands.

COB: Central Obrero Boliviano; Bolivian Workers' Union.

comunario: A person who lives within the organizational logic of the ayllu or indigenous organization of the highlands.

corregidor: A state-appointed local authority at the level of the canton.

Creole: During the colonial period this term was used to distinguish Spanish people born in the Americas from those who had been born in Spain (*peninsulares*); as a slippery term in Bolivia today, sometimes it is associated with Spanish-rooted cultural expressions and sometimes it is conflated with the adjective of racial/cultural mixing: mestizo.

cueca: A song-dance genre of Creole/mestizo association; it is in ¾ or ⁶/₈ meter; it follows a standard structure of introduction, theme, repetition of theme, quimba, jaleo; the piece is always played twice.

cumbia: A song-dance genre associated with Colombian origins; Mexican and locally recorded *cumbias,* recorded with electric guitar, bass, and keyboards, make up some of the most popular dance music in Bolivia.

ch'alla/ch'allada: General term for ritual libations performed with alcohol, corn beer, coca leaves and/or incense; these ritual libations are performed in many different occasions for everything from the first sip of a drink to the celebration of a new major purchase.

ch'arki: Dried meat.

dañanes: The Yureño men who plow and furrow the fields with their oxen; they are the composers and performers of the planting season quena genres.

diablada: A devil's dance as represented through specific costumes, masks, music, and choreography in Bolivia's principal entrada fiestas.

entrada: A ritual parade of dance troupes as accompanied by brass bands or troupes of indigenous instruments.

empírico: A musician who learns to play by listening to and watching someone play.

estudiantina: A style of ensemble found throughout Latin American countries; it usually consists of about ten musicians; the ensemble uses many plucked-string instruments with doubling and tripling of first and second melody parts.

Fiesta de Comadres: Literally, Festival of the Comothers, a term of kinship that refers to the relation established between a mother and the godmother of a baptized child; it refers to the Carnival celebrations that begin on the Thursday before the central activities of Carnival

flauta: Six-holed, vertically played duct flute made of two pieces of wood; played during the rainy season in Yura, Toropalca, and other areas of Potosi.

hermano: Literally, brother; refers to person who follows one of the protestant faiths.

huayllas: Genre name for the tunes of the ayarachis instrument.

huayño: A general term to refer to a wide range of Bolivian song-dance genres of highland or mestizo association; it is usually in a ²⁄₄ meter.

indigenismo: Political and cultural currents found in many Latin American contexts in which people who are not indigenous use references to indigenous cultures to bolster national or regional identities.

ISALP: Investigación Social y Asesoramiento Potosí, Social Research and Legal Advising, Potosi, a nongovernmental organization that operates in Yura and in other areas of Potosi.

italaques: A specific highland panpipe tradition from Italaque (Province of Camacho, Department of La Paz).

jaleo: The closing section of the cueca or bailecito, usually a loud repetition of the theme, during which the audience claps a specific rhythm and the dancers perform more energetic steps.

kamachi: Also called "alcalde," this authority in Yura, chosen by the kuraqa, acts as an assistant to the kuraqa and an intermediary between the kuraqa and local elected officials.

kantus: A specific highland panpipe performance tradition from the area of Charazani (Province of Bautista Saavedra, Department of La Paz).

kinsa rey: Wooden staff of authority as held by the kuraqas and kamachis of Yura and Toropalca.

k'oa/k'oada: Ritual burning of incense.

kolla: Person from Bolivia's highland regions; derives from *Kollasuyo,* what was once a section of the Inca Empire.

kuraqa: The indigenous authority of the ayllu organization in Yura and Toropalca, a position held by a man and a woman together; a position that is rotated among the members of the ayllu and is viewed as an obligation and responsibility of every family owning land in the ayllu.

latifundista: Large land holder; owner of a *latifundio,* a large landed estate.

llamerada: A dance representing llama herders, as presented through specific costumes, music, and choreography in Bolivia's principal entrada fiestas.

lluch'u: Woven hat with earflaps worn by men in the Andes.

mamar/mamada: Literally means to nurse or the act of nursing at the breast; in Bolivia this is an idiomatic expression to refer to a case where someone deceives (*mamar*), and to a mild act of deception (*mamada*).

maraqueta: Bread roll of La Paz that, when fresh, has a crusty exterior and a soft center.

mesa de once: Formal meal served by the sponsor of a fiesta to all people in the community or village.

mestizaje: Can refer to both racial and cultural mixing of indigenous and Spanish heritage; *mestizo* may refer to the person of this mixed heritage; *mestizaje* was the national ideology of the 1952 Revolution.

mink'a: A work party sponsored by one family and attended by many others who help with the work and then expect reciprocation for the same work activities; Yureños use these work parties during the planting season; the sponsor of the party is expected to provide the workers with three meals, chicha, and alcohol.

MNR: Movimiento Nacional Revolucionario, National Revolutionary Movement; political party of the 1952 Revolution.

mohozeño: Vertically and horizontally played cane duct flutes.

mojones: Stone boundary markers of the indigenous organizations.

morenada: A dance said to represent a combination of the enslaved African Bolivian, the movements involved in pressing grapes for wine, and the very barrels in which this wine was stored; these are all symbolized through specific costumes, masks, music, and choreography in Bolivia's principal entrada fiestas.

OTB: Organización Territorial de Base, Territorial Base Organization; the term of reference used, in the early stages of implementing the Law of Popular Participation, to refer to existing local social organizations.

paceña/paceño: Residents of the city of La Paz.

pallay: Elaborate decorative weaving along the border of an ajsu.

peninsular: Term used to refer to those individuals in the Spanish colonies who were born in the Iberian peninsula.

pífano: A six-holed, horizontally played flute, often used to accompany the awki-awki dance.

pinquillu: Term often used generically to refer to a series of different kinds of duct flutes, those flutes with insufflation canals or "built-in" embouchures.

pollera: A wide skirt worn by women of highland or mestizo association; they dress "de pollera" as opposed to "de ajsu" (more indigenous) or "de vestido" (more Western).

qhari: Man.

quena: A notched, vertically played flute that is constructed of wood, plumbing tubes, reeds, or other materials.

quimba: The quiet middle section of the cueca and bailecito song-dance forms.

rollano: A wooden duct flute that Yureños used to play in August as they fertilized their lands.

rollo: A pillar in the center of Yura's main plaza, the ritual meeting point of the four ayllus of Yura.

rosca: Term used to refer to the powerful political and economic interests in Bolivia that were structured through the owners of the tin mines.

sikus: Panpipes, also called "zampoñas," these instruments come in many forms, each particular to a specific region.

singani: Bolivian liquor made from distilled white grapes.

suris: Large feathered headdresses worn by Música de Maestros in their representation of Italaque performance.

taquirari: A song-dance form associated with the Bolivian lowlands.

tarka: Also called "anata," a six-holed duct flute carved from a single piece of wood.

toropalqueña/toropalqueño: Person from Toropalca.

unku: Knee-length pants worn by men when they are dressed "as good Yureños."

vecinos: The inhabitants of Bolivian rural villages who live outside of the logic of the ayllu, identify with an urban experience, live primarily from local commerce, and often view indigenous ways of life as obstacles to general progress.

vestido: Literally means dress; in Bolivia women who follow a more Western sense of attire will dress "de vestido" as opposed to "de pollera" or "de ajsu."

warmi: Woman.

wiphala: A rainbow-colored flag, claimed by Bolivian Aymaras as organized in the Katarista movements, and since appropriated by many different groups making indigenous claims in Bolivia.

Wisijsas: People of a pre-Conquest indigenous polity; Yureños and Toropalqueños were considered to be part of this single group.

yatiri: Aymara shaman.

yureña/yureño: Person from Yura

zampoñas: Panpipes, also called "sikus," these instruments come in many forms, each particular to a specific region.

WORKS CITED

Abercrombie, Thomas. 1998. *Pathways of Memory and Power: Ethnography and History among an Andean People.* Madison: University of Wisconsin Press.
———. 1991. "To Be Indian, to Be Bolivian: 'Ethnic' and 'National' Discourses of Identity." In *Nation-States and Indians in Latin America,* Greg Urban and Joel Sherzer, eds., pp. 95–130. Austin: University of Texas Press.
Abu-Lughod, Lila. 1991. "Writing Against Culture." In *Recapturing Anthropology: Working in the Present,* Richard G. Fox, ed. pp. 137–162. Santa Fe, New Mexico: School of American Research Press.
———. 1986.*Veiled Sentiments: Honor and Poetry in a Bedouin Society.* Berkeley: University of California Press.
Adorno, Theodor W. 1976. *Introduction to the Sociology of Music,* E. B. Ashton, trans., from German. New York: The Seabury Press.
———. 1973. *The Philosophy of Modern Music,* Anne G. Mitchell and Wesley V. Blomster, trans., from German. New York: The Seabury Press.
Aguilar Vásquez, Fernando. 1995. "La verdad de una gran mentira." *Ultima hora,* February 17.
Albó, Xavier. 1999. *Iguales aunque diferentes: Hacia unas políticas interculturales y lingüísticas para Bolivia.* La Paz: Ministerio de Educación, UNICEF, CIPCA, Cuadernos de Investigación 52.
———. 1991. "El retorno del indio." *Revista andina,* año 9 (2): 299–366.
Albó, Xavier, and Josep Barnadas. 1990. *La cara india y campesina de nuestra historia.* La Paz: UNITAS/CIPCA.
Albó, Xavier, Tomás Greaves, and Godofredo Sandoval. 1987. *Chukiyawu: la cara aymara de La Paz: IV. Nuevos lazos con el campo.* La Paz: Cuadernos de Investigación, CIPCA, 29.
———. 1983. *Chukiyawu: la cara aymara de La Paz: III. Cabalgando entre dos mundos.* La Paz: Cuadernos de Investigación, CIPCA, 24.
———. 1981. *Chukiyawu: la cara aymara de La Paz: I. El paso a la ciudad.* La Paz: Cuadernos de Investigación, CIPCA, 20.
Albó, Xavier, and Matías Preiswerk. 1986. *Los señores del Gran Poder.* La Paz: Centro de Teología Popular.
Albro, Robert. 1999. "Hazarding Popular Spirits: Metaforces of Political Culture and Cultural Politicking in Quillacollo, Bolivia." Ph.D. dissertation, University of Chicago.
Allen, Catherine. 1988. *The Hold Life Has: Coca and Cultural Identity in an Andean Community.* Washington: Smithsonian Institution Press.

Alvarez, Sonia, Evelina Dagnino, and Arturo Escobar. 1998. "Introduction: The Cultural and the Political in Latin American Social Movements." In *Cultures of Politics Politics of Cultures: Re-visioning Latin American Social Movements,* Sonia Alvarez, Evelina Dagnino, and Arturo Escobar, eds., pp. 1–29. Boulder, CO: Westview Press.

Anderson, Benedict. 1991. *Imagined Communities: Reflections on the Origin and Spread of Nationalism,* revised edition. London: Verso.

Appadurai, Arjun. 1996. "Sovereignty without Territoriality: Notes for a Postnational Geography." In *The Geography of Identity,* Patricia Yaeger, ed. pp. 40–58. Ann Arbor: University of Michigan Press.

———. 1990. "Disjuncture and Difference in the Global Cultural Economy." *Theory, Culture & Society* 7: 295–310.

———. 1986. "Introduction: Commodities and the Politics of Value." In *The Social Life of Things: Commodities in Cultural Perspective,* Arjun Appadurai, ed., pp. 3–63. Cambridge, UK: Cambridge University Press.

Archondo, Rafael. 2000. "Existencias fronterizas: ser 'chango' en El Alto: entre el rock y los sikuris." *T'inkazos.* año 3, número 6: 67–78.

———. 1991. *Compadres al micrófono: la resurrección metropolitana del ayllu.* La Paz: Hisbol.

Arguedas, Alcides. 1991 [1909]. *Pueblo infermo.* La Paz: Librería Editorial 'Juventud.'

Arias, Juan Felix. 1994. *Historia de una esperanza: Los Apoderados Espiritualistas de Chuquisaca 1936–1964.* La Paz: Aruwiyiri.

Arnold, Denise Y. and Juan de Dios Yapita. 2000. *El rincón de las cabezas: luchas textuales, educación y tierras en los Andes.* La Paz: UMSA/ILCA.

———. 1998. *Río de vellón, río de canto: cantar a los animales, una poética andina de la creación.* La Paz: Hisbol/ILCA.

Arnold, Denise Y., Domingo A. Jiménez, and Juan de Dios Yapita. 1992. *Hacia un orden andino de las cosas: Tres pistas de los Andes meridionales.* La Paz: Hisbol/ILCA.

Aruwiyiri. 1992. *Educación indígena: ¿ciudanía o colonización?* Estudios de Roberto Choque, Vitaliano Soria, Humberto Mamani, Esteban Ticona, Ramón Conde, Tomasa Siñani, Francisco Laura, Epifanio Nina, Ayllu Chari, Prólogo de Victor Hugo Cárdenas. La Paz: Aruwiyiri.

Arze Aguirre, René Danilo. 1987. *Guerra y conflictos sociales: el caso rural boliviano durante la campaña del Chaco.* La Paz: CERES.

Assadourian, Carlos Sempat. 1987. "Intercambios en los territorios étnicos entre 1530 y 1567, según las visitas de Huánuco y Chucuito." In *La participación indígena en los mercados surandinos: Estrategias y reproducción social siglos XVI a XX,* O. Harris, B. Larson, E. Tandeter, compiladores, pp. 65–110. La Paz: CERES.

Attali, Jacques. 1985. *Noise: The Political Economy of Music,* Brian Massumi, trans. Minneapolis: University of Minnesota Press.

Auslander, Philip. 1999. *Liveness: Performance in a Mediatized Culture.* London and New York: Routledge.

Balibar, Etienne. 1991. "The Nation Form: History and Ideology." In *Race, Nation, Class: Ambiguous Identities,* E. Balibar, I. Wallerstein, eds., pp. 86–106. London: Verso.

Balkin, J. M. 1987. "Deconstructive Practice and Legal Theory." *The Yale Law Journal* 96: 743–786.

Bartelson, Jens. 1995. *A Genealogy of Sovereignty.* Cambridge, UK: Cambridge University Press.

Barth, Fredrik. 1969. "Introduction." In *Ethnic Groups and Boundaries: The Social Organization of Cultural Difference,* F. Barth, ed., pp. 9–36. Boston: Little Brown and Company.

Barthes, Roland. 1985. *The Responsibility of Forms: Critical Essays on Music, Art, and Representation,* Richard Howard, trans. Berkeley: University of California Press.

Basso, Ellen. 1985. *A Musical View of the Universe: Kalapalo Myth and Ritual Performances.* Philadelphia: University of Pennsylvania Press.

Battaglia, Debbora. 1995. "On Practical Nostalgia: Self-Prospecting Among Urban Trobrianders." In *Rhetorics of Self-Making.* Debbora Battaglia, ed., pp. 77–96. Berkeley: University of California Press.

Bauman, Richard. 1992. "Performance." In *Folklore, Cultural Performances, and Popular Entertainments: A Communications-centered Handbook,* Richard Bauman, ed., pp. 41–49. New York and Oxford: Oxford University Press.

Bauman, Richard, and Patricia Sawin. 1991. "The Politics of Participation in Folklife Festivals." In *The Poetics and Politics of Museum Display,* Ivan Karp and Steven D. Lavine, eds., pp. 288–314. Washington and London: Smithsonian Institution Press.

Baumann, Max Peter. 1996. "Andean Music, Symbolic Dualism and Cosmology." In *Cosmología y música en los Andes,* Max Peter Baumann, ed., pp. 15–66. Frankfurt: Vervuert; Madrid: Iberoamericana.

———. 1985. "The Kantu ensemble of the Kallawaya at Charazani (Bolivia)." *Yearbook for Traditional Music* 17: 146–166.

———. 1981. "Music, Dance, and Song of the Chipayas (Bolivia)." *Latin American Music Review* 2: 171–221.

Bazzana, Kevin. 1997. *Glenn Gould: The Performer in the Work: A Study in Performance Practice.* Oxford: Clarendon Press.

Benjamin, Walter. 1968. *Illuminations. Essays and Reflections.* Edited and with an introduction by Hannah Arendt, Harry Zohn, trans. New York: Schocken Books.

Bhabha, Homi. 1994. *The Location of Culture.* London: Routledge.

———. 1990. "Introduction: Narrating the Nation." In *Nation and Narration.* Homi Bhabha, ed., pp. 1–7. London: Routledge.

Biersteker, Thomas J., and Cynthia Weber. 1996. "The Social Construction of State Sovereignty." In *State Sovereignty as Social Construct,* Thomas J. Biersteker and Cynthia Weber, eds., pp. 1–21. Cambridge, UK: Cambridge University Press.

Bigenho, Michelle. 1996. "Imaginando lo imaginado: las narrativas de las naciones bolivianas." *Revista andina,* año 14: 471–507.

————. 1995. "El colonialismo cultural detrás de 'la solidaridad con pueblos in-dígenas.'" *Ultima hora,* February 8.

————. 1993. "El baile de los negritos y la danza de las tijeras: un manejo de con-tradicciones." In *Música, danzas, y máscaras en los Andes,* R. Romero, ed., pp. 219–251. Lima: PUCP, Instituto Riva Agüero, Proyecto de Preservación de la Música Tradicional Andina.

Bigenho, Michelle, and Huáscar Cajías. 1996. "Participación Popular en el centro y sudeste de Potosí: una visión panorámica de las organizaciónes territoriales de base, 'OTB's." In *Reunión Annual de Etnología 1995,* pp. 198–206. La Paz: MUSEF.

Bloch, Maurice. 1974. "Symbols, Song, Dance and Features of Articulation: Is Re-ligion an Extreme Form of Traditional Authority?" *Archives Européennes de So-ciologie* 15: 55–81.

Blu, Karen. 1996. "'Where Do You Stay At?' Home Place and Community Among the Lumbee." In *Senses of Place,* S. Feld and K. Basso, eds., pp. 197–227. Santa Fe, New Mexico: School of American Research Press.

Blum, David. 1986. *The Art of Quartet Playing: The Guarneri Quartet in Conversa-tion with David Blum.* New York: Alfred A. Knopf.

Borneman, John. 1992. "State, Territory and Identity Formation in the Postwar Berlins, 1945–1989." *Cultural Anthropology* 7: 45–62.

————. 1988. "Race, Ethnicity, Species, Breed: Totemism and Horse-Breed Clas-sification in America." *Comparative Studies in Society and History* 30 (1): 25–51.

Bourdieu, Pierre. 1977. *Outline of a Theory of Practice.* Cambridge, UK: Cam-bridge University Press.

Boyarin, Jonathan. 1994. "Space, Time, and the Politics of Memory." In *Remapping Memory: the Politics of TimeSpace,* J. Boyarin, ed., pp. 1–37. Minneapolis: Uni-versity of Minnesota Press.

Boym, Svetlana. 1994. *Common Places: Mythologies of Everyday Life in Russia.* Cambridge, Massachusetts: Harvard University Press.

Brooks, Peter. 1984. *Reading for the Plot: Design and Invention in Narrative.* New York: Alfred A. Knopf.

Brown, Michael F. 1998. "Can Culture Be Copyrighted?" *Current Anthropology* 39 (2): 193–222.

————. 1996. "On Resisting Resistance." *American Anthropologist* 98: 729–749.

Bruner, Edward. 1986. "Ethnography as Narrative." In *The Anthropology of Experi-ence.* V. Turner and E. Bruner, eds., pp. 139–155. Urbana: University of Illinois Press.

Bullard, Alice. 1997. "Self-Representation in the Arms of Defeat: Fatal Nostalgia and Surviving Comrades in French New Caledonia." *Cultural Anthropology* 12: 179–212.

Cage, John. 1961. *Silence: Lectures and Writings.* Middletown, Connecticut: Wes-leyan University Press.

Cantwell, Robert. 1993. *Ethnomimesis: Folklife and the Representation of Culture.* Chapel Hill: University of North Carolina Press.

Cavour Aramayo, Ernesto. 1994. *Instrumentos musicales de Bolivia.* La Paz: Producciones CIMA.

CEDIB. 1993. "La absurda guerra de la coca." In *Violencias encubiertas en Bolivia II: coca, vida cotidiana, y comunicación,* X. Albó and R. Barrios, coordinators, pp. 15–75. La Paz: CIPCA/Aruwiyiri.

Chambers, Ian. 1994. *Migrancy, Culture, Identity.* London and New York: Routledge.

Chase, Malcom, and Christopher Shaw. 1989. "The Dimensions of Nostalgia." In *The Imagined Past: History and Nostalgia,* Christopher Shaw and Malcom Chase, eds., pp. 1–17. Manchester: Manchester University Press.

Chow, Rey. 1994. "Where Have All the Natives Gone?" In *Displacements: Cultural Identities in Question,* Angelika Bammer, ed., pp. 125–151. Bloomington: Indiana University Press.

CIPCA. 1991. *Por una Bolivia diferente: aportes para un proyecto histórico popular.* La Paz: Cuadernos de Investigación, CIPCA, 34.

Clifford, James. 1997. *Routes: Travel and Translation in the Late Twentieth Century.* Cambridge, Massachusetts: Harvard University Press.

———. 1988. *The Predicament of Culture: Twentieth-Century Ethnography, Literature and Art.* Cambridge, Massachusetts: Harvard University Press.

Collins, John. 1993. "The Problem of Oral Copyright: The Case of Ghana." In *Music and Copyright,* Simon Frith, ed., pp. 146–158. Edinburgh: Edinburgh University Press.

Colloredo-Mansfeld, Rudi. 1999. *The Native Leisure Class: Consumption and Cultural Creativity in the Andes.* Chicago: University of Chicago Press.

Comaroff, John. 1987. "Of Totemism and Ethnicity: Consciousness, Practice and the Signs of Inequality." *Ethnos* 52 (3–4): 301–323.

Condori Chura, Leandro, and Esteban Ticona Alejo. 1992. *El escribano de los caciques apoderados: kasikinakan purirarunkan Qillqiripa.* La Paz: Hisbol/THOA.

Coombe, Rosemary. 1998. *The Cultural Life of Intellectual Properties: Authorship, Appropriation, and the Law.* Durham: Duke University Press.

Dagnino, Evelina. 1998. "Culture, Citizenship, and Democracy: Changing Discourses and Practices of the Latin American Left." In *Cultures of Politics Politics of Cultures: Re-visioning Latin American Social Movements,* Sonia E. Alvarez, Evelina Dagnino, and Arturo Escobar, eds., pp. 33–63. Boulder, CO: Westview Press.

Debord, Guy. 1983. *Society of the Spectacle.* Detroit: Black and Red.

de Certeau, Michel. 1984. *The Practice of Everyday Life.* Steven Rendall, trans. Berkeley: University of California Press.

de la Cadena, Marisol. 2000. *Indigenous Mestizos: The Politics of Race and Culture in Cuzco, Peru, 1919–1991.* Durham: Duke University Press.

del Valle de Siles, María Eugenia. 1990. *Historia de la rebelión de Tupac Catari 1781–1782.* La Paz: Editorial Don Bosco.

Deleuze, Gilles, and Félix Guattari. 1987. *A Thousand Plateaus: Capitalism and Schizophrenia,* Trans. and Foreword by Brian Massumi. Minneapolis: University of Minnesota Press.

Dennis, David B. 1996. *Beethoven in German Politics, 1870–1989.* New Haven: Yale University Press.

Desjarlais, Robert. 1997. *Shelter Blues: Sanity and Selfhood Among the Homeless.* Philadelphia: University of Pennsylvania Press.

Desmond, Jane. 1997. "Embodying Difference: Issues in Dance and Cultural Studies." In *Everynight Life: Culture and Dance in Latin/o America,* Celeste Fraser Delgado and José Esteban Muñoz, eds., pp. 33–64. Durham and London: Duke University Press.

Dissanayake, Ellen. 1988. *What is Art For?* Seattle: University of Washington Press.

Doty, Roxanne Lynn. 1996. "Sovereignty and the Nation: Constructing the Boundaries of National Identity." In *State Sovereignty as Social Construct,* Thomas J. Biersteker and Cynthia Weber, eds., pp. 121–147. Cambridge, UK: Cambridge University Press.

Douglas, Mary. 1966. *Purity and Danger: An Analysis of Concepts of Pollution and Taboo.* London: Routledge and Kegan Paul.

Dumont, Louis. 1986. *Essays on Individualism: Modern Ideology in Anthropological Perspective.* Chicago: University of Chicago Press.

Durkheim, Emile. 1965 [1915]. *The Elementary Forms of Religious Life,* Joseph Ward Swain, trans. from French. New York: The Free Press.

Dussel, Enrique. 1993. "Eurocentrism and Modernity (Introduction to the Frankfurt Lectures)." *Boundary 2,* 20: 65–76.

Eco, Umberto. 1989. *The Open Work,* Anna Cancogni, trans. Cambridge, Massachusetts: Harvard University Press.

Escobar, Arturo. 1995. *Encountering Development: The Making and Unmaking of the Third World.* Princeton: Princeton University Press.

———. 1991. "Anthropology and the Development Encounter: The Making and Marketing of Development Anthropology." *American Ethnologist* 18: 658–682.

Fabian, Johannes. 1983. *Time and the Other: How Anthropology Makes its Object.* New York: Columbia University Press.

Falk, Marc. 1993. "TBMPA, OCIN y M.P. II: Investigación y composición con el Taller ARAWI y la Orquesta Contemporánea de Instrumentos Nativos." unpublished manuscript.

Falk, Richard. 1985. "The Interplay of Westphalia and Charter Conceptions of International Legal Order." In *International Law: A Contemporary Perspective,* R. Falk, F. Kratochwil, and S. Mendolvitz, eds., pp. 116–143. Boulder, CO: Westview Press.

Feld, Steven. 1994a. "From Schizophonia to Schismogenesis: On the Discourses and Commodification Practices of 'World Music' and 'World Beat.'" In *Music Grooves,* Charles Keil and Steven Feld, pp. 257–289. Chicago: University of Chicago Press.

———. 1994b. "Notes on 'World Beat.'" In *Music Grooves,* Charles Keil and Steven Feld, pp. 238–246. Chicago: University of Chicago Press.

Feld, Steven, and Aaron Fox. 1994. "Music and Language." *Annual Review of Anthropology* 23: 25–53.

Ferguson, James. 1990. *The Anti-Politics Machine: "Development." Depoliticization, and Bureaucratic Power in Lesotho.* Cambridge: Cambridge University Press.

Fernandez, James. 1986. *Persuasions and Performances: The Play of Tropes in Culture.* Bloomington: Indiana University Press.

Foucault, Michel. 1984. "What is an Author?" In *Foucault Reader,* Paul Rabinow, ed., pp. 101–120. New York: Pantheon Books.

———. 1977. *Discipline and Punish: The Birth of the Prison,* Alan Sheridan, trans. New York: Vintage Books.

Frith, Simon. 1996. *Performing Rites: On the Value of Popular Music.* Cambridge, Massachusetts: Harvard University Press.

Gamarra, Eduardo A. 1994. *Entre la droga y la democracia.* La Paz: ILDIS.

García Canclini, Néstor. 1995. *Hybrid Cultures: Strategies for Entering and Leaving Modernity,* Christopher L. Chippari and Silvia L. López, trans. Minneapolis: University of Minnesota Press.

———. 1992a. *Culturas híbridas: estrategias para entrar y salir de la modernidad.* Buenos Aires: Editorial Sudamericana.

———. 1992b. "Cultural Reconversion." In *On Edge: The Crisis of Contemporary Latin American Culture,* G. Yúdice, J. Franco, and J. Flores, eds., pp. 29–43. Minneapolis: University of Minnesota Press.

Geertz, Clifford. 1973. *The Interpretation of Cultures.* New York: Basic Books.

Gelles, Paul. 1995. "Equilibrium and Extraction: Dual Organization in the Andes." *American Ethnologist* 22: 710–742.

Gerard, Arnaud, and Marcos J. Clemente. 1996. "Ayrachis del sur de Bolivia (un primer ensayo)." In *Anales de la Reunión Annual de Etnología, 1995* (tomo II), pp. 107–134. La Paz: MUSEF.

Giddens, Anthony. 1990. *The Consequences of Modernity.* Stanford: Stanford University Press.

Gill, Lesley. 2000. *Teetering on the Rim: Global Restructuring, Daily Life, and the Armed Retreat of the Bolivian State.* New York: Columbia University Press.

———. 1997. "Creating Citizens, Making Men: The Military and Masculinity in Bolivia." *Cultural Anthropology* 12: 527–550.

Gilly, Adolfo. 1998. "Chiapas and the Rebellion of the Enchanted World." In *Rural Revolt in Mexico: U.S. Intervention and the Domain of Subaltern Politics,* Daniel Nugent, ed., pp. 261–333. Durham and London: Duke University Press.

Gilroy, Paul. 1993. *The Black Atlantic: Modernity and Double Consciousness.* Cambridge, Massachusetts: Harvard University Press.

Gironda C. Eusebio. 2001. *Coca inmortal.* La Paz: Plural.

Goffman, Erving. 1974. *Frame Analysis: an Essay on the Organization of Experience.* Cambridge, Massachusetts: Harvard University Press.

Goody, Jack. 1986. *The Logic of Writing and the Organization of Society.* Cambridge, UK: Cambridge University Press.

Gramsci, Antonio. 1971. *Selections from the Prison Notebooks,* Quintin Hoare and Geoffrey Nowell Smith, eds. and trans. New York: International Publishers.

Greenhouse, Carol J. 1996. *A Moment's Notice: Time Politics Across Cultures.* Ithaca: Cornell University Press.

Grosz, Elizabeth. 1994. *Volatile Bodies: Toward a Corporeal Feminism.* Blooming-ton: Indiana University Press.

Guillet, David. 1998. "Boundary Practice and Historical Consciousness in Spain and Peru." Paper presented at Symposium Kay Pacha: Earth, Land, Water, and Culture in the Andes, Lampeter, Wales, April 2–7.

Gupta, Akhil. 1995. "Blurred Boundaries: the Discourse of Corruption, the Cul-ture of Politics, and the Imagined State." *American Ethnologist* 22: 375–402.

Gupta, Akhil, and James Ferguson. 1997. "Discipline and Practice: 'The Field' as Site, Method, and Location in Anthropology." In *Anthropological Locations: Boundaries and Grounds of a Field Science,* A. Gupta and J. Ferguson, eds., pp. 1–46. Berkeley: University of California Press.

Gushiken, José. 1979. *El violín de Isua: Biografía de un intérprete de música folk-lórica.* Lima: Seminario de Historia Rural Andina.

Habermas, Jürgen. 1987. *The Philosophical Discourse of Modernity: Twelve Lec-tures,* Frederick Lawrence, trans. Cambridge, Massachusetts: MIT Press.

Hale, Charles R. 1994. "Between Che Guevara and the Pachamama: Mestizos, In-dians and Identity Politics in the Anti-Quincentenary Campaign." *Critique of Anthropology* 14 (1): 9–39.

Handler, Richard. 1991. "Who Owns the Past: History, Cultural Property, and the Logic of Possessive Individualism." In *The Politics of Culture,* Brett Williams, ed., pp. 63–74. Washington, D.C.: Smithsonian Institution Press.

———. 1988. *Nationalism and the Politics of Culture in Quebec.* Madison: Univer-sity of Wisconsin Press.

———. 1985. "On Having a Culture: Nationalism and the Preservation of Que-bec's *Patrimoine.*" In *Objects and Others: Essays on Museums and Material Cul-ture,* George W. Stocking Jr., ed., pp. 192–217. Madison: University of Wisconsin Press.

Harris, Olivia. 2000. *To Make the Earth Bear Fruit: Ethnographic Essays on Fertil-ity, Work and Gender in Highland Bolivia.* London: Institute of Latin American Studies.

———. 1995. "Knowing the Past: Plural Identities and the Antinomies of Loss in Highland Bolivia." In *Counterworks: Managing the Diversity of Knowledge,* R. Fardon, ed., pp. 105–123. London and New York: Routledge.

———. 1989. "The Earth and the State: the Sources and Meanings of Money in Northern Potosí, Bolivia." In *Money and the Morality of Exchange,* J. Parry and M. Bloch, eds., pp. 232–268. Cambridge, UK: Cambridge University Press.

Harrison, Regina. 1989. *Signs, Songs, and Memory in the Andes: Translating Quichua Language and Culture.* Austin: University of Texas Press.

Harvey, David. 1989. *The Condition of Postmodernity: An Enquiry into the Origins of Cultural Change.* Oxford: Basil Blackwell.

Herzfeld, Michael. 1997. *Cultural Intimacy: Social Poetics in the Nation-State.* New York: Routlege.

———. 1992. *The Social Production of Indifference: Exploring the Symbolic Roots of Western Bureaucracy.* Chicago: University of Chicago Press.

———. 1991. *A Place in History: Social and Monumental Time in a Cretan Town.* Princeton: Princeton University Press.

Hinsley, F. H. 1986. *Sovereignty.* Cambridge, UK: Cambridge University Press.

Hobsbawm, Eric. 1990. *Nations and Nationalism since 1780: Programme, Myth, Reality.* Cambridge, UK: Cambridge University Press.

ILDIS. 1993. *Lo pluri-multi o el reino de la diversidad.* La Paz: ILDIS.

ISALP. 1992. "Diagnóstico sociocultural y económico: Yura." Potosi: Investigación Social y Asesoramiento Legal Potosi (ISALP), unpublished manuscript.

Isbell, Billie Jean. 1997. "De inmaduro a duro: Lo simbólico femenino y los esquemas andinos de género." In *Más allá del silencio: las fronteras de género en los Andes,* Denise Arnold, Compiladora, pp. 253–300. La Paz: CIASE ILCA.

———. 1985. "The Metaphoric Process: 'From Culture to Nature and Back Again.'" In *Animal Myths and Metaphors in South America,* Gary Urton, ed., pp. 285–313. Salt Lake City: University of Utah Press.

Ivy, Marilyn. 1995. *Discourses of the Vanishing: Modernity, Phantasm, Japan.* Chicago: University of Chicago Press.

Jackson, Jean E. 1995. "Culture, Genuine and Spurious: the Politics of Indianness in the Vaupés, Colombia." *American Ethnologist* 22: 3–27.

Jameson, Frederic. 1991. *Postmodernism, or the Cultural Logic of Late Capitalism.* Durham: Duke University Press.

Jaszi, Peter. 1994. "On the Author Effect: Contemporary Copyright and Collective Creativity." In *The Construction of Authorship: Textual Appropriation in Law and Literature,* Martha Woodmansee and Peter Jaszi, eds., pp. 29–56. Durham: Duke University Press.

Jordan, Glenn, and Chris Weedon. 1995. *Cultural Politics: Class, Gender, Race and the Postmodern World.* Oxford: Blackwell.

Kapferer, Bruce. 1988. *Legends of People Myths of State: Violence, Intolerance, and Political Culture in Sri Lanka and Australia.* Washington and London: Smithsonian Institution Press.

Karkoschka, Erhard. 1972. *Notation in New Music.* New York: Praeger.

Keil, Charles. 1994a. "Motion and Feeling Through Music." In *Music Grooves,* Charles Keil and Steven Feld, pp. 53–76. Chicago: University of Chicago Press.

———. 1994b. "Participatory Discrepancies and the Power of Music." *In Music Grooves,* Charles Keil and Steven Feld, pp. 96–108. Chicago: University of Chicago Press.

———. 1979. *Tiv Song.* Chicago: University of Chicago Press.

Kirshenblatt-Gimblett, Barbara. 1998. *Destination Culture: Tourism, Museums, and Heritage.* Berkeley: University of California Press.

———. 1992. "Mistaken Dichotomies." In *Public Folklore,* Robert Baron and Nicholas R. Spitzer, eds., pp. 29–48. Washington and London: Smithsonian Institution Press.

———. 1991. "Objects of Ethnography." In *The Poetics and Politics of Museum Display,* Ivan Karp and Steven D. Lavine, eds., pp. 386–443. Washington and London: Smithsonian Institution Press.

Kivy, Peter. 1995. *Authenticities: Philosophical Reflections on Musical Performance.* Ithaca: Cornell University Press.

Klein, Herbert. 1982. *Bolivia: The Evolution of a Multi-Ethnic Society.* Oxford: Oxford University Press.

Krause, Elizabeth. 2001. "Ethnography Beyond Billiard Balls: Play of Reconfigured Fieldsites, Modes of Production, and Population Paradoxes," paper presented at Annual Meetings of American Ethnological Society, Montreal, Quebec.

Kruse, Thomas A. 1994. "The Politics of Structural Adjustment and the NGO's: A Look at the Bolivian Case," thesis for Cornell University Degree of Master of Regional Planning, unpublished manuscript.

Laclau, Ernesto and Chantal Mouffe. 1985. *Hegemony and Socialist Strategy: Towards a Radical Democratic Politics.* London: Verso.

Langevin, André. 1992. "Las zampoñas del conjunto de Kantu y el debate sobre la función de la segunda hilera de tubos: datos etnográficos y análisis semiótico." *Revista andina* 10 (2): 405–440.

Lauer, Mirko. 1997. *Andes imaginarios: discursos del indigenismo 2.* Lima: Centro de Estudios Regionales Andinos 'Bartolomé de Las Casas'/SUR Casa de Estudios del Socialismo.

Léons, Madeline Barbara and Harry Sanabria, eds. 1997. *Coca, Cocaine and the Bolivian Reality.* Albany: State University of New York Press.

Levi-Strauss, Claude. 1966. *The Savage Mind,* Rodney Needham, trans. Chicago: University of Chicago Press.

———. 1963. *Totemism.* Boston: Beacon Press.

Leyshon, Andrew, David Matless, and George Revill. 1998. "Introduction: Music, Space, and the Production of Place." In *The Place of Music,* Andrew Leyshon, David Matless, and George Revill, eds., pp. 1–30. New York and London: Guilford Press.

Lienhard, Martin. 1996. "Lo cosmología poética en los waynos quechuas tradicionales." In *Cosmología y música en los Andes,* Max Peter Baumann, ed., pp. 353–367. Frankfurt: Vervuert; Madrid: Iberoamericana.

Lloréns Amico, José Antonio. 1983. *Música popular en Lima: criollos y andinos.* Lima: IEP.

Locke, John. 1960 [1689]. "Second Treatise of Government." In *Two Treatises of Government,* Peter Laslett, intro. and ed., pp. 305–477. New York: Mentor.

Lord, Albert B. 1964. *The Singer of Tales.* Cambridge, Massachusetts: Harvard University Press.

Lutz, Catherine A. and Jane L. Collins. 1993. *Reading National Geographic.* Chicago: University of Chicago Press.

Luykx, Aurolyn. 1999. *The Citizen Factory: Schooling and Cultural Production in Bolivia.* Douglas Foley, forward. Albany: State University of New York Press.

Lyotard, Jean-François. 1984. *The Postmodern Condition: A Report on Knowledge,* Geoff Bennington and Brian Massumi, trans. from French. Minneapolis: University of Minnesota Press.

MacDonald, Laura. 1995. "A Mixed Blessing: the NGO Boom in Latin America." *NACLA Report on the Americas* 28 (5) March-April.

Malinowski, Bronislaw. 1984 [1922]. *Argonauts of the Western Pacific.* Illinois: Waveland Press.

Malkki, Liisa. 1995. *Purity and Exile: Violence, Memory, and National Cosmology Among Hutu Refugees in Tanzania.* Chicago: University of Chicago Press.

———. 1992. "National Geographic: The Rooting of Peoples and the Territorialization of National Identity among Scholars and Refugees." *Cultural Anthropology* 7 (1): 24–44.

Malloy, James M. 1989. *Bolivia: La revolución inconclusa.* La Paz: CERES

Mamani Condori, Carlos B. 1991. *Taraqu 1866–1935: masacre, guerra y "renovación" en la biografía de Eduardo L. Nina Qhispi.* La Paz: Ediciones Aruwiyiri-THOA.

Manuel, Peter. 1993. *Cassette Culture: Popular Music and Technology in North India.* Chicago: University of Chicago Press.

———. 1988. *Popular Musics of the Non-Western World: An Introductory Survey.* New York/Oxford: Oxford University Press.

Marcus, George. 1998. *Ethnography Through Thick and Thin.* Princeton: Princeton University Press.

———. 1995. "Ethnography in/of the World System: The Emergence of Multi-Sited Ethnography." *Annual Review of Anthropology* 24: 95–117.

Marcus, George, and Michael Fischer. 1986. *Anthropology as Cultural Critique: An Experimental Moment in the Human Sciences.* Chicago: University of Chicago Press.

Mariaca, Guillermo, Silvia Rivera, and Pablo Quisbert. 1999. "Mesa redonda: de las prácticas perversas a la exaltación del mestizaje." Carolina Loureiro, moderadora. *Historias,* número 3: 187–219.

Mariategui, José Carlos. 1985 [1928]. *Siete ensayos de interpretación de la realidad peruana.* Lima: Amauta.

Marof, Tristan. 1926. *La justicia del Inca.* Bruseles: "La Edición Latino Americana." Librería Falk Fils.

Mauss, Marcel. 1967 [1925]. *The Gift: Forms and Functions of Exchange in Archaic Societies,* Ian Cunnison, trans., E. E. Evans-Pritchard, intro. New York: W. W. Norton.

McClary, Susan. 1991. *Feminine Endings: Music, Gender, and Sexuality.* Minneapolis: University of Minnesota Press.

Mendoza, Zoila. 2000. *Shaping Society Through Dance: Mestizo Ritual Performance in the Peruvian Andes.* Chicago: University of Chicago Press.

Merleau-Ponty, Maurice. 1962. *The Phenomenology of Perception.* Colin Smith, trans. London: Routledge and Kegan Paul.

Ministerio de Comunicación Social. 1995. *¿Qué son las Organizaciones Territoriales de Base (OTB's)?* La Paz: Ministerio de Desarrollo Sostenible y Medio Ambiente/Secretaría Nacional de Participación Popular/Ministerio de Comunicación Social.

Montenegro, Carlos. 1943. *Nacionalismo y coloniaje: su expresión en la prensa de Bolivia.* La Paz: Ediciones Autonomía.

Munn, Nancy D. 1986. *The Fame of Gawa: A Symbolic Study of Value Transformation in a Massim (Papua New Guinea) Society.* Cambridge, UK: Cambridge University Press.

Murphy, Alexander B. 1996. "The Sovereign State System as Political-Territorial Ideal: Historical and Contemporary Considerations." In *State Sovereignty as Social Construct,* Thomas J. Biersteker and Cynthia Weber, eds., pp. 81–120. Cambridge, UK: Cambridge University Press.

Nader, Helen. 1990. *Liberty in Absolutist Spain: The Habsburg Sale of Towns 1516–1700.* Baltimore: Johns Hopkins University Press.

Napier, A. David. 1992. *Foreign Bodies: Performance, Art, and Symbolic Anthropology.* Berkeley: University of California Press.

Nash, June. 1992. "Interpreting Social Movements: Bolivian Resistance to Economic Conditions Imposed by the International Monetary Fund." *American Ethnologist* 19 (2): 275–293.

———. 1979. *We Eat the Mines and the Mines Eat Us: Dependency and Exploitation in Bolivian Tin Mines.* New York: Columbia University Press.

Nelson, Diane. 1999. *A Finger in the Wound: Body Politics in Quincentennial Guatemala.* Berkeley: University of California Press.

Ness, Sally Ann. 1992. *Body, Movement, and Culture: Kinesthetic and Visual Symbolism in a Philippine Community.* Philadelphia: University of Pennsylvania Press.

Nettl, Bruno. 1983. *The Study of Ethnomusicology: Twenty-nine Issues and Concepts.* Urbana: University of Illinois Press.

Orlove, Benjamin. 1991. "Mapping Reeds and Reading Maps: The Politics of Representation in Lake Titicaca." *American Ethnologist* 18 (1): 3–38.

Orta, Andrew. 2000. "Syncretic Subjects and Body Politics: Doubleness, Personhood, and Aymara Catechists." *American Ethnologist* 26 (4): 864–889.

Paerregaard, Karsten. 1997. "Imagining a Place in the Andes: In the Borderland of Lived, Invented, and Analyzed Culture." In *Siting Culture: The Shifting Anthropological Object,* Karen Fog Olwig and Kirsten Hastrup, eds., pp. 39–58. London and New York: Routledge.

Peña, Manuel. 1999a. *Música Tejana: The Cultural Economy of Artistic Transformation.* College Station: Texas A & M University Press.

———. 1999b. *The Mexican American Orquesta: Music, Culture, and the Dialectic of Conflict.* Austin: University of Texas Press.

Platt, Tristan. 1986. "Mirrors and maize: the Concept of Yanantin Among the Macha of Bolivia." In *Anthropological History of Andean Polities,* J. Murra, N. Wachtel, and J. Revel, eds., pp. 228–259. Cambridge, UK: Cambridge University Press.

———. 1982. *Estado boliviano y ayllu andino: tierra y tributo en el norte de Potosí.* Lima: IEP.

Poole, Deborah. 1997. *Vision, Race, and Modernity: A Visual Economy of the Andean Image World.* Princeton: Princeton University Press.

———. 1991. "Rituals of Movement, Rites of Transformation: Pilgrimage and Dance in the Highlands of Cuzco, Peru." In *Pilgrimage in Latin America,* N. Ross Crumrine and Alan Morinis, eds., pp. 307–338. New York: Greenwood Press.

Povenelli, Elizabeth. 1999. "Settler Modernity and the Quest for an Indigenous Tradition." *Public Culture* 11(1): 19–48.

Pratt, Mary Louise. 1999. "Modernity and Periphery: Towards a Global and Relational Analysis." paper given at Hampshire College, unpublished manuscript.

———. 1991. "Arts of the Contact Zone." *Profession* 91: 33–40.

P.A. 1995. "Concierto para los pueblos indígenas: De boca pa' afuera." *La razón*, January 28.

Radcliffe, Sarah. 1990. "Marking Boundaries between the Community, the State and History in the Andes." *Journal of Latin American Studies* 22 (3): 575–594.

Radcliffe, Sarah, and Sallie Westwood. 1996. *Remaking the Nation: Place, Identity and Politics in Latin America.* London and New York: Routledge.

Radcliffe Brown, A. R. 1965 [1929]. *Structure and Function in Primitive Society; Essays and Addresses.* New York: The Free Press.

Radhakrishnan, R. 1996. *Diasporic Mediations: Between Home and Location.* Minneapolis: University of Minnesota Press.

Ramos, Alcida Rita. 1998. *Indigenism: Ethnic Politics in Brazil.* Madison: University of Wisconsin Press.

Ranaboldo, Claudia, and Unidad de Investigación SEMTA. 1987. *El camino perdido; Chinkasqa ñan; Armat thaki: Biografía del dirigente campesino kallawaya Antonio Alvarez Mamani.* La Paz: SEMTA.

Randel, Don Michael. 1978. *Harvard Concise Dictionary of Music.* Cambridge, Massachusetts: Belknap/Harvard University Press.

Rappaport, Joanne. 1994. *Cumbe Reborn: An Andean Ethnography of History.* Chicago: University of Chicago Press.

Rasmussen, Susan J. 1991. "Modes of Persuasion: Gossip, Song, and Divination in Tuareg Conflict Resolution." *Anthropological Quarterly* 64: 30–46.

Rasnake, Roger. 1989. *Autoridad y poder en los Andes: Los kuraqkuna de Yura,* L. Brédow and L. H. Antezana, trans. La Paz: Hisbol.

Razuri. 1983. "La chicha: identidad chola en la Gran Ciudad." *Debate* 24: 72–75.

Rivera Cusicanqui, Silvia. 1993. "La raíz: colonizadores y colonizados." In *Violencias encubiertas en Bolivia I,* Xavier Albó and Raúl Barrios, coordinadores, pp. 27–139. La Paz: CIPCA/Aruwiyiri.

———. 1986. *Oprimidos pero no vencidos: Luchas del campesinado aymara y quechua de Bolivia, 1900–1980.* Ginebra: Instituto de Investigaciones de las Naciones Unidas para el Desarrollo Social.

———and THOA. 1992. *Ayllus y proyectos de desarrollo en el norte de Potosí.* La Paz: Aruwiyiri.

Rivera de Stahlie, Ma. Teresa. 1995. *Música y músicos bolivianos.* La Paz: Los Amigos del Libro.

Romero, Raúl. 1985. "La música tradicional y popular." In *La música en el Perú.* Lima: Patronato Popular y Porvenir.

Rosaldo, Michelle. 1980. *Knowledge and Passion: Ilongot Notions of Self and Social Life.* Cambridge, UK: Cambridge University Press.

Rosaldo, Renato. 1989a. *Culture and Truth: The Remaking of Social Analysis.* Boston: Beacon Press.

————. 1989b. "Imperialist Nostalgia." *Representations* 26: 107–122.

————. 1980. *Ilongot Headhunting 1883–1974: A Study in Society and History.* Stanford, California: Stanford University Press.

Rose, Mark. 1993. *Authors and Owners: The Invention of Copyright.* Cambridge, Massachusetts: Harvard University Press.

Roseberry, William. 1991. "Marxism and Culture." In *The Politics of Culture,* Brett Williams, ed., pp. 19–43. Washington and London: Smithsonian Institution Press.

————. 1989. *Anthropologies and Histories: Essays in Culture, History, and Political Economy.* New Brunswick: Rutgers University Press.

Rossells, Beatriz. 1996. *Caymari vida: La emergencia de la música popular en Charcas.* Sucre: Editorial Judicial.

Saignes, Tierry. 1987. "Ayllus, mercado y coacción colonial: el reto de las migraciones internas en Charcas (siglo XVII)." In *La participación indígena en los mercados surandinos: Estrategias y reproducción social siglos XVI a XX,* O. Harris, B. Larson, E. Tandeter, compiladores, pp. 111–158. La Paz: CERES.

Sallnow, Michael. 1987. *Pilgrims of the Andes: Regional Cults in Cusco.* Washington, DC: Smithsonian Institution Press.

Salmón, Josefa. 1997. *El espejo indígena: el discurso indigenista en Bolivia 1900–1956.* La Paz: Plural Editores/UMSA.

Salomon, Frank. 1991. "Introductory Essay: The Huarochirí Manuscript." In *The Huarochirí Manuscript: A Testament of Ancient and Colonial Andean Religion.* Frank Salomon and George L. Urioste, eds., pp. 1–38. Austin: University of Texas Press.

Sánchez Canedo, Wálter. 1996. "Algunas consideraciones hipotéticas sobre música y sistema de pensamiento: La flauta de pan en los Andes bolivianos." In *Cosmología y música en los Andes,* Max Peter Baumann, ed., pp. 83–106. Frankfurt: Vervuert; Madrid: Iberoamerianca.

Sanjinés C., Javier. 1998. "Modelos estéticos de cultura nacional: el caso boliviano." *T'inkazos,* año 1, número 2: 87–98.

San Martín Arzabe, Hugo. 1991. *El Palenquismo: movimiento social, populismo, informalidad política.* La Paz: Los Amigos del Libro.

Schafer, Murray. 1977. *The Tuning of the World.* New York: Alfred A. Knopf.

Schechter, John. 1996. "Tradition and Dynamism in Ecuadorian Andean Quichua Sanjuán: Macrocosm in Formulaic Expression, Microcosm in Ritual Absorption." In *Cosmología y música en los Andes,* Max Peter Baumann, ed., pp. 247–267. Frankfurt: Vervuert; Madrid: Iberoamericana.

Schieffelin, Edward L. 1998. "Problematizing Performance." In *Ritual, Performance, Media,* Felicia Hughes-Freeland, ed., pp. 194–207. London and New York: Routledge.

Schild, Verónica. 1998. "New Subjects of Rights? Women's Movements and the Construction of Citizenship in the 'New Democracies.'" In *Cultures of Politics, Politics of Cultures: Re-visioning Latin American Social Movements,* Sonia E. Alvarez, Evelina Dagnino, and Arturo Escobar, eds., pp. 93–117. Boulder, CO: Westview Press.

Scott, James. 1998. *Seeing Like a State: How Certain Schemes to Improve the Human Condition Have Failed.* New Haven: Yale University Press.

Seeger, Anthony. 1996. "Ethnomusicologists, Archives, Professional Organizations, and the Shifting Ethics of Intellectual Property." *Yearbook for Traditional Music* 87–105.

———. 1991. "Creating and Confronting Cultures: Issues of Editing and Selection in Records and Videotapes of Musical Performances." In *Music in the Dialogue of Cultures: Traditional Music and Cultural Policy,* Max Peter Baumann, ed., pp. 290–301. Berlin: International Institute for Comparative Music Studies and Documentation/Florian Noetzel Verlag Wilhelmshaven.

———. 1987. *Why Suyá Sing: A Musical Anthropology of an Amazonian People.* Cambridge, UK: Cambridge University Press.

Seeger, Charles. 1977. *Studies in Musicology 1935–1975.* Berkeley: University of California Press.

Seignette, Jacqueline. 1994. *Challenges to the Creator Doctrine: Authorship, Copyright Ownership and the Exploitation of Creative Works in the Netherlands, Germany and the United States.* Deventer and Boston: Kluwer Law and Taxation Publishers.

Shepherd, John. 1991. *Music as Social Text.* Cambridge: Polity Press.

Shore, Bradd. 1991. "Twice-Born, Once Conceived: Meaning Construction and Cultural Cognition." *American Anthropologist* 93: 9–27.

Smith, Steven. 1992. "Blues and Our Mind-Body Problem." *Popular Music* 11 (1): 41–52.

Spivak, Gayatri Chakravorty. 1988. "Subaltern Studies: Deconstructing Historiography." In *Selected Subaltern Studies,* Ranajit Guha and G. C. Spivak, eds., pp. 3–32. Oxford: Oxford University Press.

Starn, Orin. 1999. *Nightwatch: The Politics of Protest in the Andes.* Durham: Duke University Press.

Stearman, Allyn MacLean. 1985. *Camba and Kolla: Migration and Development in Santa Cruz,* Bolivia. Orlando: University of Central Florida Press.

Steindhardt, Arnold. 1998. *Indivisible by Four: A String Quartet in Pursuit of Harmony.* New York: Farrar Straus Giroux.

Stewart, Kathleen. 1996. *A Space on the Side of the Road: Cultural Poetics in an "Other" America.* Princeton: Princeton University Press.

———. 1988. "Nostalgia—A Polemic." *Cultural Anthropology* 3: 227–241.

Stobart, Henry. 1996a. "Tara and Q'iwa—Worlds of Sound and Meaning." In *Cosmología y música en los Andes,* Max Peter Baumann, ed., pp. 67–81. Frankfurt: Vervuert; Madrid: Iberoamericana.

———. 1996b. "The Llama's Flute: Musical Misunderstandings in the Andes." *Early Music* 24: 471–482.

———. 1988. "Pinkillos of Vitichi." unpublished manuscript.

Stoller, Paul. 1997. *Sensuous Scholarship.* Philadelphia: University of Pennsylvania Press.

Strathern, Marilyn. 1995. "Nostalgia and the New Genetics." In *Rhetorics of Self-Making.* Debbora Battaglia, ed., pp. 97–120. Berkeley: University of California Press.

Sullivan, Lawrence. 1985. "Sound and Senses: Toward a Hermeneutics of Performance." In *The History of Religions: Retrospect and Prospect: A Collection of Original Essays,* Joseph M. Kitagawa, ed., pp. 1–33. New York: Macmillan.

Tamayo, Franz. 1944 [1910]. *Creación de una pedagogía nacional.* La Paz: Editoriales de "El Diario."

Taussig, Michael. 1992. *The Nervous System.* New York: Routledge.

TBMPA (Taller Boliviano de Música Popular Arawi). 1990. "Instrumentos nativos de los Andes bolivianos: Guía de instrumentos nativos bolivianos CENDOC-MA Portales" unpublished manuscript.

Templeman, Robert. 1996. "Renacimiento de la saya: el rol que juega la música en el movimiento negro en Bolivia." In *Anales de la Reunión Annual de Etnología,* 1995 (tomo II), pp. 89–94. La Paz: MUSEF.

Thomas, Michael. 1991. "Andean Peasants in the Labyrinth of Power: Cultural Representation of Class and Ethnic Domination in the Context of Political Violence (Cuzco, Peru)," paper presented at American Ethnological Society Meeting, Charleston, South Carolina, unpublished manuscript.

Ticona Alejo, Esteban. 2000. *Organización y liderazgo aymara, 1979–1996.* La Paz: Universidad de la Cordillera/Agruco.

Titon, Jeff Todd. 1988. *Powerhouse for God: Speech, Chant, and Song in an Appalachian Baptist Church.* Austin: University of Texas Press.

Toranzo Roca, Carlos F. 1994. "Para 'nostalgiar': Entre t'unkuña y boleros." *La razón* (La Paz, Bolivia), December 18.

Torrico Villanueva, Erick R., Karina Herrera Miller, and Antonio Gómez Mallea. 1999. "Los circuitos de la cultura masiva en La Paz." *T'inkazos,* año 2, número 4: 147–160.

Tsing, Anna Lwenhaupt. 1993. *In the Realm of the Diamond Queen: Marginality in an Out-of-the-Way Place.* Princeton: Princeton University Press.

Turino, Thomas. 2000. *Nationalists, Cosmopolitans, and Popular Music in Zimbabwe.* Chicago: University of Chicago Press.

———. 1993a. *Moving Away From Silence: Music of the Peruvian Altiplano and the Experience of Urban Migration.* Chicago: University of Chicago Press.

———. 1993b. "La coherencia del estilo social y de la creación musical entre los Aymara del sur del Perú." In *Música, danzas, y máscaras en los Andes,* R. Romero, ed., pp. 61–93. Lima: PUCP, Instituto Riva-Agüero, Proyecto de Preservación de la Música Tradicional Andina.

———. 1990. "Somos el Perú [We are Peru]: "Cumbia Andina" and the Children of Andean Migrants in Lima." *Studies in Latin American Popular Culture* 9: 15–37.

Turner, Terence. 1991. "Representing, Resisting, Rethinking: Historical Transformations of Kayapó Culture and Anthropological Consciousness." In *Colonial Situations: Essays on the Contextualization of Ethnographic Knowledge,* G. Stocking ed., pp. 285–313. Madison: University of Wisconsin Press.

Turner, Victor. 1967. *The Forest of Symbols: Aspects of Ndembu Ritual.* Ithaca: Cornell University Press.

UNITAS, and Diego Cuadros (compilador). 1991. *La revuelta de las nacionalidades.* La Paz: UNITAS.

Urton, Gary. 1990. *The History of a Myth: Pacariqtambo and the Origin of the Inkas.* Austin: University of Texas Press.

———. 1984. "Chuta: El espacio de la práctica social en Pacariqtambo, Perú." *Revista andina,* año 2 (1): 7–56.

Vega, Carlos. 1966. "Mesomusic: an Essay on the Music of the Masses." *Ethnomusicology* 10: 1–17.

Velarde, Jorge. 1995. "Introducción al tema." In *Políticas culturales: La promoción estatal de la cultura,* pp. 3–7. La Paz: ILDIS, Gobierno Municipal de La Paz, Oficial Mayor de Cultura.

Vila, Pablo. 1991. "Tango to Folk: Hegemony Construction and Popular Identities in Argentina." *Studies in Latin American Popular Culture* 10: 107–139.

Wachtel, Nathan. 1977. *The Vision of the Vanquished: The Spanish Conquest of Peru Through Indian Eyes, 1530–1570,* Ben and Sian Reynolds, trans., New York: Barnes & Noble.

Wade, Peter. 1999. "Working Culture: Making Cultural Identities in Cali, Colombia." *Current Anthropology* 40 (4): 449–471.

Wallis, Roger, and Krister Malm. 1984. *Big Sounds From Small Peoples: The Music Industry in Small Countries.* Gothenburg University Department of Musicology, Sociology of Music no. 2. New York: Pendragon Press.

Wara Céspedes, Gilka. 1993. "Huayño, Saya, and Chuntunqui: Bolivian Identity in the Music of 'Los Kjarkas.'" *Latin American Music Review* 14: 52–101.

———. 1984. "New Currents in Música Folklórica in La Paz, Bolivia." *Latin American Music Review* 5: 217–242.

Warren, Kay. 1998. *Indigenous Movements and Their Critics: Pan-Maya Activism in Guatemala.* Princeton: Princeton University Press.

Waterman, Christopher. 1990. *Jùjú: A Social History and Ethnography of an African Popular Music.* Chicago: University of Chicago Press.

Weber, Cynthia. 1995. *Simulating Sovereignty: Intervention, the State, and Symbolic Exchange.* Cambridge, UK: Cambridge University Press.

Weiner, Annette B. 1992. *Inalienable Possessions: The Paradox of Keeping-While-Giving.* Berkeley: University of California Press.

Whisnant, David. 1983. *All That is Native and Fine: The Politics of Culture in an American Region.* Chapel Hill: University of North Carolina Press.

White, Hayden. 1987. *The Content in the Form.* Baltimore: Johns Hopkins University Press.

———. 1978. *Tropics of Discourse: Essays in Cultural Criticism.* Baltimore: Johns Hopkins University Press.

Williams, Brett. 1991. "Introduction." In *The Politics of Culture,* Brett Williams, ed., pp. 1–17. Washington: Smithsonian Institution Press.

Wolf, Eric. 1982. *Europe and the People without History.* Berkeley: University of California Press.

Woodmansee, Martha. 1994. *The Author, Art, and the Market: Rereading the History of Aesthetics.* New York: Columbia University Press.

Wurtzler, Steve. 1992. "'She Sang Live, But the Microphone Was Turned Off:' The Live, the Recorded and the Subject of Representation." In *Sound The-*

ory, Sound Practice, Rick Altman, ed., pp. 87–103. New York and London: Routledge.

Yano, Christine Reiko. 1995. "Shaping Tears of a Nation: An Ethnography of Emotion in Japanese Popular Song." Ph.D. dissertation, University of Hawaii.

Zavaleta Mercado, René. 1990 [1967]. *La formación de la conciencia nacional.* La Paz: Los Amigos del Libro.

———. 1986. *Lo nacional-popular en Bolivia.* Mexico: Siglo XXI.

Žižek, Slavoj. 1989. *The Sublime Object of Ideology.* London and New York: Verso.

Zulawski, Ann. 1987. "Forasteros y yanaconas: la mano de obra de un centro minero en el siglo XVII." In *La participación indígena en los mercados surandinos: Estrategias y reproducción social siglos XVI a XX,* O. Harris, B. Larson, E. Tandeter, compiladores, pp. 159–192. La Paz: CERES.

Periodicals and Newspapers

El diario (La Paz, Bolivia)
Grassroots Development: Journal of the Inter-American Foundation 20 (1), 1996.
Homenaje a Potosí, 1980
Presencia
La razón
Ultima hora

Discography

Arawi. 1990. *La Doctrina de los Ciclos: The Contemporary Orchestra of Native Instruments,* compact disc. La Paz, Bolivia. San Francisco: New Albion Records.

Buena Vista Social Club. 1997. *Buena Vista Social Club.* New York: Nonesuch Records.

Cárdenas, Jenny. 1999. *Homenaje a una generación histórica,* Jenny Cárdenas con Música de Maestros, Banda Sinfónica Militar 'Francisco Suárez Pando' e Invitados Especiales, compact disc. La Paz: Inbofon.

Grupo Amadeus de Potosí. 1992. cassette. Cochabamba: Producciones Borda.

Guerra, Juan Luis. 1990. *Bachata rosa,* cassette. Santo Domingo: Karen C. por A.

Kjarkas. 1994. *A los 500 años,* cassette. La Paz: Discolandia.

Kollamarka. 1994 [1968]. *Al Tawantinsuyo, de colección,* compact disc. La Paz: Discolandia (re-release).

Monroy Chazarreta, Manuel. 1994. *¡Bien le cascaremos!,* compact disc. La Paz: Discolandia.

Música de Maestros. 2001. *Volumen VIII,* compact disc. La Paz: Roli Producciones.

———. 2000. *Volumen VII,* compact disc. La Paz: Roli Producciones.

———. 1999. *Volumen VI Supay,* compact disc. La Paz: Roli Producciones.

———. 1998. *Volumen V, ReCanTanDo,* compact disc. La Paz: Roli Producciones.

———. 1995. *Volumen IV,* compact disc. La Paz: Discolandia.

———. 1995. *Volumen I y II,* compact disc. La Paz: Roli Producciones (re-release).
———. 1993. *Volumen III,* compact disc. La Paz: Discolandia.
Vives, Carlos. 1993. *Clásicos de la provincia,* compact disc. Mexico: PolyGram.
Wara. 1975. *Maya/Paya, de colección.* compact disc. La Paz: Discolandia (re-release).

Motion Pictures/Videos

1995. *Cuestión de fé,* motion picture, directed by Marcos Loayza. La Paz.
1990. *Qhunuskiwa: Recuerdos del Porvenir,* videocassette, directed by Silvia Rivera Cusicanqui and THOA. La Paz.

INDEX